HERE COMES

Understanding the Book of Revelation

Volume One

Graham Truscott

TRUSCOTT MISSIONS
San Diego, California
U.S.A.

HERE COMES THE BRIDE!

Understanding the Book of Revelation

Volume One

Graham Truscott

Published by:

TRUSCOTT MISSIONS
PMB G1
1765 Garnet Avenue
San Diego, CA 92109-3351
U. S. A.
graham@truscottmissions.com
www.truscottmissions.com

**Copyright © 2002 by Graham Truscott
All rights reserved**

ISBN 0-9718002-0-0

No part of this book may be reproduced, stored in a retrieval system, or transmitted in any form, or by any means—electronic, mechanical, photocopying, recording, or otherwise—without the written permission of the author. The only exceptions to this are brief quotations for articles and reviews, for which due acknowledgement must be given. Permission may be obtained by writing to the author at the above address.

AUTHOR'S NOTE: I have used bold type, italics, and capital letters for emphasis in various places throughout this text. I have also used both British and American spellings, to honour both the land of my birth, and the country where I currently reside.

*Printed in the United States of America
For Worldwide Distribution*

Other Books by the Same Author:

The Power of His Presence—The Restoration of the Tabernacle of David
First published in 1969, this book is the foundational work on David's Tabernacle and its prophetic fulfillment. 400 pages. Fully illustrated. Now in its eighth English language printing.
   Also published in:
   Japanese in Japan
   Chinese in China
   Amarhic in Ethiopia.

Also available:
Study Guide to "The Power of His Presence" by Kari Vance. Pastor Vance has written an excellent companion volume to **The Power of His Presence.** This Study Guide is a great help in studying the Restoration of the Tabernacle of David.

You Shall Receive Power—A comprehensive study of the Holy Spirit, from the Bible and history. Many have been filled with the Holy Spirit's power while reading this book.

The Only Foundation—Foundations for successful Christian living.
   Also published in:
   Bengali in Bangladesh
   Hindi in India.

Every Christian's Ministry—Based on the Tabernacle of Moses, this book teaches a Biblical ministry we can all enjoy–worship and praise.
   Also published in *Burmese* in magazine form in Burma.

Missionary Training and Discipleship—Some essentials for effective missionary training and service on the mission field.

What Does the Bible Teach About Women's Ministry?—A candid look at this controversial subject from the Bible and history.
   Also published in:
      Russian in Russia
      Spanish in Mexico.

What Does the Bible Teach About Water Baptism?—A popular study booklet that has been through many printings.
Also published in *Marathi* in India.

Books by Pamela Truscott:

I Cry Alone—Written after the Truscotts' 24-year-old daughter Debbie was killed, this book brings solace and comfort to families who have lost a child. Endorsed by President George Bush Sr.

Prayer
From a Discipline to a Delight—A practical guide to an effective and enjoyable prayer life.
   To be published in *Russian* in 2002.

To order the Truscott's books, or CDs and tapes of Graham's clarinet music, please see the end of this book for contact information.

Versions Used

Unless otherwise stated, Scripture quotations in **HERE COMES THE BRIDE! Volume One** are from *The New King James Version of the Bible*, © 1994 by Thomas Nelson, Inc., Nashville, Tennessee.

The following abbreviations are used in this book to identify which translation of the Bible is being quoted other than *The New King James Version, NKJV*:

KJV	*King James Version*
Amp	*The Amplified Bible*, © 1965 Zondervan Publishing House, Grand Rapids, Michigan.
LB	*The Living Bible*, © 1971 Tyndale House Publishers, Wheaton, Illinois.
NLT	*Holy Bible, New Living Translation*, © 1996. Used by permission of Tyndale House Publishers, Inc., Wheaton, Illinois 60189. All rights reserved
NIV	*The Holy Bible, New International Version*, © 1973, 1978, 1984 International Bible Society. Used by permission of Zondervan Bible Publishers
NAS	*New American Standard Bible*, © 1960, 1962, 1963, 1968, 1971 The Lockman Foundation, La Habra, California.
RSV	*Revised Standard Version*. Old Testament Section, © 1952, New Testament Section, © 1946 by Division of Christian Education of the National Council of the Churches of Christ in the United States of America
JBP	*Letters To Young Churches, A Translation of the New Testament Epistles* by J. B. Phillips. First Published 1947. Geoffrey Bles, London.
TEV	*Good News for Modern Man – The New Testament in Today's English*, © 1966 American Bible Society, New York.
ASV	*American Standard Version*, © 1901 by Thomas Nelson & Sons, New York.
NEB	*The New English Bible*, © 1961, 1970 The Delegates of the Oxford University Press and The Syndics of the Cambridge University Press. University Press, Oxford, Great Britain.
TM	*The Message – New Testament with Psalms and Proverbs* by Eugene H. Peterson. © 1996 by Eugene H. Peterson. Christian Art Publishers, Vereeniging, South Africa. [*Author's note:* I am aware that Mr Peterson has paraphrased the New Testament using 21st Century language, idioms, and illustrations. He has used contemporary language to capture the fact that the New Testament was written not in formal, but informal Greek – the language of the street, the market place, the common working man. I think it is both informative and refreshing to have a version of the New Testament written in our everyday English language.]
Williams	*The New Testament in the Language of the People* by Charles B. Williams. © 1966 by Edith S. Williams. Moody Press, Chicago.

Abbreviations Used

OLD TESTAMENT

Gen	Genesis	Nah	Nahum
Exo	Exodus	Hab	Habakkuk
Lev	Leviticus	Zeph	Zephaniah
Num	Numbers	Hag	Haggai
Deut	Deuteronomy	Zech	Zechariah
Josh	Joshua	Mal	Malachi

Judg	Judges		
Ruth	Ruth		

NEW TESTAMENT

1 Sam	I Samuel	Matt	Matthew
2 Sam	II Samuel	Mark	Mark
1 Ki	I Kings	Luke	Luke
2 Ki	II Kings	John	John
1 Chr	I Chronicles	Acts	Acts
2 Chr	II Chronicles	Rom	Romans
Ezra	Ezra	1 Cor	I Corinthians
Neh	Nehemiah	2 Cor	II Corinthians
Esth	Esther	Gal	Galatians
Job	Job	Eph	Ephesians
Psa	Psalms	Phil	Philippians
Prov	Proverbs	Col	Colossians
Eccl	Ecclesiastes	1 Thess	I Thessalonians
Song	Song of Solomon	2 Thess	II Thessalonians
Isa	Isaiah	1 Tim	I Timothy
Jer	Jeremiah	2 Tim	II Timothy
Lam	Lamentations	Titus	Titus
Eze	Ezekiel	Phile	Philemon
Dan	Daniel	Heb	Hebrews
Hos	Hosea	Jas	James
Joel	Joel	1 Pet	I Peter
Amos	Amos	2 Pet	II Peter
Obad	Obadiah	1 Jn	I John
Jon	Jonah	2 Jn	II John
Mic	Micah	3 Jn	III John
		Jude	Jude
		Rev	Revelation

Contents

Chapter   **Page**

	Table of Charts and Diagrams	xii
	Table of Appendices	xiv
	Dedication	xv
	Acknowledgements	xvii
	Author's Preface	xxi
	Foreword by Dr Rob Wheeler	xxv

PART ONE
THE BRIDE

1.	Here Comes the Bride!	3
2.	Bridal Language in the Old Testament	6
3.	Bridal Language in the New Testament	29

PART TWO
THE KEYS

4.	The Book Rediscovered		35
5.	The Writer		39
6.	Key One:	Panoramic Overview	44
7.	Key Two:	The Other 65 Bible Books in Revelation	46
8.	Key Three:	Types and Symbols	51
9.	Key Four:	Heaven and Earth	66
10.	Key Five:	God's Week	70
11.	Key Six:	Numbers in the Bible	88
12.	Key Seven:	The Festivals of Israel	99
13.	Key Eight:	The Tabernacle of Moses	124

PART THREE
THE CHRIST
Revelation chapter 1

14.	Here Comes the Bridegroom!	147
15.	The Sevenfold Spirit of God	167
16.	Here Comes the Bridegroom! (II)	179

Contents continued

PART FOUR
THE CHURCHES
Revelation chapters 2 and 3

Chapter		Page
17.	Introducing the Letters to the Seven Churches	201
18.	Ephesus – Overcoming Attitudes	211
19.	Smyrna – Overcoming Affliction	228
20.	Pergamos – Overcoming Associations	244
21.	Thyatira – Overcoming False Authority	263
22.	Sardis – Overcoming Apathy	280
23.	Philadelphia – Overcoming Arduous Circumstances	292
24.	Laodicea – Overcoming Affluence	307

PART FIVE
THE OVERCOMER

25.	How to Be an Overcomer	329
26.	Overcoming and Healing Your Hurts	338

THE APPENDIX

Table of Appendices	xiv
Appendices start at	355

HERE COMES THE BRIDE!

Understanding the Book of Revelation

Volume Two

Contents

Part	Title	Revelation chapters
Six	**The Throne**	4
Seven	**The Book**	5 and 6
Eight	**The Day**	7
Nine	**The Trumpets**	8, 9, and 10
Ten	**The Tribulation**	11, 12, and 13
Eleven	**The Bride**	12
Twelve	**The City**	14, 17, and 18
Thirteen	**The Bowls**	15 and 16
Fourteen	**The Marriage**	19
Fifteen	**The Millennium**	20
Sixteen	**The Lamb's Wife**	21 and 22

Table of Charts, Figures and Diagrams

Figure	Description	Page
1.	History of Restoration to the Church during the past 500 years	14
2.	Chart showing the Prophetic Types in the book of Esther	18
3.	The Ark of the Covenant	36
4.	Map showing the locations of the Island of Patmos, and the Seven Churches	40
5.	Chapter headings for the Book of Revelation	45
6.	Panoramic Overview of Revelation, with Chapter Numbers	366
7.	Chart showing the distribution of Old Testament quotations and allusions in the Book of Revelation	48
8.	Genesis/Revelation–Comparisons and Contrasts	50
9.	Table Comparing Knowledge, Wisdom, and Understanding	54
10.	The Major differences between a Type and a Symbol	64
11.	Some Symbols in the Book of Revelation	65
12.	The Revelation: The Structure of the book as a whole	69
13.	The Seven Days of God's Week	367
14.	The Feasts–Festivals of Israel	368
15.	Thirty Types and Illustrations of the Three Stages of Christian Growth	369
16.	The Feasts of the Lord–summary chart	103
17.	How Aaron and his sons prefigure the five New Testament ministries	105
18.	Signs of the Last Days illustrated in the year 1948	112
19.	Signs of the Last Days illustrated in the year 1967	113
20.	The Tabernacle of Moses	125
21.	Prototype, Type, and Antitype of Moses' Tabernacle	129
22.	Heavenly, Natural, and Spiritual Aspects of Moses' Tabernacle	130
23.	The Tabernacle of Moses in Exodus, Acts, and Revelation	370
24.	Comparisons and contrasts between the Old Testament Church and the New Testament Church	143
25.	The Graces, Gifts, and Glory of the Holy Spirit	168

Figure	Description	Page
26.	The Feast of Tabernacles as pictured in the books that contain references to the Sevenfold Spirit of God	169
27.	Comparison of the nine Gifts of the Spirit with the Sevenfold Spirit of God	176
28.	The Relationship of the Sevenfold Spirit of God with the seven Compound-Redemptive Names of the Lord	177
29.	The Relationship between the Sevenfold Spirit of God, the Compound-Redemptive Names of God, and the "I AMs" of Jesus	178
30.	The Lord Jesus Christ as seen in the Tabernacle Pattern	191
31.	The Main Groups of Seven in Revelation	202
32.	Historical Viewpoint of the Letters to the Seven Churches	205
33.	Comparison between the Kingdom Parables and the Seven Churches	206
34.	Summary of the Book of Ephesians	215
35.	The Loss and Restoration of the Ascension Gift Ministries	220
36.	The Doctrine of Balaam (Rev 2:14)	256
37.	Summary of Christ and His Five Ministries as typified in Moses' Tabernacle	269
38.	The Three Levels of the Operation of the Gift of Prophecy	274
39.	Three Essentials for the Overcomer in the Laodicean Age	324
40.	Some Illustrations of the Three Major Stages of Christian Growth	330
41.	How Christ Overcame Temptation in the Wilderness	336

Table of Appendices

Appendix Number	Title	Page
1	The Differences Between a "Visitation" and a "Revival"	355
2	Some Questions asked in the Book of Job	359
3	"Be not ignorant"	360
4	Further Details of the Feast of Passover	361
5	Further Details of the Feast of Pentecost	362
6	10 Questions to Consider When Examining a Teaching, a Ministry, or a "New Spiritual Move"	364
7	*Figure 6:* Panoramic Overview of Revelation with Chapter Numbers	366
8	*Figure 13:* The Seven Days of God's Week	367
9	*Figure 14:* The Feasts – Festivals of Israel (Deut 16: 15,17; Lev 23)	368
10	*Figure 15:* Thirty Types and Illustrations of the Three Stages of Christian Growth	369
11	*Figure 23:* The Tabernacle of Moses in Exodus, Acts and Revelation	370
*	Addresses to Order Books by Other Authors	371
*	About the Author	372
*	To Order Books, Music tapes and CDs, from the Truscotts	373

Dedication

To Pamela, my bride for 44 years, and my wonderful Proverbs chapter 31 wife, who encouraged and helped me so much in the production of this book,

and

To Bible students all over the world, who have encouraged me by purchasing well over 100,000 copies of my books. I pray you have been as blessed in reading as I have been in writing the books.

Acknowledgements

When I became a Christian, the first book I read about my newfound faith was *Peace with God* by Billy Graham. In this book Dr Graham has a chapter on the importance of Scripture memorization. He says how sad it is that the only Bible verse most Christians can quote is John 3:16.

Reading this made me feel ashamed. I could not quote John 3:16. I didn't know who John was! I decided there and then it was time for me to start reading the Bible seriously.

I read and studied for two years, then preached my first Sunday morning sermon in 1954. This year, 2002, I celebrate 48 years uninterrupted ministry of God's Word.

Even though I had begun preaching I was very hungry to know God better. I knew that this would only happen as I grew in the knowledge of His Word.

Therefore, first and foremost, at the top of this list of my acknowledgements is my Saviour, the **Lord Jesus Christ**. I give thanks and praise to Him for His blessing on my life, for creating this hunger in my heart, and for His Word, the Bible.

In 1959, as Pamela and I were preparing to leave New Zealand to be faith missionaries in India, there was birthed within me an even greater longing for more of God. I was deeply aware that my knowledge and experience of Him were limited. Surely the Lord would not cause this desire for more of Him, if there was nothing more for Him to give?

It was at this time we met **Rob Wheeler**.[1] The first time I heard Rob preach I knew he had answers to my quest. There was more of God after Pentecost. I learned it is called the Feast of Tabernacles. I heard God has a plan to restore His Church before Jesus comes again. I believed the Lord Jesus Christ will marry a perfected Bride.

I would like to have delayed our departure for India and spent more time studying with Rob. But this was not possible. Our reservations on the ship to India could not be changed. However, through the years, there have been many other opportunities for fellowship with, and learning from Rob. I am grateful for all I have received from him these past 43 years. And I heartily recommend the latest edition of Rob's excellent book, *Present Day Truths & Last Day Events*.[2]

---

[1] Rob Wheeler came to Christ in Auckland, New Zealand, when he was just five years old. He attended Bible colleges in both New Zealand and Australia. After pastoring for a few years, in the mid-1950s he began several successful years of tent evangelism throughout New Zealand. Hundreds came to Christ. Hundreds more received the baptism in the Holy Spirit. Scores of churches were established. During his more than 50 years of ministry, Rob has functioned as pastor, apostle, teacher, and evangelist, and has encouraged many young men and women into the ministry. He has preached in several nations. He is the founding pastor of Auckland Christian Fellowship, and currently resides with his wife, Beryl, in Stanmore Bay, Auckland, New Zealand.

[2] See the end of this book concerning ordering information for these recommended books.

On our arrival in India I began to study the Bible at least eight hours a day. From these study times came my first seven books, all written and first published in India.

Soon after our arrival in India in 1960, I ordered from America a copy of a book that has been very foundational in my understanding of Scripture, *God and His Bible—the Harmonies of Divine Revelation* by Rev W.H. Offiler.[3]

Although he passed away in 1957, and I never had the privilege of meeting him, I acknowledge the help and blessing the books of **Pastor Offiler** have been to me, and to many other Bible students. As Kevin Conner says in his foreword to the 1991 edition of Pastor Offiler's book, *God and His Bible*:

> "When I think of Brother Offiler, I think of the great truths of the name of God, the glorious Church as the Bride of Christ, and then, beyond these, I think of keys to eschatology—end-time events! ...
> "I have personally used these *divine keys* over many years to unlock the Word of God to the Body of Christ and will continue to use them."[4]

I acknowledge the great debt I owe to **Kevin Conner**, and thoroughly recommend all his books, especially *Interpreting the Book of Revelation*, which should be read along with **HERE COMES THE BRIDE!**[5] I thank Kevin for giving me permission to quote from his works, and reproduce some of his diagrams and charts. Those readers who wish to study a detailed exposition of Revelation should see Kevin's excellent textbook, *The Book of Revelation (An Exposition.)*[6]

Both Kevin Conner and Rob Wheeler read the manuscript of this book before it went to the press, and I am grateful to them for their encouraging words and helpful suggestions.

I am grateful to **Alister Lowe** for his four volumes on *End Time Events*, and for his permission to adapt some diagrams from *Volume 4, A Guide to Things that Are To Be*,[7] for publication in **Volume Two** of **HERE COMES THE BRIDE!**

---

[3] William Offiler was born in England in 1875, and moved to the United States in 1899. He founded Bethel Pentecostal Temple in Seattle, Washington in 1914, and pastored there until 1948. Many missionaries were sent out, especially to Indonesia, where over 10,000 churches give testimony to their "Bethel roots." Pastor Offiler was an outstanding teacher of the Bible, and his deep insight into last day events have inspired and challenged many. He passed away in 1957, preceded in death by his wife and three children.

[4] Kevin J. Conner in his foreword to *God and His Bible–the Harmonies of Divine Revelation* by Rev W.H. Offiler. Bethel Temple, Seattle, Washington; 1991. Emphasis Kevin Conner's.

Kevin Conner was born in 1927 in Melbourne, Australia, and saved at the age of 14. At 21 he began his ministry, which has taken him to many nations, including over 10 years at Bible Temple in Portland, Oregon. Upon his return to Melbourne, he served as Senior Pastor of Waverley Christian Fellowship, and saw tremendous growth in that church. Since 1995 he has been released to the body of Christ, and is in much demand as a Bible teacher. He resides with his wife, Rene, in Melbourne.

[5] *Interpreting the Book of Revelation* by Kevin J. Conner. K.J.C. Publications, Vermont, Victoria, Australia; 1995.

[6] *The Book of Revelation (An Exposition)* by Kevin J. Conner. K.J.C. Publications, Vermont, Victoria, Australia; 2001.

[7] *End Time Events, Volume 4: A Guide to Things that Are to Be* by A.J. Lowe. End Time Publications, Brisbane, Australia; 1982.

To other books, sermons, and sources that have helped me express my thoughts, but the origin of which has been forgotten, I am thankful. While I am grateful to everyone for their input into my understanding of the Book of Revelation, I need to state that the final conclusions found in this book are my own. But, I need to add, these views are shared by a number of Bible scholars and teachers.

Furthermore, it is not my intention to write a detailed study of the various views different schools of thought have on subjects in the Revelation. Kevin Conner has done this extremely well in his three books on Revelation.

I first taught the Book of Revelation in our churches in India. The basic material of this book was taught in Friday night Bible Studies when I was the pastor of the church we founded in San Diego (now called The Life Church, Mission Bay). I am indebted to **Dana Cottrell** for his many hours of hard work in transcribing these tapes for me. In editing the tapes for publication, I have endeavoured to maintain the pastoral and practical applications of the teachings.

My thanks to **Cliff Philip** for helping me with computer work beyond my very limited abilities. Also to **Paul Garratt**, my friend of 52 years, for working with me on the final layout of the text. I am extremely grateful to **Richard Rappley** for his editorial and proof-reading assistance. My thanks to **David and Linda Larson** for help with the art work. I acknowledge the invaluable help of **Rick Moran**, printer, and brother in Christ, and all his staff at Carbon Copy, San Diego.

Last but not least, I want to express my heartfelt gratitude to the large number of people who, over many years, have encouraged me to write this book. It has been a labour of love–an expression of my love for the Lord Jesus Christ, and my love for you, the reader.

Graham Truscott
San Diego, California
February 2002

Author's Preface

I began to study the Book of Revelation seriously in early 1960, soon after our arrival as missionaries in India. During the next 40 years I taught Revelation many times, especially in churches of which I was the founding pastor. But it was not until March 2001, when I began preparing the text for **HERE COMES THE BRIDE!** that I wrote the first draft of this Preface.

None of us will forget where we were on September 11, 2001 when we heard the news of the terrorist attacks on the United States. Pamela and I were in San Diego working on this book. That morning our younger son, Mark, telephoned us early in the morning and told us to turn our television on to CNN. As many newscasters said, "September 11 was a day that changed the history of the world." Through the media coverage of the events of that day, images of the shocking terrorist attacks on the Twin Towers in New York and the Pentagon in Washington, D.C., together with the plane crash in Pennsylvania, are indelibly printed on our minds.

That fateful day the need to understand the Book of Revelation, and its relevance to current events, took on even greater importance. Since then I have been asked many times, "What, in the light of Bible prophecy, do I think happened?" My answer is this – Could the dreadful terrorist attacks of September 11, 2001 be the commencement of the fulfillment of the prophecy which states:

> "Thus says the Lord God: 'On that day it shall come to pass that thoughts will arise in your mind, and you will make an evil plan:
> You will say, 'I will go up against a land of unwalled villages; I will go to a peaceful people, who dwell safely (*margin*, 'securely'), all of them dwelling without walls, and having neither bars nor gates'—
> To take plunder and to take booty, to stretch out your hand against the waste places that are again inhabited, and against a people gathered from the nations, who have acquired livestock and goods, who dwell in the midst of the land."
> (Ezek 38:10-12)?

Though this prophecy was spoken to the nation of Israel, there certainly could be an *application* to the nation of America (or even other nations like America) being attacked by her enemies.[1] This current war seems to be a further opening of the second seal, the ability "to take peace from the earth, and that people should kill one another" (Rev 6:4). And I wonder if this is the commencement of that which the Lord Jesus called "the beginning of sorrows" (Matt 24:8)?

Because of the events of the past six months it is with a deep sense of urgency that I rewrite this preface to **HERE COMES THE BRIDE! – Understanding the Book of Revelation, Volume One.**

---

[1] There will be a detailed study of Ezekiel chapters 38, 39 in **HERE COMES THE BRIDE! Volume Two**.

I am aware there are diverse views among Christians concerning the interpretation of the Book of Revelation. I realize too it is dangerous to place an over-emphasis on last day events to the exclusion of other Biblical truth.

I have therefore endeavoured to present a balanced view of the Book of Revelation. "Balances of deceit are an abomination to the Lord: but a just weight is His delight." (Prov 11:1–*KJV, margin*)

In the Book of Revelation we find many facets of Bible truth. A few of these are:

- The Lord Jesus Christ, our exalted High Priest, Saviour, King.
- The importance of being an overcomer.
- The necessity for an ever-growing personal relationship with the Lord.
- The obligation to preach the Gospel to all nations.
- The order of last day events.
- The final judgment of God against the devil, and all that is evil.
- The marriage of the Lord Jesus Christ to His Bride.
- The resurrection of the dead in Christ to eternal life.
- The resurrection of the ungodly dead to eternal punishment.
- The reality of the eternal new heaven and new earth.

I realize, that at first reading some of the views expressed in **HERE COMES THE BRIDE!** may appear different, and even extreme,. But let us imagine you met a person on a street in Jerusalem thirty years before Christ was born, and you told him: "God's Messiah is going to come as a babe in Bethlehem. He will be born of a virgin, live a normal life until He is thirty, and then begin to demonstrate God's power by doing great miracles. After three and one half years of teaching and doing miracles, He will die a criminal's death at the hands of the Romans by being nailed to a wooden cross. He will rise from the dead after three days, then ascend to Heaven."

Even though these things are prophesied in Scripture, the chances are you would be ridiculed for holding such beliefs. "No, no! You're crazy! That's not how it will happen," you would be told. "Messiah will come from Heaven a mighty military commander, breaking the Roman yoke we are under. He will liberate us from Roman oppression, reign as our Supreme Commander, and we will again live unrestricted in our own land. That is how Messiah will come. This is what Messiah will do."

Well ... He didn't.

So if there is anything in this book you don't understand, just put that thought on the shelf for another day. And take time to be a good "Berean." Search the Scriptures to see if these things are so.[2] (I am sure that questions not answered in this book, will be addressed in **Volume Two**).

---

[2] See Acts 17:11.

When I published my second book, *The Power of His Presence—The Restoration of the Tabernacle of David*, I received much criticism and ostracism at the hands of many Pentecostal leaders who, in 1969, considered that book heresy. One of these leaders even demanded I recant, and confess that what I had written about the Restoration of David's Tabernacle was false teaching. But today, that same book is widely accepted in the Church, and last year we produced our Eighth English Edition of *The Power of His Presence*. While I have not purposely sought to be controversial in **HERE COMES THE BRIDE!** I realize history has a habit of repeating itself!

Our understanding of events yet in the future, if properly received and acted upon, will change the way we live today. Try telling a couple engaged to be married that an event in the future has no effect on the way they live today. Of course it does.

I am deeply conscious we are living in days of unfolding, ever-increasing revelation. The Lord will give new insights into the Book of Revelation as the time of the end draws closer. As Paul said, "now we see in a mirror, dimly."[3] Jesus warned us: "Of that day and hour no one knows."[4] "You know neither the day nor the hour."[5] "An hour you do not expect."[6] "It is not for you to know."[7] But then, at the opposite end of the spectrum, He also said, "Take heed; see, I have told you all things beforehand."[8] Somewhere between these two extremes is our experience. Because the strong inference of Scripture is this: The Bible's predictive prophecies will most definitely come to pass, but usually through means and ways we least expect!

On this subject, I value the wisdom of the man who is still called "The Prince of Expositors," Dr G. Campbell Morgan:

> "The whole Book of Revelation reveals the final stages in the work of God with humanity. No one has perfectly understood all its teaching. Its great principles are evident. It shows the final overthrow of evil, and the setting up of the eternal Kingdom of God. It moreover teaches us that that overthrow and that setting up will be realized through Jesus the anointed King."[9]

One thing is certain: when we take the truths contained in the Book of Revelation into our hearts, they will demand radical changes in our personal lives. We will desire to give ourselves in total dedication to the Lord Jesus Christ. We will want to prepare to meet

---

[3] 1 Cor 13:12.
[4] Matt 24:36.
[5] Matt 25:13.
[6] Matt 24:44.
[7] Acts 1:7.
[8] Mark 13:23.
[9] *The Letters of Our Lord – A First Century Message to Twentieth Century Christians*, by Dr G. Campbell Morgan; Pickering & Inglis Ltd, London, England, *First Printed* 1945 – page 8.

G. Campbell Morgan was born in Tetbury, a remote village in Gloucestershire, England. In 1900 he moved to East Northfield, Massachusetts, from where he carried on the preaching mission of Dwight L. Moody. Preacher, teacher, evangelist, and author, Dr Morgan became one of the most famous expositors of the Bible of his generation. His books are still widely read by Bible-lovers today.

Him. We will be challenged to share His wondrous salvation with others so they too can make preparation for His coming.

That is my prayer for the ministry of this book.

Dr Graham Truscott
San Diego, California
February 2002

Foreword

Dr Rob Wheeler

It has been my great honour and privilege to read the early transcripts of Dr Graham Truscott's latest book **HERE COMES THE BRIDE!–Understanding the Book of Revelation**. Even though I have believed this interpretation for many years, I was still challenged and convicted by his many applications in this presentation.

I was not brought up in, or taught the generally accepted "Futuristic" or "Historical" schools of interpretation of the Book of Revelation. Therefore, as a result of my early Christian experience in the Scriptures, I did not find it difficult to accept this quite different school of thought. Because, to my mind, it made Scriptural sense, and there was a strong agreement and witness within my spirit. To some, these thoughts Pastor Graham suggests will come as quite a shock, and may even seem "outlandish" to others.

This treatise will challenge you! It may even disturb you!

If you have been schooled in the generally accepted views of modern interpretations it may cause you some sleepless nights as you wrestle with the Scriptures that do not "fit" those standard explanations of Revelation. But as you compare Scripture with Scripture, let the Bible interpret itself by typology and repetitive principles. This, together with the inner witness of God's Holy Spirit in your spirit and understanding, will lead you into a vast new dimension of truth and revelation–one that so many other people of God, around the world, are already entering into!

Be prepared to "put the cat among the pigeons" of traditions. You will see nicely categorized interpretations of the past, with their neat little charts and graphs, upset. For this understanding of Revelation is something quite different. It will make you either "Mad!" or very "Glad!"

However, whatever your reaction and response, it will not change the opinion of four generations of respected Bible teachers who have taught these truths from the Northern hemisphere to the equatorial regions, into the Southern hemisphere, and all places in between–in many different cultures and climates. These teachings are here to stay!

These teachings do not fit into "hype" or unbalanced emotionalism. They demand, and when accepted, will result in new vision, new dedication, and holiness in the awesome fear of God. It is not an easy task to put these convictions into print, because they will cause offence to a number of people, and, in some cases, even separation. But then, true Scriptural unity was never based upon "easy believism" or compromise, but always on conviction, and vision of true purpose.

Having honestly read to the last page of this treatise, you will either have to change, or miss out on God's very best for your life. You just cannot remain the same!

Blessed reading.

Dr Rob Wheeler
Stanmore Bay, New Zealand
January 2002

PART ONE

THE BRIDE

PART ONE   THE BRIDE

Chapter 1

Here Comes the Bride!

I led the way. Behind me were my two tall, handsome sons. Stephen, the bridegroom, was the first of our children to be getting married. His younger brother Mark was his best man.

It was a warm sunny morning in Palm Springs. We walked through the beautiful gardens of Ingleside Inn to the music of "The Chorale from Bach's Cantata 147" (known today as "Jesu, Joy of Man's Desiring").

As we approached the floral canopy where the wedding ceremony would take place, there was an excited buzz of conversation from the audience of close friends and family members. The best man and the groomsmen escorted the maid of honour and the bridesmaids to the canopy. All the bridesmaids looked lovely, but one special blonde caught my attention—our daughter Ruthie.

As the bridal party stood waiting, the music changed. We heard the strains of the ever-familiar Wedding March, "Here Comes The Bride."[1]

And there she was! As the guests rose to their feet, all eyes were fixed on the bride. Cindy, our new daughter-in-law, looked radiant in her beautiful white wedding gown.

After the usual preliminaries were finished, I reminded everyone that, while the Bible has many instructions concerning marriage, there is only one definition of marriage in Scripture—marriage is *"a covenant of companionship."* [2]

There was much love expressed as I led Stephen and Cindy in their covenant vows. It was a memorable wedding from start to finish. I felt so privileged to be given such a vital part in Stephen and Cindy's special day.

What the Bible Teaches About Marriage

We all enjoy the beauty and excitement of a marriage ceremony. But did you know the Bible commands every one of us to prepare for the most beautiful and exciting Marriage Ceremony ever seen—the wedding of the Lord Jesus Christ and His Bride? The Scriptures often use marriage terminology—weddings, brides, and bridegrooms. God uses

---

[1] The music for the Wedding March is from the opera *Lohengrin* written by the German composer Wilhelm Richard Wagner (1813–1883).
[2] See Prov 2:17 and Mal 2:14.

marriage to teach us about the relationship He desires with His people. He wants fellowship with us in a "covenant of companionship."

He sent His Son Jesus to seal the new covenant—this wonderful agreement—with His Own blood. And throughout the Bible, particularly in the Book of Revelation, God promises, to all who receive His salvation, everlasting fellowship and companionship with Him.

God confirms His approval of marriage with the words: "Marriage is honorable among all, and the bed undefiled." (Heb 13:4) In the eyes of God, marriage is the highest and holiest relationship between two people on this earth. Marriage is a covenant of companionship between a man and a woman who love one another. Indeed, marriage is covenant unity in every area of human life.

God is a Trinity—Father, Son, and Holy Spirit—Three in One. So are we. The Bible teaches we are tripartite beings:

> "Now may the God of peace Himself sanctify (*margin*, 'set apart') you completely; and may your whole *spirit, soul,* and *body* be preserved blameless at the coming of our Lord Jesus Christ.
> He who calls you is faithful, who also will do it." (1 Thess 5:23,24)

Marriage is a:

1. Unity between two spirits: worshipping together (Psa 34:3);

2. Unity between two souls: agreeing, and flowing together (Amos 3:3; Jer 31:12);

3. Unity between two bodies: expressing love together (Gen 2:24; Matt 19:4-6).

In **HERE COMES THE BRIDE! Volume Two**, we shall study, in Revelation chapter 12, the pregnant Bride of Christ, and how she conceived. Therefore, it is important that we state here—the relationship between husband and wife is unique. The intimacy enjoyed between husband and wife should be reserved for only one person, the spouse.

The Beginning and the Ending

The Bible begins and ends with a wedding.

In Genesis, the book of beginnings, we read how God created Mrs Adam for Adam. (Adam called her "Eve" after they had sinned.)[3] This first marriage was consummated in Genesis 4:1. Eve conceived, bore a son, and said, "I have acquired a man from the Lord."

In Revelation, the book of ultimates, we read of the Bride of Christ in chapters 12, 19, and 21. In chapter 12 the Bride's marriage has been consummated—she has conceived,

---
[3] Gen 3:20.

and brings forth a man child. In Revelation chapters 19 and 21 we read further details concerning the marriage of the Lamb and His Bride.

John, the writer of the Book of Revelation, tells us in his Gospel that the Lord Jesus began His public ministry at a wedding, where He miraculously turned water into wine. The narrative of this wedding opens: "On the third day there was a wedding in Cana of Galilee" (John 2:1).

We will see the full significance of "on the third day" in a later chapter. Suffice to say here, the Bible makes it clear: "But, beloved, do not forget this one thing, that with the Lord one day is as a thousand years, and a thousand years as one day" (Psa 90:4; 2 Pet 3:8).

The second chapter of John's Gospel continues: "Now both Jesus and His disciples were invited to the wedding."[4]

All who will receive Jesus Christ into their lives as Lord and Saviour are invited to a wedding. At this wedding Jesus is the Bridegroom and His people are His Bride.

---

[4] John 2:2.

Chapter 2

Bridal Language in the Old Testament

The Old Testament is filled with picturesque Bridal language. Sometimes God speaks of Old Testament Israel as His "bride." He has always desired to enjoy a covenant of companionship with His people:

> "'For your Maker is your husband, the Lord of hosts is His name; and your Redeemer is the Holy One of Israel; He is called the God of the whole earth. For the Lord has called you like a woman forsaken and grieved in spirit, like a youthful wife when you were refused,' says your God." (Isa 54:5,6)

Later the prophet Isaiah says:

> "I will greatly rejoice in the Lord, my soul shall be joyful in my God; for He has clothed me with the garments of salvation, He has covered me with the robe of righteousness, as a bridegroom decks himself with ornaments, and as a bride adorns herself with her jewels." (Isa 61:10)

But the nations of Israel and Judah broke their covenant with Jehovah:

> "The Lord said also to me in the days of Josiah the king: 'Have you seen what backsliding Israel has done? She has gone up on every high mountain and under every green tree, and there played the harlot.
> 'And I said, after she had done all these things, 'Return to Me.' But she did not return. And her treacherous sister Judah saw it.
> 'Then I saw that for all the causes for which backsliding Israel had committed adultery, I had put her away and given her a *certificate of divorce;* yet her treacherous sister Judah did not fear, but went and played the harlot also.
> 'So it came to pass, through her casual harlotry, that she defiled the land and committed adultery with stones and trees.'" (Jer 3:6-9)

Through the prophet Isaiah, God says to those who were His people:

> "Thus says the Lord:
> 'Where is the *certificate of your mother's divorce,*
> *Whom I have put away?*
> Or which of My creditors is it to whom I have sold you?
> For your iniquities you have sold yourselves,
> And for your transgressions your mother has been put away.'" (Isa 50:1)

God divorced them because they committed spiritual adultery with other gods. And His law commands that a woman who had been divorced from her husband could not return to him again as his wife:

> "Then her former husband who divorced her must not take her back to be his wife after she has been defiled; for that is an abomination before the Lord, and you shall not bring sin on the land which the Lord your God is giving you as an inheritance." (See Deut 24:1-4)

The Lord will never break His Own law. Therefore He will never re-marry the wife He divorced.

The whole of Ezekiel chapter 16 should be read in this context. Just two quotations–from verses 32, and 59: "You are an adulterous wife, who takes strangers instead of her husband ... I will deal with you as you have done, who despised the oath by breaking the covenant" (Eze 16:32, 59). Strong words indeed. But then, after words of judgment come words of promise to Israel: " ... I will establish my covenant with you. *Then* you shall know that I am the Lord, that you may remember and be ashamed." (verses 62 and 63)

"Then." Future. When will the Lord re-establish His covenant with Israel? Under the ministry of the two witnesses and Enoch during the Great Tribulation. Not that every Jew will be saved then—only those who turn from sin and unbelief, and receive Christ as their Saviour. For the so-called "Jewish problem"—the problem with national Israel today, is the same problem as the "American problem," the "Indian problem," the "New Zealand problem"–the problem of people of every nation. It is, in God's eyes, the "sin problem." Because it is sin and unbelief that separate us from fellowship with God.[1] Regardless of national and ethnic origin, unless a person turns to Christ, that individual's "sin problem" remains.

There are more harsh words from the Lord concerning Israel, this time through the prophet Hosea: "She is not My wife, nor am I her Husband!" (Hos 2:2). But again, God's gracious promise: "Afterward the children of Israel shall return and seek the Lord their God and David [a prophetic Name for the Lord Jesus Christ] their king. They shall fear the Lord and His goodness in the latter days" (Hos 3:5). What "latter days"? The 1,260 days of the ministry of the two witnesses.[2]

Jesus told the Jewish chief priests and elders: "The kingdom of God will be taken from you and given to a nation bearing the fruits of it" (Matt 21:43). It is interesting to note, "when the chief priests and Pharisees heard His parables, they perceived (margin, 'knew') He was speaking of them."[3] The fruit-bearing nation of which Jesus speaks here is, of course, His Church. His Church includes Jews who believe in Him, together with believing Gentiles:

---

[1] Isa 59:2; Heb 3:19.
[2] Rev 11:3.
[3] Matt 21:23-46.

> "For by one Spirit are we all baptized into one body, whether we be Jews or Gentiles, whether we be bond or free; and have been all made to drink into one Spirit." (1 Cor 12:13–*KJV*)

For this reason Peter assures the Church:
> "But you are
> a chosen generation,
> a royal priesthood,
> a holy nation,
> His own special people ..." (1 Pet 2:9)

It could not be any clearer. Those who have received Christ as Messiah and Saviour, both Jews and Gentiles, are God's *"holy nation,"* "His own special people."

Concerning Jews and Gentiles being one in Christ, Paul says:

> "Having abolished in His flesh the enmity, that is, the law of commandments contained in ordinances, so as to create *one new man from the two,* thus making peace ...
> Now, therefore, you are no longer strangers and foreigners, but *fellow citizens* with the saints and members of the household of God." (Eph 2:15,19)

Salvation is no longer by race, but by grace. His Church is international. He now invites people of every tribe and tongue and people and nation to be redeemed by the precious blood of His Son, Jesus Christ.[4]

Therefore it is imperative that we obey the Lord's command to preach the gospel to all nations. The Bride of Christ will be made up of Jews and Gentiles whose sins have been washed away by His blood. And those who go on in the Lord, and prepare themselves for the wedding, will marry their Heavenly Bridegroom.

When the Lord poured out His Spirit at the commencement of the Church Age, it was upon the Jews. "And there were dwelling in Jerusalem Jews, devout men, from every nation under heaven."[5] But then, as now, Jewry, as a nation, rejected both Jesus their Messiah, and the outpouring of the Holy Spirit. As a result, hear carefully what the great Jewish apostle Paul said to them. The Bible records:

> " ... Paul was compelled by the Spirit, and testified to the Jews that Jesus is the Christ.
> But when they opposed him and blasphemed, he shook his garments and said to them, 'Your blood be upon your own heads; I am clean. From now on I will go to the Gentiles.'" (Acts 18:5,6)

---

[4] Rev 5:9.
[5] Acts 2:5.

However, I am mindful that the Bible teaches in the last days, before the second coming of Christ, there will be one last worldwide outpouring of the Holy Spirit "upon all flesh."[6] This will, of course, include Israel as we recognize that nation today. God's promise, through the prophet Ezekiel is, "'I will not hide My face from them anymore; for I shall have poured out My Spirit on the house of Israel,' says the Lord God" (Eze 39:40). When? Immediately after the events described in Ezekiel chapters 38 and 39. For Ezekiel 39:40 speaks of the Spirit being poured out, before the Great Tribulation.[7] Israel will have the same opportunity to respond to the Holy Spirit as all other nations during that worldwide revival and harvest. Not only this, but as we shall see in **Volume Two** when we study Revelation chapter 11, the Lord will give Israel, under the ministry of the two witnesses, a "special chance" (*not* a "*second* chance") to turn to the Messiah.

BRIDES IN THE OLD TESTAMENT

The Old Testament is a true record of Bible history. But it is much more than that. The Old Testament is filled with people, places, man-made objects, numbers and symbols, which have important prophetic significance. This includes a number of brides in the Old Testament.

Referring to Old Testament people and events, Paul teaches:

> "Now these things befell them by way of a figure—as an example and warning (to us); they were written to admonish and fit us for right action by good instruction, we in whose days the ages have reached their climax—their consummation and concluding period." (1 Cor 10:11 – *Amp*)

Before we can understand the Bride of Christ in the Book of Revelation, it is necessary for us to first learn some important lessons from notable brides in the Old Testament. The following brides are examples—figures and prophetic pictures—of the Bride of Christ. Space forbids a complete study, for whole books could be written about each one.[8]

1. EVE—the Bride from the Body

> There are four prominent brides in Genesis, known as the book of beginnings. Each foreshadows the Bride of Christ in the Book of Revelation. The first of these is Eve.
>
> God caused a deep sleep to fall upon Adam. While Adam slept, the Lord took Adam's bride from his side.[9] This is a prophetic picture of what happened to Jesus.

---

[6] See, for example, Joel 2:28, Jas 5:7,8.
[7] We will study Ezekiel chapters 38 and 39 in **HERE COMES THE BRIDE! Volume Two**, when we look at the second seal of Revelation chapter 6.
[8] For example, Asenath the wife of Joseph and Zipporah the wife of Moses could be added to this list. They are pictures for us of Gentile brides married to God's covenant sons.
[9] Gen 2:20-24.

When our Lord Jesus died on the cross, His side was pierced with a spear. From the blood and water that flowed from His body, the Church was birthed (John 19:34; 1 Jn 5:6-8). I must emphasize that Jesus did not just sleep on the cross. He died.

And in these last days, from this slumbering giant, the body of Christ, the Church, God will bring forth the Lord's living Bride described in Revelation.

Adam and Eve were united in marriage—became one flesh—on the sixth day of the re-creation.[10] At the end of the sixth day of the week of redemption, Christ and His Bride will be united in marriage.

2. SARAH—the Bride of Restoration

We are all familiar with the story of Abraham and Sarah. Sarah was beautiful, but she was barren:

> "Abraham and Sarah were old, well advanced in age; and Sarah had passed the age of childbearing." (Gen 18:11)

The Lord appeared to them. He promised them a son. She was restored:

> "By faith Sarah herself also received strength to conceive seed, and she bore a child when she was past the age, because she judged Him faithful who had promised." (Heb 11:11)

Just as Sarah was restored to fruitfulness, so will the Lord's last day Church be restored to fruitfulness. The Bible teaches that Jesus cannot come again until this great restoration has taken place:

> "Repent therefore and be converted, that your sins may be blotted out, so that times of refreshing ['and reviving'–*Amp*] may come from the presence of the Lord,
> and that He may send Jesus Christ, who was preached to you before,
> whom heaven must receive [retain, hold back] until the times of restoration of all things, which God has spoken by the mouth of all His holy prophets since the world began." (Acts 3:19-21)

These verses do not promise that everything will be restored. Nor do they say every person on earth will be saved. They do state that everything *the prophets foretold* concerning restoration will take place before the Lord Jesus comes again.

Restoration is not just a teaching—it is a personal experience, as demonstrated in David's prayer:

---

[10] See Chapter 10 of this book, "God's Week."

"I am sick at heart. How long, O Lord, until you restore me?" (Psa 6:3–*LB*)

Here are just a few areas in which God promises restoration:

- The joy of salvation (Psa 51:11,12);

- Our soul–mind, emotions, will, purpose, intellect, affections and motivations (Psa 23:3);

- Years that have been wasted (Joel 2:25);

- Paths to dwell in (Isa 58:12);

- Comforts in time of mourning (Isa 57:18);

- Lands, vineyards, olive groves, houses, corn, wine, oil (each speaking of the fullness of God's blessings) (Neh 5:11);

- The tabernacle of David (Amos 9:11; Acts 15:16).[11]

How exciting it is for us to be living in these wonderful days of restoration!

3. REBEKAH—the Bride of Separation

The story of Rebekah is found in Genesis chapter 24, which is the longest chapter in the book of beginnings. The narrative is filled with prophetic insight.

Abraham the father, sent his servant to find a bride for his son. God, our Father, has sent the Holy Spirit to prepare a Bride for His Son.

Some of the characteristics of the bride chosen for Isaac by Eliezer, together with their New Testament prophetic fulfillment, are:

- Rebekah was related to Abraham by blood (Gen 24:4).

The Bride of Christ is related to God by being washed from sin in the blood of Jesus (Rev 1:5; Eph 2:13).

- Rebekah was a beautiful virgin (verse 16).

The Bride of Christ will be beautiful, and will not have committed spiritual adultery with other gods (Eph 5:22; 2 Cor 11:2; Matt 25:1-13).

---

[11] For more teaching on restoration, see my book *The Power of His Presence*, chapter one, "The Complete Restoration." *The Power of His Presence* contains an in-depth study on The Tabernacle of David, and praise and worship.

- Rebekah was found drawing water from the well at evening time (verses 16-20).

    The Bride of Christ will draw water from the wells of salvation at this evening hour of time (Isa 12:3).

- Rebekah was diligent in dispensing water (verses 16-20).

    The Bride of Christ will be diligent in ministering the water of the Word of God (Eph 5:26).

- Rebekah received gifts from the servant for her ears and hands (verse 22).

    The Bride of Christ will have blessed ears to hear the Spirit, and hands to minister for the Lord (Rev 2:7).

- Rebekah was attentive to the servant's words (verse 23ff).

    The Bride of Christ will be obedient to the voice of the Holy Spirit (Rev 2:11; Rom 8:14).

- Rebekah, by faith, was willing to separate herself to follow the servant and marry the son (verse 58).

    The Bride of Christ will, by faith, be willing to separate herself to follow the Holy Spirit all the way to the appearing of God's Son (Matt 19:29; Heb 9:28).

- Rebekah met Isaac in the field (verses 63, 64).

    The Bride of Christ will also meet her Bridegroom as she obeys His command to work for Him in the field (John 4:35; Matt 13:38).

- Rebekah was loved by Isaac, and he married her (verse 67).

    The Bride of Christ will experience the Bridegroom's great love in increasing measure, and He will marry her (1 Jn 3:1-3; Rev 19:7).

4. RACHEL–the Shepherd Bride

We read of Rachel in Genesis chapter 29. Just as Rebekah was introduced to us at a well, so is Rachel (verse 6). The story of the love of Jacob for Rachel is filled with prophetic significance. Again, I can only mention a few brief comparisons with the Bride of Christ:

There were three flocks of sheep waiting to drink at the well (Gen 29:2).

There are three distinct stages in spiritual growth. John, the author of the Book of Revelation, informs us these three stages are illustrated as "little children," "young men," "fathers" (1 Jn 2:12,13,14). We will develop this teaching later.

Therefore these three flocks can represent believers at different stages of maturity in God.

There was a large stone over the well's mouth (verse 2). Jacob rolled it away (verse 10).

The history of the Church for the past 500 years has been a history of strong men and women of God removing the stones that closed His wells—stones of error and unbelief that blocked the flow of the water of His Word. They opened the wells of Biblical truth. The chart on page 14 summarizes this history. (*Figure 1: "History of Restoration to the Church During the Past 500 Years."*)

There still remain stones to be removed, and even more wells to be opened in these last days!

Jacob worked one week (seven years) for Rachel (Hebrew, "a lamb"), but Laban gave him her sister Leah (Hebrew, "weary") instead (verse 25).

God re-created the world in seven days, but Adam and Eve sinned.

Jacob worked a second week (seven years) and was given his beloved Rachel (verses 26 &27).

God is at work a second week. A week with God is seven 1,000-year days.[12] This is His week of redemption, during which the Bride He desires for His Son will be prepared (Rev 19:8).

Rachel was a keeper of sheep, a shepherd (verse 9).

The Lord is raising up true shepherds in these last days who will guard, guide, and feed the flocks of God, challenging them to grow to maturity.

5. RUTH—the Bride of the Visitation

In Bible times the book of Ruth was written on a separate scroll, and read each year at the Feast of Pentecost, the harvest festival. The events and the characters in this book contain so much that foreshadows what the Lord is doing in the earth today.

---

[12] Psa 90:4; 2 Pet 3:8.

Figure 1: **History of Restoration to the Church During the Past 500 Years**

YEAR	RESTORED THROUGH	COUNTRY	WELLS OPENED
1517	Martin Luther	Germany/Europe	Salvation through faith in Christ alone
1525	Anabaptists	Switzerland/Europe	Water baptism by immersion after conversion
1555	John Knox	Scotland/Europe	Presbytery leads church Hymns of worship
1730	John and Charles Wesley	England/USA	Personal holiness and discipline; Methodism; Inspired hymns of worship
1827	Brethren Movement	Ireland/England	Body ministry; Lord's supper; sanctification
1900	Pentecostal Visitation	1890s Scotland, England 1900 USA, whole world	Baptism into Holy Spirit with sign of tongues
1928	Welsh Revival	Wales/England British Commonwealth	Apostles and prophets; Evangelism
1948	Latter Rain Visitation	Canada, whole world	Praise and worship; laying on of hands
1960s	Charismatic Renewal	USA, whole world	Baptism in Spirit for all believers; unity; new charismatic churches

Ruth is the story of a Moabitess—a Gentile woman—who finds a place of unusual acceptance and honour in the household of faith. She marries Boaz, who portrays for us Christ, the Owner of the field, our great Kinsman-Redeemer.

I have divided the book of Ruth into five parts, showing her progression in becoming the bride of Boaz:

a. **Ruth, the STRANGER—1:1-5**

During the time of the Judges, famine conditions prevailed in Canaan. There was no bread. Amos warns us:

"'Behold, the days are coming,' says the Lord God, 'that I will send a famine on the land, not a famine of bread, nor a thirst for water, but of hearing the words of the Lord.'" (Amos 8:11)

Because of the famine, Elimelech and Naomi traveled with their family to the land of Moab. Their sons married women of Moab–Ruth and Orpah. Ruth was a stranger to God, His covenants, His blessings, His promises. So were we. But now, in Christ:

"you are no longer strangers and foreigners, but fellow citizens with the saints and members of the household of God, having been built on the foundation of the apostles and prophets, Jesus Christ Himself being the chief cornerstone." (Eph 2:19)

b. Ruth STEADFAST—1:6-22

When Naomi, Ruth and Orpah "heard that the Lord had visited His people by giving them bread" they began their journey back to the land of Judah (chapter 1:6,7). We too can confidently expect another great visitation of the Lord's power, presence and provision: "Thou hast granted me life and favour, and thy visitation hath preserved my spirit" (Job 10:12 – *KJV*).

Peter exhorts us how to live in the season of God's visitation:

"Having your conduct honorable among the Gentiles, that when they speak against you as evildoers, they may, by your good works which they observe, glorify God in the day of visitation." (1 Pet 2:12)

Jesus wept over Jerusalem with the words: " ... because you did not know the time of your visitation" (Luke 19:44). Let us be careful not to miss the visitation of the Lord in these last days!

On the return journey, Orpah turned back to Moab. Naomi also missed out on being blessed in the land, because her heart was bitter. But Ruth was steadfast. She wanted to receive from the visitation. So will the Bride of Christ. It will be the Bride's foremost aim to participate in God's last day visitation.[13]

c. Ruth SERVING—2:1-23

Ruth began to glean in the field of Boaz. In adverse circumstances, she was humble, faithful, and hard-working.

The Bride of Christ will not only be a faithful hard worker in the Master's field, but will also be humble, exalting Him.

---

[13] See *Appendix 1,* "The Differences Between a 'Visitation' and a 'Revival.'"

d. Ruth SEEKING–3:1-13

In preparation for her meeting with Boaz, Ruth was commanded to do three things:

i. "Wash yourself"

The Bride of Christ will be washed by the Word (Eph 5:26);

ii. "Anoint yourself"

As we shall soon see, the Bride of Christ will have sufficient oil (the anointing of the Holy Spirit) to enter the door to the marriage supper of Christ (see Matthew chapter 25);

iii. "Put on your best garment"

It will be essential to be clothed with a wedding garment for the marriage of the King's Son (Matt 22:11).

Ruth lay on the threshing floor at the feet of Boaz at the midnight hour (3:8). The word "midnight" is found fourteen times in the Bible, and is of great significance concerning the hour in which we live. We will look at this in detail when we study Matthew chapter 25. But "midnight" never means "the end." Conversely, midnight heralds a transition from something good to something better!

e. Ruth SATISFIED–4:1-22

Ruth marries Boaz, and brings forth a man child, Obed, destined to be "a restorer of life" (Ruth 4:15). Ruth became the great-grandmother of King David (verse 17), and is listed in the genealogy of Jesus Christ.[14]

Similarly, in the Book of Revelation, the Bride of Christ marries Him. She gives birth to a man child, whose birth precipitates the "restoration" of heaven because Satan is cast out.[15]

6. ABIGAIL–the Overcoming Bride

When we carefully study the letters to the seven churches, we will see one of the main teachings of the Book of Revelation is learning how to be an overcomer.

---

[14] Matt 1:5.
[15] Rev 12:1-10.

Being an overcomer is not just overcoming the judgments of the trumpets, vials, plagues, earthquakes, wars, and all the "big, bad stuff." God wants us to learn how to be victorious in the adverse circumstances we encounter in everyday life. Abigail, whose life, and ultimate marriage, is recorded in First Samuel chapter 25, is an example of such an overcomer–she overcame negative circumstances and became the bride of a king.

Samuel had died. The mighty judge and prophet was gone. Saul was still on the throne. David was out in the wilderness with 600 men. The kingdom was being shaken. There was uncertainty and fear in the land–just as in many places today.

Abigail's first husband, Nabal, though wealthy, was a foolish scoundrel. His name means "fool." The Bible says, "he was harsh and evil in his doings" (1 Sam 25:3). Conversely, Abigail's name means "source or cause of delight." The Scripture says "she was a woman of good understanding and beautiful appearance" (verse 3).

While David was in the wilderness, he sent a message to Nabal asking him for provisions. Nabal refused. David's anger was kindled, and he came to kill Nabal and his men. Abigail heard of David's plan, and despite her difficult circumstances at home, she did three things:

She brought gifts to David, who was soon to become king (verse 18).

The Bride of Christ will be kind, generous, giving sacrificially to her coming King;

She interceded with David on behalf of those he was going to put to death (verses 25, 26).

The Bride of Christ will be made up of believers who pray and intercede;

She humbled herself before David (verse 28).

The Bride of Christ will be made up of those who have humbled themselves in the sight of the Lord (Jas 4:10).

After ten days Nabal died. Later Abigail became the wife of David (verses 37 and 42). Abigail overcame all the difficulties of living with a husband who was a greedy scoundrel, and became the bride of him who would soon be crowned king.

7. ESTHER–the Captive Orphan who became the Bride of a King

There are only two books in the Bible in which there is no direct reference to God–Esther, and the Song of Solomon. Nevertheless, both these books contain, hidden in the types and shadows, wonderful teachings about the Bride of Christ.

There are eight main characters and people groups in the book of Esther. To help you study this book, I suggest the types in the following chart:

Figure 2: **Chart Showing the Prophetic Types in the Book of Esther**

	People	Prophetic Picture of
1.	Ahasuerus	the king, a type of God the Father;
2.	Mordecai	adopted Esther because of his blood relationship with her, a type of the Lord Jesus Christ;
3.	Hegai (Hege)	prepared Esther to be the King's Bride, a type of the Holy Spirit;
4.	Esther	a type of the last day Bride of Christ;
5.	Jews	a type of the whole Church in the last days;
6.	Haman	an Agagite of Amelekitish descent who tried to destroy Mordecai, Esther, and her people, a type of Satan;
7.	Vashti	the queen who was deposed because of her disobedience to the king, a type of national Israel at the time of Christ's first coming (John 1:11);
8.	The king's officers	sent to every province of the kingdom to gather the virgins to the king, a type of the five ascension gift ministries (Eph 4:8,11).

As I divided the book of Ruth into five major sections, so I have done with the book of Esther. The truths contained in each section are prophetic pictures pertaining to the Bride of Christ:

a. Esther PREPARING–1:1–2:16

Esther was an orphan. She was a beautiful woman who found favour with many. Mordecai, with whom she had a blood relationship, adopted her.

Esther was taken to the palace to be prepared to meet the king. Hegai ordered "beauty treatments" (*LB*) for twelve months, as he "changed her" (2:9–*margin*, *KJV*). Six months with oil of myrrh, and six months with perfumes and other preparations for the beautifying of women (2:12). Our Father is preparing a Bride for His Son. He has sent the Holy Spirit to mould and change us, conforming us to His will. It is a long, and sometimes painful, process. But, just as Esther submitted to the massages, pummellings, and heat, we must submit to the dealings of God to be in that company spoken of in Revelation 19:7:

> "Let us be glad and rejoice and give Him glory, for the marriage of the Lamb has come, and His wife has made herself *ready*."

b. Esther PREFERRED–2:16-2:23

The king chose Esther, the captive, orphan girl, and married her:

> "The king loved Esther more than all the other women, and she obtained grace and favor in his sight more than all the virgins; so he set the royal crown upon her head and made her queen instead of Vashti." (2:17)

In verse 18 the great wedding feast begins.

c. Esther PERISHING–chapters 3 and 4

The words and plans of Haman in chapter 3 are prophetic of Satan's quest to destroy Christ and His Bride. Satan's plans have their climax in Revelation chapter 12:

> "And when the dragon saw that he was cast unto the earth, he persecuted the woman which brought forth the man child." (Rev 12:13–*KJV*)

Because of Haman's wicked decree, Esther and her people were as good as dead.

d. Esther PRAYING–5:1–8:10

Esther was determined to intercede for her people:

> "Now it happened on the third day that Esther put on her royal robes and stood in the inner court of the king's palace, across from the king's house, while the king sat on his royal throne in the royal house, facing the entrance of the house.
> So it was, when the king saw Queen Esther standing in the court, that she found favor in his sight, and the king held out to Esther the golden scepter that was in his hand. Then Esther went near and touched the top of the scepter." (5:1,2)

It was Esther's bold entrance to the inner court of the king's palace, and her supplication to him, that reversed the whole situation. Haman was hanged on the very tree (5:14–*margin, KJV*) that was prepared for Mordecai. This was prophetic of the fact it would not be Jesus who was conquered on the cross–it would be the devil:

> "For this purpose the Son of God was manifested, that He might destroy the works of the devil." (1 Jn 3:8b)

The Bride of Christ will be willing to perish, if needs be, but will boldly intercede in prayer, ministering to the Lord, and for Him. Jesus taught us:

> "He who finds his life will lose it, and he who loses his life for My sake will find it." (Matt 10:39)

e. Esther POWERFUL–8:11-10:3

Mordecai is exalted:

> "So Mordecai went out from the presence of the king in royal apparel of blue and white, with a great crown of gold and a garment of fine linen and purple; and the city of Shushan rejoiced and was glad." (8:15)

From her new position as Queen, Esther, together with Mordecai, "wrote with full authority to confirm this second letter about Purim" (9:29).

The orphan girl became the bride of the king, with great authority.

The Bride of Christ is His by new birth, and by adoption, and, in the last days, will have great authority.

8. THE QUEEN OF SHEBA – the Sign-Bride of the End Times

The record of the Queen of Sheba's visit to King Solomon is found in First Kings chapter 10. However, to discover the full significance of the Queen of Sheba, we must turn to the New Testament.

The scribes and Pharisees asked Jesus, "Teacher, we want to see a sign from you" (Matt 12:38). They had already seen the Lord do many signs and wonders. What they were asking for now was a sign, definite proof, that He was Whom He claimed to be, the Son of God.

Jesus answered them by telling them about not one, but two signs. Firstly, He gave them the sign of Jonah:

> "... no sign will be given [this generation] except the sign of the prophet Jonah.
>
> For as Jonah was three days and three nights in the belly of the great fish, so will the Son of Man be three days and three nights in the heart of the earth."
> (Matt 12:39,40)

Jesus also said:

"For as Jonah became a sign to the Ninevites, so also the Son of Man will be to this generation." (Luke 11:30)

The Lord Jesus fulfilled the sign of Jonah when He died on the cross of Calvary, was buried for three days and three nights, and rose triumphantly from the dead. For our Lord was crucified on Wednesday, not Friday, as is generally supposed.[16]

After Jesus told them about the sign of Jonah, both Matthew and Luke record that Jesus immediately spoke of the sign of the Queen of Sheba:

"The queen of the South will rise up in the judgment with this generation and condemn it, for she came from the ends of the earth to hear the wisdom of Solomon; and indeed a greater than Solomon is here." (Matt 12:42)

Jesus did not fulfill the sign of the Queen of Sheba during His earthly ministry. He will fulfill this sign in His Bride in the last days. This same word, "sign," is used to describe the Bride of Christ in the Book of Revelation (Rev 12:1).

So Jesus gave two outstanding signs.

The first one was for the generation in which He lived as a Man on the earth. He died on the cross, and rose again, to usher in the Church age. The second sign was for the last generation, to end the Church age. These are signs, which if men will not receive them, they will be left without excuse. These are not signs of healings or miracles. These signs are central to the message of the kingdom of God. These signs are worldwide in their influence and impact. These signs bring blessing to those who believe, and act upon them. But judgment to those who refuse them.

Most significantly, these two signs cannot be imitated by the devil, even though, in the last days, the antichrist will appear to do "miracles."[17] Jesus gave these two signs to illustrate His ministry at the beginning and the ending of the Church age. These signs Satan will never be able to counterfeit.

Who was this Queen of Sheba? She was a stranger, a foreigner, who came to the king. We were strangers too, until we came to King Jesus.

The narrative in First Kings chapter 10, describing her coming to the king, is filled with prophetic pictures and types. Here are just a few:

---

[16] There were two Sabbaths during the Passover week in which Jesus died. These were the special Feast Sabbath on Thursday (the "high day" referred to in John 19:31), and the weekly Sabbath (Saturday).
For further details, see *The Three Days and Three Nights* by Kevin J. Conner; Conner Publications, Melbourne, Australia, 1988.

[17] "The coming of the lawless one is according to the working of Satan, with all power, signs, and lying wonders." (2 Thess 2:9)

a. **"The queen of Sheba heard of the fame of Solomon concerning *the name of the Lord.*"** (1 Ki 10:1)

And in these last days, as a result of this current restoration-revival, the Name and salvation of the Lord Jesus Christ is being preached throughout the earth.

b. **"She came to Jerusalem ... with camels that bore *spices.*"** (verse 2)

If you have eaten Indian food, you will know that it is the spices that give the unique flavour. Spices represent the nine fruit of the Spirit, listed in Galatians 5:22 and 23. It is these fruit–love, joy, peace–and all the others that demonstrate the character of Christ in our lives.

> "Awake, O north wind, and come, O south! Blow upon my garden, that its spices may flow out. Let my beloved come to his garden and eat its pleasant fruits." (Song 4:16)

"You are God's garden." (1 Cor 3:9)[18] Our Beloved Lord wants to come to His garden to enjoy the aroma and taste of its spices and fruits. From time to time God allows seasons of chilling winds – winds of adversity and contradiction–to blow in our lives. This is because He desires that the fruit of His Spirit develop and mature in us.

Orchards in New Zealand produce a variety of delicious apples. We don't enjoy the cold winter weather; however, cold is required to develop the fragrance and sweet flavour of the fruit. The icy winds of winter are quickly forgotten when we bite into our first crisp apple of the new season. We relish the flavour as it explodes in our mouth. Sugary juices run down our chin. This mature fruit is not only nourishing our body; it is delighting our senses!

Verse 10 says: "There never again came such abundance of spices as the queen of Sheba gave to King Solomon."

c. **"She came to Jerusalem with ...very much *gold.*"** (verse 2)

> "She gave the king one hundred and twenty talents of gold." (verse 10)

In the Bible gold often speaks of faith:

> "In this you greatly rejoice, though now for a little while, if need be, you have been grieved by various trials, that the genuineness of your faith, being much more precious than gold that perishes, though it is tested by fire, may be found to praise, honor, and glory at the revelation of Jesus Christ."
> (1 Pet 1:6, 7)

---

[18] *The Living Bible*; Holman Illustrated Edition, Philadelphia, 1973–page 1065

Faith is both a fruit and a gift of the Holy Spirit. The Bride of Christ will be filled with faith. Not presumption. Not arrogance. But the Bride will have a vibrant trust in God, believing He answers prayer, and fulfills His Word.

Faith will be tested and purified. The number 120 represents "the end of all flesh." The Bride will not be fleshly or carnal, but cleansed and pure.

d. "She came to Jerusalem with ... *precious stones*." (verse 2)

When "gold" and "precious stones" are mentioned together, they speak of authority, power and reigning. For example:

> "Then he [David] took their king's crown [the king of Rabbah] from his head. Its weight was a talent of gold, with precious stones. And it was set on David's head." (2 Sam 12:30)

The Bride of Christ will live and minister in the authority of the Name and power of the Lord Jesus Christ, in the knowledge that He "has blessed us with every spiritual blessing in the heavenly places in Christ." (Eph 1:3)

> "To Him who loved us and washed us from our sins in His own blood, and has made us kings and priests to His God and Father, to Him be glory and dominion forever and ever. Amen." (Rev 1:5 & 6)

e. She came because of His *wisdom* (verse 7).

The Bible says that Jesus Christ "became for us wisdom from God." (1 Cor 1:30)

"She came to test him with *hard questions*." (verse 1) The more we grow in the Christian life, the more difficult may be the questions and situations we face.

In her book *Prayer–From a Discipline to a Delight*, in the chapter entitled "The Silences of God," my wife Pamela says this about difficult questions:

> "It is in those periods of silence the Lord works some of His greatest changes in our lives. During the waiting He sometimes allows circumstances which appear to contradict all we have believed.

> "Our Lord Jesus endured contradiction:

> 'Looking unto Jesus the author and finisher of our faith; who for the joy that was set before him endured the cross, despising the shame, and is set down at the right hand of the throne of God. For consider him that endured such *contradiction* of sinners against himself, unless you be wearied and faint in your minds.' (Hebrews 12:2,3–*KJV*)

"In the Greek language the word 'contradiction' is *antilogia,* from:

anti = 'against'

logo = 'to speak.'

"Sometimes the Lord will allow us to experience circumstances, just as Jesus did, which seem to contradict the very Word of God ...
"What did Jesus, our example, do in contradiction? The Bible says He 'endured.' This word means to 'abide under,' 'to bear up courageously,' 'to wait patiently with faith and hope.' It is difficult to endure. But be persistent:

'... don't become weary and give up.' (Hebrews 12:3–*LB*)

"Understand that your negative circumstances are not because God is angry with you, nor because you have committed some great sin. Rather, the Lord is teaching you that as you stand firm during times of contradiction, your heart will be changed."[19]

f. She spoke with the king "about *all that was in her heart.*" (verse 2)

In like manner, the Bride of Christ will enjoy intimate, heart-to-heart fellowship and communion with her Bridegroom.

g. She was amazed when she saw the king's *house he had built.* (verse 4)

The Lord is building His house, His Church (Matt 16:18). Concerning this house, it is written:

"Christ as a Son over His own house, whose house we are if we hold fast the confidence and the rejoicing of the hope firm to the end." (Heb 3:6)

A very important part of what God is building and restoring today is the Tabernacle of David (see Amos 9:11 and Acts 15:16). When David is speaking of the glories of God's heavens, He says:

"In them He has set a tabernacle for the sun,
Which is like a bridegroom coming out of his chamber..." (Psa 19:4,5)

h. She was amazed when she saw *the food on the king's table.* (verse 5)

This food speaks to us of the Word of God. In Malachi 3:10 and 11 we read:

"'Bring all the tithes into the storehouse, that there may be *food* in My house, and try Me now in this,' says the Lord of hosts, 'If I will not open for you the

---

[19] *Prayer – From a Discipline to a Delight* by Pamela Truscott; Truscott Missions, San Diego, 2000 – pages 120-122.

windows of heaven and pour out for you such blessing that there will not be room enough to receive it.'"

Pamela and I have been very encouraged these past few years, to find a great new hunger for God's Word among His people. In every nation Christians want to be fed, not just with "milk of the Word," but with "solid food."[20] God's promise is: "He has given *food* to those who fear Him; He will ever be mindful of His covenant." (Ps 111:5)

The words of our Lord Jesus challenge us:

> "Who then is that faithful and wise steward, whom his master will make ruler over his household, to give them their portion of *food* at the right time?" (Luke 12:42–*margin*)

i. She was amazed at the *seating of the king's servants*. (verse 5)

In normal circumstances, servants don't sit. But even as the love slaves of Jesus are serving Him, they experience the blessings of Ephesians 2:6:

> "[God has] raised us up together, and made us sit together in the heavenly places in Christ Jesus."

j. She was amazed at the *"service of his waiters."* ["attendance of his ministers"– *KJV*] (verse 5)

We must be ever mindful of the fact that the word "minister" has no other meaning but "servant." Our Lord Jesus was emphatic about this:

> "So likewise you, when you have done all those things which you are commanded, say, 'We are unprofitable servants. We have done what was our duty to do.'" (Luke 17:10)

k. She was amazed at *their apparel*. (verse 5)

In Matthew chapter 22, Jesus relates the parable of the king who arranged a marriage for his son. It is clear the king is a type of God the Father, and the Son, of course, our Lord Jesus Christ. He emphasizes the necessity of wearing a wedding garment to this marriage.

The complete wedding garment comprises five major articles of clothing:

i.	Salvation	Isa 61:10	iv.	Humility	1 Pet 5:5
ii.	Righteousness	Isa 61:10	v.	Love	Col 3:14
iii.	Praise	Isa 61:10			

---

[20] Heb 5:13,14.

Isaiah 61:10 reads:

> "I will greatly rejoice in the Lord,
> my soul shall be joyful in my God;
> for He has clothed me with the garments of salvation,
> He has covered me with the robe of righteousness,
> as a bridegroom decks himself with ornaments,
> and as a bride adorns herself with her jewels."

Of the Bride of Christ, the Book of Revelation says:

> "And it was given to her to clothe herself in fine linen, bright and clean; for the fine linen is the righteous acts of the saints." (Rev 19:8–*NAS*)

l. The Queen of Sheba was amazed at the king's *cupbearers*. (verse 5)

These cupbearers are a prophetic picture of the five kinds of ascension gift ministries, who minister the wine of the Gospel:

> "Therefore He says: 'When He ascended on high, He led captivity captive, and gave gifts to men.'
> And He Himself gave some to be apostles, some prophets, some evangelists, and some pastors and teachers." (Eph 4:8,11)

We can expect to see more of these anointed ascension gift ministries in these last days, together with an increase of miraculous signs and wonders from the Lord:

> "Here am I and the children whom the Lord has given me! We are for signs and wonders in Israel from the Lord of hosts ..." (Isa 8:18)

m. She was amazed at *the king's entry way* by which he went up to the house of the Lord. (verse 5)

There was a glorious pathway to the house of the Lord. The Bride of Christ also has an abundant entrance into His presence with:

i.	Holiness and purity	Psa 24:3
ii.	Praise and worship	Psa 100:1-4
iii.	Gladness	Psa 122:1

n. She was amazed the king's house was filled with *happiness and praise*.
(1 Kings 10:8-9)

> "The king made ... *harps and stringed instruments* for singers." (verse 12)

The prophet Isaiah says that not only does God give *us* joy. We are also to give joy to *Him*:

> "As the bridegroom rejoices over the bride, so shall your God rejoice over you." (Isa 62:5)

In Jeremiah we read of "the voice of the bridegroom and the voice of the bride" four times. In this great "restoration chapter" he describes the restoration of praise:

> "the voice of joy and the voice of gladness, the voice of the bridegroom and the voice of the bride, the voice of those who will say:
> Praise the Lord of hosts,
> For the Lord is good,
> For His mercy endures forever' – and of those who will bring the sacrifice of praise into the house of the Lord." (Jer 33:11)

God is restoring the joy of salvation to the people of God (Psa 51:12). He is restoring Biblical worship and praise. The Book of Revelation is also a Book about worship:

> "And I heard the sound of harpists playing their harps. They sang as it were a new song before the throne." (Rev 14:2,3)

o. The king gave the Queen of Sheba *"all she desired, whatever she asked."* (verse 13).

The Bride of Christ will have such intimate fellowship with the Lord, that the Lord's desires shall become her desires:

> "Delight yourself also in the Lord, and he shall give you the desires of your heart." (Psa 37:4)

John records that Jesus promised:

> "Until now you have asked nothing in My name. Ask, and you will receive, that your joy may be full." (John 16:24)

And John says in his first letter:

> "Now this is the confidence that we have in Him, that if we ask anything according to His will, He hears us. And if we know that He hears us, whatever we ask, we know that we have the petitions that we have asked of Him." (1 Jn 5:14,15)

These Two Signs

These two signs, the sign of Jonah, and the sign of the Queen of Sheba, bring both blessing and judgment. Many missed the first sign–the sign of the prophet Jonah. They did not believe that Jesus was the promised Messiah. They did not believe that three days after His crucifixion the Lord Jesus was raised from the dead.

Let us be careful not to miss the second sign–the sign of the Queen of Sheba. This is the Lord's sign to our generation. The sign of the glorious Bride of Christ.

PART ONE THE BRIDE

Chapter 3

Bridal Language in the New Testament

The Song of Solomon

Before we look at New Testament bridal language, further mention must be made of the Song of Solomon.

The Song of Solomon is the marriage manual for Christian couples. My wife and I have been privileged to lead Marriage Enrichment Seminars in many parts of the world. In these seminars we teach, using the Song of Solomon, that romantic expression between a husband and his wife can be enhanced and increased.[1]

There is also a great devotional message in the Song of Solomon–the growing love between the Shulamite and her beloved illustrates the growing love of the Bride of Christ for her beloved Saviour. This love reaches its consummation and fulfillment in the Book of Revelation. For example: "Who is this coming up from the wilderness, leaning upon her beloved?" (Song 8:5) has its fulfillment in Revelation 12:6.

BRIDAL LANGUAGE IN THE NEW TESTAMENT

As we have already seen, Jesus Christ began His public ministry at a wedding. Later, He clearly referred to Himself as "the Bridegroom":

> "And Jesus said to them, 'Can the friends of the bridegroom mourn as long as the bridegroom is with them? But the days will come when the bridegroom will be taken away from them, and then they will fast.'"
> (Matt 9:15)

Jesus used the language of marriage in two of His parables:

- Matthew 22, the parable of the marriage of the king's son; and

---

[1] An excellent book we recommend on this subject is *Solomon on Sex* by Joseph C. Dillow, Thomas Nelson, Inc., New York/Nashville, 1977. In our Marriage Enrichment Seminars we encourage married couples to read this book.

- Matthew 25, the parable of the five wise and the five foolish virgins.

We will study these parables in detail in subsequent chapters.

Engaged to Christ

The Church is not yet married to Christ. Rather, the Bible teaches that the Church is engaged, or betrothed, to Christ:

> "For I am jealous for you with godly jealousy. For I have betrothed you to one husband, that I may present you as a chaste virgin to Christ." (2 Cor 11:2)

The Greek meanings of some of these words shed important light on this verse:

"Jealous":	
Greek, *zēloo*	"zealous"
"betrothed":	"to be fitted together, to fit, to join"
Greek, *harmozo*	The roots of this word are *harmos*, which means "a joint, joining" and *ar*, signifying "to fit"
	From this Greek word we get our English words "harmony" and to "harmonize" (two or more musical notes making a beautiful sound together).
"chaste":	"consecrated."
Greek, *hagnos*	

In Bible times, engagement, or betrothal, was a binding contract, made in the presence of witnesses. [During our years as pastors, we had an "engagement ceremony" for couples planning to marry. This usually took place during a Sunday morning service. It was made clear sexual union was not permitted to take place until after marriage. But the couple would exchange vows of promise, give gifts to one another, and receive the prayers and blessing of the congregation.]

According to Matthew 1:18, Mary and Joseph were only betrothed. Nevertheless, verse 19 refers to Joseph as Mary's "husband"—the identical word used in 2 Corinthians 11:2 to describe our present relationship with Jesus. When he discovered Mary was pregnant:

> "Joseph her husband, being a just man, and not wanting to make her a public example, was minded to put her away secretly." (Matt 1:19)

To do this, he would have to give her "a certificate of divorce" (see Deut 24:1).

Therefore we understand that being betrothed to the Lord Jesus is a great blessing, and an awesome responsibility.

Bridal Preparation

Bridal preparation is an extremely important subject in Scripture, and this theme will be developed further in later Chapters.

Ephesians chapter 5, verses 22 through 33, gives us a very clear picture of what the Lord is doing today to prepare the Bride of Christ:

> "Husbands, love your wives, just as Christ also loved the church and gave Himself for her,
> that He might sanctify and cleanse her with the washing of water by the word,
> that He might present her to Himself a glorious church, not having spot or wrinkle or any such thing, but that she should be holy and without blemish." (Eph 5:25-27)

Christ loves His Church. He is sanctifying and cleansing His Church. He will present to Himself a glorious Bride. No spots. No wrinkles. No blemishes. Perfect!

An eternally perfect Bridegroom. A perfected Bride. Married. A great mystery. Christ and His Church.

The will of God is that the Bride of Christ be *ready* (see Matt 25:10; Rev 19:7). This, I believe, is one of the main themes of the Book of Revelation.

The word "Bride" appears four times in the Book of Revelation, and the word "Bridegroom" once. We will look closely at these references later. But notice the last reference to the Bride in the Book of Revelation is in conjunction with preaching the Gospel. It is an invitation to come to the Lord:

> "And the Spirit and the bride say, 'Come!' And let him who hears say, 'Come!' And let him who thirsts come. Whoever desires, let him take the water of life freely." (Rev 22:17)

Here Comes the Bridegroom!

Referring to the Lord Jesus, John the Baptist said:

> "He who has the bride is the bridegroom; but the friend of the bridegroom, who stands and hears him, rejoices greatly because of the bridegroom's voice.
> Therefore this joy of mine is fulfilled.
> He must increase, but I must decrease." (John 3:29,30)

I have called this book **HERE COMES THE BRIDE!** to emphasize the necessity for us to get ready if we want to be in the Bride of Christ.

But first and foremost, the Book of Revelation is a Book about the Bridegroom. As we see from the following Scriptures, the climax of His ministry in Revelation is His Second Coming in power and great glory:

- Rev 1:3   "the time is near,"
- Rev 1:7   "Behold, He is coming,"
- Rev 2:25   "till I come,"
- Rev 3:11   "Behold, I am coming quickly!"
- Rev 22:5,10   "the time is at hand,"
- Rev 22:12   "I am coming quickly,"
- Rev 22:20   "Surely I am coming quickly.

Indeed, He *is* coming soon. The reason I have written this book is to show how we can be fully prepared for that great day–and how we can assist others in their preparation.

Soon we shall study how the Bridegroom is revealed in Revelation chapter one.

But before this, I need to give you the main keys to unlock the door of this wonderful Book of Revelation.

PART TWO

THE KEYS

| PART TWO | THE KEYS |

Chapter 4

The Book Rediscovered

The News Ahead of the News

If you could hold in your hands a newspaper that contained the headlines of the major events of the past 100 years, you would have a wealth of knowledge concerning historical events and lots of interesting information.

But what if you were given a newspaper that contained, not the headlines of the past 100 years, but rather the headlines that will appear in our newspapers for the next 30 years? Every time you pick up your Bible you are holding such a newspaper!

The Bible is "the news ahead of the news." This is especially true of the Book of Revelation. Because this Revelation was given to John "to show His servants things which must shortly take place" (Rev 1:1).

The Book Rediscovered

The Bible contains many prophetic pictures illustrating the things God is doing in these last days. Not only is the Old Testament a true record of Bible history. It also contains many important lessons for us today:

> "For whatever things were written before were written for our learning, that we through the patience (*margin*, 'perseverance') and comfort of the Scriptures might have hope." (Rom 15:4)

In Second Kings, chapter 22, we read of the rediscovery of the Book of the Law in the house of the Lord. This Book of the Law was placed beside the ark of the covenant. (See *Figure 3*[1])

The ark of the covenant was an oblong-shaped box, 3¾ feet long, 2¼ feet wide, and 2¼ feet high. The box was made of wood, and was overlaid, both inside and out, with gold. On top of the box was the "mercy seat" which had a golden molding around it, called a "crown." Two angelic-looking beings—"cherubim"—were at each end of the top of the ark. There were poles each side of the box to carry it.

---

[1] This diagram is taken from my book, *The Power of His Presence*, page 34. For further details concerning the ark of the covenant, see chapter 4 of that book, "The Ark of the Covenant."

Figure 3: **The Ark of the Covenant**

In Hebrews 9:9 we learn that the facts about Moses' tabernacle, and the ark of the covenant, were "a parable–a visible symbol or type or picture of the present age" (*Amplified Bible*). Or, as the *New Living Translation* renders this verse:

> "This is an illustration pointing to the present time."

The ark was situated in the holy of holies, and was the visible, audible presence of God to Old Testament Israel. It was their "Immanuel—God is with us." We understand God is Omnipresent. He dwells everywhere. But this was the place where God appeared to the high priest, once a year, on the day of atonement:

> "I will appear in the cloud above the mercy seat." (Lev 16:2)

Not only did the Lord appear there. He promised to speak with them:

> "And there I will meet with you, and I will speak with you from above the mercy seat, from between the two cherubim which are on the ark of the Testimony." (Exo 25:22)

There were four things associated with the ark of the covenant. Inside the ark of the covenant were:

THE BOOK REDISCOVERED

    a. The two Stone Tablets on which were written the ten commandments;

    b. The Golden Pot of manna;

    c. Aaron's Rod that budded.

In addition there was:

    d. The Book of the Law by the side of the ark.

> "Take this Book of the Law, and put it beside the ark of the covenant of the Lord your God, that it may be there as a witness against you." (Deut 31:26)

This Book of the Law was taken out and read during the Feast of Tabernacles.

When we go back to Second Kings chapter 22, we find that Josiah, whose name means "Jehovah supports," was king at that time. He was one of the good "restoration kings." Even as a youth, he wanted the house of God repaired and restored. He collected finances to pay "carpenters, and builders and masons–and to buy timber and hewn stone to repair the house." (verse 6).

As they repaired, they rediscovered the Book of the Law:

> "Then Hilkiah the high priest said to Shaphan the scribe, 'I have found the Book of the Law in the house of the Lord.' And Hilkiah gave the book to Shaphan, and he read it." (verse 8)

Shaphan read the Book of the Law to the king, who, upon hearing its contents, tore his clothes. The Book had been lost. Its contents forgotten. The Book's warnings had gone unheeded. Surely, God's judgments would follow?

The king gathered all the people. "And he read in their hearing all the words of the Book of the Covenant which had been found in the house of the Lord." (2 Ki 23:2)

The king and his people responded to the Book of the Law by renewing their covenant relationship with God:

> "Then the king stood by a pillar and made a covenant before the Lord, to follow the Lord and to keep His commandments and His testimonies and His statutes, with all his heart and all his soul, to perform the words of this covenant that were written in this book. And all the people took a stand for the covenant." (2 Ki 23:3)

Josiah cleansed the priesthood and the temple. He instructed the people to keep a great feast of Passover. He was assured they would escape the coming judgments if they kept God's commandments written in the Book of the Law.

This Book of the Law is a prophetic picture of the Book of Revelation. For many years the Book of Revelation has been "lost" by the people of God. This is a Book of the Bible that has been locked away. It has not been taught. It has been closed; forgotten. But, thank God, it is being rediscovered!

As in the days of King Josiah, so it shall be in these last days–those who respond to God's commands in the Book of Revelation, and keep, not just the Feast of Passover, but also the Feast of Tabernacles, will escape the worst of God's severest judgments.

This is the day. This is the hour for the unveiling of the Book of Revelation.

PART TWO   THE KEYS

Chapter 5

The Writer

The writer of the Book of Revelation is the apostle John. Of Jesus' twelve apostles, we know Peter, James and John had the closest relationship with their Master. John was "the disciple whom Jesus loved … who also had leaned on His breast at the supper."[1] He was well qualified to write about the Lord Jesus. He had "seen and heard" Jesus for well over three years during His earthly life and ministry.[2] He had "seen and heard" Jesus in visions on the Island of Patmos.[3] This same John assures us he was personally commanded to write the Book of Revelation:

> "Write the things which you have seen, and the things which are, and the things which will take place after this." (Rev 1:19)[4]

The Author of the Book of Revelation—indeed, of all the books of the Bible—is the Holy Spirit:

> "Holy men of God spoke as they were moved by the Holy Spirit."
> (2 Pet 1:21)

Like Moses, John wrote five books of the Bible. Moses wrote the first five, the Old Testament Pentateuch. Chronologically, John wrote the last five books of the Bible, the New Testament "Pentateuch"—John's Gospel, the First, Second, and Third Letters of John, and the Book of Revelation.

John wrote Revelation about A.D. 95. Twenty-five years before, in A.D. 70, Prince Titus and his Roman armies had destroyed the city of Jerusalem. History strongly suggests that by the time John wrote the Revelation, the other ten apostles, and Paul, had been martyred. Christ's young Church was being brutally persecuted by the Emperor Domitian, the most cruel of all the Roman emperors. Contemporary historical records state that because the early Christians refused to worship Domitian as god, at least 40,000 of them had suffered martyrdom under his bloodthirsty reign. They were killed by being burned alive at the stake, thrown to lions, wrapped in wild animal skins and fed to dogs, dipped in tar and, still alive, set alight as torches at night-time in the emperor's garden. Historical records report the emperor delighted in hearing the screams of the burning Christians. They were crucified. They were boiled in oil.

---

[1] John 21:20.
[2] John 1:14; 1 John 1:3.
[3] Revelation chapter 1 and following chapters.
[4] The writer's name occurs four times in the Book of Revelation: 1:1,4,9; 22:8.

Tradition tells us that during this persecution, when the enemies of the Church arrested John, they tried to kill him by boiling him in oil for 24 hours. But he remained unharmed. Because they could not kill him, they banished John to the Isle of Patmos, accusing him of witchcraft. Patmos is located about 60 miles south west of the city of Ephesus. Ephesus was a large city that had thrived under the Greeks in the 300s B.C., and now was the capital of the Roman province of Asia. (See *Figure 4*)

Figure 4: **Map showing the locations of the Island of Patmos, and the Seven Churches**

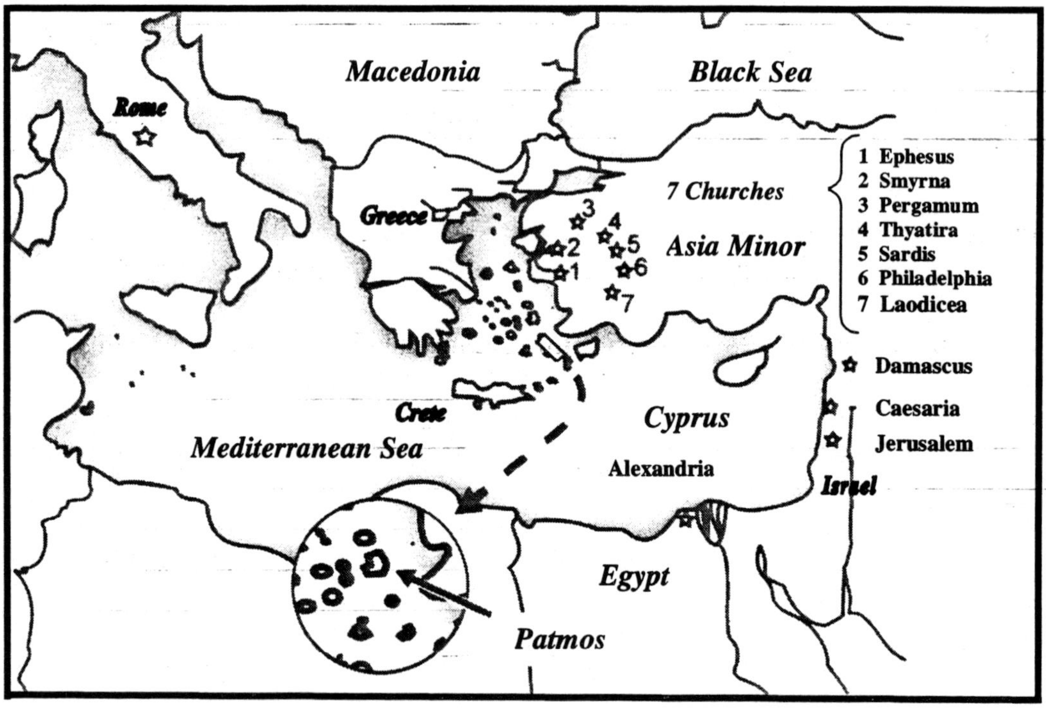

An unknown writer has called Patmos "an island that owes its fame to its prisoner." Patmos is a rugged isle, about ten miles long, and six wide; treeless, rocky, barren, and infested with snakes, large lizards, and scorpions. Because Patmos was so rocky and uninhabitable, the Roman government used it as a penal colony for criminals. John was put in a prison reserved for the worst kind of law-breakers. The prisoners were forced to perform hard, manual labour in the mines of the island, probably digging for, cutting, and carrying heavy blocks of marble. This would have been very difficult and strenuous for John because of his age. Of his personal suffering he writes:

> "I, John, your brother, who share with you in the suffering and the sovereignty and the endurance which is ours in Jesus–I was on the island called Patmos because I had preached God's word and borne my testimony to Jesus." (Rev 1:9—*NEB*)

Exiled on Patmos, John was separated from all encouragement and support. He was cut off from his family, his friends, his church, his city. His body ached. His heart was lonely. Yet, in the midst of unspeakable solitude and suffering, John is about to receive the Revelation of Jesus Christ!

Do you feel exiled on a "personal Patmos"? Are you enduring solitude and suffering? Maybe your "Patmos" is a family in which you are the only Christian. Maybe your "Patmos" is a sickbed. Maybe your "Patmos" is the isolation and banishment of rejection. Possibly you are far from family and friends. A "personal Patmos" can come to us in many different ways. But be encouraged. And be patient. Perhaps the Lord is isolating you for a season because He desires to reveal His beauty, power and glory to you. He will be revealed in a way you have never previously seen Him! Maybe He will use this time in your life to create a stronger passion in your heart to serve Him with renewed strength and zeal.

Once more, history and tradition tell us that some time after John received the Revelation, another, final attempt to kill him was made. Again his enemies were unsuccessful. John became such an embarrassment to his persecutors they released him from prison during the reign of the next Emperor, Nerva, A.D. 96. He returned to the mainland, and continued his ministry in the Ephesian church, living into the reign of the Emperor Trajan, which began in A.D. 98. John finally passed away in old age, the only one of the twelve apostles to die of natural causes.

The past tense, "I *was* on the island called Patmos," seems to indicate that, while he received the inspired visions while on Patmos, he could have written them after his release from captivity, between the persecutions of Domitian and Trajan.

The Message

This is not the book of "revelations." It does not contain many different revelations. It is "The Revelation [singular] of Jesus Christ." It is the apocalypse (Greek, *apokalupsis*), the unveiling, the appearing of the Lord's Christ. The theme of this book is the showing forth of His glory, His love, His power, His triumph, His salvation, His second coming, His eternal Kingdom. The Book of Revelation also contains some of the direst warnings and most precious and blessed promises of all Scripture.

By the very words "The Revelation," God is saying to us: "Read and study this book, and I will draw aside the veil–I will open the curtain—and reveal My Son, Jesus Christ. I will reveal to you what is going to happen in the last days." *"Reveal"*–not conceal! The title which is given this Book in our English Bible–"The Revelation" is derived from the Latin word, *revelatio* (from *revelare*, "to reveal or unveil that which has been previously hidden.")

The uniqueness of Revelation is this: it is the only book in the Bible that has a special blessing pronounced on those who read, those who hear, and those who keep the things written in it:

> "Blessed is he who reads and those who hear the words of this prophecy, and keep those things which are written in it; for the time is near." (Rev 1:3)

From this verse we see it is not just sufficient to fill our minds with facts about this Book. Rather, as we begin to understand the message of Revelation, we will be changed, by receiving not only information, but also inspiration, motivation, and blessing.

As Anne Graham Lotz writes in the introduction to her excellent devotional book on Revelation, *The Vision of His Glory:*

> "Even when the worst conceivable nightmares become reality ... there is one splendid, shining, sure hope for the future–and His Name is Jesus!
> "The book of Revelation was originally written to give hope to the early church when Christians were being fed to lions, nailed to crosses, burned at the stake, and boiled in tar. It was written *by* a Christian who himself was suffering 'because of the word of God and the testimony of Jesus.'[5] It was written specifically *to* a generation of Christians yet to come who will experience what Jesus described as 'great distress, unequaled from the beginning of the world until now–and never to be equaled again.'[6]
> "... Revelation is, above all, a book of hope ..."[7]

One of the main messages of hope to the Church from the Book of Revelation is this—God's will for His people is that they become victorious overcomers, even in difficult times:

> "He who overcomes shall inherit all things, and I will be his God and he shall be My son." (Rev 21:7)

The Various Schools of Interpretation

All writers and scholars agree that the main object of Revelation is to show forth the ultimate triumph of Christ. Someone has well described Revelation as "a song of victory before the battle." But there are some differences as to attitudes and details of meaning. Therefore, at this point we need to take a very brief look at the various schools of interpretation of the Book of Revelation. The five major opinions are:

1. **The Praeterists** believe the greater part of Revelation was fulfilled in early church history. Revelation, they say, only describes the time in which John was living. It is past. The Book refers chiefly to events of its own day, written to comfort a persecuted church, and in code that the first century Church would understand. Thus, in the Praeterist's view, the only teaching of Revelation is the victory of Christ over the Roman Empire, which, according to them, is symbolized by the beast. Thus the seven

---

[5] Rev 1:9–*NIV*.
[6] Matt 24:21–*NIV*.
[7] *The Vision of His Glory–Finding Hope Through the Revelation of Jesus Christ* by Anne Graham Lotz; Word Publishing, 1996–pages xiv and xv. Emphasis hers.

Anne Graham Lotz, the second child of Billy and Ruth Graham, is the founder and president of AnGeL Ministries based in Raleigh, North Carolina. She has been ministering God's Word worldwide for 25 years, and is an award-winning and best-selling author.

seals are symbolic of the terrible judgments about to fall on the Empire, and the Church's safety through those judgments. The seven bowls of God's wrath are the final judgments that bring about the fall of Rome.

2. **The Historists (or Presentists)** believe the Book of Revelation contains God's prophetic program from apostolic days to the end of time. This view considers that the Book was designed to forecast a general view of the whole period of Church history from John's time to the end–a kind of panorama–a series of pictures, in which are delineated the successive steps and outstanding features of the Church's struggle to final victory.

3. **The Idealists** believe that in Revelation spiritual realities are taught under various symbols, and very little is taught about specific historical events.

4. **The Futurists** believe that the events of Revelation are mainly future—in the years just preceding, then following, the second coming of Christ. Chapters four through twenty describe a seven-year period immediately preceding the Second Coming of Christ. Some extreme believers from this Dispensationalist school teach that the Jewish temple in Jerusalem will be rebuilt, and "pure Judaism," including animal sacrifices for sin, will be restored on earth after this Second Coming. Yet other Futurists hold that King David will be resurrected to rule over this Jewish kingdom. In the light of Jesus' "once for all" sacrifice for the sin of the world, such teaching is a blasphemous affront to Calvary, and unworthy of our consideration.[8]

5. **The Spiritualists** believe the whole Book of Revelation is only an allegory, with very little historical or practical significance. Like the Idealists, the Spiritualists separate the imagery of the Book entirely from reference to historical events, and regard it as a pictorial representation of the great principles of divine government applicable to all times. They believe Revelation is but a symbolic representation, in highly figurative language, of "the conflict, described in terms of the first century, that rages between good and evil, through all times, capable of infinite application," "the moral forces that are working out the destiny of the world."

As you will discover in subsequent chapters, I recognize there is–with the exception of the extreme Futurist-Dispensationalist teaching that God will restore Old Testament law in its entirety including animal sacrifices–a portion of truth in each of these schools of thought. However, in my understanding, Revelation covers a time period from the early Church to the end of the Millennium. Most of the chapters follow on one after another chronologically, with a few passages, sometimes not in sequence, in parenthesis. As someone has said, sometimes looking at the Book of Revelation is like standing on the seashore. The waves come in, appear to go out, and then the next wave comes closer. Some major events are described two or three times in different places in the Book. I will do my best to give clear indication of the time factor as I write.

Now for those keys I promised you.

---

[8] Heb 10:10; John 1:29.

| PART TWO | THE KEYS |

Chapter 6

Panoramic Overview

Imagine you are standing in front of a magnificent mansion that has many rooms. The owner is at the door with a set of keys in his hand.

He extends this invitation to you: "Every room of this vast house contains great and valuable treasures. From each room you unlock, you can take possession of as many precious items as you desire. The golden cups, the priceless china, the crystal chandeliers, the carpets, the exquisite paintings, the expensive furniture–everything. It's all yours for the taking. But you will need a different key to open each room door."

I know you would be interested in having those keys.

The Bible contains great treasures. But we must use the keys provided by the Lord. He has given us numerous keys to help us unlock and understand His Word.

There are eight major keys we need to unlock the Book of Revelation:

1. **A Panoramic Overview of the whole book of Revelation;**

2. **The Relevance of the other 65 books of the Bible to the Book of Revelation;**

3. **Understanding the use of Types, Prophetic pictures, and Symbols in Revelation;**

4. **Is the Vision from a "Heavenly" or "Earthly" Viewpoint;**

5. **Heaven's Timetable–the Seven Days of God's Week of Redemption;**

6. **The Significance of Numbers in the Bible;**

7. **The Feasts–Religious Festivals–of Old Testament Israel;**

8. **The Tabernacle of Moses as seen in the Book of Revelation.**

A whole book could be written on each of these keys. Indeed, whole books have been written, and my recommendations are noted.

Key Number One:
A Panoramic Overview of the Whole Book of Revelation

I am aware there were no chapter and verse numbers in the original Biblical manuscripts. They were added for our convenience. But to introduce you to an overall view of the Book, I have given a chart of headings over each chapter of Revelation from my personal preaching Bible. (*Figure 5*)

Figure 5: Chapter Headings for the Book of Revelation

Chapter	Main subject
1	Christ, our Great High Priest, in the Midst of the Churches
2 and 3	The Letters to the Seven Churches
4	The Throne, the Seven Spirits, the Four Living Ones
5	The Lamb and the Sealed Book
6	The Opening of the First Six Seals
7	The Day of Atonement
8 and 9	The First Six Trumpets
10	The Seventh Trumpet Sounds. The Little Book Opened
11	The Temple Measured. The Two Witnesses
12	The Sun-clad woman, man child, and dragon
13	The Great Tribulation. The Unholy Trinity
14	The 144,000. The Tribulation Saints
15	The Tribulation Saints Victorious
16	The Great Tribulation. The Seven Bowls of God's Wrath
17	The Fall of Ecclesiastical Babylon
18	The Fall of Political-Economic Babylon
19	The Marriage Supper of the Lamb. The Judgment of the Beast and the False Prophet
20	The Millennium. The Judgment of the Devil
21	Heaven
22	Final Heavenly Blessings, Commands, and Invitation

Placing the chapters of the Book on our time chart, we now have a clear introduction to the order of events in Revelation. (See *Figure 6* in *Appendix 7*, page 366)

By using this Panoramic Overview, we can observe the time frame of each chapter of the Book of Revelation, and see the Book as one harmonious whole.

In the next chapter we will study our Second Key, *The Relevance of the other 65 books of the Bible to the Book of Revelation.*

PART TWO   THE KEYS

Chapter 7

The Other 65 Bible Books In Revelation

Key Number Two: **The Relevance of the other 65 books of the Bible to the Book of Revelation**

The only written Testament the New Testament Church writers had was the Old Testament. This is why they quoted from the Old Testament, and alluded to, ("their Bible") so often in their writings.

Indeed, in the words of the adage concerning the Old and New Testaments:

> "The New is in the Old, concealed;
> The Old is in the New, revealed.
> The New is in the Old, contained
> The Old is in the New, explained."

The Old Testament in Revelation

Matthew's Gospel and the Book of Hebrews each contain approximately 100 quotes or references from the Old Testament. The Book of Revelation contains nearly 350 references, and allusions, to the Old Testament.

In his book *Interpreting Revelation*, Merrill C. Tenney has an excellent chapter entitled "The Old Testament Background of Revelation."[1] This chapter begins with these words:

> "The reader of Revelation will not have perused many of its pages before he realizes that much of its language sounds familiar. It is filled with references to events and characters of the Old Testament, and a great deal of its phraseology is taken directly from the Old Testament books."

Tenney goes on to say that H.B. Swete, in his *Commentary on the Apocalypse*, states that out of the 404 verses in the Book of Revelation, 278 refer to the Old Testament.[2]

---

[1] *Interpreting Revelation* by Merrill C. Tenney; Wm B. Eerdmans Publishing Company, Grand Rapids, 1957, Reprinted 1988–page101-104.

Merrill C. Tenney, who died in 1985, was for many years Dean of the Graduate School and Professor of Bible and Theology at Wheaton College, Wheaton, Illinois. It has been written of Dr Tenney, "He is able to present difficult and complicated issues in a simple and intelligent manner."

[2] *The Apocalypse of St. John* by H.B. Swete; Macmillan & Co., London, England, 1906.

Tenney then defines for us the difference between a *citation*, a *quotation*, and an *allusion* to the Old Testament in the New Testament.

1. "**A citation** is a fairly exact reproduction of the words of the original text, accompanied by a statement of the fact they are being quoted by an identification of the source.

2. "**A quotation** is a general reproduction of the original text, sufficiently close to give the meaning of its thought and to establish unquestionably the passage from which it is taken. The quotation may be loose, and still be a quotation.

3. "**An allusion** consists of one or more words which by their peculiar character and general content are traceable to a known body of text, but which do not constitute a complete reproduction of any part of it."

Two of these three different kinds of references to the Old Testament are found in Revelation. This is very relevant for the purpose of these studies, for, as we have already noted, it is very difficult to understand the Book of Revelation without a good working knowledge of the Old Testament.

There are no direct citations, as defined above, in the Book of Revelation. However, there are 348 quotations and allusions to the Old Testament. This is demonstrated in the accompanying charts adapted from those in Tenney's book.

And, as Tenney correctly notes:

> "The books most often quoted are Psalms, Isaiah, Daniel, Ezekiel, Jeremiah, Exodus and Zechariah. These contain the bulk of *predictive* prophecy in the era before Christ, and thus they form the framework for the further development of prophecy in Revelation." (emphasis mine.)

Genesis/Revelation Comparisons and Contrasts

While we are considering the Old Testament, I need to bring to your attention a few of the many comparisons and contrasts between the Books of Genesis and Revelation.

The Book of Genesis—the book of beginnings—contains, in "seed form", every major subject in Scripture. Because these themes have their origin in Genesis it is imperative every student of the Bible gives himself to the study of the first book of the Bible.

In the Book of Revelation—the book of ultimates—we see these subjects completed. In the many Bible Schools around the world where I have taught, I tell my students:

> "If you have a good knowledge of Genesis and Revelation, the other 64 books in between will become much easier to understand.
> "Conversely—It is impossible to understand Genesis and Revelation without a good knowledge of those other 64 books!"

Figure 7: **Distribution, by Sections of the Book of Revelation, of Old Testament Quotations and Allusions**

Revelation Reference	Section	No. of References	
Rev 1:1-8	PROLOGUE	11	
Rev 1:9-3:22	VISION I	38	
Rev 4:1-16:21	VISION II	164	
Rev 17:1-21:8	VISION III	95	
Rev 21:9-22:5	VISION IV	24	**Total 348**
Rev 22:6-21	EPILOGUE	16	

The chart below shows there are references to 24 of the 39 books in the Old Testament, and each of the main divisions of the Old Testament is represented.[3]

Revelation Contains References From These Old Testament Books

Books	Number	Books	Number
Genesis	13	Isaiah	79
Exodus	27	Jeremiah	22
Leviticus	4	Ezekiel	43
Numbers	3	Daniel	53
Deuteronomy	10	**MAJOR PROPHETS**	**197**
PENTATEUCH	**57**	Hosea	2
Joshua	1	Joel	8
Judges	1	Amos	9
II Samuel	1	Habakkuk	1
II Kings	6	Zephaniah	2
I Chronicles	1	Zechariah	15
Nehemiah	1	Malachi	1
HISTORIC	**11**	**MINOR PROPHETS**	**38**
Psalms	43		
Proverbs	2	**Total of OT books referenced**	**24**
POETRY	**45**	**Quotations, Allusions in Revelation**	**348**

---

[3] The Old Testament can be divided into five sections:
(1) *Pentateuch:* (the five books of Moses). The 5 books from Genesis to Deuteronomy.
(2) *History:* The 12 books from Joshua to Esther.
(3) *Poetry*: The 5 books from Job to Song of Solomon.
(4) Major *Prophets:* (the longer books of the prophets). The 5 books from Isaiah to Daniel.
(5) *Minor Prophets:* (the shorter books of the prophets). The 12 books from Hosea to Malachi.

Satan hates Genesis and Revelation. This is because his origin, his aims, his works, and his ultimate end are revealed in them. Revealed also is man's power to overcome him through the authority of the Name of our Lord Jesus Christ.

Modernistic "theologians" have tried to disprove the truths contained in these books. "Genesis and Revelation are mere mythical stories," they say. It is interesting to me that the two books in the Bible that Satan has attacked the most are the Book of Genesis and the Book of Revelation.

The chart, *Figure 8*, on the next page lists some of the comparisons and contrasts between the Books of Genesis and Revelation. This chart reinforces how Biblical truth flows from its beginning in Genesis to its consummation in Revelation. Or, in the words of Ecclesiastes 1:7:

> "All the rivers run into the sea,
> Yet the sea is not full;
> To the place from which the rivers come,
> There they return again."

The Other 26 Books of the New Testament in Revelation

Before we move on to Key Number Three, it must be emphasized that not only quotes and allusions from the Old Testament are used in Revelation. Many subjects that are found in the four Gospels, the Book of Acts, and the Epistles have their final fulfillment in Revelation.

For example, Jesus was asked by His apostles, "When will these things be? And what will be the sign of Your coming, and of the end of the age?" (Matt 24:3). He replies by warning them (and us!) against the dangers of deception. He speaks of wars, famines, pestilences, earthquakes, persecution, the great tribulation, His second coming. And all of these are described in graphic detail in Revelation.

In their letters, Paul, Peter, James, and John, all teach about the last days, and the ultimate triumphant second coming of Christ, which happens in the Book of Revelation.

What a miracle! Forty different writers, writing over a period of about 1,500 years, write 65 books. Then John, writing under the inspiration of the same Author, the Holy Spirit, pens the Book of Revelation, using nearly 350 quotations, citations and allusions from the Old Testament, together with many more from the New. And yet there are no contradictions. No opposing views or statements. Every book agrees and unfolds as one harmonious whole.

The Bible is indeed Divinely inspired!

As we continue in our study, we shall discover just how much the Book of Revelation draws from the other 65 books of the Bible to illustrate last day truths.

Figure 8: Genesis and Revelation: Comparisons and Contrasts

	GENESIS	**REVELATION**
1.	Beginning, First book of Bible	Ending, Last Book of Bible
2.	Book of Beginnings	Book of Ultimates
3.	Great themes in seed form	Great themes in full fruition
4.	All main doctrines commence	All main doctrines consummated
5.	Heaven and Earth created	First Heaven and Earth pass away
6.	Light is sun	Lord God gives light
7.	Satan's first rebellion	Satan's last rebellion
8.	Darkness called night	No night there
9.	Sun, moon, stars (1:14)	Sun, moon, stars (12:1)
10.	Waters called seas	No more seas
11.	River for garden	River for new earth
12.	Man in God's image	Man in Satan's image (The Antichrist)
13.	Man falls from God's image	Man restored to God's image
14.	Serpent enters	Serpent bound and cast out
15.	Serpent's doom pronounced	Serpent's doom complete
16.	Curse through sin (3:14-19)	No more curse (21:3)
17.	Death through sin (2:17; 3:19)	No more death (21:4)
18.	Sorrow and pain	No more sorrow and pain
19.	Man cut off from tree of life	Man regains right to tree of life
20.	Man loses river	Pure river of life
21.	False worship begins (Cain, 4:3)	False worship destroyed (ch.18)
22.	Flood from God to destroy ungodly	Flood from serpent trying to destroy Bride
23.	Nimrod and Babylon (ch.10)	The beast and Babylon (chs.13 and 17)
24.	Rainbow, sign of deliverance (9:13)	Rainbow and the Deliverer (10:1,2)
25.	Two angels judging sin (ch.19)	Two witnesses judging man's rebellion (ch. 11)
26.	Perfect bride for Adam	Perfected Bride for Jesus (ch.12)
27.	Bride for son who was offered up (ch. 24)	Bride for Son Who was offered up (19:7)
28.	Marriage (ch.2)	Marriage (19:7)
29.	Blessing upon 12 tribes (ch.49)	Those out of 12 tribes on Zion (chs 7,14)
30.	Man's dominion ends; Satan's begun	Satan's dominion ends; Man's restored

PART TWO   THE KEYS

Chapter 8

Types and Symbols

Key Number Three: **The Use Of Types, Prophetic Pictures, and Symbols In Revelation**

The sub-title of this book is **"Understanding the Book of Revelation."** The Bible has so much to teach us about "understanding." For example:

> "...in all your getting, get understanding.
>
> Exalt her, and she will promote you;
> She will bring you honor, when you embrace her.
>
> She will place on your head an ornament of grace;
> A crown of glory she will deliver to you." (Prov 4:7b-9)

We live in the "give me"-"I want to get" generation. Yet here the Bible says there is one thing we should get above all else–understanding. What tremendous blessings are promised to those who do!

When King Solomon was faced with the awesome challenge of leading Israel, God said to him, "Ask! What shall I give you?" Solomon replied, "Give to Your servant an *understanding* (*margin*, 'hearing') heart to judge Your people." The next verse says, "The speech pleased the Lord, that Solomon had asked this thing." (See 1 Kings 3:3-14).

As we have already seen in Chapter two of this book, Abigail was blessed because "she was a woman of good *understanding*" (1 Sam 25:3).

The King called Daniel to help him because "This man Daniel ... was found to have a keen mind and knowledge *and understanding*, and also the ability to interpret dreams, explain riddles and solve difficult problems." (Dan 5:12)

The sons of Issachar were commended because they had "*understanding* of the times, to know what Israel ought to do" (1 Chr 12:32).

It is clear from Matthew chapter 13, the chapter that contains the teachings of Jesus concerning the seven parables of the kingdom of heaven, He wants us to understand His Word. He asked His disciples, "Have you *understood* all these things?" (verse 51)

In verse 15 of this chapter, our Lord Jesus defines "understanding":

i. to *see* with our eyes–to see with the eyes of our spirit; spiritual vision;
ii. to *hear* with our ears–hearing with the ears of our spirit (See Rev 3:22);
iii. to *understand* with our hearts–insight; spiritual comprehension in our inner-most being;
iv. to *be converted*–to turn again and be healed (*Amp* and *JBP*). Here Jesus is not just referring to "conversion to Christ," but rather to the fact that understanding is not passive. Understanding will result in active changes, corrections, and healings as we respond to what we understand.

KNOWLEDGE, WISDOM, AND UNDERSTANDING

With reference to our studies here in the Book of Revelation, there are three helpful, but different, words repeated many times in the book of Proverbs:

1. "Knowledge" (mentioned 44 times in Proverbs)

Knowledge is defined as "to be aware of the facts," and covers past and present realities. "Yes, a man of knowledge increases strength." (Prov 24:5)

Gaining knowledge begins as a function of the *body*–seeing, reading, hearing facts that are stored in the mind. Thus we are able to develop our intellect.

It is important for us to know the facts contained in the Book of Revelation. But to knowledge, another ingredient must be added–

2. "Wisdom" (mentioned 53 times in Proverbs)

Wisdom can be defined as "knowledge applied"–the ability to apply the facts we know, our knowledge, to all of life's situations. Thus, wisdom is both present and future. How great it is to learn that wisdom will eliminate hindrances and stumbling from our lives:

"I have taught you in the way of wisdom;
I have led you in right paths.

When you walk, your steps will not be hindered,
And when you run, you will not stumble." (Prov 4:11,12)

Thus wisdom is to do with the way we live our lives. It is the ability to take knowledge, and apply it to all life's opportunities, challenges, and circumstances. Gaining wisdom begins as a function of the *soul*. The Bible teaches man is a "tripartite" being. According to 1 Thessalonians 5:23 we are spirit (Greek, *pneuma*), soul (Greek, *psuche*), and body (Greek, *soma*). Hebrews 4:12 teaches that one of the works of the sword of the Spirit, the Word of God is "piercing even to the division of soul and spirit." The soul is the seat of the following seven elements that greatly effect our character, personality and actions:

1. Mind
2. Emotions
3. Will
4. Purpose
5. Intellect
6. Affections
7. Motivation

Through intuition and experience we apply the facts we know to areas of everyday living. Thus we are able to develop, for good, our restored soul. This will result in godly character.

The Book of Revelation is a very practical book. From it we can learn many lessons for daily life, particularly in the realm of overcoming.

In addition to knowledge and wisdom, there is a third quality we must get:

3. "Understanding" ("understand", "understanding" mentioned 67 times in Proverbs)

"Understanding" is to do with seeing, and is defined as "the power to perceive and discern; to recognize, to comprehend, and thus be able to interpret the facts correctly." Much blessing is promised to those who will obey the Lord's commandment to "get understanding." For example:

"Understanding is a wellspring of life to him who has it." (Prov 16:22)

Gaining understanding begins as a function of the human *spirit*—that God-conscious part of us that was made alive when we received Christ into our lives, and we were "born again."[1] As a result of our being born of the Holy Spirit "the Spirit Himself bears witness with our spirit that we are children of God" (Rom 8:16).

It is only as the Lord inspires our spirit, with the anointing of His Holy Spirit upon His Word, that we begin to receive understanding of the Bible, including

---

[1] "But he who is joined to the Lord is one spirit with Him." (1 Cor 6:17) When the human spirit is made alive in Christ, it begins to develop the same five senses as the human body (see Hebrews 5:14–*KJV*. This verse in Hebrews tells us we must exercise our spiritual senses so as to grow and mature in the Lord.)

Here is a summary of these five spiritual senses, together with Scripture references, and the five ministries that assist in their development. (See Eph 4:8,11) These spiritual senses are our ability to:

1.	*Hear*	Rev 3:22	The Teacher
2.	*Smell* (Discern)	Heb 5:14; 1 Cor 12:17; Song 7:13	The Apostle
3.	*See*	Rev 3:18b	The Prophet
4.	*Taste*	Psa 34:8; John 6:53	The Evangelist
5.	*Touch* (feel God's presence)	Col 2:20,21	The Pastor

the Book of Revelation. The same Holy Spirit, Who gave this Book to the Apostle John, will anoint us to understand it.[2]

> "But there is a spirit in man: and the inspiration of the Almighty giveth them understanding." (Job 32:8–*KJV*)

The *Amplified Bible* renders this verse:

> "But there is [a vital force] a spirit [of intelligence] in man, and the breath of the Almighty gives men understanding."

Here is one more powerful Scripture. Note that the Lord promises all three qualities—knowledge, wisdom, and understanding—in this verse:

> "For the Lord gives skillful and godly Wisdom; from His mouth come knowledge and understanding." (Prov 2:6–*Amp*)

We can summarize these vital qualities which we must develop in the following chart.

Figure 9: **Knowledge, Wisdom, and Understanding**

Quality	In Proverbs	Definition	Gives us	Promised Blessing	Origin of Function
1. KNOWLEDGE	44 times	Possession of facts	SIGHT	Prov 24:5	Begins in body
2. WISDOM	53 times	Application of facts	FORESIGHT	Prov 4:11,12	Begins in soul
3. UNDERSTANDING	67 times	Interpretation of facts	INSIGHT	Prov 16:22	Begins in spirit

And so, to understand the Book of Revelation, we must first understand the different ways God speaks to us from His inspired Word.[3]

"IN DIFFERENT WAYS GOD SPOKE"

In Hebrews chapter 1, verses 1 and 2 we read:

> "In many separate revelations–*each of which set forth a portion of the Truth*– and *in different ways God spoke* of old to [our] forefathers in and by the prophets.

---

[2] See Revelation 1:10
[3] 2 Tim 3:16

[But] in the last of these days He has spoken to us in [the person of a] Son, Whom He appointed Heir and lawful Owner of all things, also by and through Whom He created the worlds and the reaches of space and the ages of time–[that is,] He made, produced, built, operated and arranged them in order." (*Amp*)

Here are just a few of the "different ways God spoke," together with a brief definition:

1. Parables:

A parable is an earthly story with a heavenly meaning. A parable uses known and understood facts to reveal spiritual truth.

For example, the Lord Jesus did not tell the parable of the sower to give us a lesson in horticulture. Rather, Matthew 13:3-9 describes the parable, then in verses 18-23 Jesus interprets this parable, explaining what the things He talked about represent–the seed, the wayside, the stony places, the thorns, the good ground, and the harvest.

2. Dark Sayings:

The Hebrew word for "dark," *chidah*, means "a knot, an acute hidden saying." This word is used five times in the Bible. For example, Asaph sings in the seventy-eighth Psalm:

"I will open my mouth in a parable–in instruction by [numerous] examples; I will utter dark sayings of old [that hide important truth]." (Psa 78:2–*Amp*)

Only when the light of the Holy Spirit shines on a "dark saying" will we receive the illumination necessary to understand the meaning of that dark saying.[4] The words of Jesus in Luke 17:36 and 37 concerning the field, the body, and the eagles are a "dark saying," but when we study Revelation chapter 12 together we will understand what Jesus meant.

3. Similitudes:

The Greek word for "similitude," *homoiōma*, simply means "likeness, resemblance, comparison." An example:

"And it is yet far more evident: for that after the *similitude* of Melchisedek there ariseth another priest." (Heb 7:15–*KJV*)

A very similar Greek word *homoios* is used often in the Book of Revelation, and is translated "like unto" (*KJV*) or "like" (*NKJV*). For example:

---

[4] See John 16:13.

1:15	"His feet were *like* fine brass"
4:3	"He who sat there was *like* a jasper and a sardius stone in appearance"
4:7	"The first living creature was *like* a lion ... "
9:7	"The shape of the locusts was *like* horses prepared for battle"
11:1	"Then I was given a reed *like* a measuring rod"
16:13	"And I saw three unclean spirits *like* frogs coming out of the mouth of the dragon ..."

I have noticed one very interesting thing. When a parable or symbol is used, natural things–sheep, goats, coins, houses, rain, pearls–are employed to illustrate spiritual truths or principles. But when a similitude is used, the opposite happens. For example, throughout the Book of Revelation John sees and hears spiritual visions, and uses natural things to illustrate spiritual matters, as can be seen in these verses:

> "And he carried me away in the Spirit to a great and high mountain, and showed me the great city, the holy Jerusalem, descending out of heaven from God,
> having the glory of God. Her light was *like* a most precious stone, *like* a jasper stone, clear as crystal." (Rev 21:10,11)

4. Riddles:

A riddle is a question or statement made puzzling to test the understanding. Usually a riddle will have a deeper meaning or teaching hidden in the language used. Two examples:

Samson's riddle about honey from the lion's carcass (Judges chapter 14);

Ezekiel's riddle about the house of Israel, and the great eagles (Eze 17:1-10).

5. Dreams:

Dreams are images, or pictures, seen in sleep. When a dream is given by the Lord, there is a message, the interpretation of which is usually prophetic. Just four examples:

Joseph's dreams (Genesis chapter 37);
The dreams of Pharaoh's butler and baker (Genesis chapter 40);
God's promise concerning prophets: "If there is a prophet among you ... I speak to him in a dream" (Num12:6);
God's warning to the three wise men in a dream (Matt 2:12,13).

6. Visions:

Visions are images, or pictures, seen while awake. We can be encouraged by the Lord's promise concerning visions. For the following promise is not just for the Church in the Book of Acts, but also for these days:

> "And it shall come to pass afterward
> That I will pour out My Spirit on all flesh;
> Your sons and your daughters shall prophesy,
> Your old men shall dream dreams,
> Your young men shall see visions.
>
> And also on My menservants and on My maidservants
> I will pour out My Spirit in those days." (Joel 2:28,29; see also Acts 2:16-18)

God conveys a distinct message by means of a vision. For example:
* Saul (later Paul) had a vision of Ananias laying hands on him so that his sight could be restored (Acts 9:11,12);
* Peter's vision of the creatures in the sheet to show him that the Gentiles were not unclean (Acts chapter 10);
* The many visions John saw in the Book of Revelation, e.g. "And thus I saw the horses in the vision." (Rev 9:17)

7. Proverbs:

A proverb is a short, pithy saying with a deep, sharp meaning. A good New Testament example is Peter's teaching about backsliding in 2 Peter 2:20-22 where he quotes Proverbs 26:11.

8. Examples:

An example is using the pattern, or model, of some character, incident, place or truth to warn us, and/or teach us an important lesson. The Greek word can mean "sample," "exhibition," "model," or "copy."

The example of Israel to the Church: "Now these things became our examples, to the intent that we should not lust after evil things as they also lusted" (1 Cor 10:1-6);

The example of the disobedient who were refused entry into the promised land: "Let us therefore be diligent to enter that rest lest anyone fall according to the same example of disobedience" (Heb 4:11);

The example of Sodom and Gomorrah to the ungodly (2 Pet 2:6). This same example is again used in Jude verse 7.

9. Figures:

A figure is an incident, character, event, or descriptive passage that prophesies of, and points to, something greater:

In some ways, Adam was a "figure of Him that was to come" (Rom 5:14–*KJV*).

The Mosaic order was "a figure for the time then present." The sacrifices were "the figures of the true" (Heb 9:9,24–*KJV*).

Abraham received Isaac from the dead "in a figurative sense" (Heb 11:19).

10. Shadows:

A shadow is the outline of a real object or person, made when the real object or person is intercepted by light. Light falls on the real, and its shadow is cast. The Bible contains many shadows of real people and events, which, when viewed in the light of the Holy Spirit's illumination, give wonderful outlines to teach us of, and point us to, real events and people.

Old Testament ordinances and festivals "are a shadow of things to come, but the substance is of Christ" (Col 2:17);

The Old Testament law contains only a "shadow of the good things to come" (Heb 10:1).

11. Patterns:

A pattern is a model, a blueprint, or a design to refer to and copy while working to make the real thing. The peculiar point to notice about a pattern (both in the natural and in the spiritual) is that it is practical. A pattern serves a useful purpose, and is put to work.

> "Moses was divinely instructed when he was about to make the tabernacle. For He said, 'See that you make all things according to the pattern shown you on the mountain.'" (Heb 8:5)

Speaking of Old Testament blood sacrifices, Hebrews says, "It was therefore necessary that the patterns of things in the heavens should be purified with these; but the heavenly things themselves with better sacrifices than these" (Heb 9:23).

12. Meanings of the Names of People and Places:

Almost all proper names in the Bible have meanings that convey a message. When seen in their proper context, the meanings of the names of people and places can assist in our understanding. We will observe this principle in the Book of Revelation. The meanings of names can be found in a good concordance or Bible dictionary.

The interpretation of King Melchizedek's name helps us identify Him (Heb 7:1-3). The naming of Simon Peter by Jesus (John 1:41,42).

13. Signs:

The Greek word most often translated as "sign" is *sēmeion* and means "a sign, mark, or signal." A sign gives warning, or communicates some special message.

Jesus taught the sign of the prophet Jonah will be a prophetic signal in these last days (Matt 12:39).[5]

> "Now a great sign appeared in heaven." (Rev 12:1)
> "Then I saw another sign in heaven, great and marvelous." (Rev 15:1)

TYPES AND SYMBOLS

Knowledge of the "different ways God speaks" will help in your study of the Bible, and in particular, the Book of Revelation.

We must now turn to the two ways in which God speaks to us most often in the Book of Revelation–types and symbols. Firstly, let us look at types.

In this book, I have repeated a number of times that the Old Testament is filled with types and prophetic pictures for the New Testament Christian. Speaking of the Old Testament Scriptures, the Apostle Paul says:

> "For whatever things were written before were written for *our* learning, that *we* through the patience and comfort of the Scriptures might have hope."
> (Rom 15:4)

When teaching the lessons we can learn from Old Testament Israel, Paul writes to the church at Corinth:

> "All these things happened to them as examples for others, and they were written down as a warning for *us*. For *we* live at the time when the end is about to come."(1 Cor 10:11–*TEV*)

Peter teaches, referring to salvation, " ... not to themselves, but to *us* they [the Old Testament writers] were ministering the things which have been reported to *you* through those who have preached the gospel to *you* by the Holy Spirit sent from heaven" (1 Pet 1:12).

---

[5] See Chapter two of this book.

What Is a Type?

Our English word "type" is translated from the Greek word *tupos*. According to Vine's *Expository Dictionary of New Testament Words*:

"*TUPOS* primarily denoted a blow (from a root *tup–*, seen also in *tuptō*, to strike), hence

- **a.** an impression, the mark of a blow, John 20:25 ['Unless I see in His hands the *print* of the nails, and put my finger into the *print* of the nails ...']

- **b.** the impress of a seal, the stamp made by a die, a figure, image, Acts 7:43 ['*figures* which ye made to worship them'–*KJV*]

- **c.** a form or mould, Rom 6:17 ['But thanks be to God that though you were slaves of sin, you became obedient from the heart to that *form* of teaching to which you were committed'–*NAS*]

- **d.** the sense or substance of a letter, Acts 23:25 ['He wrote a letter in the following *manner*']

- **e.** an ensample, pattern, Acts 7:44 ['Our fathers had the tabernacle of witness in the wilderness, as he had appointed, speaking unto Moses, that he should make it according to the *fashion* that he had seen'–*KJV*]." [6]

This important Greek word *"tupos"* is variously translated in the *King James Version* of the Bible in the following eight ways:

Word	Times used in New Testament	References
"ensample"	5 (*margin*, 'type' 1)	1 Cor 10:11; Phil 3:17; 1 Thess 1:7; 2 Thess 3:9; 1 Pet 5:3
"example"	2 (*margin*, 'figure' 1)	1 Cor 10:6; 1 Tim 4:12
"fashion"	1	Acts 7:44
"figure"	2	Acts 7:43; Rom 5:14
"form"	1	Rom 6:17
"manner"	1	Acts 23:25
"pattern"	2	Titus 2:7; Heb 8:5
"print"	2	both in John 20:25

TOTAL   16 times

---

[6] *Expository Dictionary of New Testament Words* by W.E. Vine; Oliphants Ltd, London, England, Thirteenth impression, 1963–Vol II, page 33.

Definition of a Type

We can, then, define a type as: "A type is a person or incident in Scripture, which is a picture, parable, or pattern, that resembles and points prophetically to something or someone greater."

The peculiar feature of a type is that it contains teaching for our instruction. This teaching may be veiled, but the veil is taken away by the power of our Lord Jesus Christ:

> "But their minds were blinded. For until this day the same veil remains unlifted in the reading of the Old Testament, because the veil is taken away in Christ. Nevertheless when one turns to the Lord, the veil is taken away." (2 Cor 3:14,15)

For example, in Matthew chapter 13 we have the seven parables of the kingdom. In this whole chapter there are no clear doctrinal teachings. These parables are "mysteries of the kingdom" and it is necessary to interpret each of the types–seed, fields, weeds, mustard seed, leaven, pearls, fish, and many more–to understand the meanings of the parables.

Finis Dake defines a type:

> "A type is a pre-ordained representation wherein certain persons, events, and institutions of the Old Testament stand for related and corresponding persons, events, and institutions of the New Testament."[7]

A type is a prophetic symbol or parable–a parabolic method of revealing truth. The Greek word *parabole* is translated in the the *King James Version*:

| comparison | 1 | parable | 40 |
| figure | 2 | proverb | 1 |

A Few Observations About Types:

1. There Is No Perfect Type

There is no perfect type because of sin. The people in the Bible who are used as types and prophetic pictures were sinners. So it follows that we must:

2. Know Where a Type Begins and Ends

> Paul teaches that Aaron is a type of our Great High Priest, the Lord Jesus Christ. (See Heb 9:1-14). But Aaron built a golden calf for the people to worship!

---

[7] *Dake's Annotated Reference Bible* by Finis Jennings Dake; Dake Bible Sales, Atlanta, *Second Printing*, June 1965.

Jesus used Noah, and the times in which Noah lived, as a type–a prophetic illustration of conditions in the last days (Matt 24:37,38). We can begin those thoughts with the corrupt condition of the world and Noah's righteousness. But we must end with Noah's ark, because later Noah got drunk!

3. Everything and Everyone We Use As Types Are Never Types to Themselves

While they are types of things to come, they are, of course, never types to themselves. They are actual, historical, literal people, experiences, and things. For example, the Book of Hebrews speaks of the literal veil in the tabernacle, but also that this veil is a type of Christ's flesh.[8]

4. The Literal is in the Spiritual, and the Spiritual Is in the Literal

1 Corinthians 15:46 speaks not only of the resurrection, but also of the way God speaks to us from His Word:

> "However, the spiritual is not first, but the natural, and afterward the spiritual."

As we have already noted, the first three chapters of Genesis are the foundation for the remainder of the Bible. The natural things of creation become the language of redemption. This is emphasized in Psalm 19, where the sun, moon and stars–created by God–are said to be witnesses of His greatness.

5. The Type Becomes the Prophecy

The fulfillment of the prophecy is always greater than the type. For example, it is written in Exodus chapter 12 that not a bone of the passover lamb was to be broken (Exo 12:46). This passover lamb was a prophetic type of the Lord Jesus, our Passover Lamb, whose bones were not broken on the cross (John 19:36; 1 Cor 5:7).

6. The Doctrine and Teaching is Hidden in the Type

While it is difficult for some to receive this fact, the reality is this–New Testament writers built whole doctrines on types.

In Galatians, the whole teaching of our freedom from the law of Moses, as believers in Jesus, and the liberty we enjoy in Christ, is built upon the Genesis account of Moses, Sarah, Hagar, Ishmael and Isaac.

In Hebrews chapter five the doctrine of the High Priesthood of Christ, and our salvation through Him, is built on one type, also from Genesis, Melchizedek.

---

[8] Heb 10:20.

7. The Bible Interprets Its Own Types

John 1:14 interprets the tabernacle of Moses as a type of Christ.

John 1:51 interprets Genesis 28:12 ("Jacob's ladder").

John 3:14 and 15 interpret Numbers 21 (the serpent in the wilderness).

8. Christ Himself is the Main Key to All Types

The Bible records:

> "And beginning at Moses and all the Prophets, He expounded *(margin, 'explained')* to them in all the Scriptures the things concerning Himself ...
> Then He said to them, 'These are the words which I spoke to you while I was still with you, that all things must be fulfilled which were written in the Law of Moses and the Prophets and the Psalms concerning Me.'
> And He opened their understanding, that they might comprehend the Scriptures." (Luke 24:27,44,45)

In the Law, the Psalms, and the Prophets–the total Bible of the early New Testament Church–the Lord Jesus Christ is the key to the understanding of prophetic pictures and types.

What Is a Symbol?

The Concise Oxford Dictionary defines a symbol:

> "Thing regarded by general consent as naturally typifying or representing or recalling something by possession of analogous qualities or by association in fact or thought."[9]

While the word "symbol" does not actually occur in the Bible, there is a prolific use of symbols in Scripture, especially in the Book of Revelation.

In reality, the language of the symbol is the language of creation. God has used the language of created things–about which we know–to teach us spiritual truths unknown to us. He takes the natural to reveal the spiritual. He takes finite things to teach us about our Infinite God. We could say that the language of the symbol is God's "secret code."

Throughout His Word, God uses symbols that we know–animals, colours, rain, snow, plants, metals, precious stones, oil, rainbows, sunsets, names, people, birds, bread, milk, clouds, doors, cities, fields, trees–and many more symbols we can easily comprehend–to teach us spiritual lessons.

---

[9] *The Concise Oxford Dictionary*, Oxford University Press, Calcutta, India, 1968–page 1311.

The Lord Jesus constantly used symbols in His teachings. He used created, known things to illustrate spiritual truths. He spoke of houses, storms, floods, sheep, shepherds, building, farming, seeds, harvest, fishing, weddings, brides, bridegrooms–everyday things, events, and people–as symbols to teach us divine truths of the kingdom of God.

The Difference Between Symbols and Types

Symbols are *representative* –they represent something greater than themselves.

Types are *prophetic* –they prophetically prefigure a future revelation of truth.

This chart from Kevin Conner's book shows us the main differences between a symbol and a type[10]:

Figure 10: **The Major Differences Between a Type and a Symbol**

A Symbol	A Type
May represent a thing, either past, present or future.	Is essentially a prefiguring of something future from itself.
Is a figure of something either past, present or future.	Is a figure of that which is to come.
Has in itself no essential reference to time.	Has inherent in itself a reference to time.
Is designed to represent certain characteristics or qualities in that which it represents.	Is designed to be a pre-ordained representation of something or someone to come.
To be interpreted, requires a pointing out of the characteristics, qualities, marks or features common to both the symbol and that which it symbolizes.	To be interpreted, generally requires a setting forth of an extended analogy between the type and that which it typifies.

Symbols in the Book of Revelation

There are scores of symbols used in the Book of Revelation. But here, in brief table form, are just six. There are many more symbols in Revelation that we will study together.

A study of the contents of this Chapter will greatly help in your understanding of the Bible.

---

[10] *Interpreting the Symbols and Types* by Kevin J. Conner; Bible Temple Publishing, Portland, Oregon, *Revised Edition* 1992–Page 85.

Figure 11: **Table of Some Symbols in the Book of Revelation**

SYMBOL	Reference In REVELATION	MEANING	Other References in the BIBLE
Trumpet	1:10, 4:1,8:2,9:14	The voice of the Lord, warnings, prophecies	Joel 2:1,15, Zech 9:14
Candlesticks (Lampstands)	1:12,13,20,2:1,11:4	The seven churches in Asia	Exo 25:31-40; Zech 4:2,11; Matt 5:15
White garments	3:5,18, 7:9,13,14	"The righteous acts of the saints" (Rev 19:8)	Exo 28:39-41; 2 Chron 5:12; Eccl. 9:8
Incense	5:8	Prayers of God's people	Exo ch. 30 Psa 141:1,2
Sun-clad woman	12:1	The Bride of Christ	Eph 5:23-32; Song 8:5
Pure river of water of life	22:1	Eternal refreshing flow of rivers of Holy Spirit	Gen 2:10-14; Eze 47:1-12; John 7:37-39

Now we move on to our next key–the need to note if the vision is from a "heavenly" or "earthly" viewpoint.

| PART TWO | THE KEYS |

Chapter 9

Heaven And Earth

Key Number Four: **Note if the Vision is from a "Heavenly" or an "Earthly" Viewpoint**

"Heaven and earth" is a wonderful subject of study. Time and space prevent us from taking a full look at this great truth, but a glance at the following verses will help us. Because God's plan is this:

- To put heaven in the heart of man while man still lives on earth (John 3:3);

- To have man seek first the kingdom of heaven while he is on earth (Matt 6:33);

- To give man, when he has completed his life here on earth, eternal life in heaven (1 Pet 1:4).

Just look at these powerful verses about "heaven and earth."

- The Bible opens with the words:

    "In the beginning God created the heavens and the earth" (Gen 1:1).

- Melchizedek blessed Abraham, saying:

    "Blessed (favored with blessings, made blissful, joyful) be Abram by God Most High, possessor and maker of heaven and earth." (Gen 14:20–*Amp*)

- The statement that the Lord is God of heaven and earth occurs frequently in Scripture. For example:

    "Therefore know this day, and consider it in your heart, that the Lord Himself is God in heaven above and on the earth beneath; there is no other." (Deut 4:39)

- God promises the outpouring of the early and latter rains of blessing upon those who obey His commandments–upon those who love and serve Him with all their heart and soul. Then comes the promise of blessings "as the days of heaven upon the earth" (Deut 11:13-21–*KJV*). What a promise. "Days of heaven upon the earth"!

- Our Lord God owns heaven and earth:

    "Yours, O Lord, is the greatness,
    The power and the glory,
    The victory and the majesty;
    For all that is in heaven and in earth is Yours;
    Yours is the kingdom, O Lord,
    And You are exalted as head over all." (1 Chr 29:11)

- Our Lord God fills heaven and earth:

    "'Can anyone hide himself in secret places,
    So I shall not see him?' says the Lord;
    'Do I not fill heaven and earth?' says the Lord." (Jer 23:24)

- The Lord lifted up the prophet Ezekiel between earth and heaven, where he saw visions:

    "… the hand of the Lord God fell upon me …
    He stretched out the form of a hand, and took me by a lock of my hair; and the Spirit lifted me up between earth and heaven, and brought me in visions of God to Jerusalem …" (Eze 8:1-3)

- In the New Testament, our Lord Jesus commanded us to pray:

    "Our Father in heaven,
    Hallowed be Your name.
    Your kingdom come.
    Your will be done
    On earth as it is in heaven." (Matt 6:9,10)

- And our Lord Jesus promised us authority in His Name:

    "'And I will give you the keys of the kingdom of heaven, and whatever you bind on earth will be bound in heaven, and whatever you loose on earth will be loosed in heaven.'" (Matt 16:19)

- When our Master commissioned us to make disciples throughout the world, He promised:

    "'All authority has been given to Me in heaven and on earth.
    Go therefore and make disciples of all the nations, baptizing them in the name of the Father and of the Son and of the Holy Spirit,

Teaching them to observe all things that I have commanded you; and lo, I am with you always, even to the end of the age.'" (Matt 28:18-20)

- The Apostle Paul teaches that God's purpose is:

"That in the dispensation of the fullness of the times He might gather together in one all things in Christ, both which are in heaven and which are on earth–in Him." (Eph 1:10)

- And because of all that the Lord Jesus accomplished on the Cross:

"God also has highly exalted Him and given Him the name which is above every name,
that at the name of Jesus every knee should bow, of those in heaven, and of those on earth, and of those under the earth,
and that every tongue should confess that Jesus Christ is Lord, to the glory of God the Father." (Phil 2:9 -11)

- In the Book of Revelation, we find the term "heaven and earth" mentioned at least six times. Just one example:

"And every creature which is in heaven and on the earth and under the earth and such as are in the sea, and all that are in them, I heard saying:
'Blessing and honor and glory and power
Be to Him who sits on the throne,
And to the Lamb, forever and ever!'" (Rev 5:13)

1. Visions in Heaven and on Earth in Revelation

Keeping in mind these wonderful truths about heaven and earth, we find when reading the Book of Revelation that sometimes John appears to be in heaven but describing a vision of things on earth. At other times, he seems to be on earth, but describing events in heaven. When John sees a vision in heaven, this immediately causes corresponding or resultant events on earth. Therefore, to have insight into *what* is happening in Revelation, we need to see *where* it's happening–on earth, or in heaven.

This is best illustrated in the accompanying table on the structure of the Book of Revelation adapted from *The Companion Bible*.[1] In this chart we see that there are seven visions in heaven, and each of these is followed by a vision on earth.

In the Book of Revelation, we see God's ultimate eternal purpose is to create for man a new heaven and a new earth for the "holy city, New Jerusalem, coming down out of heaven from God, prepared as a bride adorned for her husband" (Rev 21:2). Here God

---

[1] *The Companion Bible, King James Version*; Kregel Publications, Grand Rapids, Michigan, 1990–page 1883. The notes in The Companion Bible state this Structure is taken from Dr. E.W. Bullinger's treatise, *The Apocalypse*.

does what He has been progressively doing for thousands of years. In and through and by our Lord Jesus Christ, He finally brings heaven and earth together!

Noting if the vision is from an "earthly" or "heavenly" viewpoint is an important key to our understanding of the Book of Revelation.

Our next essential key is God's Week.

Figure 12: **Revelation – the Structure of the Book as a whole**

Vision	Location	Chapter	Details
		1	Introduction
		2 and 3	The People on the Earth; The seven Churches
VISION 1	Vision in heaven	4 and 5	The Throne, the Book, and the Lamb
	Vision on earth	6:1–7:8	The Six Seals and 144,000
VISION 2	Vision in heaven	7:9–8:6	The Great Multitude and the Seventh Seal
	Vision on earth	8:7–11:14	The Six Trumpets, the Two Witnesses
VISION 3	Vision in heaven	11:15–11:19	The Seventh Trumpet
	Vision on earth	11:19	The Ark of His Covenant, Earthquake, Hail
VISION 4	Vision in heaven	12:1-12	The Woman, Man child, Dragon; the Remnant
	Vision on earth	12:13–13:18	The Dragon and the Two Beasts
VISION 5	Vision in heaven	14:1-5	The Lamb and 144,000
	Vision on earth	14:6-20	The Six Angels
VISION 6	Vision in heaven	15:1-8	The Seven Angels with Seven Vials
	Vision on earth	16:1–18:24	The Seven Vials; both Babylons destroyed
VISION 7	Vision in heaven	19:1-16	The Marriage of the Lamb; Second Coming;
	Vision on earth	19:17–20:15	The Final Five Judgments
		21:1–22:5	Bride, the Lamb's Wife; God's People in the New Heavens and New Earth
		22:6-21	Conclusion

PART TWO   THE KEYS

Chapter 10

God's Week

Key Number Five: **Heaven's Timetable — The Seven Days of God's Week of Redemption**

As has been briefly noted, God has a timetable. His timetable is called "God's Week." (See *Figure 13* in *Appendix 8*, page 361).

Without doubt, God's Week is one of the important keys to an understanding of the Bible as one harmonious whole. As Alister Lowe says, this truth is "The Foundation of Prophetic Truth."[1] Knowledge of God's Week is essential to the study of the Book of Revelation.

It is interesting to note that the book of Job, the first book of the Bible to be written, contains all the main questions asked by men, including a question about God's days.[2] In Job 24:1, the question is asked:

> "Since times are not hidden from the Almighty, why do those who know Him *see not His days?*"

Nothing is hidden from God. He delights in revealing hidden things to those who seek Him. Why then is this verse asking, "Why don't those who know Him see His days?" God's days? God's week?

But God not only asks questions. He gives answers!

> "But, beloved, be not ignorant of this one thing, that one day is with the Lord as a thousand years, and a thousand years as one day." (2 Pet 3:8–*KJV*)

"Be not ignorant." This is not a suggestion. This is a command. The word "ignorant" (Greek, *agnoeō*) means "without knowledge." God is clearly stating: He wants us to know about His days.

This command, "Be not ignorant," occurs only seven times in the New Testament. Five times the context is Bible teaching; twice personal matters. I have listed these references

---

[1] *End Time Events, Volume 1, The Creative and Redemptive Weeks–The Foundation of Prophetic Truth* by A.J. Lowe; End Time Publications, Brisbane, Australia, 1982.
[2] See *Appendix 2,* "Some Questions Asked in the Book of Job."

for you in the Appendix.[3] When God wants to bring something to our attention, He often uses the phrase "I would not have you ignorant."

Peter is quoting from Psalm 90. Moses, the writer of Genesis chapter one, also wrote Psalm 90: "For a thousand years in Your sight are like yesterday when it is past ..." (Psa 90:4)

The word "day" is found many times in the Bible. Whether we are studying the Old Testament (especially the prophets), or the New, we must examine the context to find out the "day" to which the writer is referring. Here are just some examples of what the word "day" can mean in Scripture:

- The 24-hour period from midnight to midnight (John 2:1);

- The 12 hours from 6 am to 6 pm (Matt 27:5,6; Acts 2:15);

- The fulfillment of the Day of Atonement (Isa 4:2-6, 66:8-11; Heb 10:25; 1 Thess 5:2);

- The day of salvation (Isa chapter 12; 1 Cor 5:5);

- The day of judgment (Isa 61:2; Acts 17:31; Rom 2:5,16);

- The day of Christ's second coming (2 Thess 2:1,2; Phil 1:10; 1 Cor 1:7,8);

- One of seven 1,000-year periods of time.

The Hebrew word for week, *shabua*, is translated as both "week" and "seven." There is no separate word for "week" in the Hebrew language.

Referring again to our diagram, we will first study three major aspects of God's week under the following headings:

I.   **LITERAL–God's Week of *RE-CREATION***

II.   **HISTORICAL–God's Week of *REDEMPTION***

III.   **SPIRITUAL–God's Week of *RESTORATION***

---

[3] See *Appendix 3*, "Be Not Ignorant."

I.   LITERAL–God's Week of *RE-CREATION*

Genesis 1:1 records:

> "In the beginning God created the heavens and the earth."

This was a perfect creation. Nothing God does is incomplete or imperfect.

However, verse two reads:

> "The earth was without form, and void [*Hebrew, bohu*, 'empty, emptiness']; and darkness was on the face of the deep."

Something dramatic happened, spoiling God's perfect creation.

Verse two *cannot* refer to God's perfect creation. God never makes anything without form. With reference to the Lord's creation of heaven and earth, we read in Isaiah 45:18, He "created it not a worthless waste."[4]

God is never associated with emptiness. On the contrary, in Ephesians 1:22 and 23, He speaks of His people as "the church, which is His body, the fullness of Him who fills all in all."

And darkness? No! "God is light and in Him is no darkness at all." (1 Jn 1:5)

What happened between verses one and two? Satan was cast out of Heaven for his rebellion against God. And when Satan (Lucifer) was cast down, he spoiled God's creation. Note the five "I wills" of Satan in this passage:

> "How you are fallen from heaven,
> O Lucifer, son of the morning!
> How you are cut down to the ground,
> You who weakened the nations!
>
> For you have said in your heart:
> '*I will* ascend into heaven,
> *I will* exalt my throne above the stars of God;
> *I will* also sit on the mount of the congregation
> On the farthest sides of the north;
>
> *I will* ascend above the heights of the clouds,
> *I will* be like the Most High.'
>
> Yet you shall be brought down to Sheol,

---

[4] *Amplified Bible.*

>To the lowest depths of the Pit.
>Those who see you will gaze at you,
>And consider you, saying:
>'Is this the man who made the earth tremble,
>Who shook kingdoms,
>
>*Who made the world as a wilderness*
>And destroyed its cities
>Who did not open the house of his prisoners?'"(Isa 14:12-17)

Jesus confirmed the fall of Satan. The eternal Son of God told His disciples, "I saw Satan fall like lightning from heaven" (Luke 10:18).

Ezekiel chapter 28 is the prophet's lamentation for the king of Tyre. But there are many reasons to believe this passage can also be applied to the rebellion of Satan, and his being cast out of Heaven. For example, it states, "You were in Eden, the garden of God" (verse 13). The king of Tyre was never in Eden. But Satan was. This once-beautiful angel created by God–the chief musician of Heaven–was cast out of God's presence because of pride, deception, sin and rebellion:

>"Thus says the Lord God:
>
>'You were the seal of perfection,
>Full of wisdom and perfect in beauty.
>
>You were in Eden, the garden of God;
>Every precious stone was your covering ...
>The workmanship of your timbrels and pipes
>Was prepared for you on the day you were created.
>
>You were the anointed cherub who covers;
>I established you;
>You were on the holy mountain of God;
>You walked back and forth in the midst of fiery stones.
>You were perfect in your ways from the day you were created,
>Till iniquity was found in you.
>
>By the abundance of your trading
>You became filled with violence within,
>And you sinned;
>*Therefore I cast you as a profane thing*
>*Out of the mountain of God ...*
>
>*I cast you to the ground ...*'" (See Ezek 28:12-19)

HERE COMES THE BRIDE!

We read the consequences of the casting down of Satan in Jeremiah: "I beheld the earth, and indeed it was without form, and void; And the heavens, they had no light." (See Jer 4:23-27)

Genesis 1:2 should more correctly read, "The earth *became* formless, and empty." The Hebrew word translated "was" is the same word that is used in Genesis 2:7, "... and man *became* a living being."

Thus God began to re-create the heavens and the earth. This He did through the moving of His Spirit, and by speaking forth His Word. The Spirit and the Word always work together to bring order out of chaos, to bring light to the darkness, and to bring deliverance from the work of Satan.

God's Week of Re-creation may be summarized:

Day one:	Creation of Light
Day two:	Dividing of the waters; Heaven
Day three:	Dry land and plants
Day four:	Sun, moon, and stars
Day five:	Fish; and birds of the air
Day six:	Animals; man and woman
Day seven:	God rested.

There are two very different Hebrew words for our English word "create":

a. *asah* means "to make again", or to "accomplish [by virtue of the fact that it has been done before]"

b. *bara* means "to prepare, to form, to fashion, to create for the first time."

In Genesis chapter one, the word *bara* is only used of:

- The original heaven and earth (verse 1);
- The great sea creatures (e.g. whales) and birds;
- Man.

Everything else had been previously created. This is the reason these seven days are called God's Week of *Re-creation*.

II.   HISTORICAL–God's Week of *REDEMPTION*

God created a perfect heaven and earth. It was spoiled by Lucifer's sin.

God created a perfect man and woman. They were also spoiled by sin.

God had given Adam clear warning: "But of the tree of the knowledge of good and evil you shall not eat, for in the day that you eat of it you shall surely die." (Gen 2:17). And he did. Time began when Adam sinned (not when he was created), and 930 years later Adam died, well within the first 1,000-year day of God's week.[5] Adam took 930 years, and left us with 70!

As a result of his sin, Adam's life, and the lives of all his descendants, became empty. He began to dwell in spiritual darkness. However, God, demonstrating His love and grace, began His Week of Redemption.

Jacob worked a week (seven years, counting a year for a day) for his bride. He did not get her. So he worked a second week ("Fulfill her week"–Gen 29:27), and received his beloved Rachel.

God worked the Week of Re-creation for His Bride. He did not get her. So the Lord is currently working a second week, His Week of Redemption, to prepare His Bride, a great company, who will sing to the Redeemer their song of redemption:

> "You were slain, and have redeemed us to God by Your blood out of every tribe and tongue and people and nation." (Rev 5:9)

Two important things happened in Genesis chapter 3. Firstly, by shedding the blood of an innocent victim (to make the coats of skin for their covering) God introduced Adam and Eve to the first principles of redemption.

Secondly, God promised the serpent:

> "Because you have done this ...
>
> I will put enmity
> Between your seed and her Seed;
> He shall bruise your head,
> And you shall bruise His heel." (Gen 3:14,15)

The bruising of Christ's heel happened when He died on the cross. The ultimate fulfillment of the seed of the woman bruising the serpent's head will take place in Revelation chapter 12, when the Bride's seed, the man child, is "caught up to God and His throne" (verse 5).

---

[5] See Psalm 90:10. It is interesting to note this is the same Psalm of Moses that tells us (in verse 4) that 1,000 years are a day of God's Week.

It does not disturb me if scientists claim to have discovered skeletons or bone fragments millions of years old. The Bible gives us no indication as to when the original creation (Gen 1:1) took place. It could have been millions of years ago.

Time, as we know it, only began when Adam and his wife fell into sin. We are not told how long the time was between Mr and Mrs Adam's creation, and their subsequent fall.

The arrival of the man child at the throne of God precipitates war in heaven, and "that serpent of old, called the Devil and Satan, who deceives the whole world; he was cast to the earth, and his angels were cast out with him" (verse 9). This casting out of Satan makes way for the manifestation of the Antichrist, who is none other than the Devil incarnate in a man.

The Seven Days of God's Week of Redemption

The seven days of God's Week of Redemption are each 1,000-year periods of time[6]:

Day one	(1,000 years):	Adam's fall to the translation of Enoch
Day two	(1,000 years):	Enoch's translation to Abraham
Day three	(1,000 years):	Abraham to the translation of Elijah
Day four	(1,000 years):	Elijah to our Lord Jesus Christ
Day five	(1,000 years):	The Day of Pentecost to the middle of what are known as the "dark ages"
Day six	(1,000 years):	The middle of the "dark ages" to the Second Coming of Christ
Day seven	(1,000 years):	The 1,000-year reign of Christ over the earth; the Millennium; the rest for the people of God

In the Week of Re-creation, the last act of creation performed by God before He rested on the seventh day was to create a bride for Adam. In the Week of Redemption, the final consummation of Day six will be the creation of a Bride for Christ.

Please note that Day six, and the 2,000 years of the Church Age, commence with the outpouring of the Holy Spirit in Acts chapter two. The Day of Pentecost took place (depending on whose chronology you follow) somewhere between A.D. 37 and 41. I am not suggesting that Jesus will come again in the year 2037. But this does explain why He didn't come in the year 2,000!

We do not know the day nor the hour (Matt 24:36). Nor do we know the month or the year. But we do know the signs of the times. And we do know the Lord is working according to Heaven's Timetable. God's Week of Redemption.

---

[6] It must be emphasized that today, when time can be measured with such precision, these "1,000-year days," though historically correct, are nevertheless approximate. One reason for small inconsistencies is that in measuring time, we know a Jewish year is only 360 days, not 365. Also, there are some minor discrepancies in modern endeavours to measure Old Testament chronology.

It is more important to grasp the *principles* of God's Week, than to focus on pinpointing exact years and dates.

III. SPIRITUAL–God's Week of *RESTORATION*

These truths have a personal and practical application to our spiritual lives. They speak of our growing Christian experience.

God made man from the dust of the earth. As we have seen, just as the earth was spoiled by Satan, so was man. The earth was:

   a. "Without form [a waste]"–Man was created to enjoy fellowship with God through His Son Jesus Christ. Any life that does not have this fellowship is a "waste."

   b. "Void [empty]"–Without Christ, we have stretched out over us "the line of confusion and the stones of emptiness" (Isa 34:11). Only Christ can fill the aching void in the empty hearts of people today.

   c. In "darkness"–"They ... became vain in their imaginations, and their foolish heart was darkened" (Rom 1:21–*KJV*). Until Jesus, the Light of the world, comes into our lives, we dwell in darkness.

God's answer is re-creation and restoration:

> "Therefore, if anyone is in Christ, he is a new creation; old things have passed away; behold, all things have become new." (2 Cor 5:17)

> "For we are His workmanship, created in Christ Jesus for good works ..." (Eph 2:11)

To be re-created and restored in Christ is both an event and a process. The best summary of the "elementary principles" we must experience to grow in the Lord is found in Hebrews 6:1 and 2:

> "Therefore, leaving the discussion of the elementary principles of Christ, let us go on to perfection (*margin*, 'maturity'), not laying again the foundation of
>
> repentance from dead works
> and of faith toward God,
> of the doctrine of baptisms,
> of laying on of hands,
> of resurrection of the dead,
> and of eternal judgment."

This Scripture encourages us to grow and mature to perfection!

This spiritual re-creation and restoration are prefigured in the literal Seven Days of God's Week of Re-creation:		
Day one	Literal:	Creation of Light
	Spiritual:	"Repentance from dead works" and "Faith towards God" through the Light of the Gospel
Day two	Literal:	Dividing the Waters; Separation
	Spiritual:	"Doctrine of Baptisms"–water baptism (for separation from sin and the old man; see Rom 6:3-7)
Day three	Literal:	Dry land, plants to bring forth fruit
	Spiritual:	"Doctrine of Baptisms"–baptism in the Holy Spirit (for fruitfulness; see Acts 1:8)[7]
Day four	Literal:	Sun, moon and stars (for signs and light)
	Spiritual:	"Laying on of Hands" to receive confirmation, impartation, and illumination.
Day five	Literal:	Fish; Fowl of the air (rising above earth)
	Spiritual:	"Resurrection Life" and "Eternal Judgments"
Day six	Literal:	Animals; Perfect Man and Woman
	Spiritual:	"Perfection, maturity" of Bride at end of Day six
Day seven	Literal:	God Rested. Re-creation and Restoration complete
	Spiritual:	Reigning and Living in His sight (Rev 20; Hos 6:2)

Finally, a quick look at the four points at the top of our diagram of God's Week:

1. The Three Heavenly Witnesses

> "For there are three that bear witness in heaven: the Father, the Word, and the Holy Spirit; and these three are one." (1 Jn 5:7)

As I wrote in my book *The Only Foundation*:

> "The word 'Trinity' is not used in the Bible, but this word does describe what the Bible teaches concerning God–one God Who has revealed Himself in three Persons–the Father, the Son, and the Holy Spirit.

---

[7] For further teaching about Repentance, Water Baptism, and Baptism in the Holy Spirit, see my book *The Only Foundation*.

The following few pages have been adapted, with additional material, from *The Only Foundation*; Restoration Temple, San Diego, *Third Edition*, 1987–pages 71 to 75.

> "The Father, the Son, and the Holy Spirit are all Co-Eternal. All stand equally superior to time, and free from the temporal distinctions of past and future:
>
> The Eternal Father–Gen 21:33
> The Eternal Son–Rev 1:8
> The Eternal Spirit–Heb 9:14
> The Eternal Godhead–Rom 1:20."

By joining the first six days of God's Week to form couplets, we discover three major periods of time–dispensations, each approximately 2,000 years long–from the fall of Adam to the second coming of Christ. Each Person in the Godhead has placed His special imprint on a dispensation.

   a. **The Father:** He is emphasized during the first 2,000-year period of time. He walked with Enoch. He sent the flood. He made covenants with Noah and Abraham.

   b. **The Son:** The second 2,000-year span begins with the offering up of a son, and ends with the offering up of *the* Son. It is the dispensation of blood atonement. All the sacrificial blood shed on earth prophesied of the Witness in Heaven–He Who would come and shed His perfect blood, once for all, for forgiveness of sin.

   c. **The Spirit:** The third dispensation of 2,000 years begins with the outpouring of the Holy Spirit on the Day of Pentecost. He has been active throughout this Church age. God promises a mighty move of His Spirit in the days just prior to the second coming of Christ.

2. The Name of the Godhead

> "Who has ascended into heaven, or descended?
> Who has gathered the wind in His fists?
> Who has bound the waters in a garment?
> Who has established all the ends of the earth?
> *What is His name, and what is His Son's name,
> If you know?"* (Prov 30:4)

Just as Agur asked this question, so do many people today. "What is God's name?" they enquire. "And what is the name of the Son of God?"

God has given many promises to those who know, and honour, His Name. Here are three:

> "Because he has set his love upon Me, therefore I will deliver him; I will set him on high, because *he has known My name.*" (Psa 91:14)

"Then those who feared *the Lord* talked with each other, and *the Lord* listened and heard. A scroll of remembrance was written in his presence concerning those who fear *the Lord* and honored *his name*." (Mal 3:16–*NIV*)

"The man of wisdom shall *see thy name*." (Mic 6:9–*KJV*) In another translation this promise is rendered, "The Lord, the fear of whose *name* brings success" (*NEB*).

The early church understood that Father, Son, and Holy Spirit are not names, but titles. I am both a father and a son. But these are only titles, not my names. The early followers of Jesus knew the names of the Father, Son, and Holy Spirit. The Bible also teaches us their Names.

The Name of the Father

What is the Father's name?

> "The Lord is a man of war;
> *The Lord is His name*." (Exo 15:3)

> "I am *the Lord; that is my name*!" (Isa 42:8)

In Jeremiah we read:

> "Therefore I will teach them–this time I will teach them my power and might. They will know that *my name is the Lord*." (Jer 16:21–*NIV*)

> "This is what the Lord says, He who made the earth, the Lord who formed it and established it–*the Lord is his name*." (Jer 33:2–*NIV*)

The Name of the Son

What is the Son's name?

The angel of God instructed:

> "You are to give him the name *Jesus*, because he will save his people from their sins." (Matt 1:21–*NIV*)

> "His name was called *Jesus*, the name given by the angel." (Luke 2:21)

The Name of the Holy Spirit

"Christ" is the name in which the presence and person of the Holy Spirit are recognized. For the Holy Spirit is the *Chrism* (the Greek word for "anointing"). It was the Holy Spirit's Person as the anointing which made Jesus *the* "Christ." ("Christ" from the Greek *Christos*).

Jesus is the Christ, and believers are Christians by reason of the Person, presence, and anointing of the Holy Spirit in their lives. (See Col 1:27; Acts 2:36)

Jesus–Both Lord and Christ

The fullness of His glorious name was revealed to Peter on the day of Pentecost when Peter preached:

> "God has made this **Jesus**, whom you crucified, both **Lord** and **Christ**." (Acts 2:36)

Thus was announced, for all to hear, the Name of our Triune God, and the way in which the Church can obey the commandment of Jesus regarding water baptism: "Go therefore and make disciples of all the nations, baptizing them in the name of the Father and of the Son and of the Holy Spirit."[8] The fullness of the Godhead–His Nature and His Name–dwells bodily in the Son of God.[9] So the New Testament Church, in obedience to His command, went everywhere baptizing in the Name of the Lord Jesus Christ.[10] In fact, they were commanded to do *everything* in the Name of the Lord Jesus.[11]

An understanding of this truth makes it possible to appreciate the full meaning of the words the Lord Jesus spoke to the church at Pergamos, "You hold fast to My Name," and to the church at Philadelphia, "You have not denied My Name." And in the last verse of the Book of Revelation, the final benediction honours the fullness of that Name: "The grace of our Lord Jesus Christ be with you all. Amen." (Rev 22:21)

3. The Three Created Heavenly Witnesses, or Symbols, in the Heavens

In Genesis 1:14 we saw that on the fourth day of God's Re-creative Week, He made the sun, moon and stars.

Throughout the Bible, God uses the language of created things to teach us spiritual truths. He takes natural things to teach us of His supernatural power and glory. In the words of Paul to the Corinthians: "The spiritual is not first, but the natural, and afterward the spiritual" (1 Cor 15:46).

In the Book of Revelation:

- The word "sun" appears 11 times.

- The word "moon" appears 4 times.

---

[8] Matt 28:19.
[9] Col 2:9.
[10] For more details, see my book, *What Does the Bible Teach About Water Baptism?*
[11] Col 3:17.

- The words "star" or "stars" appear 14 times.

In Revelation 12:1 we see all three words used to describe a pregnant woman who is clothed with the sun, standing on the moon, and who has a crown of twelve stars on her head.

A Christian does not become involved in astrology, nor consult horoscopes. But astronomy–the study of the signs created to show forth the splendour of the Godhead–is both encouraged and necessary.

The psalmist emphasizes the significance of the sun, moon, and stars:

> "The heavens declare the glory of God;
> And the firmament shows His handiwork.
>
> Day unto day utters speech,
> And night unto night reveals knowledge.
>
> There is no speech nor language
> Where their voice is not heard.
>
> Their line (*margin*, 'sound') has gone out through all the earth,
> And their words to the end of the world.
> In them He has set a tabernacle for the sun,
>
> Which is like a bridegroom coming out of his chamber,
> And rejoices like a strong man to run its race.
> Its rising is from one end of heaven,
> And its circuit to the other end;
> And there is nothing hidden from its heat." (Psa 19:1-6)

These glorious signs in the heavens point beyond themselves to something far greater–God's eternal power and Godhead:

> "For since the creation of the world His invisible attributes are clearly seen, being understood by the things that are made, even His eternal power and Godhead, so that they are without excuse." (Rom 1:20)

The sign of the sun, moon, and stars is God's creation, drawing our attention to the Great Creator. Therefore, those who deny the existence of the One True God are left without excuse.

The sun, then, is a visible symbol of our Invisible God. The Scripture says:
> "For the Lord God is a sun and shield." (Psa 84:11)

> "Bless the Lord, O my soul!
> O Lord my God, You are very great:
> You are clothed with honor and majesty,

> Who cover Yourself with light as with a garment,
> Who stretch out the heavens like a curtain." (Psa 104:1,2)

"Who alone has immortality, dwelling in unapproachable light." (1 Tim 6:16)

"God is light and in Him is no darkness at all." (1 Jn 1:5)

In the Song of Solomon we read:

> "Who is she who looks forth as the morning,
> Fair as the moon, Clear as the sun,
> Awesome as an army with banners?" (Song 6:10)

Couple this with the promise of Jesus, that "the righteous will shine forth as the sun in the kingdom of their Father" (Matt 13:53). Both these Scriptures prefigure the sun-clad Bride of Revelation chapter 12.

The sun in Scripture is a symbol of God the Father.

The moon reflects the light of the sun. When He was on earth, the Lord Jesus said His mission was to reflect His Father's glory:

> "Most assuredly, I say to you, the Son can do nothing of Himself, but what He sees the Father do; for whatever He does, the Son also does in like manner." (John 5:19)

There are three verses in Scripture which state that the moon will become like blood in the last days–Joel 2:31; Acts 2:20; Rev 6:12.

The moon in Scripture is a symbol of God the Son.

The stars in the heavens cannot be numbered.[12] They are unlimited in their influence in every place–as is the ministry of the Holy Spirit.

The Spirit-filled pastors of the seven churches in Revelation are spoken of as stars in God's hand (Rev 1:20).

Concerning stars, Daniel prophesied:
> "Those who are wise shall shine
> Like the brightness of the firmament,
> And those who turn many to righteousness
> Like the stars forever and ever." (Dan 12:3)

Spirit-empowered believers who turn many to Christ are spoken of as stars.

---

[12] Gen 15:5 and Heb 11:12.

The Lord told Job about stars singing:

> "When the morning stars sang together,
> And all the sons of God shouted for joy." (Job 38:7)

The second dream of Joseph, and his father's interpretation of it, illustrates the symbolism of the sun, moon and stars:

> "Then he dreamed still another dream and told it to his brothers, and said, 'Look, I have dreamed another dream. And this time the sun, the moon, and the eleven stars bowed down to me.'
>
> So he told it to his father and his brothers; and his father rebuked him and said to him, 'What is this dream that you have dreamed? Shall your mother and I and your brothers indeed come to bow down to the earth before you?'" (Gen 37:9,10)

Here Jacob interprets sun, moon and stars as his earthly family–father, mother, sons.

The Family of God in Heaven–the Father, Son, and Holy Spirit–are symbolized by these three created signs in the heavens–the sun, moon and stars.

Stars in Scripture are a symbol of God the Holy Spirit.

4. The Three Earthly Witnesses

> "And there are three that bear witness on earth: the Spirit, the water, and the blood; and these three agree as one." (1 Jn 5:8)

Water speaks of the 2,000-year dispensation of the Father. There is a clear imprint of water on this period of time. The water of the rivers in Eden. The waters of the flood.

Blood speaks of the 2,000-year dispensation of the Son. Blood is the witness and seal of the Son of God. From Abraham to Christ, all the blood sacrifices at altars, in the Tabernacle of Moses, and in the Temple of Solomon, were a prophecy pointing to Jesus shedding His blood on the cross.

The 2,000 years of the **Spirit** began on the Day of Pentecost, and speak of the dispensation during which the Holy Spirit works through the Church.

Some Prophetic Pictures and Types of God's Week:

1. Exo 12:1-6: The passover lamb was kept four days, from the tenth to the fourteenth day, before being slain.

    * God's Passover Lamb, the Lord Jesus, was "kept" four 1,000-year days from Adam's sin until Calvary.

2. Exo 16:5: A double portion of manna was gathered on the sixth day.

    * This speaks of a double portion of the bread of God's Word in the sixth day of God's Week.

3. Exo 19:11: "Let them be ready for the third day."

    * Counting from the Day of Pentecost, the 1,000-year Millennial reign of Christ will be the third day. We must prepare.

4. Exo 24:16: The glory cloud covered Mount Sinai six days. On the seventh day God called to Moses, and all saw the glory of the Lord as a consuming fire.

    * Despite sin, God's glory has, from time to time, dwelt on the earth. On the seventh day God will call His people, and destroy sin and sinners with consuming fire. (Mal 4:1; Heb 12:29; 2 Thess 2:8)

5. Exo 25-40: The dimensions of the Tabernacle of Moses:

    - Fence = 1,500 sq cubits.
      The 1,500 years of the Law, from Moses to Christ.

    - Holy Place = 2,000 cubic cubits.
      The 2,000 years of the Church age.

    - Holy of Holies = 1,000 cubic cubits.
      The Millennium (see Rev 20).

6. Lev 25:1-22: Field sown six years. Triple portion in sixth year.
    Seventh year an agricultural sabbath.

    * Blessing on the sixth day of God's Week. Seventh day a sabbath rest.

7.	Lev 25:	Number of Jubilee (50) multiplied by number of end of all 4.

* We are entering a great Jubilee for the people of God, when works of the "flesh" shall cease, and the Holy Spirit will move as never before.

8.	Josh 3:4:	2,000 cubits between the Ark of the Covenant and the people while crossing Jordan.

* Jesus died on the cross, and 2,000 years later will marry His Bride.

9.	2 Chr 4:1:	The bronze altar in Solomon's Temple was 20x20x10, i.e. 4,000 cubic cubits.

* During the 4,000 years from Adam's fall to Calvary, sacrifice for sin was offered on altars.

10.	1 Ki 7:26 & 2 Chr 4:5:	The 2,000 and 3,000 measurements of water in the bronze "Sea" in Solomon's Temple.

* Prophetic of the Church age, and the Church age plus the Millennium.

11.	Eze 47:1-14:	Four 1,000-cubit measurements.

* Measuring prophetic "1,000-cubit" time periods from Abraham, the father of faith, brings us to the present time, the time of waters in which to swim.

12.	Hos 6:2:	"After two days He will revive us; on the third day He will raise us up, that we may live in His sight."

* At the close of the second day of the Church age God will send a great revival to His people. Day three commences with the dead in Christ being raised to live with Him.

13.	Mark 5:13:	2,000 devil-possessed swine ran violently into the sea and drowned.

* Prophetic of the casting down and binding of Satan at the end of the 2,000 years' Church age (Rev 12:9; 20:2).

14.	Mark 9:2:	After six days, Jesus appeared on the mount transfigured, radiant in His glory.

* At the end of the sixth day of God's Week the glorified Lord will appear to His Bride. (Heb 9:28; 1 Jn 3:3)

15. Luke 10:35: Innkeeper given two denarii to care for the wounded man until the good Samaritan returned.

    * This was two days' wages. Our Good Samaritan has provided for His Church to be a place for the care and healing of the wounded for two days–2,000 years.

16. Luke 13:32: "Behold, I cast out demons and perform cures today and tomorrow, and the third day I reach My goal." (*NAS*)

    * Jesus promises to minister for two days, and during the third day, His goal of reigning over a perfected earth will be realized.

17. John 2:1: Marriage in Cana on the third day.

    * Measuring from the Day of Pentecost, there will be a great marriage between day two and day three–the marriage of Christ and His Bride.

18. John 2:6: Six waterpots at the wedding.

    * Illustrate the six days of God's Week of Redemption. Christ's last day Bride will be filled with the wine of the Holy Spirit, and prepared for the wedding

19. John 4:40: Jesus stayed two days with the Samaritans.

    * A prophetic picture of the Gospel being preached to the Gentiles for the two days of the Church age.

20. John 11:39: Lazarus dead four days.

    * Illustrates the four 1,000-year days from Adam to Christ, when man was dead in trespasses and sins, for the Saviour had not yet come.

21. Rev ch 20: The 1,000-year reign of Christ.

    * The seventh day of God's Redemptive Week.

God's Week is an essential key to unlock the Book of Revelation.

Chapter 11

Numbers in the Bible

Key Number Six: **Numbers in the Bible**

Most Bible students are familiar with the fact that certain numbers have an important meaning in the Word of God. In this chapter we will discover that numbers have significance and symbolic interpretation. Numbers are inseparably linked with themes that wind as unbroken cable wires through the whole Bible.

It is a scientific fact that every branch of nature is based on a mathematical system. Someone has said, "Great mathematical laws govern the activities of the entire universe." Examine the human body. Delve into music. Note the gestation periods of animals. Look into physics. Study botany. Inquire into chemistry. Certain definite fixed mathematical laws, patterns, and proportions govern all these realms of study.

Why?

Because God is their Creator. All creation is signed with His mathematical signature. His creation is stamped with the "seal of God" in numerics. God has made man himself a creature of time, and therefore, a creature of number. Jesus said, "The very hairs of your head are all numbered."[1]

It is consistent with the very nature and being of God that His Book, the Bible, should be stamped with this same "seal"–Bible numbers.

The Psalmist says:

> "Praise the Lord! ...
> He counts the number of the stars;
> He calls them all by name." (Psa 147:1-4)

Isaiah the prophet asks:

> "Who has measured the waters in the hollow of His hand,
> Measured heaven with a span[2]
> And calculated the dust of the earth in a measure?

---

[1] Matt 10:30.
[2] "A span = ½ cubit, 9 inches; or the width of His hand." (*margin*)

> Weighed the mountains in scales
> And the hills in a balance?"
>
> "Lift up your eyes on high,
> And see who has created these things,
> Who brings out their host by number ..."
> (Isa 40:12 and 26)

"The Wonderful Numberer"

In Daniel 8:13 we read:

> "Then I heard one saint speaking, and another saint said unto that certain saint which spake, How long shall be the vision concerning the daily sacrifice, and the transgression of desolation, to give both the sanctuary and the host to be trodden under foot?" (*KJV*)

In the *King James Version*, the marginal rendering for "that certain saint" is "Or, *the numberer of secrets*, or, *the wonderful numberer*. Heb. *Palmoni*." Indeed, our Great God is the wonderful numberer!

Numbers most definitely have important significance in the Book of Revelation. In the words of Henry Halley:

> "Certain numbers are used so extensively [in Revelation] that it seems evident they were intended to be in themselves a language, having a meaning apart from their numerical value."[3]

Basic Principles of Interpretation of Numbers

Before I show you the symbolic significance of numbers, I want to give you some basic principles of interpretation of Bible numbers. These principles will keep students of Scripture from error or extremes.

1. God is consistent throughout His Word. The sixty-six books of the Bible were written by forty different writers over about fifteen hundred years. Yet there is manifest, throughout all the books, the same marvelous meaning and harmony in the use of numbers. This begins in Genesis, flows through each book, and consummates in Revelation.

---

[3] *Pocket Bible Handbook–An Abbreviated Bible Commentary* by Henry Hampton Halley; self published, Chicago, Illinois, *Sixteenth Edition*, 1944–page 526.

2. The simple numbers 1 through 13 have symbolic significance.[4]

3. Multiples of these numbers, or doubling and trebling, carry basically the same meaning, only intensifying the truth. For example, 1,000 is 10 raised to the 3rd power to convey superlative greatness; 144 is 12 times 12 and conveys the meaning of 12 intensified.

4. The first use of the number in Scripture generally conveys its spiritual meaning.

5. The symbolic significance of a number is not always stated, but may be veiled, or hidden, or seen by comparison with other Scriptures.

6. Generally there are good and evil, true and counterfeit, Godly and Satanic aspects in numbers.

7. Remember: the number is not always stated in the text of the Bible. Many times we have to count a list of names, statements, places, or blessings. For example, there are found in various places in Scripture, the five things that come out of the rock–water, snow, honey, oil, and fire–each of which represents a blessing from the Lord.

Symbolic Meanings of Some Numbers in the Bible

The following list of numbers, and their symbolic meanings, is brief. Only a few examples are given for each number. You can search out many more. For further study of Bible numerics refer to the books listed in the footnote on this page.[5]

ONE: Expresses Beginning, Source of Commencement (Which God Is)

* The number one is the source of all numerals:
* "The Lord our God, the Lord is one!" (Deut 6:4)

* One expresses unity:
* "For by one Spirit we were all baptized into one body." (1 Cor 12:13)

---

[4] Bible numerics must not be confused with "numerology." Numerology implies that numbers affect people and circumstances in some mystical way. This concept is witchcraft and is forbidden in Scripture. However, in the study of Bible numerics, we find that numbers have symbolic significance in Scripture, and this discovery assists us in the interpretation of Bible truth.

[5] These are four books I recommend:
1. Keys to Scripture Numerics by Ed. F.Vallowe; Ed. F. Vallowe Evangelistic Association, Forest Park, Georgia, *Eighth Printing* 1977.
2. Interpreting the Scriptures–A Textbook on How to Interpret the Bible by Kevin J. Conner and Ken Malmin; Bible Temple–Conner/Malmin Publications, Portland, Oregon, 1976–Chapter 20, "The Numerical Principle."
3. The Arithmetic of God by Don Kistler; Self-published, Kings Mountain, North Carolina, 1976.
4. Number in Scripture, Its Supernatural Design and Spiritual Significance by Ethelbert W.Bullinger; Kregel Publications, Grand Rapids, Michigan, 1978 *(first edition published 1894)*.

TWO: Number of Witness and Testimony

* "It is also written in your law that the testimony of two men is true. I am One who bears witness of Myself, and the Father who sent Me bears witness of Me." (John 8:17,18)

THREE: Number of the Godhead and Perfect Testimony

* The Triune Godhead–Father, Son, and Holy Spirit.
* The Name of the Godhead–the Lord Jesus Christ.[6]
* The 3 men who visited Abraham, each of whom he called "Lord." (The Bible narrative also calls them "Lord"–Hebrew, *adonai*).

* The Tabernacle of Moses had 3 sections, 3 colours, 3 doors, 3 coverings, contained 3 metals, and 3 Festivals were celebrated there in 3 different months of each year.

* The body of Jesus lay in the tomb 3 days and 3 nights, so as to fulfill the sign of the Prophet Jonah.

FOUR: Number of Earth, World, Creation and the Worldwide Nature of the Gospel

* The waters of the river in Eden parted into 4 head-streams to water the garden (Gen 2:10).

* In Scripture there are 4 divisions of the day (the first, 6 am, third, sixth, and ninth hours); 4 seasons; 4 points of the compass; order of 4-fold outreach for witnessing (Acts 1:8); 4 Gospels; 4 living ones in Revelation.

FIVE: Number of the Cross, Salvation by Grace, and the Outworking of the Gospel Through the Five Ministries

* The 5 "I wills" of Lucifer (Isa 14:12-14).
* Man fell through the 5 physical senses (Gen 3:1-6).

* The 5 spiritual senses (Heb 5:14).
* The 5 animals of Abraham's sacrifice (Gen 15:9).

In the Tabernacle of Moses:
* 5 cubits square was the dimension of the brazen altar (Exo 27:1).
* 5 vessels at the brazen altar (Exo 27:3).
* 5 different offerings on the brazen altar (Lev chapters 1-5).
* 5 pillars into the Holy Place (Exo 36:38).
* 5 anointed priests (Num 3:2,3).[7]

---

[6] See Chapter 10, "God's Week."
[7] See Chapter 12, "The Feasts of Israel."

* 5 ingredients of the holy anointing oil (Exo 30:23,24).
* 5 ingredients of the incense (Exo 30:34,35).
* 5 shekels of silver was the redemption money (Num 3:47).

* David chose 5 smooth stones to slay the giant (1 Sam 17:40).

* 5 thousand fed with 5 loaves and 2 fish (Matt 14:15-21).
* 5 wise and 5 foolish virgins (Matt 25:1-13).
* 5 times Jesus foretold of His atoning death to his disciples.
* 5 bleeding wounds of Christ on the Cross to cancel out and defeat the 5 "I wills" of Satan:
2 in His hands (to change and heal our works);
2 in His feet (to change and heal our walk);
1 in His side (to change and heal our hearts).

* 5 signs that follow believers (Mark 16:17,18).
* 5 ascension gift ministries (Eph 4:8,11).

SIX: Number of Man, Beast, and Satan

* Man created on the 6th day (Gen 1:26-31).
* 6 generations of Cain (Gen 4:17,18).
* 6 cities of refuge (Num 35:15).
* 6 pieces of Goliath's armor. His height was 6 cubits plus a span (1 Sam 17:4-7).
* 6 working days of God's week.[8]

SEVEN: Number of Dispensational Completeness, and Perfection of That Which Is Temporary

* 7 days of re-creation including day of rest (Gen 2:1-3).
* 7 days of God's week (including the millennium).[9]
* At Jericho: 7 priests, blowing 7 trumpets, marched 7 times on 7th day (Joshua chapter 6).
* 7 letters to 7 churches in Revelation.

* "Seven" appears 54 times in the Book of Revelation, sometimes emphasizing that which is finished. For example:

* "In the days of the sounding of the seventh angel, when he is about to sound, the mystery of God would be finished." (Rev 10:7)

* "Then the seventh angel poured out his bowl into the air, and a loud voice came out of the temple of heaven, from the throne, saying, 'It is done.'" (Rev 16:17)

---

[8] See Chapter 10, "God's Week."
[9] See Chapter 10, "God's Week."

EIGHT: Number of Resurrection Life and a New Beginning

* Male children commanded to be circumcised the 8th day (Gen 17:12).
* Cleansed leper presented by the priest on the 8th day (Lev 14:10,11).
* Christ rose from the dead the first day of a new week, the 8th day (Matt 28:1).
* In music, the 8th note of a scale is the beginning of a new octave.

NINE: Number of Fullness, Especially of The Holy Spirit

* 9 beatitudes–blessings (Matt 5:3-11).
* 9 fruit of the Holy Spirit (Gal 5:22,23).
* 9 miraculous gifts of the Holy Spirit (1 Cor 12:8-10).
* The term "Latter Rain" occurs 9 times in the Bible.

TEN: Number of the Perfection of Divine Order. Also the Number of Law and Testimony

" ...*ten* ... *signifies the perfection of Divine order*, commencing, as it does, an altogether new series of numbers ...
"Completeness of order, marking the entire round of anything, is, therefore, the ever-present signification of the number *ten*. It implies that nothing is wanting; that the number and order are perfect; that the whole cycle is complete."[10]

* 10 times in Genesis chapter one it is written, "God said."
* 10 plagues on Egypt (Exodus chapters 7 through 12).
* 10 commandments (Exo 34:28).
* 10 percent of increase for the Lord–tithe (Lev 27:32).
* Holy of Holies in Moses' Tabernacle 10 x 10 x 10 cubits.
* 10 curtains for the Tabernacle of Moses (Exo 26:1).
* David sang to the Lord with a harp of 10 strings (Psa 144:9).
* 10 toes of Daniel's image (Dan 2:41).
* 10 horns on the beast (Dan 7:7 and Rev 12:3).

Also, Ten is the Number of Testings and Trials

* Abraham asked God to spare Sodom if there were only 10 righteous people in that wicked city (Gen 18:32,33).
* Rebekah drew water for 10 camels (about 400 gallons!). But that which she watered carried her to the bridegroom, Isaac. (Genesis chapter 24).
* The Passover lamb was taken on the 10th day of the month (Exo 12:3).
* 10 times Israel put God to the test (Num 14:22).
* Abigail was tested another 10 days before her wicked husband died, and she was free to marry David (1 Sam 25:38).
* The woman who lost one of her 10 silver coins (Luke 15:8).
* 10 virgins–5 wise and 5 foolish–the "oil test" (Matt 25:1-13).

---

[10] Bullinger, *op.cit*. Emphasis his.

* 10 minas (about 3 months' salary) given to 10 servants to test their faithfulness. One was rewarded by being given authority over 10 cities (Luke 19:13-25).

* The disciples of Jesus had to wait for 10 days in the upper room before the Holy Spirit was poured out upon them (Acts 1:3, 2:1).

* "The devil will put some of you in prison to test you, and you will suffer persecution for ten days." (Rev 2:10–*NIV*)

ELEVEN: Number of Disorder, Incompleteness, and Judgment

* 11 sons of Jacob–Benjamin not yet born (Gen 32:22, 35:16-18).

* 11 stars–which Joseph saw representing his father Jacob's other 11 sons (Gen 37:9).

* 11 Judgments upon the Egyptians–10 plagues plus their overthrow at the Red Sea (Exodus chapters 7-14).

* Jehoiakim and Zedekiah each reigned 11 years. Because they did evil, judgment came, and Israel was taken captive to Babylon (Jeremiah chapter 52).

* Judas' betrayal and suicide left only 11 disciples who witnessed the death, resurrection, and ascension of the Lord Jesus (Matt 28:16).

TWELVE: Number of Governmental Perfection, Apostolic Fullness, and Eternal Order

> "This number symbolizes God's perfect, divine accomplishment actively manifested. It shows a COMPLETENESS of a GROWTH or ADMINISTRA-TION. TWELVE marks GOVERNMENTAL PERFECTION and is used as the SIGNATURE of Israel. This number is used 187 times in the Bible. It is used 22 times in the Book of Revelation."[11]

* 12 sons of Jacob, who became the heads of the 12 tribes (Gen 49:28).

* 12 wells of water at Elim (Exo 15:27).

* 12 stones in the High Priest's breastplate representing the 12 tribes (Exo 28:17-21).

* 12 stones and 12 men of Joshua (Josh 4:3,4,9).

* 12 apostles of the Lamb chosen by Jesus at the beginning of the Gospel age (Matt 10:1-5).

* 12 apostles of the Bride will be chosen by the Holy Spirit at the end of the Gospel age–to make up the 24 elders of the Book of Revelation (Rev 4:4).

* 12 stars make up the Bride's crown (Rev 12:1).

* 12 gates, 12 angels, 12 names of 12 tribes, 12 foundations, 12 precious stones, 12 pearls, in conjunction with the wall of the holy city, New Jerusalem, the Bride, the Lamb's wife (Rev 21:12-21).

[It is interesting to note how that as the Book of Revelation draws to a close, the emphasis shifts from number 7 to number 12.]

---

[11] Vallowe, *op.cit*. Emphasis his.

THIRTEEN: Number of Depravity and Rebellion

"Twelve years they served Chedorlaomer [King of Elam] and in the thirteenth year they rebelled." (Gen 14:4) The number 12 is used with the reign of the government of the King. But the number 13 is associated with rebellion against that government.

* Nimrod, who rebelled against God and in his depravity introduced witchcraft, was the 13th from Adam (Gen 10:10).
* Ishmael was 13 years old when he was circumcised (Gen 17:25).
* Haman, the enemy of the Jews, had a decree to kill all Jews on the 13th day of the 12th month signed on the 13th day of the 1st month (Esth 3:8-13, 9:1).

FOURTEEN: Number of Passover, Deliverance and Salvation

"FOURTEEN is the number that represents DELIVERANCE or SALVATION. It is used some 26 times in the Bible. It was the FOURTEENTH day of the first month of the year when the children of Israel were DELIVERED from Egyptian bondage, and from the stroke of judgment which fell upon the firstborn of the Egyptians. (Exo 12:6-7; Exo 12:12-13; Lev 23:4-5)

"The number FOURTEEN is found three times connected with Christ's coming into the world, and He came to SAVE, or DELIVER His people from their sins … Matthew 1:17."[12]

Note that the number 14 is twice times 7.

TWENTY: Number of Payment on Demand

* Jacob served Laban 20 years for his wives and cattle (Gen 31:38,41).
* Joseph was sold by his brothers for 20 pieces of silver (Gen 37:28).
* The payment of redemption money was 5 shekels of silver, which equals 20 gerahs in weight (Num 18:16).[13]
* On the long sides of Moses' Tabernacle, the North and South sides, were 20 pillars of brass.
* Israel did evil, and "the Lord sold them into the hand of Jabin king of Canaan … for twenty years" (Judg 4:2,3).

TWENTY-FOUR: Number of Complete Priesthood and Governmental Perfection

* In the Tabernacle of David 24 priests governed the work of the sanctuary (1 Chr 24:1-18). The next chapter, 1 Chronicles 25, lists the 24 courses of musicians at David's Tabernacle.

---

[12] *Ibid.* Emphasis his.
[13] "Gerah (Heb. *Gerah*, a *kernel*) … smallest weight and also the smallest piece of money …worth about three cents." *Unger's Bible Dictionary* by Merrill F. Unger; Moody Press, Chicago, *Twenty-second Printing* 1975–page 724.

* In the Book of Revelation, John sees 24 elders sitting on 24 thrones (Rev 4:4).
* Remember, the number 24 is 2 x 12.

THIRTY: Number of Dedication, and Maturity For Ministry

* Joseph was 30 years old when he stood before Pharaoh (Gen 41:46).
* The curtains of goats' hair for the tent of the Tabernacle of Moses were 30 cubits long (Exo 26:8).
* The sons of Kohath, the children of Levi, began serving in the Tabernacle of Moses at 30 years of age (Num 4:1-4).
* David was 30 years old when he began to reign (2 Sam 5:4).
* Jesus began his ministry on earth at about 30 years of age. So, it appears, did John the Baptist (Luke 3:23).
* In 2 Cor 6:4-10 we read of 30 qualifications that approve ministers of God. (The first of these is "much patience"–*margin*, "much endurance!")

FORTY: Number of Trials, Probation, and Testings

This number occurs 146 times in the Bible.

* There were 40 days and 40 nights of rain to destroy all the living in the time of Noah (Gen 7:4).
* The 12 spies were sent to Canaan for 40 days (Num 13:25).
* Israel wandered 40 years in the wilderness as judgment for their disobedience (Num 14:33-35).
* Moses spent 40 days and 40 nights on Mount Sinai where he received the law (Exo 24:18).
* Elijah was 40 days in Horeb after his experience on Mount Carmel (1 Ki 19:8).
* Jonah preached for 40 days that God's judgment would come upon Nineveh (Jon 3:4).

* The Lord Jesus Christ fasted 40 days and 40 nights in the wilderness, and overcame temptation (Matt 4:1-11). After His resurrection, he was seen by His disciples for 40 days before His ascension (Acts 1:3).

FIFTY: Number of Holy Spirit, Liberty, and Jubilee

The number 50 is found 154 times in the Bible.

* 50 loops and 50 gold clasps were made for the curtains of the Tabernacle of Moses (Exo 26:6,7).
* The Levites entered into their rest from Tabernacle work at 50 years of age (Num 8:25,26).
* In the Year of Jubilee (*KJV margin*, "loud of sound"), which was observed every 50th year:

i.	It was a holy year;
ii.	The trumpet of Jubilee sounded on the day of atonement;
iii.	Liberty was proclaimed throughout all the land;
iv.	Every man returned to his possession;
v.	Every man returned to his family;
vi.	It was a year of rest;
vii.	The priests possessed the fields which were released that year (Lev 25:10,11; 27:21).

* The Holy Spirit was poured out upon the disciples 50 days after the day Jesus offered Himself on Calvary's cross as God's eternal Passover Lamb (Acts 2:1-4).

ONE HUNDRED TWENTY: The Number of the End of All Flesh, and a New Moving Into the Power of The Spirit

* God said that man's days shall be 120 years (Gen 6:3).
* Moses was 120 years old when he died (Deut 34:7).
* In Solomon's Temple, the vestibule that was in front of the sanctuary was 120 cubits high (2 Chr 3:4).
* When the singers and the 120 priests sounded with 120 trumpets, the glory of God filled the Temple, so that the priests could not continue ministering because of the cloud of God's glory (2 Chr 5:12-14).
* Also at the dedication of the Temple, King Solomon offered a sacrifice of 120 thousand sheep (2 Chr 7:4-6).

* Jesus said, "Do you not say, 'There are still four months and then comes the harvest?'" (John 4:35) In Bible days, 4 months equaled 120 days.
* On the Day of Pentecost, 120 disciples waited for, and received, the power of the Spirit, which enabled them to obey Christ's command to be His witnesses to all nations.

ONE HUNDRED FORTY-FOUR: The Number of the Bringing Forth of God's Ultimate Purpose

144,000 is the square of 12 (the number of Governmental Perfection) multiplied by 1,000.

It is interesting to note that the number of those instructed to sing skilfully the songs of the Lord in the Tabernacle of David was 12 squared (12 x 12) multiplied by 2 = 288 (1 Chr 25:7).

In the Book of Revelation, the holy city, New Jerusalem, the measurement of the wall is 144 cubits (Rev 21:17).

Also in Revelation, there are two references to a company of people who number 144,000 (Rev 7:1-8, 14:1-5).

SIX HUNDRED SIXTY-SIX: **The Number of the Beast, the Antichrist**

"There were three men in Scripture who stand out as the avowed enemies of God and His people. Each is branded with the number SIX that we may not miss their significance.

* GOLIATH, whose height was 6 cubits, and who had 6 pieces of armour. His spear's head weighed 600 shekels of iron (1 Samuel 17:4-7).

* NEBUCHADNEZZAR, whose 'image' which he set up, was 60 cubits broad (Daniel 3:1), and which was worshipped when the music was heard from 6 specified instruments.

* ANTICHRIST, whose number is 666 as revealed in Revelation 13:18.

"In the first we have one SIX connected with the PRIDE of FLESHLY might.

"In the second we have two SIXES connected with the PRIDE of absolute DOMINION.

"In the third we have three SIXES connected with the PRIDE of SATANIC guidance."[14]

Revelation 13:18 clearly tells us:

"Here is wisdom. Let him who has understanding calculate the number of the beast, for it is the number of a man: His number is 666."

Truly, the Lord our God is "The Wonderful Numberer"!

---

[14] Vallowe, *op. cit.* Emphasis his.

PART TWO   THE KEYS

Chapter 12

The Festivals of Israel

Key Number Seven: The Feasts–Religious Festivals–of Old Testament Israel

God commanded Israel to gather together three times a year to celebrate special religious Festivals. These Festivals, or Sacred Feasts, are, without doubt, one of the greatest of all Old Testament prophetic pictures. Understanding the Festivals of Israel is a principle key to help us unlock the Book of Revelation.[1]

THREE TIMES A YEAR

The Lord told His people:

> "Three times a year all your males shall appear before the Lord your God in the place which He chooses: at the
>
> 1. Feast of Unleavened Bread   [or Passover], at the
> 2. Feast of Weeks   [or Pentecost], and at the
> 3. Feast of Tabernacles   [or Ingathering];
>
> and they shall not appear before the Lord empty-handed." (Deut 16:16)

In Leviticus chapter 23 we see the first and last Feasts were tripartite, "three-in-one" Feasts. Thus three Feasts became seven separate celebrations. From Leviticus chapter 23 we can list the seven Feasts:

A. Unleavened Bread (Passover)
v 5   1.   Feast of Passover
v 6   2.   Feast of Unleavened Bread
v 10   3.   Feast of Firstfruits

B. Pentecost (Weeks; Harvest)
V 16   4.   Feast of Pentecost

---

[1] In this chapter we can only consider a brief summary and overview of these Feasts. Those wishing to pursue this subject further should read Kevin Conner's excellent study book, *The Feasts of Israel*, Bible Temple-Conner Publications, Portland, Oregon, 1980.

C. Tabernacles (Ingathering)

v 24	5.	Feast of Trumpets
v 27	6.	Day of Atonement
v 34	7.	Feast of Tabernacles

DEFINITION OF "FEASTS"

According to Young's Concordance, the Hebrew word *chagag* means "To hold, keep, or observe a festival."

Strong's Concordance defines "Feasts":

> "To revolve" (i.e. to dance);
>
> To move in a circle,
>
> To march in a sacred procession,
>
> To observe a festival";

By implication "To be giddy; celebrate, dance;

> keep, hold a solemn feast (holiday);
>
> reel to and fro."

The other Hebrew word, *moed*, means an "appointed meeting." The Greek word, *heortazo*, means "to hold a feast."

The English dictionary defines "festival" as "A joyous or period-ical celebration."[2]

FULFILLMENT OF THE FEASTS

1. Actual Fulfillment In Israel (What God Did in Israel)

This is called *Observation*.

Firstly, we look for the Historical Fulfillment in Israel. God gave Israel, through Moses and Aaron, the commandment to keep the Feasts.

---

[2] *Webster's Unified Dictionary and Encyclopedia*; H.S. Stuttman Co., New York, 1957–page 1544.

Each Feast points to a particular historical event in God's dealings with Israel. It was as if God said: "You are to keep an annual memorial–a Festival–so you don't forget what I have just done for you."

2. Prophetical Fulfillment In The Lord Jesus (What God Did in Christ)

This is called *Interpretation*.

Everything in the law of Moses has its fulfillment in the Lord Jesus Christ. The Lord Jesus said:

> "Do not think that I came to destroy the Law or the Prophets. I did not come to destroy but *to fulfill*." (Matt 5:17)

In John's Gospel Jesus said, "*Moses ... wrote about Me.*" (John 5:46)

And in Luke:

> "Then He [Jesus] said to them, 'These are the words which I spoke to you while I was still with you, that all things must be fulfilled which were *written in the Law of Moses* and the Prophets and the Psalms *concerning Me*.'" (Luke 24:44)

Once again, in Matthew's Gospel, Jesus states, "*The law prophesied*" (Matt 11:13).

3. Experiential Fulfillment In The Life Of The Believer (What God Does in the Church)

We call this *Application*.

In First Corinthians chapter 10, Paul applies lessons learned from Moses and the children of Israel to the Church:

> "Now these things happened as examples (Greek, *tupos*, 'a type, a model') for us, that we should not crave evil things, as they also craved.
> And do not be idolators, as some of them were ...
> Nor let us act immorally, as some of them did ...nor let us try the Lord, as some of them did ..."(1 Cor 10:6-9–NAS)

Referring to the Tabernacle of Moses, and the law–which includes the Feasts of Israel– Hebrews 10:1 says these are

- "a shadow of the good things to come."

In Hebrews 9:9 it is stated concerning these things:

- "a parable–a visible symbol or type or picture of the present age." (*Amp*)
- "This has an important lesson for us today." (*LB*)
- "This is a illustration pointing to the present time." (*NLT*)

The Lord promises blessing to those who know the truths of the Feasts:

> "Blessed–happy, fortunate [to be envied]–are the people who know the joyful sound *[who understand and appreciate the spiritual blessings symbolized by the feasts]*; they walk, O Lord, in the light and favor of Your countenance!" (Psa 89:15–*Amp*)

How wonderful that we can understand, appreciate, and experience the spiritual blessings symbolized by the feasts!

One of the main aspects of Christian life illustrated in the Feasts is growing to maturity. God wants us to grow in Him:

> "Grow in the grace and knowledge of our Lord and Savior Jesus Christ." (2 Pet 3:18)

> "Grow up in all things into Him who is the head–Christ." (Eph 4:15)

This growth takes place as we experience Passover, Pentecost–then Tabernacles. *Figure 15* in *Appendix 10*, page 369 shows thirty types and illustrations of the three stages in Christian growth.

We can liken the Feasts to a road map. Most Christians know where they are in the Lord. Most Christians know where the Lord wants them to be. But how do we get from where we are to where God wants us? By progressing through the Feasts. God's purpose for us is that:

- We experience *Passover* to bring us to the *SON*;

- We experience *Pentecost* to live in the power of the *HOLY SPIRIT*;

- As we experience *Tabernacles* we enable the *FATHER* to prepare us to be a part of the Bride of His Son.

Figure 16 on the next page is a summary of the Three Feasts:

THE FESTIVALS OF ISRAEL

Figure 16: **The Feasts of the Lord–Summary Chart**

Name of Feast	Religious Month	Civil Month	Historical Fulfillment	Christological Fulfillment	Experiential Fulfillment	Growing in God	Fruitfulness	Bible Books
PASSOVER	1	7	Egypt	Died on the Cross	Salvation	Children	30-fold	Gospels
PENTECOST	3	9	Wilderness	Sent Holy Spirit	Spirit Baptism	Youths	60-fold	Acts and Letters
TABERNACLES	7	1	Promised Land	Rent Veil; Resurrection Ascension	God's Fullness; Christ Appears	Adults ("Fathers")	100-fold	Hebrews and Revelation

Figure 14 in *Appendix 9*, "The Feasts–Festivals–of the Lord," gives a summary of the Historical, Christological, and Experiential fulfillments of the Feasts of Passover and Pentecost. Further details about Passover and Pentecost can be found in *Appendix 4* and *Appendix 5*.

While all three Feasts are alluded to in the Book of Revelation, it is in Revelation that we have the ultimate climax and glorious, final fulfillment of the Feast of Tabernacles. It is to this Feast, the Feast at the end of the year, we will devote the remainder of this chapter.

It is clear from *Figure 14* that God has taken the Old Testament rituals of Passover and Pentecost, and made them for us personal, practical experiences of His grace and power. However, we are unable to discover a complete fulfillment of the Feast of Tabernacles to the Church–not in the New Testament, nor in Church History, nor in the Church of this generation. The Church has been in existence for nearly 2,000 years, but, only in the past 50 years or so, has seen the commencement of the first part of this Feast.

Why?

To answer this question, we turn to what happened in Israel, which is a prophetic picture for us. Old Testament Israel had experienced their Passover (Exodus chapters 11 and 12), and their Pentecost (Exodus chapters 19 and 20). They should have arrived in the promised land and experienced their Feast of Tabernacles just six months after leaving Egypt. Instead, this journey took them 40 years!

Why?

Disobedience, fear, and lack of faith caused them to wander in the wilderness for 40 years. There was a 40-year delay. God did not break His promise. But because of the people's unbelief, He postponed the fulfillment of the promise. Thus there was a 40-year breach of promise and breach of time.

The New Testament Church experienced the spiritual fulfillment of Passover and Pentecost. But they disobeyed their Lord's command to take the Gospel to all nations. Time and again we read in the Book of Acts the apostles, for the most part, stayed in Jerusalem.[3] This situation has changed little. 2,000 years later, 90 percent of the Church's resources–personnel, finances and development–support 10 percent of the (mainly Western) Church. [Pamela and I count it a privilege to be a small part of the 10 percent going to the remaining 90 percent, millions of whom have never once heard the Name of Jesus.]

And so, because of disobedience, fear, lack of faith (and lack of teaching), the Church has not gone into the "promised land" of the Festival of Tabernacles. The Church's delay has been not 40 years, but 40 Jubilees–that is, 40 (the number of trial and testing) multiplied by 50 (the number of Jubilee, Hebrew, *Yobel*, "time of shouting") which equals 2,000 years.

But now we can be encouraged! The Feast of Tabernacles has commenced!

In Leviticus 23:23-44 we read there were three parts to this great Festival:

	Name	Day of month	Bride	Fulfillment
A.	**Trumpets:**	1st	*Preparation*	Awakening through 5 ministries
B.	**Day Of Atonement:**	10th	*Perfection*	Sin removed; intimate communion
C.	**Tabernacles:**	15th to 21st	*Performance* then *Protection* in Great Tribulation	Worldwide harvest of souls (Evangelism), Marriage supper of the Lamb

We are living in the time of the Feast of Trumpets. So we will study that Festival first.

A. THE FESTIVAL OF TRUMPETS

During the Feast of Trumpets, trumpets were blown for the first ten days of the last month of the religious year.

The Bible has much to say about the blowing of trumpets. Trumpets are wonderful instruments in the hands of the Lord's servants. Great men of God–for example, Joshua and Gideon–blew trumpets as part of their strategy for victory. Trumpets blew at the coronation of kings. Trumpets were blown by 120 priests at the dedication of Solomon's Temple, and the glory of God filled the house. The Book of Revelation opens with a trumpet sound for the messengers to the seven churches,[4] and contains many more "trumpet sounds."

---

[3] For example, see Acts 8:1.
[4] Rev 1:10.

In the Old Testament, the most detailed teaching concerning the blowing of trumpets is found in Numbers chapter 10.

God commanded Moses to make two silver trumpets (verse 2). Silver speaks of redemption (Lev 5:15; 1 Pet 1:18-20). These two trumpets represent Christ and His Bride. The very last invitation recorded in the Bible reads, "The Spirit and the bride say, 'Come!' " (Rev 22:17). The Lord and His Bride working together.

God further commanded that Aaron's four sons were to blow the trumpets (verse 8). Aaron and his sons total five. These five prefigure the five ascension gift ministries listed in Ephesians 4:11. The names of Aaron's four sons are found in Exodus 6:23. The meaning of names in Scripture is always significant.

We can summarize the prophetic significance of Aaron and his four sons as follows:

Figure 17: **Showing How Aaron and His Four Sons Prefigure the Five New Testament Ministries**

	Name	**Meaning of name**	**New Testament ministry**
1.	Aaron	"Enlightened"	Apostle (foundational, Eph 2:20)
2.	Nadab	"Liberal" (giving freely, generously)	Evangelist
3.	Abihu	"He is my Father"	Prophet (foundational, Eph 2:20)
4.	Eleazar	"God is my Helper"	Pastor
5.	Ithamar	"Palm tree"	Teacher[5]

In Bible days God's leaders and ministers blew on actual trumpets to convey a distinct message to His people. These trumpets are called "signal trumpets" (Num 31:6).

---

[5] The palm tree:
1. The palm tree can withstand abuse. The heart of the palm tree is alive, so attacks on the bark of its trunk do not affect the tree.
2. The palm tree can endure storms. In heavy wind and rain the palm tree is supple enough to bend without breaking.
3. Because of its deep roots the palm tree can survive drought.
4. The older the palm tree becomes, the sweeter its fruit, especially from 50 years old and beyond.

These are just a few of the reasons the meaning of Ithamar's name resembles the ministry of a teacher of God's Word. "The righteous shall flourish like a palm tree." (Psa 92:12)

At other times the leaders were commanded to speak with the intensity and urgency of a trumpet blast:

> "Cry aloud, do not hold back
> Lift up your *voice* like a trumpet;
> *Tell* My people their transgression,
> And the house of Jacob their sins." (Isa 58:1)

In Numbers chapter 10 nine reasons for the blowing of trumpets are listed. Each prefigures a distinct message God wants to convey to His Church today, through the preaching and teaching of His ministers. The nine trumpet sounds, and their anti-typical fulfillment in the New Testament Church, are:

1. **verse 2–Calling the Congregation**

    This speaks of a message of Unity–the coming together of Christians from various national and doctrinal backgrounds. The prayer of Jesus for unity among His followers will be answered. The showing forth of God's glory through His people in the last days depends on it:

    > "I do not pray for these alone, but also for those who will believe in Me through their word ...
    > And the *glory* which You gave Me I have given them, that they may be one just as We are one:
    > I in them, and You in Me; that they may *be made perfect* in one, and that the world may know that You have sent Me, and have loved them as You have loved Me." (See John 17:20:23)

    When the two trumpets blew, it required two priests to blow together. God is leading His ministers to work together. In the coming days this will be especially true of apostles and prophets.

    The congregation was to gather together at the door of the tabernacle. This door speaks to us of our Lord Jesus, Who said: "I am the door. If anyone enters by Me, he will be saved" (John 10:9). The Person of our Lord Jesus Christ is the focal point of our unity.

2. **verse 2–Directing the Movement ("journeying"–*KJV*) of the Camps**

    As Israel traveled through the wilderness, they came to new places. This trumpet message is prophetic, speaking of our need to be awakened and encouraged to receive New Truths as we go on in the Lord.

    There are, of course, no "new truths" in the Bible. Nor is anything to be added to the complete Canon of Scripture.[6] But from time to time we hear or read truths

---

[6] Rev 22:18.

that are new *to us*. When this happens, we should neither hastily accept nor reject the teaching. Rather, like the Bereans, we should begin to search the Scriptures to see if these things are so.[7]

Hebrews, one of two New Testament books containing detailed teaching on the Feast of Tabernacles[8] describes this trumpet message:

> " ... we have much to say, and hard to explain, since you have become dull of hearing.
> For though by this time you ought to be teachers, you need someone to teach you again the first principles of the oracles of God; and you have come to need milk and not solid food ...
> But solid food belongs to these who are mature (*margin*)." (Heb 5:11-14)

3. verse 4–Gathering the Leaders

> "But if they blow only one [trumpet], then the leaders, the heads of the divisions of Israel, shall gather to you [at the door of the tabernacle of meeting–verse 3]."

The blowing of just one trumpet is very clearly the message proclaiming the need for *Unity Among Church Leaders*. In our ministry travels through more than 60 nations during the past 43 years, Pamela and I have been delighted to see this growing unity. May it continue and increase!

4. verses 5, 6–Sounding the Advance

> "When you sound the advance, the camps that lie on the east side shall then begin their journey.
> When you sound the advance the second time, then the camps that lie on the south side shall begin their journey; they shall sound the call for them to begin their journeys."

During their journey from Egypt to the promised land, the children of Israel moved their camp a total of 42 times. At any time of day the cloud that was leading them could move. The people were alerted to begin their journey by the sounding of the trumpets. At any time in the night, no matter how inconvenient it was for the people, the fiery pillar over the tabernacle could move. The trumpets blew, and the people packed up and moved on.[9]

God does not change (Mal 3:6). But He moves (Gen 1:2). And He wants us to follow Him, and move on spiritually as we mature in the Lord. Not unstable–

---

[7] Acts 17:11.
[8] The other is, of course, the Book of Revelation.
[9] Num 9:15-23.

always moving from place to place; church to church. But, rather, this second trumpet message is *Move on in God! Grow up! Go on to Maturity! Advance!*

5. **verse 9–Going to War Against the Enemy**

> "When you go to war in your land against the enemy who oppresses you, then you shall sound an alarm with the trumpets ..."

Bugles and trumpets are associated with armies and war. This trumpet message is twofold:

a. Evangelism and Missions

Anyone who has been actively involved in evangelism, at home or overseas, knows that redeeming souls from the hand of the enemy is a spiritual battle:

> "O my soul, my soul!
> I am pained in my very heart!
> My heart makes a noise in me;
> I cannot hold my peace,
> Because you have heard, O my soul,
> The sound of the trumpet,
> The alarm of war." (Jer 4:19)

But God's promise to Israel is for us too:

> "When you go to war ... you will be remembered before the Lord your God, and you will be saved from your enemies." (Num 10: 9)

The greatest harvest of souls in history is about to take place. The message to the Church today is to "put in the sickle, for the harvest is ripe." (Joel 3:13)

We are all watchmen. Let us blow the trumpet to warn the people, so that their blood will not be required at our hands. (See Eze 33:3-6)

b. Alarm Against False Teachings

In Matthew chapter 24 the disciples of Jesus asked Him the sign of His coming and the end of the world (verse 3). While Jesus gave them a number of signs, I think it is extremely significant that He repeats one sign four times in just 24 verses. That sign is deception![10] He taught that false Christs will arise. False prophets. False signs and wonders. False doctrines.

For a long time I could never fully understand what Jesus meant when he said, "If it were possible, they shall deceive the very elect" (Matt 24:24–*KJV*). But

---

[10] Matt 24: 4,5,11,24.

now I shudder when I recall how, a few short years ago, I observed a young pastor who, as a result of pride, was totally deceived. He also led his congregation into deception. People I knew well were deceived by the devil. It was like a nightmare. But it happened. I saw it. And I grieved because of it. (See *Appendix 6,* "10 Questions to Consider When Examining a Teaching, a Ministry, or a 'New Spiritual Move.'")

As the Church age draws to a close, we must be vigilant. This trumpet alarm, warning of false teachings and false ministries, must be sounded loud and clear for all to hear! Nehemiah records that every man involved in restoring the walls of the city "had his sword girded at his side as he built. And the one who sounded the trumpet was beside me." The command was: "Wherever you hear the sound of the trumpet, rally to us there. Our God will fight for us." (Neh 4:17-20)

That's what we need–the sword of God's Word, together with the trumpet's alarm to unite us when we are attacked.

Each trumpet blast listed in Numbers chapter 10 had a distinctive sound. Every Israelite had to be able to recognize the different trumpet messages, so he could act accordingly. Incorrect hearing would result in an incorrect response. They needed "ears to hear."

> "If the trumpet makes an uncertain (Greek, *adelos*, 'not manifest, not clearly evident or understandable') sound, who will prepare for battle?" (1 Cor 14:8)

For the people to respond correctly, those who blew the trumpets–the messengers–had to blow a clear, distinct sound. The messenger had to get the message right! For where there is misunderstanding, confusion and disobedience soon follow.

I commenced high school just three years after the end of World War II. Because New Zealand had experienced dangerous situations during the war, our government decided that all high school boys would be involved in regular military training.

I well remember, in the middle of winter, being at a military camp in New Zealand's frozen south. It was impossible to get warm in those army huts. And early each morning, while it was still dark, the trumpet would blow reveille. Anyone who was not outside on parade in three minutes was punished by having to run around the parade ground, which was white with frost, in bare feet.

The early morning trumpet gave a certain, understandable sound, and evoked an immediate, obedient response!

6. **verse 10–In the Day of Your Gladness**

    This speaks to us of the message of Worship, Praise, and Rejoicing. We have already seen the importance of praise and worship in Chapter two, "Bridal Language in the Old Testament."

7. **verse 10–In Your Solemn Days** *(KJV)*

    This is the message of *Prayer, Fasting, and the Dealings Of God.* God's commandment is: "These are the feasts of the Lord, holy convocations which you shall proclaim at their appointed times." (Lev 23:4)

    Ministers must proclaim the truth of these solemn Feast days, and, with a clear trumpet sound, teach them to the Church. Otherwise, how will God's people know how to respond when they face contradictions and the dealings of God? As Asaph sang to the Chief Musician: "Blow the trumpet ... on our solemn feast day" (Psa 81:3).

8. **verse 10–At the Beginning of Your Months**

    This speaks to us of *Knowing Times and Seasons.*

    Churches, families, and individual Christians go through different times and seasons. God's people must understand that there will be both good times and bad times. We must take care how we respond in these varying seasons.

    In Ecclesiastes 3:1 we read:

    > "To everything there is a season,
    > A time for every purpose under heaven."

    This chapter goes on to enumerate 28 different seasons of human experience.

    The Lord commends the sons of Issachar, not just because they were great warriors, but they also "had understanding of the times, to know what Israel ought to do" (1 Chr 12:32).

    There must be a clear trumpet message taught concerning the seasons of life so that Christians will be able to recognize these seasons.

9. **verse 10–Over Their Offerings (Sacrifices–*KJV*)**

    We don't like the word "sacrifice." Unfortunately, this attitude can give rise to the false teaching that says Jesus offered the full sacrifice on the cross, so sacrifice has no part in the life of a Christian.

Jesus did indeed offer the full sacrifice for our sins. Certainly nothing can ever be added to that. But, we all, as New Testament priests, are encouraged to offer these sacrifices to the Lord:

a. Our bodies–Rom 12:1,2

"I urge you therefore, brethren, by the mercies of God, to present your bodies a living and holy sacrifice, acceptable to God, which is your spiritual service of worship.
And do not be conformed to this world, but be transformed by the renewing of your mind, that you may prove what the will of God is, that which is good and acceptable and perfect." (*NAS*)

b. Our praise–Heb 13:15

"Therefore by Him let us continually offer the sacrifice of praise to God, that is, the fruit of our lips, giving thanks to His name."

c. Our finances–Phil 4:18

"Indeed I have all and abound. I am full, having received from Epaphroditus the things sent from you, a sweet-smelling aroma, an acceptable sacrifice, well pleasing to God."

"Keep Your Appointed Feasts"

Many Christians seem to be concerned only with the Last Trumpet–the Trumpet that heralds the Second Coming of Christ. But what about these other trumpet messages? What about the Feast of Trumpets? If we are Church leaders, are we trumpet voices, proclaiming these truths? Are our people hearing them? Can they hear the clear distinctions between the trumpet sounds? Have they been taught how to respond to the various trumpet blasts?

Too often our focus is only on the Last Trumpet. But the Book of Revelation teaches us there are six other trumpets before the seventh, the Last Trumpet, sounds.

Jeremiah 6:17 is a sad verse:

"I set watchmen over you, saying,
'Listen to the sound of the trumpet!'
But they said, 'We will not listen.'"

But I pray we *will* listen. For the Lord commands:

"Keep your appointed feasts,
Perform your vows." (Nah 1:15)

THE FEAST OF TRUMPETS–HISTORICAL

It is my personal conviction that we are living in the season of the Feast of Trumpets. I believe this Feast commenced in 1948.

God has always had trumpeters–those who faithfully proclaimed His message. Luther, Knox, Wesley, Spurgeon, Booth, Wigglesworth, just to mention a few, were among the faithful messengers. But in 1948 something very special happened.[11]

In February of that year God visited a small Bible School that was meeting in an abandoned airport building in North Battleford, Saskatchewan, Canada. The Spirit of the Lord moved, and truth from the Word–worship, the laying on of hands, unity, and much more–was restored. This Visitation of God became known as the "Latter Rain Movement," and its message quickly spread throughout many countries of the world, including New Zealand.[12]

To understand the full significance of a special time or season in the last days, there are seven areas to which we look for signs. This chart lists these signs, and their particular prophetic fulfillment in the year 1948.

Figure 18: **Signs of the Last Days, and Their Prophetic Fulfillment in 1948**

	SIGNS IN	1948
1.	Israel	Re-established as a nation
2.	Nations of the World	Independence of many nations (e.g. India) Rise of United Nations Organization for future world government established
3.	Nature	Famines, pestilences, earthquakes all increase.
4.	Commerce, Finance	Bretton Woods conference decisions implemented World trade pegged to U.S. Dollar and Pound Sterling
5.	Prophetic Types	Noah–violence and corruption increase
6.	False Church	Ascendancy of World Council of Churches
7.	True Church	Feast of Trumpets commences

---

[11] Some of the "trumpet voices" raised up during that 1948 season are still faithfully preaching– we honour the ministries of Billy Graham and Oral Roberts–just to mention two.

[12] For a more complete history of the Latter Rain Movement, see *Latter Rain–The Latter Rain Movement of 1948 and the Mid-Twentieth Century Evangelical Awakening* by Richard M. Riss; Honeycomb Visual Productions Ltd, Mississauga, Ontario, Canada, 1987.

See also *The Eternal Church* by Dr Bill Hamon; Christian International Publishers, Phoenix, No date– chapter 10, "The Latter Rain Movement."

THE FESTIVALS OF ISRAEL

We can examine any given year or season for these seven signs. Here is a chart for another special year, 1967.

Figure 19: Signs of the Last Days, and Their Prophetic Fulfillment in 1967

	SIGNS IN	1967
1.	Israel	6-day war. Jerusalem retaken
2.	Nations of the World	Treaty of Rome Power of European Economic Community
3.	Nature	New and strange plagues (AIDS) Further increase in famines, earthquakes, floods and other disasters
4.	Commerce, Finance	December, Pound Sterling severely devalued Ascension of International Monetary Foundation (IMF) with power of control
5.	Prophetic Types	Lot–rise of homosexuality and occult
6.	False Church	Liberation theology (political) "Hippies" lay foundation for "New Age Movement" based on Hinduism Social Gospel "Theologian" proclaims "God is dead"
7.	True Church	Charismatic renewal for all denominations and many new churches commenced

B. THE FEAST DAY OF ATONEMENT

The Day of Atonement was celebrated on the tenth day of the seventh month–at the close of the religious year. This was the high and holy day when the High Priest went beyond the second veil that separated the Holy Place from the Holy of Holies. In the Holy of Holies the High Priest sprinkled blood on the mercy seat of the Ark of the Covenant. Hebrews, the New Testament companion book to Revelation, states:

> "Into the second part the high priest went alone once a year, not without blood, which he offered for himself and for the people's sins ..." (Heb 9:7)

The details concerning the Day of Atonement are found in Leviticus chapter 16, and in Leviticus 23:26-32.

We can see the **Historical** fulfillment of the Day of Atonement in Old Testament Israel.

We can see the **Christological** fulfillment–how the Lord Jesus fulfilled the Day of Atonement–in the Gospel record. When He died, the veil in the temple, which separated the Holy Place from the Holiest of all, was torn from top to bottom. Later Christ ascended to God's throne to present His Perfect Atoning Blood before His Father (Matt 27:51; Heb 9:11-14).

However, we cannot find, in the New Testament, nor in Church history, nor in the Church today, any record of God's people having experienced the fulfillment of the Day of Atonement.

There are eight principal prophetic types that will be fulfilled when the Lord manifests Himself to the Church on the New Testament fulfillment of the Day of Atonement. These are:

1. A Day–a Literal 24-Hour Day

Passover was fulfilled on a literal 24-hour day. The hours of the day are mentioned in the Bible.

Pentecost was fulfilled on a literal 24-hour day. The hours of the day are mentioned in the Bible.

The Day of Atonement will also be fulfilled on a literal 24-hour day. It was a set 24-hour day in Bible times (Lev 23:27), and so it will be in these last times.

2. A Day of Unity and Expectation in Local Churches

> "Not forsaking the assembling of ourselves together, as is the manner of some, but exhorting one another, and so much the more as you see the Day approaching." (Heb 10:25)

Here the Bible categorically states there is a Day coming when we must be assembled together in our local churches. Do we need to be in church to participate in Christ's second coming? No. Do we need to be in church to experience, personally and collectively, the fulfillment of the Day of Atonement? Indeed, we do.

3. A Day of Perfection

> "On that day the priest shall make atonement for you, to cleanse you, that you may be clean from *all your sins* before the Lord." (Lev 16:30)

On the Day of Atonement Christ's Bride will become the Church described in Ephesians 5:27–the "glorious church, not having spot or wrinkle or any such thing, but that she should be holy and without blemish." This Bride will have "[gone] on to perfection–full maturity" (Heb 6:1). As it says in Proverbs:

> "The path of the just is like the shining sun,
> That shines ever brighter unto the *perfect day.*" (Pro 4:18)

4. A Day of His Appearing

> "I will appear in the cloud above the mercy seat." (Lev 16:2)

The New Testament makes a clear distinction between the "appearing" of the Lord Jesus Christ, and His second coming. At His second coming "every eye shall see Him" (Rev 1:7). But not at His appearing. At His appearing, only those who are looking for Him will see Him:

> "To those who eagerly wait ('look'–*KJV*) for Him He will appear a second time, apart from sin, for salvation." (Heb 9:28)

Is the whole world eagerly waiting for His appearing? No. Therefore the whole world won't see Him at His appearing. But, eagerly waiting or not, every eye will indeed see the Lord at His coming in power and great glory.

And why does Hebrews 9:28 use the word "salvation"? Because the truth is this:

- We have been saved;
- We are being saved;
- We will be saved.

Peter also speaks of a salvation that will be revealed in the last days. He says there will be believers:

> " who are protected by the power of God through faith for a salvation ready to be revealed in the last time." (1 Pet 1:5–*NAS*)

Paul writes to the church at Rome:

> "Why all this stress on behaviour? Because, as I think you have realised, the present time is of the highest importance–it is time to wake up to reality. Every day brings God's salvation nearer." (Rom 13:11–*JBP*)

In the *New King James Version* this last phrase is rendered "for now our salvation is nearer than when we first believed." Didn't we receive salvation when we first believed?

Hebrews 10:23 says: "Now we can look forward to the salvation God has promised us." (*LB*) What salvation has God promised us?

Full and complete salvation! The Feast of Tabernacles is the "third installment" of salvation, to prepare and perfect a Bride for the appearing of Christ.

5. A Day of Incense

> "Then he shall take a censer full of burning coals of fire from the altar before the Lord, with his hands full of sweet incense beaten fine, and bring it inside the veil.
> And he shall put the incense on the fire before the Lord, that the cloud of incense may cover the mercy seat that is on the Testimony [the Ark of the Covenant], lest he die." (Lev 16:12,13)

Many times in Scripture, incense speaks of prayer and praise. For example:

> "Let my prayer be set before You as incense,
> The lifting up of my hands as the evening sacrifice." (Psa 141:2)

Today, in the Church worldwide, there is a renewed emphasis on "incense"–ministering to the Lord in prayer, worship, and praise.[13] This will have its climactic fulfillment in the Book of Revelation:

> "Then another angel, having a golden censer, came and stood at the altar. He was given much incense, that he should offer it with the prayers of all the saints upon the golden altar which was before the throne.
> And the smoke of the incense, with the prayers of the saints, ascended before God from the angel's hand.
> Then the angel took the censer, filled it with fire from the altar, and threw it to the earth." (Rev 8:3-5)

6. A Day of Entrance Inside the Veil

Leviticus 16, verses 2 and 12, state the High Priest went inside the veil. This was the most intimate fellowship with God possible. For on the Day of Atonement:

- The High Priest drew aside the veil;
- There was the shedding of blood;
- He had face-to-face communion.

Does this not sound like the language of a wedding night? Yes. It does. The fulfillment of the Day of Atonement will be the wedding night of Christ and His Bride. The meaning of Hebrews 6:18-20 now becomes evident:

> "That by two immutable things, in which it is impossible for God to lie, we might have strong consolation, who have fled for refuge to lay hold of the hope set before us.

---

[13] For further details about "Ministry to the Lord" see my book *Every Christian's Ministry*, Gordon Donaldson Missionary Foundation, Calgary, Alberta, Canada, 1977.

> This hope we have as an anchor of the soul, both sure and steadfast, and which enters the Presence behind the veil,
> where the forerunner has entered for us, even Jesus, having become High Priest forever according to the order of Melchizedek."

We have a hope beyond the veil! This hope anchors our souls during the storms of life. Titus tells us this hope is the appearing of Christ, with redemption from all iniquity:

> "Looking for the blessed hope and glorious appearing of our great God and Savior Jesus Christ,
> who gave Himself for us, that He might redeem us from every lawless deed ('all iniquity'–*KJV*) and purify for Himself His own special people, zealous for good works." (Titus 2:13,14)

Blessed hope indeed!

7. A Day of the Slain Body and Shed Blood

> "He shall take some of the blood of the bull and sprinkle it with his finger on the mercy seat on the east side; and before the mercy seat he shall sprinkle some of the blood with his finger seven times.
> Then he shall kill the goat of the sin offering, which is for the people, bring its blood inside the veil, do with that blood as he did with the blood of the bull, and sprinkle it on the mercy seat and before the mercy seat."
> (Lev 16:14,15)

Israel soon became very familiar with this truth–that to cover their sins, an innocent victim must be killed, and its blood used in atonement (Hebrew, *kippurim*, "covering"). The slain body; the shed blood. When the priests looked at the bread and wine at the Table of Showbread in the Holy Place of the Tabernacle, they had a continual prophetic reminder of the body and blood.

Twelve loaves of bread were on the table. At the table was also a flagon of wine, a drink offering (Num 28:7; Exo 25:29). The priests fellowshipped at this table "every Sabbath" (Lev 24:8). The bread was set in order, and the drink offering poured out on the desert floor. This was prophetic of Christ, "the Bread of life," Who would pour out His blood to wash our sins away.

Today, we look back to the Cross, and remember our Saviour's sacrifice for us in the breaking of bread. The importance of the communion table in the life of a Christian cannot be overemphasized. I am continually amazed as I read in First Corinthians chapter 10 that Paul, in order to emphasize the power of the Lord's presence at His table (and to warn us against idolatry) talks about the power of demons behind idols, and God's power in the bread and the cup at the communion table, in the same teaching.

And Jesus said something astounding in Matthew 26:29:

> "I will not drink of this fruit of the vine from now on until that day when I drink it new with you in My Father's kingdom."

Communion services in Heaven? No. But Christ appearing one day to His Bride worldwide in the communion service? Yes! And that's just the beginning. Remember, in Revelation chapter 12 the Bride is nourished for 3½ years in a place of protection. A 3½-year communion service! What a marriage supper that will be! [We will study this further in **Volume Two**].

Do I hear someone say, "That's absurd. Jesus never used the term 'Day of Atonement.'" You're right. But He never used the term Feast of Pentecost, either. All He commanded his disciples was they were to "wait for the Promise of the Father" (Acts 1:4). He did not tell them He was going to fulfill the Feast of Pentecost. But fulfill it He did.

Imagine what the response would be if you were to tell someone during that period of waiting: "Do you know what is going to happen? While the Jews are in the temple keeping the Feast of Pentecost, God is going to give the followers of Jesus of Nazareth the spiritual reality of which the Feast is but a prophecy. A sound like a mighty rushing wind will fill the house where they will gather. Tongues of fire will be seen on each person. They will be filled with the Holy Spirit. They will praise God in languages they have never learned. And after Peter preaches, 3,000 souls will be baptized in water!"

Absurd? But that's exactly what happened. And just as the Lord fulfilled the Day of Pentecost in His disciples as recorded in Acts chapter two, so He will fulfill every detail of the Day of Atonement.

8. A Day of the Scapegoat

> "He [Aaron] shall take the two goats and present them before the Lord at the door of the tabernacle of meeting." (Lev 16:7)

Each animal about to be sacrificed was examined for blemishes. Both these goats had to be without "spot or blemish." One goat died as a sin offering (verse 9). This is prophetic of the Lord Jesus, the perfect sacrifice, dying for our sins. The other goat was presented alive before the Lord (verse 10). The Church lives because He died. Indeed, Christ and His Church are united in the ministry of atonement. He died to make atonement; His Church lives to witness of His atonement.

Here, on the Day of Atonement, is a beautiful prophetic picture of Christ and His glorious Church, His Bride.

The scapegoat (Hebrew–"the goat for escape, dismissal, departure") is "[sent] away into the wilderness by the hand of a suitable man" (verse 21). The ultimate prophetic fulfillment of this is seen in Revelation chapter 12, where the Bride of Christ escapes into the wilderness for protection and nourishment during the Great Tribulation.

"BLOW THE TRUMPET IN ZION"

The commandment is given in Joel, chapter 2:

> "Blow the trumpet in Zion,
> And sound an alarm in My holy mountain!
> Let all the inhabitants of the land tremble;
> For the day of the Lord is coming,
> For it is at hand." (Joel 2:1)

"Blow the trumpet in Zion." Zion means "fortress." It was situated in the southwest of Jerusalem. Zion was higher than the rest of the city. King David dwelt in this fort, and built up Zion and its walls.[14]

It was in Zion, this "city within a city," that David built a tabernacle to receive the Ark of the Covenant. God promises to restore the Tabernacle of David.[15]

"A CITY WITHIN A CITY"

I must issue a word of caution here. Some are disturbed by the phrases, "a city within a city," or "a church within the Church." Many say that there is great danger in describing God's people as being in groups, companies, and different stages of Christian maturity. If this were true, then the Bible is a very dangerous book. For the Bible speaks of the Bride and the remnant of her seed;[16] the temple and the outer court Christians;[17] the wise and the foolish virgins;[18] children, young people, and adults;[19] believers who receive the seed of the Word into their hearts and bear 30, 60, or 100-fold fruit.[20] Jesus and Paul taught that Christians will experience various levels of glory and authority in the resurrection.[21]

The fact is, without being judgmental, we all realize that believers love and serve the Lord with varying measures of fervency. As C.H.Spurgeon, the man still known as the "Prince of Preachers" explains:

> "Christ is the same, but believers do not all see him in the same clear light, nor do they all approach to the same nearness of fellowship. Some only know his offices; others only admire his character; far fewer commune with his person; but there be some who have advanced still further, who have come to feel the unity of all the Church with the person of Christ Jesus their Lord…

---

[14] 2 Sam 5:6 -10.
[15] For further details about Zion, see *The Power of His Presence* chapter 9, "The Church Within the Church."
[16] Rev 12:1,17.
[17] Rev 11:1,2.
[18] Matt 25:1-13.
[19] 1 Jn 2:12-14.
[20] Matt 13:23.
[21] Luke 19:12-27; 1 Cor 15:40-57.

> "All Christians know Christ, but they do not all know him to the same degree and in the same way...
>
> "There was one of the disciples at least who knew Jesus Christ even better than [just as Rabbi]. There was one chosen out of the twelve, as the twelve had been chosen out of the rest, who knew Christ as a *dear companion*, and as a sweet friend ... I fear that those who advance as far as John did are not very many ... May the Lord teach each of us more and more how to walk with Jesus and to know his love!"[22]

The danger is that no-one should become proud, judgmental, or puffed up because of his or her knowledge, ministry, or experience. Nothing is worse than believers thinking they belong to some special category of Christians. God alone knows the hearts of all His children. Our responsibility is to humbly respond to the Word of God, and mature in our relationship with Him.

ANNOUNCING THE DAY

"For the day of the Lord is coming." This trumpet announces that the Day of Atonement is coming. As a result of the Day of Atonement, a mighty army will be raised up:

> "A people come, great and strong,
> The like of whom has never been;
> Nor will there ever be any such after them ...
>
> The Lord gives voice before His army." (Joel 2:2,11)

This is the same army spoken of in the Song of Solomon:

> "Who is she who looks forth as the morning,
> Fair as the moon,
> Clear as the sun,
> Awesome as an army with banners?" (Song 6:10)

The Bride of Christ will minister as God's mighty army, smashing the strongholds of the devil, and winning multitudes to Christ.

Again in verse 15 of Joel chapter two the commandment is given: "Blow the trumpet in Zion." This trumpet sound calls for a "sacred assembly"–fasting, unity, sanctification, weeping. Again, Bridal language is used here:

---

[22] *Sermons on the Book of Revelation*, by C.H. Spurgeon; Marshall, Morgan & Scott, London, 1962–pages 7-9 (Emphasis his).

Charles Haddon Spurgeon (1834-1892) was born in Essex, England. He was converted to Christ at 15 years of age, preached his first sermon at 16, and became a pastor at 17. By his early 20s he was preaching to 10,000 people at each of his services. He pastored the famous Metropolitan Tabernacle for 30 years. In his day he was called "the prince of preachers." Many still call him this today. During his lifetime, Spurgeon preached over 3,000 sermons, hundreds of which are still being published in selected volumes of his preaching.

> "Let the bridegroom go out from his chamber,
> And the bride from her dressing room." (Joel 2:16)

C: THE FEAST OF TABERNACLES

The term "Feast of Tabernacles" is sometimes used in Scripture to include all three parts of this Feast–Trumpets, Day of Atonement, and Tabernacles.

The prophetic fulfillment of all the three stages of the Feast of Tabernacles will span three major periods of time:

a. From the commencement of the Festival of Trumpets until the fulfillment of the Day of Atonement to the Bride of Christ—1948-20??

b. The period from the appearing of Christ on the Feast Day of Atonement until the birth of the man child. This will probably be one year. The main events to occur during this time are:
- The Bride celebrates the last "Year of Jubilee";
- The Bride reaps a great harvest of souls;
- The gestation of the man child in the womb of the Bride.

c. The period from when the Bride is taken out into the wilderness for protection, to the second coming of Christ in power and great glory. This period of time is the 3½-year Great Tribulation.

This third part of the Feast of Tabernacles, from which the whole Feast takes its name, was celebrated from the 15th to the 21st days of the seventh month. We can summarize the main points concerning the Feast of Tabernacles as follows:

1. The Festival of Joy and Worship

> "You shall rejoice before the Lord your God for seven days." (Lev 23:40)

> "And you shall rejoice in your feast." (Deut 16:14)

Rejoicing before the Lord from the beginning to the end of this festival! Little wonder we are encouraged to:

> "Sing to God, sing praises to His name;
> Extol Him who rides on the clouds (*margin*, 'heavens'),
> By His Name YAH,
> And rejoice before Him." (Psa 68:4)

2. The Festival of Ingathering

> "You shall keep ...
> the Feast of Ingathering at the end of the year, when you have gathered in the fruit of your labors from the field." (Exo 23:15,16)
> "Also on the fifteenth day of the seventh month, when you have gathered in the fruit of the land, you shall keep the feast of the Lord seven days." (Lev 23:39)

After she has experienced the Day of Atonement, the impact of the Gospel ministry of the Bride of Christ will be extremely powerful. The result will be the greatest ingathering of souls in the history of the world.

3. The Festival of Rest

There were two sabbaths during the Feast of Tabernacles:

> "On the fifteenth day of the seventh month ... you shall keep the feast of the Lord for seven days; on the first day there shall be a sabbath-rest, and on the eighth day a sabbath-rest." (Lev 23:29)

We remember also that no work was done on the Feast Day of Atonement. This Day was the most high and holy Day of rest for the people of Israel. These "no-work days" remind us that it is not by our own works that we can be a part of this great Festival, but by God's grace alone.

These sabbaths also speak of entering into Christ's rest and peace after the great harvest is over.

4. The Festival of Temporary Dwelling Places

> "And you shall take for yourselves on the first day the fruit (*margin*, 'foliage') of beautiful trees, branches of palm trees, the boughs of leafy trees, and willows of the brook ...
> You shall dwell in booths (*margin*, 'tabernacles; shelters made of boughs') for seven days." (Lev 23:40,42)

In the words of the prophet Hosea:

> "I will again make you dwell in tents,
> As in the days of the appointed feast." (Hos 12:9)

As we have seen, this will have its ultimate prophetic fulfillment when the Bride is taken out to a temporary dwelling place in the wilderness.

JESUS AT THE FEAST OF TABERNACLES

> "On the last day, that great day of the feast, Jesus stood and cried out, saying,
> 'If anyone thirsts, let him come to Me and drink.
> He who believes in Me, as the Scripture has said, out of his heart
> will flow rivers of living water.'
> But this He spoke concerning the Spirit, whom those believing in Him would receive; for the Holy Spirit was not yet given, because Jesus was not yet glorified." (John 7:37-39)

Jesus spoke these words on the last, the great day of the Feast of Tabernacles (see verse 2). [Please note, for our further study in **HERE COMES THE BRIDE! Volume Two**, that verse 10 says, "He also went up to the feast, not openly, but as it were in secret." Then later in the feast, according to verse 14, He went up openly to the temple, where everyone could see Him.]

Tradition says that, in the time of Jesus, during the Feast of Tabernacles some of the temple priests marched around the brazen altar seven times, in memory of Joshua's victory at Jericho. This was followed by the offering of sacrifices on the altar.

Other priests brought water in golden vessels, which was poured out in remembrance of Joel's prophesied outpouring of the Spirit as rain.[23] The words of Isaiah 12, "Therefore with joy you will draw water from the wells of salvation" were sung, accompanied by the blowing of trumpets.[24]

But despite all the ceremony and religious pageantry, the people were going away empty. For them, coming to Jerusalem to keep the Feast had been a ritual. It was only tradition, and dead form. They were thirsty for spiritual reality!

Jesus knew this. And that is why He stood and cried, "If any man thirst ..." He recognized they were thirsty. The only way their thirst could be quenched was to come to Him and drink the waters He offered–the waters of everlasting life.

As He did in Bible times, in these last days Jesus is about to manifest Himself in the Feast of Tabernacles. The trumpets are already sounding. The Day of Atonement is coming. Let us be done with dead form. Rather, let's respond to His invitation to come to Him, and be refreshed by drinking of the Holy Spirit. Again, the words of Hosea:

> "What will you do on the day of the appointed festival
> And on the day of the feast of the Lord?" (Hos 9:5)

This is God's challenge to us.

---

[23] Joel 2:23.
[24] Isa 12:1.

| PART TWO | THE KEYS |

Chapter 13

The Tabernacle of Moses

Key Number Eight: The Tabernacle of Moses as Seen in the Book of Revelation

The tabernacle of Moses is an extremely important subject, and another essential key to understanding God's Word.

The details of the creation of "man's dwelling place"–this earth–occupy just two consecutive chapters of the Book of Genesis. Mankind marvels at this vast, temporal creation. Many spend a lifetime studying its mysteries and wonders. Yet infinitely greater is the mystery and wonder of that which the Bible calls "God's dwelling place"–the tabernacle of Moses.

Forty-three consecutive chapters are given to the account of Moses' tabernacle–Exodus chapters 25–40, together with the 27 chapters of Leviticus. Numbers and Deuteronomy contribute many more.

Also, the New Testament contains a number of references to the tabernacle of Moses, especially in the books of Hebrews and Revelation.

If just two chapters pertaining to the earthly home of man generate such an enormous field of study and research, how much more should be generated by these many chapters concerning, what was then, the habitation of God! And once we do begin to study this vast subject, we soon discover that the tabernacle of Moses is a portion of God's visual aid education–a prophetic blueprint of His plan and purposes for His Church throughout the ages.[1]

The Tabernacle of Moses

The tent of Moses' tabernacle was surrounded by an outer fence, 150 feet long and 75 feet wide.[2] (See *Figure 20*). This outer fence was 7½ feet high. On the east side of this fence, facing the rising sun, was a gate 30 feet wide.[3]

---

[1] Those wanting to make a fuller study of this subject are referred to *The Tabernacle of Moses* by Kevin J. Conner; Bible Temple Inc., Portland, Oregon, 1974.
[2] Exo 27:9-15.
[3] Exo 38:18.

Figure 20: **The Tabernacle of Moses**

(Not drawn to scale)

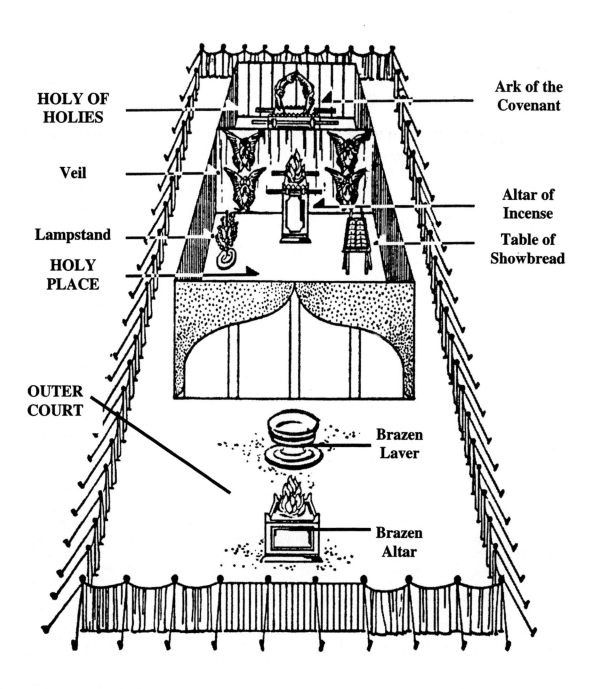

In the "outer court" area were two articles of tabernacle furniture. These were an altar made of brass where animal sacrifices were offered (known as the brazen altar), and a washstand, also made of brass, where the priests washed their hands and feet (the brazen laver).

The tabernacle proper was a small, portable tent, 45 feet long, 15 feet wide, and 15 feet high.

The tent was divided into two rooms. The "front room"–called "the holy place," or the "first sanctuary"–which was 30 feet long, and contained three pieces of tabernacle furniture–the lampstand or candlestick, the table of showbread, and the golden altar of incense. The "back room" was separated from the holy place by a curtain (or veil), and was a cube, 15 feet x 15 feet x 15 feet. This room contained the ark of the covenant (see *Figure 3*)[4] and is called "the most holy place," or "the holy of holies."

In Bible days all measurements were in cubits.[5] The area of the outer court fence was 1,500 cubits, symbolizing the 1,500 years of the law of Moses. The cubic measurement of the holy place in cubits–20 x 10 x10–equals 2,000, and symbolizes the 2,000 years of the fifth and sixth days of God's week. The cubic measurement of the most holy place is 1,000 cubic cubits, which speaks to us of the seventh day of God's week.[6]

The Bible records that when Moses finished the work of building the glory of the Lord appeared:

> "Then the cloud covered the tabernacle of meeting, and the glory of the Lord filled the tabernacle.
> And Moses was not able to enter the tabernacle of meeting, because the cloud rested above it, and the glory of the Lord filled the tabernacle."
> (Exo 40:34,35)

"An Important Lesson For Us Today"

In Hebrews 9:9 we read that the facts concerning Moses' tabernacle were "a parable–a visible symbol or type or picture of the present age,"[7] or as the same verse is rendered in The Living Bible:

> "This has an important lesson for us today."

The lessons we learn from the tabernacle of Moses as it is seen in the Book of Revelation are:

---

[4] *Figure 3*, The Ark of the Covenant, is found in Chapter 4 of this book, "The Book Rediscovered."
[5] The cubit was "an important and constant measure among the Hebrews ... and other ancient nations. It was from the joint of the elbow to the end of the middle finger, about 18 inches." Unger, *op. cit.*–page 720.
[6] See Chapter 10, "God's Week."
[7] *Amplified Bible*.

i. Each piece of tabernacle furniture is mentioned (or, in one case, alluded to) in the Book of Revelation;

ii. In the Book of Revelation a different group of God's people (for example, the 24 elders, the martyrs, the pregnant bride) is found at each piece of furniture;

iii It is necessary for us to press in and serve the Lord Jesus with all our hearts that we may wholly and fervently follow Him.

The word "tabernacle" occurs three times in the Book of Revelation. In the first reference the beast blasphemes not only God's Name, and God's people, but also His tabernacle (Rev 13:6). In Revelation 15:5 "the temple (*margin*, 'sanctuary') of the tabernacle of the testimony in heaven was opened."

In Revelation chapter 21, John sees the holy city "coming down out of heaven, prepared as a bride adorned for her husband." Then the victorious proclamation:

> "And I heard a loud voice from heaven saying, 'Behold the tabernacle of God is with men, and He will dwell with them, and they shall be His people. God Himself will be with them and be their God.'" (Rev 21:2,3)

The language of Revelation chapter one is clearly tabernacle of Moses language. John beholds our Lord Jesus Christ, our great High Priest, clothed with garments of glory and beauty.

The companion New Testament book to the Book of Revelation is Hebrews. The writer of Hebrews speaks of the tabernacle of Moses, and of Jesus our Great High Priest. He is called our "merciful and faithful High Priest."[8]

As well as describing Moses' tabernacle in considerable detail in chapters 8 and 9, the book of Hebrews also tells us there is a tabernacle not made by man:

> "Now this is the main point of the things we are saying: We have such a High Priest, who is seated at the right hand of the throne of the Majesty in the heavens,
> a Minister of the sanctuary and of the true tabernacle which the Lord erected, and not man." (Heb 8:1,2)

> "But Christ came as High Priest of the good things to come, with the greater and more perfect tabernacle not made with hands, that is, not of this creation." (Heb 9:11)

What does this mean?

---

[8] Heb 2:17. The word "priest" occurs 17 times in Hebrews, and the word "priesthood" 4 times.

PROTOTYPE, TYPE AND ANTITYPE

The tabernacle of Moses is, for us, a type. There are three main aspects of a type. Because Bible truths, as we have already seen, are in "tri-unity" when we use the principles of types and shadows in Scripture. These three aspects are:

1. The **prototype:** the original model from which something is made.

2. The **type:** the historic reality that becomes the prophecy.

3. The **antitype:** the complete spiritual fulfillment in the New Testament Church.

Consider a natural example of this: When your car was originally designed, the manufacturers made a wax or clay model. This was the prototype. Based on this prototype, they then made a few cars. They tested those cars. These first automobiles were, if you like, "prophetic"–they were "types" of the cars that would finally be marketed. Lastly, the vehicles were mass-produced, and sold to the public.

The prototype of the tabernacle of Moses–the original–is in heaven. This is "the greater and more perfect tabernacle not made with hands, that is, not of this creation" (Heb 9:11). This is one of "the patterns of things in the heavens" (Heb 9:23–*KJV*). This tabernacle in heaven is the one Moses saw when God commanded him, "See to it that you make them according to the pattern which was shown you on the mountain" (Exo 25:40; Heb 8:5).

The light of God shone on the original tabernacle, and cast a shadow on the earth. Moses saw it, and he built it:

> "...there are priests who offer the gifts according to the law;
> who serve the copy and shadow of the heavenly things, as Moses was
> divinely instructed when he was about to make the tabernacle ...
> For the law, having a shadow of the good things to come ..."
> (Heb 8:4,5; 10:1).

The tabernacle that Moses saw is the same tabernacle John saw in heaven. Remember, one of our keys to the Book of Revelation is to note if the vision is from an earthly or heavenly perspective. Moses built the type. Of course, the tabernacle in the wilderness was not a type to Moses and the people of Israel. But it is a type to us. That which is written about Moses and Israel admonishes us. From the type, we receive instruction, advice and warning.[9] Thus the type becomes, for us, the prophecy.

According to the Oxford Dictionary, an antitype is defined as "that which a type or symbol represents." The antitype of the tabernacle is Christ and His Church. The type thus becomes spiritual reality and experience for the New Testament Christian. This reality has a threefold interpretation:

---

[9] 1 Cor 10:11.

i. The antitype–the New Testament reality–is firstly the Lord Jesus Christ. John's Gospel says of Him: "The Word became flesh and dwelt (Greek, *skenoo* 'to tent, to tabernacle') among us" (John 1:14). This verse continues, "and we beheld His glory, the glory as of the only begotten of the Father." This is tabernacle language.

Jesus clearly said, "Moses ...wrote of me" (John 5:46).

ii. The antitype–the New Testament reality–is also the individual believer in Him. Peter referred to his human body as a "tabernacle" or "tent" (2 Pet 1:13,14). Paul spoke of his body as "the earthly house of this tabernacle" (2 Cor 5:1–*KJV*).

iii. The antitype–the New Testament reality–is also a prophetic picture of the Church. Moses and the people of Israel are called "the church in the wilderness" (Acts 7:38–*KJV*).

We can summarize this in the following chart, and the diagram on the next page:

Figure 21: **Prototype, Type, and Antitype of Moses' Tabernacle**

	Place	**Description**	**Nature**
1. PROTOTYPE	In heaven	Heavenly	Heaven's perfect original, the pattern
2. TYPE	In Israel	Natural	Typical, prophetic
3. ANTITYPE	In Christ and His Church	Spiritual	New Testament reality and experience; corresponds to, and points to, prototype

TABERNACLE FURNITURE IN THE BOOK OF REVELATION

1. The Brazen Altar–Revelation 6:9

> "When He opened the fifth seal, I saw under **the altar** the souls of those who had been slain for the word of God and for the testimony which they held."

As can be seen in the diagram of the tabernacle of Moses, the brazen altar was the first piece of tabernacle furniture encountered on entering the gate into the outer court. In the Bible, brass (or "bronze") always speaks of judgment against sin and self.[10]

---

[10] Some examples of brass:
*Israel had to look to the serpent made of brass to be healed (Num 21:8,9);
* God promised the heavens would be as brass if they disobeyed His commands (Deut 28:23);
* Blind Samson was imprisoned and bound with fetters of brass (Judg 16:21);
* Zedekiah was also bound with brass (2 Ki 25:7).

Figure 22: **Heavenly, Natural, and Spiritual Aspects of the Tabernacle**

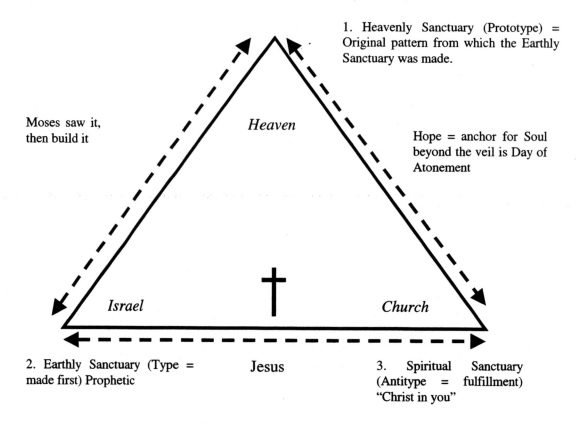

The curtains of the fence were attached to 60 brass pillars. The altar and the washstand were brass. As we enter the tabernacle, first we "touch" brass–we experience God's judgment against sin. As we progress we "touch" silver, which speaks of redemption.[11] If we continue to go on in the Lord, we finally come to gold, which speaks of the glory of God.

Sin offerings were sacrificed on this altar of brass. The blood of innocent victims was shed to cover the sins of the guilty.

The brazen altar was five cubits square. It was hollow, with a grill, or grate, inside it to hold the sacrifices. A total of five different kinds of offerings were sacrificed upon this altar–the sin, the trespass, the grain, the burnt, and the peace offerings.[12]

Five priests ministered at this altar–Aaron and his four sons.[13] There were five kinds of vessels employed in the ministry at this altar–the ash pan, the shovel, the

---

[11] The sockets upon which boards of the fence stood were made of silver, as were the hooks and bands of the pillars (Exo 26:12,25; 27:10,17). At census time every Israelite had to pay half a shekel of silver in atonement money. God commanded Moses to "take the atonement money of the Israelites and use it [exclusively] for the service of the tent of meeting" (Exo 30:16–*Amp*).
[12] Leviticus chapters 1 through 5.
[13] Num 3:1-3.

basin, the flesh hooks or forks, and the fire pans.[14] Notice that John saw a vision of the brazen altar when the Lamb opened the 5th seal of the scroll.

We have already seen the significance of the number 5.[15] Five represents the cross, salvation, atonement–and their outworking. The number 5 always reminds us that Jesus bore five bleeding wounds in His body for our redemption.

At the tabernacle of Moses the priest poured the blood of the sacrifice at the base of the brazen altar. This blood would make atonement for the soul of the guilty by covering his sin.

When John sees the brazen altar in heaven, he also sees there a company of people who have been slain for their testimony. They have died for their faith, and their blood is crying out to be avenged.[16] These saints at the brazen altar are the Christians who die a martyr's death before the 3½ years of the time period called the Great Tribulation.

2. The Sea of Glass (the Brazen Laver)–Revelation 4:6 and 15:1

"Before the throne there was **a sea of glass**, like crystal."

"And I saw something like **a sea of glass** mingled with fire."

The second piece of furniture in the tabernacle of Moses was the washstand made of brass. During the course of their ministry, the hands and feet of the priests became very dirty. They were soiled with blood, flesh, feathers, hair, soot, and sand from the desert floor. It was therefore necessary for the priests to wash their hands and feet before entering the tent of meeting.

When Solomon's temple was built, everything was larger than in the tabernacle of Moses. For example, the holy of holies was 20 x 20 x 20 cubits.[17] In the temple of Solomon, the molten sea took the place of the brazen laver. But whether we speak of the brazen laver, the molten sea, or the sea of glass, it is essentially the same truth.

In Revelation chapter 4 John beholds a sea of glass, "clear as crystal"[18] But as yet, no one has taken his place at the sea of glass.

But notice the contrast when we reach Revelation chapter 15. Now the sea of glass is mixed with fire, and there are people standing on the sea of glass:

---

[14] Exo 27:3.
[15] See Chapter 11, "Numbers in the Bible."
[16] Rev 6:10,11.
[17] For further details see *The Temple of Solomon* by Kevin J. Conner; Conner Publications, Blackburn South, Victoria, Australia, 1988.
[18] Rev 4:6–*TEV*.

> "And I saw something like a sea of glass mingled with fire, and those who have the victory over the beast, over his image and over his mark and over the number of his name, standing on the sea of glass, having harps of God." (verse 2)

This company of believers is victorious over the image, mark, and number of the antichrist's name. And verse 3 records they are singing the song of Moses, and of the Lamb.

When God set His people free from Egypt, each family first had to shed the blood of their Passover lamb. They were set free from 144,000 days of captivity.[19] As they left the land they came to the Red Sea. (First the blood, then the water.) To Israel, Pharaoh was their "beast," who came after them to destroy them. But God miraculously caused His people to go through the Red Sea, and be victorious over Pharaoh. Moses–the man child of the tabernacle–and the children of Israel sang a song of praise to their Great Deliverer. We could call this "the song of Moses and the Passover Lamb."[20]

Today, we do not sing the song of Moses. We sing the song of the Lord Jesus Christ–He Who is the Lamb–the One Who takes away the sin of the world.[21] The Lamb Who opens the seals in the Book of Revelation. In Revelation chapters 4 and 5 John sees the throne of God. The Great Tribulation period has not yet commenced. The beast–the antichrist–has not yet been manifested. So the sea is clear as crystal. And nobody is there.

However, in Revelation chapter 15 the sea of glass is mingled with fire. The water is no longer calm and clear. I suggest the fires of the Great Tribulation have begun for Christians who have only experienced Passover.[22]

The beast appears to have the victory during his 3½-year reign over the earth. But the members of this company of Christians refuse his mark. They overcome the beast spiritually, but he overcomes them physically. They die for their faith. And now, with instruments from the tabernacle of David–harps–they sing the song of Moses and of the Lamb.

This company of believers takes its place, not at the brazen altar, but at the sea of glass, the equivalent of the brazen washstand. Both these pieces of furniture, representing blood and water, are in the outer court. When John was commanded to measure the temple of God, he was instructed to leave out the outer court,

---

[19] 400 years of 360 days. 400 x 360 = 144,000.
[20] Exodus chapters 12 -15. This song of Moses and the children of Israel in Exo 15:1-19, at the beginning of his ministry, is the first recorded song, or psalm, in Scripture. The song of Miriam the prophetess is the second (Exo 15:20,21). The Bible records a second song of Moses at the end of his ministry (Deut 31:30-32:44).
[21] John 1:29.
[22] See Chapter 12, "The Festivals of Israel."

because those in the outer court would be trodden underfoot for the 3½ years of the Great Tribulation.[23]

From the outer court we now proceed into the holy place of the tabernacle.

3. The Candlesticks (Lampstands)–Revelation chapters 1-3

> "Then I turned to see the voice that spoke with me. And having turned I saw seven golden **lampstands**." (Rev 1:12)

It is interesting to note that when John was introduced to the tabernacle of Moses, he was brought straight into a holy place scene where he saw the seven lampstands.[24] The lampstand, or candlestick, was the only source of light in the holy place. There are a number of ways we can interpret this light.

Light speaks to us of:

a. The Lord Jesus Christ

Concerning Him, it is written:
"In Him was life, and the life was the light of men." (John 1:4)

Jesus said:
"As long as I am in the world, I am the light of the world." (John 9:5)

b. The written Word, the Bible

The Psalmist said:
"Your word is a lamp to my feet
And a light to my path …
The entrance of Your words gives light." (Psa 119:105,130)

c. The individual believer

Jesus taught us:

"You are the light of the world." (Matt 5:14)

David sang to the Lord:

"For you will light my lamp;
The Lord my God will enlighten my darkness." (Psa 18:28)

The candlestick in the tabernacle of Moses was made from one piece of gold, but

---

[23] Rev 11:1,2.
[24] Rev 1:12.

was molded into 66 segments. Each of the six branches had three ornamental knobs, three flowers, plus three almond blossoms, totalling nine segments in all.[25] There were 12 segments on the central shaft, or "stick." Add the total number of segments of three of the branches plus the shaft, and we have 39, the number of books in the Old Testament. Add the total number of the segments of the three remaining branches and we have 27, the number of books in the New Testament. 66 segments from one piece of gold. Our Bible–our source of light for living–contains 66 books from one Author.

The nine segments of each branch speak to us of the nine gifts and nine fruit of the Holy Spirit.[26] The twelve segments of the central shaft remind us of the fullness of apostolic doctrine,[27] the seven lamps on the lampstand the sevenfold Spirit of God,[28] the oil the anointing of the Holy Spirit.[29]

d. The local church

Jesus said: "Nor do they light a lamp and put it under a basket, but on a lampstand, and it gives light to all who are in the house." (Matt 5:15)

There is no room for error here. The Lord tells John:

"The seven lampstands which you saw *are* the seven churches." (Rev 1:20)

Zechariah the prophet saw one lampstand.[30] He was seeing the Church prophetically from God's standpoint. From Heaven's viewpoint there is one Church, universal. God has ordained that this one Church on earth be made up of many geographical expressions of His body, called local churches.

Aaron the high priest stood by the lampstand in the tabernacle to make sure it continually gave light. He removed burnt pieces and supplied the lampstand with fresh oil every morning and evening. In the Book of Revelation we see Jesus standing in the midst of the churches. The main function of each local church is to give light.[31] But Jesus says to these seven churches, "I know your works." He knows the heart of each individual in every church.

In the seven churches some had left their first love; some were lukewarm; some had embraced false doctrine. What a mixture! And most important of all–in His dealings with the seven churches, the Lord emphasizes that in the final analysis there are only going to be two kinds of Christians–those who overcome, and

---

[25] Exo 25:33.
[26] 1 Cor 12:8-10; Gal 5:22,23.
[27] Rev 12:1.
[28] Rev 4:5.
[29] Psa 92:10. There were five ingredients in the holy anointing oil–pure myrrh, sweet cinnamon, sweet calamus, cassia, and olive oil. (Exo 30:22-25).
[30] Zech 4:2.
[31] Rom 13:12; Eph 5:8.

those who are overcome. It is time for us to "buy" oil so we can be overcomers, and shine as lights in this dark world!

In Revelation chapter 11 the two witnesses are called lampstands. Their ministry will be to give special witness and light during the dark days of the 3½-year Great Tribulation period.

At Belshazzar's feast the fingers of a man's hand wrote words of judgment against his Babylonian kingdom. Where? "Opposite the lampstand on the plaster of the wall of the king's palace." (Dan 5:5) As the Lord's lampstand–His Church–shines brightly in these last days, judgment will surely fall upon every kingdom opposed to God.

4. The Golden Altar Of Incense–Revelation 8:1- 5; 9:13; 11:1

> "And another angel, having a golden censer, came and stood at the altar. He was given much incense, that he should offer it with the prayers of all the saints upon the **golden altar** which was before the throne." (Rev 8:3)

> "Then the sixth angel sounded: And I heard a voice from the four horns of the **golden altar** which is before God." (Rev 9:13)

> "Then I was given a reed like a measuring rod. And the angel stood, saying, 'Rise and measure the temple of God, **the altar**, and those who worship there.'" (Rev 11:1)

In the tabernacle of Moses, the golden altar of incense was the article of furniture nearest to God's glory.[32] This altar was made of acacia wood overlaid with gold.[33] The top was bordered with a crown of gold to prevent the fire and the incense from falling to the ground.[34] The four horns of this altar speak to us of the power and authority of intercession–the power of prayer for every tribe and nation reaching to the four corners of the earth. Because, for the New Covenant believer, the golden altar represents prayer and praise, intercession and worship.

a. Christ's Intercession–and Ours

How wonderful it is to know that our Lord Jesus Christ is our Intercessor! The promise concerning Him is:

> "But He, because He continues forever, has an unchangeable priesthood.

---

[32] Exo 40:5.
[33] Exo 30:1-10.
[34] Exo 30:3.

Therefore He is also able to save to the uttermost those who come to God through Him, since He always lives to make intercession for them." (Heb 7:24,25)

Not only this. We have a High Priest Who sympathizes with our weaknesses:

"Seeing then that we have a great High Priest who has passed through the heavens, Jesus the Son of God, let us hold fast our confession.
For we do not have a High Priest who cannot sympathize with our weaknesses, but was in all points tempted as we are, yet without sin.
Let us therefore come boldly to the throne of grace, that we may obtain mercy and find grace to help in time of need." (Heb 4:14-16)

b. Prayer and Praise

David cried out to the Lord:

"Let my prayer be set before You as incense,
The lifting up of my hands as the evening sacrifice." (Psa 141:2)

The Hebrew word used for prayer here is *tephillah*, which means "that which is offered up," and can refer to both prayer and worship.

In the Book of Revelation chapter eight, the Greek word for "prayers" is proseuchē, which literally means "a pouring out," and can also refer to both prayer and worship.

The incense made at the tabernacle of Moses contained five ingredients[35]:

i. **Stacte**–The stacte tree was found in the mountain area of Gilead. Without breaking a branch, or piercing the tree, there flowed out a creamy substance.

   This ingredient speaks to us of the spontaneity of prayer and worship.

ii. **Onycha**–Onycha was taken from a perfumed crab found in the depths of the Red Sea. A drop of this costly fragrance was extracted from the crab. The extract yielded a musky odour when burned.

   This speaks of worship and prayer from the depths of a sincere heart.

iii. **Galbanam**–This substance came from the Galbanam shrub which grew 6-10 feet high. The stem had to be cut or broken for the fragrant sap to flow out. This speaks of our need for brokenness in prayer and worship.

---

[35] Exo 30:34,35.

iv. **Frankincense**–Frankincense is a pale yellow, pungent resin, which is very fragrant when burned. The Bible speaks of the hill of frankincense and the trees of frankincense (Song 4:6,14).[36]

This speaks to us of the stabilizing power of prayer and worship.

v. **Salt**–Salt reminds us of "the salt of the covenant"–the life of Christ flowing through the prayer and worship of those who are in covenant relationship with Him (Lev 2:13).

This is the incense that was burned as a sweet fragrance to the Lord.[37] The offering of incense had to be sweet, pure, holy, fragrant, and perpetual. So does our prayer and worship.

In Revelation chapter eight, the Lamb, our Lord Jesus, is given much incense– incense which is offered with the prayers of the people who are at the golden altar. Their prayers, together with the incense, ascend to God.

Verse 5 says: "Then the angel took the censer,[38] filled it with fire from the altar, and threw it to the earth. And there were noises, thunderings, lightnings, and an earthquake." As we shall see in **Volume Two** in more detail, God really answers their prayers! The seventh seal has been opened, and now "the seven angels who had the seven trumpets prepared themselves to sound them" (Rev 8:6–*NAS*).

In the tabernacle of Moses the golden censer was used only on the Day of Atonement. On that Day, God's command to Aaron, through Moses, after Aaron had slain the bull for the sin offering, was to:

> "take a censer full of burning coals of fire from the altar before the Lord [i.e. the golden altar of incense], with his hands full of sweet incense beaten fine, and bring it inside the veil.
> And he shall put the incense on the fire before the Lord, that the cloud of incense may cover the mercy seat that is on the Testimony [the ark of the covenant], lest he die." (Lev 16:12,13)

As we draw closer to the fulfillment of the Day of Atonement to the Church, we can expect to see a worldwide increase in the ministries of prayer and worship.

Zacharias the priest was ministering at the altar of incense when he received the glorious revelation concerning the birth of John the Baptist and the coming of the Messiah.[39] As we press into the ministry of prayer and worship, the way is also

---

[36] For example, see Psa 1:3; Jer 17:7,8.
[37] Heb 9:4.
[38] The censer was a small portable vessel made of metal, which was fitted to receive burning coals from the brazen altar, and on which the incense for burning was sprinkled.
[39] Luke 1:5-25.

opened for us to receive divine revelation. At the altar of incense Zacharias received illumination concerning the first coming of Jesus the Messiah. Those who stand at this piece of furniture today will receive illumination concerning the second coming of the Lord Jesus. May the Spirit of intercession and worship descend upon us!

5. The Table of Showbread–Revelation 4:4

The table of showbread in the tabernacle of Moses was made of acacia wood overlaid with pure gold. There were 12 loaves of bread on the table. This was the "bread of the Presence," "the bread of the Face," "the continual bread."[40] Every seven days the priests ate this bread in the holy place.[41]

There was a golden bowl of wine, a drink offering, at the table. This wine was poured out to the Lord as an offering.[42]

The table of showbread was a glorious prophecy of our Lord Jesus Christ. The priests ate the bread as a prophetic picture of Him Who came and said, "I am the bread of life" (John 6:48). They poured the wine out on the desert floor as a prophecy that Messiah would come, and His blood would be poured out for His people.

As His death approached, Jesus, at the last supper, took bread and wine with his disciples, and commanded them to fellowship regularly with bread and wine–just as the Old Testament priests had done in the holy place of Moses' tabernacle.

The New Testament Church obeyed by celebrating the body and blood of Jesus at the communion table every first day of the week.[43] The Church today continues to do this in remembrance of Him.[44] As we saw in the Chapter entitled "The Festivals of Israel" the communion service will increase in significance and importance as we come closer to the fulfillment of the Day of Atonement.

The Number 24, and the Crowns

The table of showbread is the only article of furniture in the tabernacle of Moses not specifically named in the Book of Revelation. But there is an allusion to the table of showbread. In Revelation 4:4 we read:

> "Around the throne were twenty-four thrones, and on the thrones I saw twenty-four elders sitting, clothed in white robes; and they had crowns of gold on their heads."

---

[40] Num 4:7.
[41] Exo 25:23-30; Lev 24:5-9.
[42] Exo 25:28,29; Num 28:7.
[43] Acts 20:7.
[44] 1 Cor 11:24.

In verses 10 and 11 the twenty-four elders fall down before the Lord and cast their crowns before His throne, beginning to worship Him. We have seen the unique significance of the number 24.

There are two distinctive features in the type, that is, the actual table of showbread in Moses' tabernacle. Firstly, the table of showbread is associated with the number 24. On the table were 12 loaves of bread, and each loaf was made of 2 tenths of an ephah of finely crushed flour:

> "And you shall take fine flour, and bake twelve cakes with it; two tenths of an ephah shall be in each cake [of the showbread or bread of the Presence]. And you shall set them in two rows, six in a row, upon the table of pure gold before the Lord." (Lev 24:5,6–*Amp*)

That is, the total weight of the flour used each week was 24 tenths of an ephah. Thus the table of showbread was associated with the number 24.

The second unique thing about the table of showbread was this–it was surrounded by two golden moldings, called crowns. The Bible says, "make thereto a crown of gold round about," and "thou shalt make a golden crown to the border thereof round about" (Exo 25:24,25–*KJV*).

The altar of incense had one crown around the top of it.

The ark of the covenant had one crown around the top of it.

The table of showbread had two crowns around the top of it.

The table of showbread is, therefore, associated with the number "twenty-four" and "crowns." Twenty-four elders and their crowns in Revelation chapter 4. A rather obscure inference, I agree. But an allusion, nevertheless.

But there is no doubt that John clearly sees the next article of tabernacle furniture

6. The Ark of the Covenant–Revelation 11:19

> "Then the temple of God was opened in heaven, and **the ark of His covenant** was seen in His temple. And there were lightnings, noises, thunderings, an earthquake, and great hail."

We have seen a brief description of the ark of the covenant in Chapter four of this book.

The ark of the covenant in Moses' tabernacle was an oblong-shaped box, 3¾ feet long, and 2¼ feet wide and 2¼ feet high.[45] When we look at the ark of the covenant, we see a

---

[45] See *Figure 3*, The Ark of the Covenant, in Chapter 4.

glorious depiction of the triune God—the two cherubim speak of God the Father and God the Holy Spirit—the mercy seat, sprinkled with atonement blood, speaks of God the Son. Remember, God promised that He would appear, and that He would speak, from the ark of the covenant:

> "I will appear in the cloud above the mercy seat." (Lev 16:2)

> "You shall put the mercy seat on top of the ark, and in the ark you shall put the Testimony that I will give you.
> And there I will meet with you, and I will speak with you from above the mercy seat, from between the two cherubim which are on the ark of the Testimony." (Exo 25:21,22)

While we know that God is everywhere, the ark of the covenant was, for Old Testament Israel, their "Immanuel—God with us." It was the place where, once a year, in the person of the high priest, they could see God's glory and hear Him speak. This was, of course, on the Day of Atonement.

For the New Testament Christian, the ark of the covenant is a prophetic picture of the fullness of the power, presence and glory of our Lord Jesus Christ.

Turning again to John's heavenly vision, we understand the tabernacle he saw was the prototype of Moses' tabernacle. Revelation 11:19 should be the first verse of chapter 12. The temple of God is opened in heaven, revealing the ark of the covenant. And the Bride of Revelation 12:1, a company made up of believers who will go all the way with God, has also seen the ark, and enjoyed her Day of Atonement experience.

The Bride of Christ has entered within the veil. This is why the writer of Hebrews could say these amazing words concerning our hope:

> "That by two immutable (*margin*, 'unchangeable') things, in which it is impossible for God to lie, we might have strong consolation, who have fled for refuge to lay hold of the *hope* set before us.
> This *hope* we have as an anchor of the soul, both sure and steadfast, and which enters the Presence behind the veil,
> Where the forerunner has entered for us, even Jesus, having become High Priest forever according to the order of Melchizedek." (Heb 6:18-20)

This glorious hope anchors our soul. We are steadfast in our faith.

What is our hope? The appearing of the Lord Jesus Christ on the day when God fulfills the Day of Atonement to His Church! Titus expresses it this way:

> "…we should live soberly, righteously, and godly in the present age,
> looking for the blessed *hope* and glorious appearing of our great God and Savior Jesus Christ." (Titus 2:12,13)

What is our hope? To have such intimate fellowship and communion with God that we see His glory on the Day of Atonement!

> "Christ in you, the *hope* of glory." (Col 1:27)

What is our hope? To be like Him. To be married to Him when He appears on the Day of Atonement:

> "Dear friends, now we are children of God, and what we will be has not yet been made known. But we know that when He appears we shall be like Him, for we shall see Him as He is.
> Everyone who has this *hope* in Him purifies himself, just as He is pure."
> (1 Jn 3:2,3–*NIV*)

As we have studied, the tabernacle of Moses on earth was the shadow of the heavenly tabernacle. Also, the temple of Solomon on earth was the shadow of the heavenly temple. In Revelation 15:5, John sees the prototypes of both tabernacle and temple:
> "After these things I looked, and behold, the temple of the tabernacle of testimony in heaven was opened."

And what else does John see? God's glory and power!

> "The temple was filled with smoke from the glory of God and from His power." (Rev 15:8)

SUMMARY TABERNACLE OF MOSES IN REVELATION

We have now seen in the Book of Revelation different groups of God's people at the various pieces of furniture of the tabernacle of Moses:

1. Brazen altar — Those who fail the "measuring test." They do not lose their salvation, but they do lose their lives. They die for their faith.

2. Brazen washstand — Those who go into the fire of the Great Tribulation and lose their lives, being beheaded for their faith. These two groups are not overcomers, but, sad to say, are overcome.

3. Lampstand — The local churches, but what mixture there is in them. Five of the seven churches are commanded by the Lord to "Repent, or else!"

4. Golden altar — His praying and worshipping saints.

5.	Table of Showbread	Church eldership and government cast their crowns before the Lord's throne and glorify only Him.
6.	Ark of the Covenant	The Bride of Christ, married to Him on the Day of Atonement.

"LET US GO ON"

One of the most important truths I want to emphasize in this book is our need for preparation. It is time to get ready. "And those who were ready went in with Him to the wedding." (Matt 25:10)

An essential part of preparation is learning how to obey God's command to "grow in the grace, and knowledge of our Lord and Savior Jesus Christ" (2 Pet 3:18).

As can be seen from *Figure 23* in *Appendix 11* on page 370, each article of furniture in Moses' tabernacle represents a distinct New Covenant redemptive truth and experience. Israel was "the church in the wilderness" (Acts 7:38).

The first time the word "church" is used after the death, resurrection, and ascension of Christ is on the birthday of His Church, the Day of Pentecost. "And the Lord added to the church daily those who were being saved." (Acts 2:47)

This account of the birth of the Church in Acts chapter 2 is a pattern for subsequent generations of the Church. Seven major redemptive truths are listed in Acts chapter 2. In the tabernacle of Moses, there were seven major steps into the fullness of God's glorious presence.

We need to experience each redemptive truth–but not to stop and settle down at any one of them. For, when listing these truths, the writer to the Hebrews exhorts us:

> "Therefore, leaving the discussion of the elementary principles of Christ, *let us go on* to perfection (*margin*, 'maturity'), not laying again the foundation of repentance from dead works and of faith toward God,
> of the doctrine of baptisms, of laying on of hands, of resurrection of the dead, and of eternal judgment.
> And this we will do (*margin*, 'let us do') if God permits." (Heb 6:1-3)

By comparing the various articles of furniture in the tabernacle of Moses–the Old Testament "church in the wilderness"–with the birthday of the New Testament Church on the Day of Pentecost, we can see how accurately Moses' tabernacle prophesied. We can also see that the steps into the fullness of God's presence are almost the same in both instances. The formality of the type has become the reality of the antitype.

Figure 24: **Comparison and Contrast Between Old and New Testament Churches**

	OLD TESTAMENT CHURCH (Acts 7:38)	NEW TESTAMENT CHURCH (Acts 2:36-47)
	Moses over his house (Heb 3:1)	**Christ over His house (Heb 3:6)**
1	**Brazen Altar**	"Repent" (verse 38)
2	**Brazen Washstand**	"Be baptized" (verses 38 and 41)
3	**First Curtain:** to enter the Holy Place, the priest had to be clothed with the special priestly garments	"Receive the Holy Spirit" (verse 38). Luke 24:49: "Be endued (clothed) with power"
4	**Golden Lampstand**	"Continued steadfastly in apostles' doctrine" (the Word of God) (verse 42)
5	**Table of Showbread**	"Fellowship in the breaking of bread" (verse 42). Submitted to godly eldership in local church
6	**Altar of Incense**	"Prayers" (verse 42) and "praise" (verse 47)
7	**Ark of the Covenant**	Maturity and perfection (Heb 6:1)
"So Moses finished the work" (Exo 40:33)		**"I have finished the work" (John 17:4)**

One of the great tragedies of Church history is that many sincere believers have stopped and built their churches around only one article of furniture–for example, the brazen altar, or the brazen washstand. We must experience the blessings these pieces of furniture represent, but not camp there. "Let us go on" is the Lord's command to us.

The Three Feasts

From our diagram of the tabernacle of Moses, we can readily see it was divided into three main sections–the outer court, the holy place, and the holy of holies.

The outer court speaks to us of the Feast of Passover.

The holy place speaks of the Feast of Pentecost and the commencement of the Feast of Tabernacles.

The holy of holies points to the fulfillment of the Day of Atonement and the fullness of Tabernacles.

"Let us go on." Which Feasts have you kept? How many pieces of furniture have you experienced? Where do you desire to be?

PART THREE

Revelation chapter 1

THE CHRIST

PART THREE   THE CHRIST

Chapter 14

Here Comes The Bridegroom!

Revelation chapter 1

Christ, our Great High Priest, in the Midst of the Churches

"THE REVELATION OF JESUS CHRIST" (VERSE 1)

The greatest revelation contained in the Bible is the revelation of the Person of the Son of God – the Lord Jesus Christ. This revelation of Him in all His fullness is *the* revelation of all revelations. This is the *apokalupsis* – the drawing aside of the covering veil.[1] The opening of the curtain – the full manifestation – of our marvellous Lord.

Each book of the Bible uncovers a fragment of this wonderful revelation of Christ. But here, in this last Book of the Bible, the revelation is complete. More than any other subject in the Book of Revelation, the revelation of the Lord Jesus is pre-eminent.

When our Lord Jesus came to this earth in the flesh, very few people recognized Him. John records: "He came to His own (*margin*, 'His own people') and His own did not receive Him."[2] They did not receive Him, because they did not recognize who He was. He was so "under the covering veil" that the religious leaders did not know He was the Messiah. At His trial the high priest said to Him, "I put You under oath by the living God: Tell us if You are the Christ, the Son of God!"[3] Members of His Own earthly family did not believe in Him.[4] His Own disciples understood so little of the atonement, they tried to dissuade Him from His principal purpose.[5] But as we read the words of this prophecy, we discover the covering veil is lifted, and we can now see our Lord Jesus infinitely clearer than those who were with Him during His earthly life and ministry.

In this Book, the Lord Jesus Christ is revealed to us as:

1. Him who is and who was and who is to come (1:4):

> Jesus always was. He always is. He always will be. And He is going to come again – at His glorious Second Coming with power and great glory:

---

[1] *Apokalupsis* is the Greek word for "revelation."
[2] John 1:11.
[3] Matt 26:63.
[4] John 7:1-10.
[5] Matt 16:21,22.

"This Jesus, who was taken up from you into heaven, will come back in the same way that you saw him go to heaven." (Acts 1:11 – *TEV*)

2. The Faithful Witness (Greek, *martus*, "martyr") (1:5):

In Revelation 1:5 we have a powerful revelation of our Lord Jesus in connection with His three most important redemptive acts – His death, His resurrection, and His ascension.

Firstly, Jesus was *the* faithful martyr. He died on the cross as our sin substitute. When revelation of this great redemptive truth – Christ's death for us – comes to men and women, it sets them gloriously free from the bondage of sin and the fear of death.

The fact that Jesus was dead identifies Him with the most tragic of all man's experiences. No mere mortal can conquer death. But our Lord Jesus Christ did. Because He was dead but is now alive, we who honour Jesus as Saviour and Lord, though we die, will live forever with Him. Hallelujah!

"The Faithful Witness." His testimony – His word – is faithful, true, sure, and eternal. During His earthly ministry He spoke the truth without compromise, even though it cost Him His life.[6]

Revelation of Jesus as the Faithful Witness should make us faithful and true in our testimony for Him. We should witness without compromising, though we be persecuted, or even slain, for doing so.

Old Testament saints stood uncompromisingly for the truth. They were "stoned, … sawn in two, were tempted, were slain with the sword."[7] In the New Testament Stephen was a faithful martyr.[8] So was the Apostle Paul.[9] So was Antipas, whom Jesus calls "My faithful martyr, who was killed among you, where Satan dwells."[10] As we will see, there are many more faithful martyrs in the Book of Revelation.

Today, rather than deny their Master, many of our brothers and sisters in Christ are dying a martyr's death. In countries of the African Continent, Asia, and South America, Christians are being tortured, drowned, poisoned, crucified, shot, stabbed, and burned to death. This should move us to pray for the persecuted Church of our day – and cause us to be faithful witnesses for our Lord wherever we are.

The Lord Jesus Christ is also revealed in the Book of Revelation as:

---

[6] John 18:33-40.
[7] Heb 11:37.
[8] Acts 22:20.
[9] Acts 21:13.
[10] Rev 2:13.

3. The Firstborn from the Dead (1:5):

He has conquered death. Revelation of the resurrection of Christ challenges us to be overcomers in this world. As a result of our being baptized into Jesus Christ, and His death, we can now "walk in newness of life." We are "united together ... in the likeness of His resurrection." That is why we are commanded to "reckon [our]selves to be dead indeed to sin, but alive to God in Christ Jesus our Lord" (Rom 6:3-11).

Jesus, the firstborn from the dead? The Bible records that many died and were raised from the dead before Jesus.[11] Therefore, to understand Revelation 1:5, we must also read Revelation 1:18:

"'I am He who lives, and was dead, and behold, I am alive forevermore. Amen. And I have the keys of Hades and of Death.'"

Jesus is the first to rise from the dead and *live forevermore*. All who had previously been raised from the dead died – or will die – again. For example, Moses died, and the Lord buried him. But he was raised from the dead, and was seen by the disciples with Jesus on the mountain of transfiguration, together with Elijah.[12] Moses must return to earth to die. Otherwise he would be the first to rise from the dead and live forevermore, thus contradicting Revelation 1:5.

Moses and Elijah (who up to this present time has escaped death), will return as the two witnesses during the Great Tribulation. Both will be killed, and then resurrected after 3½ days. Thus Jesus is confirmed as the *first* to rise from the dead and *live forevermore*.

He is also:

4. The Ruler over the Kings of the Earth (1:5):

Not only must the Church have a revelation of Christ's death and resurrection. A revelation of His ascension is also necessary.

He was murdered by being nailed to a tree. After three days God raised Him from the dead. "God has exalted [Him] to His right hand to be Prince and Savior." (Acts 5:30,31) Christ "is the head of all principality (margin, 'rule and authority') and power." He "disarmed principalities and powers, He made a public spectacle of them, triumphing over them in [the cross]" (Col 2:10,15). Now we see His exaltation and glorification!

---

[11] For example, the widow of Zarephath's son (1 Ki 17:23); the Shunammite's son (2 Ki 4:34); the dead man placed in Elisha's tomb (2 Ki 13:21); the ruler's daughter (Matt 9:25); the widow's son (Luke 7:15); Lazarus (John 11:44).
[12] Jude 9; Matt 17:1-13.

There are many battles in the Book of Revelation. Other kings and princes who make war against the Lamb and His followers are mentioned in this Book. But the Ascended Christ wins each and every battle, finally assuming the pre-eminence of this title: "The Ruler of the kings of the earth."

Revelation of Christ's ascension, and our position together with Him, will give us great victory. For God "has raised us up together, and made us sit together in the heavenly places in Christ Jesus" (Eph 2:6).

We are crucified with Christ.[13] We died with Him.[14] We were buried with Him.[15] We were raised with Him.[16] We sit together with Him. Our identification with Christ is complete. The Father "has blessed us with *every* spiritual blessing in the heavenly places in Christ" (Eph 1:3). What more could we possibly ask for?

5. The "I AM" (1:8):

It was through a revelation of this Name of God–"I AM"–that Israel was delivered from the bondage of Egypt. God commanded Moses to tell the children of Israel, "I AM has sent me to you" (Exo 3:3,14).

And here in Revelation 1:8 Jesus is revealed as the eternal "I AM." Ever present tense. Never changing. Unchangeable. "Jesus Christ is the same yesterday, today, and forever."[17] It is through the revelation of the unchanging Christ that we have entered into a personal relationship with God.

The apostle John records in his Gospel, that while the Great I AM was on earth, He declared:

> "I AM the bread of life." (John 6:35)
>
> "I AM the light of the world." (John 9:5)
>
> "I AM the door of the sheep." (John 10:7)
>
> "I AM the good shepherd [Who] gives His life for the sheep."(John 10:11)
>
> "I AM the resurrection and the life." (John 11:25)
>
> "I AM the way, the truth, and the life." (John 14:6)
>
> "I AM the true vine." (John 15:1)

Jesus our great "I AM" is everything we will ever need!

---

[13] Gal 2:20.
[14] Rom 6:2-5a.
[15] Rom 6:4,7.
[16] Rom 6:5b.
[17] Heb 13:8.

6. The Alpha and the Omega (1:8, 21:6, 22:13):

The first and last letters of the Greek alphabet. Our Saviour is the beginning, ending, and everything in between. What assurance and security is ours as we accept this fact!

From His throne comes this promise:

> "I am the Alpha and the Omega, the Beginning and the End. I will give of the fountain of the water of life freely to him who thirsts." (Rev 21:6)

7. The Beginning and the End (1:8, 21:6, 22:13); the First and the Last (1:17, 22:13):

Our Lord Jesus Christ has no beginning or end. Beginnings and endings as applied to the Lord are used only in connection with His redemptive work. Because, as we have seen, time began only when man sinned. When sin is done away with, time will be no more.

Jesus is the beginning of our redemption from sin, and He is the ending. He is the One "Who is able to keep you from stumbling, and to present you faultless before the presence of His glory with exceeding joy" (Jude 24).

"The First and the Last." This aspect of revelation concerning Jesus, our Great Redeemer, was prophesied by Isaiah:

> "Thus says the Lord, the King of Israel,
> And his Redeemer, the Lord of hosts:
> I am the First and I am the Last;
> Besides Me there is no God." (Isa 44:6)[18]

In addition, Jesus is the Beginning and Ending – the First and the Last – of all successful Christian service:

> "For of Him and through Him and to Him are all things, to Whom be glory forever. Amen." (Rom 11:36)

"Of Him"	–	God's *will* governs the beginning;
"Through Him"	–	God's *power* governs the doing;
"To Him"	–	God's *glory* governs the end.

Indeed, our Lord Jesus is the Beginning and the End, the First and the Last.

---

[18] See also Isa 48:10.

8. Our Great High Priest (chapter 1):

The Old Testament high priest stood by the lampstand to trim the wicks of the lamps by cutting out the blackened ashes. He then poured oil into the bowls so the lamp would give light continually.

In Revelation chapter one we see Jesus, our New Testament High Priest, standing in the midst of seven lampstands – seven local churches – ready to trim the lamps. He purposes, by the power of His Word, to cut away sin, remove lukewarmness, and pour out the oil of His Holy Spirit upon them. He desires the members of His churches to burn brightly with God's fiery light.

Let it be emphasized that the lampstands are not the sources of light, but the bearers of light. God is each church's source of light. By the power of His anointing, every assembly must shine for Him.[19]

9. The Slain Lamb (5:6):

The word "lamb" appears more often in the Book of Revelation than in any other New Testament book. In fact, outside the writings of John, "lamb," referring to Jesus, is found only twice.[20]

In John's Gospel, there are two references to Jesus as the Lamb of God.[21] John recorded the Baptist's words, who, upon seeing Jesus, declared, "Behold! The Lamb of God who takes away the sin of the world!"[22]

It excites me to find Jesus described as the Lamb of God 28 times in the Book of Revelation! Through the sacrifice of Himself, Jesus, our sinless substitute, there is atonement. In the Book of Revelation we find the consummation of perfect atonement through God's Lamb. Not only this; the Lamb is the One Who opens the seals of the seven-sealed book.[23]

In Revelation 5:6, the Lamb is described as having seven horns. This indicates that even though He is a Lamb, He manifests the fullness of God's power, might, and authority. The Lamb has seven eyes. We will study these seven eyes in the next Chapter, The Sevenfold Spirit of God.

When John beheld the Bride-city, the Lamb's wife, He said:

> "But I saw no temple in it, for the Lord God Almighty and the Lamb are its temple.

---

[19] Matt 5:14-16.
[20] Acts 8:32; 1 Pet 1:19.
[21] John 1:29, 36.
[22] John 1:29.
[23] Rev 5:9, 6:1.

The city had no need of the sun or of the moon to shine in it, for the glory of God illuminated it. The Lamb is its light." (Rev 21:22,23)

God's Lamb ultimately becomes the temple and the light of the Bride city!

10. The Angel (Messenger) having the seal of God (7:2):

The word "angel" appears in the Book of Revelation more often than in any other book of the Bible. The word translated "angel" is found 76 times in Revelation.

In Scripture we must look within the context to discover to whom the word "angel" is referring. Both the Hebrew word *malak*, and the Greek, *angelos*, mean "messenger." In the Bible, "angel" can refer to:

i. The Lord Jesus Christ, Who appeared as "The Angel of the Lord" many times in the Old Testament.[24] In Revelation chapter 7 Jesus appears as the "Sealing Angel" to "[seal] the servants of our God on their foreheads."[25]

ii. The Lord's angels, which are created, sinless, invisible, immortal spirit beings, existing in great numbers, and as special messengers of God.[26] These angels are "all ministering spirits sent forth to minister for those who will inherit salvation."[27]

iii. Satan, who "transforms himself into an angel of light" (2 Cor 11:14). Satan's final destiny is to be "cast into the lake of fire and brimstone" (Rev 20:10).

iv. The demons, devils – angels who rebelled with Satan, and were cast out of heaven. Jesus said their fate is "the everlasting fire, prepared for the devil and his angels" (Matt 25:41).

v. Men of God who are leaders and pastors in churches:

"The seven stars are the angels of the seven churches."[28]

"You received me [the Apostle Paul] as an angel of God."[29]

vi. The signifying angel-messenger sent by God to John to give him "the words of this prophecy"[30] – the Book of Revelation. This angel appears again in Revelation 14:6 and 22:16.

---

[24] For example, to Joshua (Josh 5:13,14); to Gideon (Judg 6:11); in the fiery furnace (Dan 3:28).
[25] Rev 7:2,3.
[26] Acts 27:23; 1 Pet 1:12.
[27] Heb 1:14.
[28] Rev 1:20.
[29] Gal 4:14.
[30] Rev 1:3.

In the Book of Revelation, I believe the Lord Jesus Christ is revealed as the Angel having the seal to stamp His mark of ownership, safety, and security upon the servants of God (7:1,2).[31] He is also the other "Mighty Angel" Whom John saw in chapter 10 – where Jesus is the Mighty Messenger-Angel "coming down from heaven, clothed with a cloud. And a rainbow was on his head, his face was like the sun, and his feet like pillars of fire."[32]

11. Lord of lords and King of kings (17:14, 19:16):

In the Book of Revelation, we are about to read of repeated, violent, worldwide attempts by earthly personalities and peoples, who are energized and directed by demonic powers and led by Satan, to oppose and prevent God's intention to establish Christ's rule and reign on the earth. But the Lord Jesus Christ is always victorious. The beast and the 10 kings "will make war with the Lamb, and the Lamb will overcome them, for He is Lord of lords and King of kings" (Rev 17:14).

Our Lord Jesus is the Great Overcomer, and through Him, we can overcome all the power of the enemy.[33]

In Revelation chapter 19 we see Jesus with the name "King of kings and Lord of lords" written on His robe and on His thigh.

12. The Lamb-Bridegroom (19:7, 21:2):

We have previously noted that in Revelation chapter 19, the Bride of the Lord has made herself ready for marriage with her Bridegroom, Jesus, the Lamb of God. Revelation chapter 21 describes the Bride as the holy city, "prepared as a bride adorned for her husband."[34]

13. Faithful and True (19:11):

> "Now I saw heaven opened, and behold, a white horse. And He who sat on him was called Faithful and True, and in righteousness He judges and makes war." (Rev 19:11)

As we have seen, Jesus is our "merciful and faithful High Priest in things pertaining to God."[35] He is "the faithful witness."[36] And He Who is faithful to us requires us to be faithful to Him – even to death. "Now it is required that those

---

[31] This is prophesied in Ezek 9:1-6.
[32] Rev 10:1.
[33] Luke 10:19; Rev 21:7.
[34] Rev 21:2.
[35] Heb 2:17.
[36] Rev 1:5.

who have been given a trust must prove faithful."[37] "Be faithful until death, and I will give you the crown of life."[38]

14. The Word of God (19:13):

In the opening of John's Gospel, Jesus is revealed to John as the eternal Word of God:

> "In the beginning was the Word, and the Word was with God, and the Word was God.
> He was in the beginning with God ...
> And the Word became flesh and dwelt among us ..." (John 1:1,2,14)

In the closing chapters of John's Revelation, Jesus is again revealed as the eternal Word of God. He Who is sitting on the white horse:

> "had a name written that no one knew except Himself.
> He was clothed with a robe dipped in blood, and His name is called The Word of God." (Rev 19:12,13)

15. The Root and Offspring of David (22:16):

> "I, Jesus, have sent My angel to testify to you these things in the churches. I am the Root and the Offspring of David, the Bright and Morning Star." (Rev 22:16)

This is the first time the word "church" has occurred in Revelation since the letters to the seven churches. (The word "church" is found only in chapters 1, 2, 3, and 22.) Jesus makes it clear He wants not only the seven letters read in each individual local church. He also desires that the whole Book of Revelation be read and taught in all the churches.

That Jesus would be "the Root and Offspring of David" was foretold long ago by the Prophets.[39] In Ezekiel 34:23-26 Jesus, prophetically, is called David, the shepherd and prince of God's people. [This portion of Scripture ends with the words of the familiar hymn, "There shall be showers of blessing."]

16. The Bright and Morning Star (22:16):

> "I, Jesus, have sent My messenger (angel) to you to witness and to give you assurance of these things for the churches (assemblies). I am [both] the Root

---

[37] 1 Cor 4:2 – *NIV*.
[38] Rev 2:10.
[39] Isa 11:1,2; 55:1- 5; Jer 23:5,6; Eze 37:24-26: The only "everlasting covenant" was sealed by the blood of Jesus.

(the Source) and the Offspring of David, the radiant and brilliant Morning Star." (*Amp*)

In our study on "Stars" we saw they represent the Holy Spirit and His anointing. The last Name our Anointed Saviour calls Himself in the Book of Revelation is "The Bright and Morning Star." In nature, the bright morning star precedes the full glory of the sun's light in daytime. This certain star is the herald of the new day.

This is the harbinger of the brightness and glory of the Bride-city, because the Lamb, our Lord Jesus Christ in all His glory, is the light of that city.

Not only this. Stars are guides. So is our Lord, and so are His true and faithful ministers. How many wanderers, stranded in the ocean, or lost on a mountain or in the jungle, have been led to safety by following the patterns in the starry heavens in the black of night. Today, if darkness seems to surround us, we can have confidence in the Son of Man, our Bright and Morning Star. He will guide us to His light.

Truly the Book of Revelation is "The Revelation of Jesus Christ."

The Angel-Messenger to John (Revelation 1:1 – continued)

"Which God gave Him to show His servants – things which must shortly (*margin*, 'quickly or swiftly') take place. And He sent and signified it by His angel to His servant John."

The order of the giving of the Revelation is clear –

- God the Father gave the Revelation to Jesus Christ;
- Jesus gave the Revelation to His angel;
- His angel gave the Revelation to Christ's servant John;
- John was to give the Revelation to Christ's servants – not only to the pastors of the seven churches, but to each and every believer: "John, to the seven *churches* which are in Asia" (Rev 1:4).

Who was this angel – this messenger – by whom the Lord sent to John the message of the Book of Revelation?

I would like to suggest this messenger was Enoch. After the birth of Enoch's son, Methuselah, Enoch walked with God for 300 years, and was translated bodily to heaven. "He was not, for God took him," the record reads.[40]

---

[40] Gen 5:21-24.

In the New Testament, we are told Enoch was a prophet who prophesied concerning the Second Coming of Christ, and last day events.[41] Enoch was the seventh from Adam, speaking of the fullness and purity of his message.[42]

Enoch is unique in many ways, but the most significant thing about him is this – he is the only man in Scripture of whom it is written he did not see death:

> "By faith Enoch was taken away so that he did not see death, 'and was not found, because God had taken him'; for before he was taken he had this testimony, that he pleased God." (Heb 11:5[43])

Enoch prefigures those Christians who in the last days will reach perfection – complete fullness and maturity – and who, like Enoch, will not see death. Speaking prophetically of this Bridal company, the Psalmist said:

> "Let this be recorded for the generation yet unborn, and a people yet to be created shall praise the Lord.
> For He looked down from the height of His sanctuary, from Heaven did the Lord behold the earth,
> To hear the sighing and groaning of the prisoner, to loose those who are appointed to death." (Psa 102:18-20 – *Amp*)

In other translations, this last phrase reads as follows:

- " ... release those condemned to death." (*NIV*)

- "[God] ... heard the groans of his people in slavery – they were children of death – and released them." (*LB*)

- "The Lord ... looks down ... to listen to the groaning of the prisoners and set free men under sentence of death." (*NEB*)

- "to set free those who were doomed to death (*margin*, 'the sons of death')." (*NAS*)

This truth is again seen prophetically in Asaph's Psalm:

> "Let the groaning of the prisoner come before You;
> According to the greatness of Your power
> Preserve those who are appointed to die." (Psa 79:11)

How does the Bride of Christ escape death? The answer is found in Revelation chapter 12, where we learn the serpent cannot harm her:

---

[41] Jude 14,15.
[42] 1 Chr 1:1-3.
[43] Quoting Gen 5:24.

> "And when the dragon saw that he was cast down to the earth, he went in pursuit of the woman who had given birth to the male child.
> But the woman was supplied with the two wings of a giant eagle, so that she might fly from the presence of the serpent into the desert (wilderness, to the retreat) where she is to be kept safe and fed for a time, and times, and half a time [three and one-half years, or twelve hundred sixty days]." (Rev 12:13,14 – *Amp*)

Also, Paul clearly teaches there is a company of believers who are loosed from their appointment with death. This is confirmed in the following verses:

> "For this we say to you by the word of the Lord, that *we who are alive and remain* until the coming of the Lord will by no means precede those who are asleep (*margin*, 'dead').
> For the Lord Himself will descend from heaven with a shout, and with the voice of an archangel, and with the trumpet of God. And the dead in Christ will rise first.
> Then *we who are alive and remain* shall be caught up together with them in the clouds to meet the Lord in the air. And thus we shall always be with the Lord." (1 Thess 4:15-17)

When our Lord Jesus comes again in His splendour and glory, all believers in Him will be found in one of two groups:

a. "The dead in Christ;"
or
b. "We who are alive [on the earth] and remain."

Those "who are alive and remain" have been loosed from their appointment with death. [Please note for future reference that in this verse the apostle Paul uses the personal-inclusive pronoun, "*we* who are alive and remain."]

Paul writes the same thing in different words to the Corinthian church:

> "Take notice! I tell you a mystery – a secret truth, an event decreed by the hidden purpose or counsel of God. We shall not all fall asleep [in death], but we shall all be changed (transformed)." (1 Cor 15:51 – *Amp*)

Once again, not all believers will die. But all believers will be changed. For at the last trumpet, sin will be removed, and all who enjoy personal faith in the Saviour will put on immortality.

In Revelation 14:1 we see the Lamb, and in verse 6 we read of "another angel flying in the midst of heaven, having the everlasting gospel to preach to those who dwell on the earth." If I am correct in my identification of the angel-messenger, I believe this is, once again,

Enoch. Because the three "men" of the four living ones[44] – Enoch, Moses, and Elijah – will, I believe, be involved in the preaching of the Gospel during the Great Tribulation, encouraging those who are Christ's to stand firm in their faith.[45]

There are only four that have lived on the earth who were physically translated to Heaven. Two of these – Enoch and Elijah – did not die. The other two – Moses and our Lord Jesus – died, and were raised from the dead. [As we have seen, during the Great Tribulation, when their ministry to the people on earth draws to a close, Elijah and Moses will die, be raised from the dead, and ascend to Heaven.[46]] These four – Enoch, Moses, Elijah, and Jesus – are, I am persuaded, the four living ones.[47]

Enoch appears at the beginning, in the middle, and at the end of the Book of Revelation. The last reference to him is Revelation chapter 22:

> "Now I, John, saw and heard these things (*margin*, 'am the one who heard and saw'). And when I heard and saw, I fell down to worship before the feet of the angel who showed me these things *[everything contained in the previous 21 chapters of Revelation].*
> Then he said to me, 'See that you do not do that. For I am your fellow servant, and of your brethren the prophets, and of those who keep the words of this book. Worship God.'" (Rev 22:8,9)

This messenger testifies he is John's fellow servant, a "brother-prophet," and that he himself [Enoch] kept the words of this book – the Book of Revelation. Angels, wonderful as they are, are not fellow-servants with an apostle, neither are they prophets. Furthermore, the Bible makes it clear angels do not experience redemption.[48]

John then bears witness that the Book of Revelation is the Word of God, is the testimony of Jesus Christ, and that he is about to describe *"all* the things he saw" (verse 2).

The Blessing (1:3)

There is a danger that if a reader of Revelation read the Book superficially, he may consider it is only about frightening visions and terrifying events. True, there are severe warnings and judgments recorded in Revelation. But there are blessings promised too!

It is no exaggeration to say I have read Revelation hundreds of times. But I only discovered by checking my Bible Concordance this morning, that there are seven blessings, or beatitudes, in this Book.[49] I list them for your encouragement:

---

[44] Rev 4:6b.
[45] Moses and Elijah as the two witnesses in Revelation chapter 11.
[46] Rev 11:7-12.
[47] See **Volume Two** of this book, *"The Four Living Ones."*
[48] 1 Pet 1:12.
[49] There are *nine* beatitudes in the teachings of Jesus in His sermon on the mount (Matt 5:3-12).

> **a.** "Blessed is he who reads and those who hear the words of this prophecy." (1:3)
> **b.** "Blessed are the dead who die in the Lord from now on." (14:13)
> **c.** "Blessed is he who watches, and keeps his garments." (16:15)
> **d.** "Blessed are those who are called to the marriage supper of the Lamb!"(19:9)
> **e.** "Blessed and holy is he who has part in the first resurrection. Over such the second death has no power." (20:6)
> **f.** "Blessed is he who keeps the words of the prophecy of this book." (22:7)
> **g.** "Blessed are those who do His commandments (*margin*, 'wash their robes')." (22:14)

The promise in Revelation chapter one is:

> "*Blessed* is he who reads and those who hear the words of this prophecy, and keep those things which are written in it; for the time is near." (1:3)

Every book of the Bible can be a blessing to us. But the Book of Revelation is the only Book that promises a special blessing to the obedient student. However, according to this verse, to receive this blessing we must:

> **a.** **"Read"** – it takes only a few minutes to read the Book of Revelation. However, when we turn to the Greek word for "read," we learn the blessing is not promised to those who casually skip-read this Book. The Greek word for "read," *anaginōskō* (from the roots *ana*, again, *ginosko*, to know) means "to know well," "to know certainly," "to know again."

> Paul instructed Timothy:

>> "Till I come, give attention to reading, to exhortation, to doctrine (*margin*, 'teaching')." (1 Tim 4:13)

> Here Paul may be encouraging the public reading of the Scriptures in church services. But for those teachers and preachers reading this book, I say, never forget the adage, "If you don't read, you won't feed."

> As we continue to read and study the Bible, the Word of the Lord will be so built into our lives that our automatic responses to life's situations and challenges will be according to God's Word. God's will for us is that we so resemble the Word of God, we live as "living letters" of Scripture: "You are our epistle written in our hearts, [you are] known and read of all men." (2 Cor 3:2)

> What do others read from our lives as they get to know us?

> **b.** **"Hear"** – we have already noted that the human spirit made alive in Christ has the same five faculties as the human body.[50] The ability to hear is one of these.

---

[50] See Chapter 8, "Types and Symbols."

Our faith is quickened and strengthened as we hear God's Word.[51] The Lord says repeatedly to the believers in the seven churches, "He who has an ear, let him hear what the Spirit says to the churches." Let us be careful to hear Him.

    c. **"Keep"** – Jesus said, "Blessed are those who hear the word of God and keep it!" (Luke 11:28) In James we are commanded to "be doers of the word, and not hearers only, deceiving yourselves" (Jas 1:22).

    As with the other books of the Bible – so with Revelation. God wants His Word to change us, purify us, mature us, make us overcomers. This can take place only as we apply the lessons we learn from this Book to our daily lives. Reading and hearing alone will not accomplish God's purpose. We must *respond* to His Word, and His Spirit, as we read and hear the Revelation. Keeping, doing, responding, repenting, believing, changing, seeking, receiving, embracing, preparing – all these, and much more, will take place in us as we experience the truths of the Book of Revelation.

The blessing promised in Revelation 1:3 is more than just the blessing we receive when we discover a gem in God's Word. Rather, this is the "blessing of all blessings" that is bestowed on those who read, hear, and keep the things that are written.

This is *the* blessing promised in Psalm 24:

> "Who shall ascend into the hill of the Lord? Or who shall stand in his holy place?
> He that hath clean hands, and a pure heart; who hath not lifted up his soul unto vanity ('an idol' – *NKJV*), nor sworn deceitfully.
> He shall receive *the* blessing from the Lord, and righteousness from the God of his salvation.
> *This is the generation* of them that seek him, that seek thy face, O Jacob (*margin*, 'O God of Jacob')." (Psa 24:3-6 – *KJV*)

What is *the* blessing? What do you consider to be the greatest blessing you could receive from the Lord. Some spiritual gift? Finances? A better job?

The greatest blessing – making us truly "happy, to be envied"[52] – is to receive the revelation of Jesus Christ, who is the "Blesser." He is the Giver of every blessing. This revelation will make us overcomers. This revelation will prepare us to be in His Bride. This revelation will get us ready for that great Wedding Day – the Marriage of the Lamb. The psalmist prophesies there will be a generation that seeks His face. A generation with clean hands and pure hearts. No idols. A generation with a great desire to ascend the hill of the Lord. A generation longing to stand in His holy place.

Let us be that generation and be sure to read, hear, and keep the Book of Revelation!

---

[51] Rom 10:17.
[52] Rev 1:3 – *Amp*.

"Grace" and "Peace" (1:4)

In the New Testament, the apostles were not just saying "Hello" in their written salutations. By their prayers and their giftings, they sought in their letters to impart faith to their readers, so the believers could receive "grace" and "peace."

The majority of the New Testament epistles contain these two words – "grace" and "peace" – in their greetings at the beginning or end of each letter. For example:

> "Grace to you and peace from God our Father and the Lord Jesus Christ." (Eph 1:2)

> "To Timothy, a true son in the faith: Grace, mercy, and peace from God our Father and Jesus Christ our Lord." (1 Tim 1:2)

"Grace" is usually defined as "God's unmerited favour." And so it is. "For by grace you have been saved."[53] But grace means so much more than this.

The Greek word for grace is *charis*, one of the roots from which we get the term in common usage today, "charismatic." Grace is not a passive blessing, but an active power at work in us, causing us to mature in the Lord: "Grow in the grace and knowledge of our Lord and Savior Jesus Christ" (2 Pet 3:18).

"Peace" is also a powerful blessing. The Church of John's day was intensely persecuted. Many were dying for their faith. But the Lord speaks peace to His people – both then, and now. We hear Him say in the midst of storms raging around us:

> "Peace I leave with you, My peace I give to you; not as the world gives do I give to you. Let not your heart be troubled, neither let it be afraid."
> (John 14:26)

"Kings and Priests" (1:5, 6)

> "To Him who loved (*margin*, 'loves us and freed') us and washed us from our sins in His own blood,
> And has made us kings (*margin*, 'a kingdom') and priests to His God and Father, to Him be glory and dominion forever and ever. Amen."

This statement amazes me. The first people spoken of as "kings" in the Book of Revelation are the redeemed!

Jesus loved us. He loves us still. As John says in another place, "The love I speak of is not our love for God, but the love he showed to us in sending his Son as the remedy for the defilement of our sins."[54] He washed and loosed us from our sins by the power of His

---

[53] Eph 2:8.
[54] 1 Jn 4:10 – *NEB*.

blood. Remember, this is being written to the seven churches. The message to the Christians in those seven churches is, "Be an overcomer." It is overcomers who are kings and priests. Because the Lord says specifically that only overcomers will sit as kings with Him on His throne:

> "To him who overcomes I will grant to sit with Me on My throne, as I also overcame and sat down with My father on His throne." (Rev 3:20)

The kings and priests of Revelation 1:5 are, then, the overcomers. John says the Lord has made us (notice he includes himself):

a. "kings" – who possess supreme power and authority. The overcoming Christian will possess a supreme power to reign over, to overcome, both sin and his carnal soulish nature.

Christians do not receive this power over sin, of course, because of their own natural strength.

Rather, it is by the power of the Holy Spirit. It is to bring us to this place of victory and reigning, that God sometimes allows trials and testings in our lives:

> "If we suffer (Greek, 'endure, to remain under,') we shall also reign with Him." (2 Tim 2:12 – *KJV*)

b. "priests" – with ability to minister unto Him. "[You are] a holy priesthood ... a royal priesthood" (1 Pet 2:5,9).[55] Notice the high qualifications of this priesthood – a chosen generation, a holy nation, a peculiar people. This is a generation chosen to be overcomers.

"He is coming with clouds" (1:7)

> "Behold, He is coming with clouds, and every eye will see Him, even they who pierced Him."

The word translated "pierced" here occurs only one other time in the New Testament, significantly in John's Gospel: "And again another Scripture says, 'They shall look on Him whom they pierced.'" (John 19:37)[56]

When the Lord Jesus ascended, the Bible records "He was taken up, and a cloud received Him out of their sight" (Acts 1:9). One cloud – singular.[57]

---

[55] Peter is quoting in part the promise of God to Moses, made 1,500 years before: "You shall be to Me a kingdom of priests and a holy nation" (Exo 19:6).
[56] Quoting Zech 12:10.
[57] Here is a thought for your consideration: Luke records that as the disciples were looking toward heaven, two men in white apparel said to them, "Men of Galilee, why do you stand gazing up into heaven? This same Jesus, who was taken up from you into heaven, *will so come in like manner* as you saw Him go into heaven" (Acts 1:11). In what manner is He coming? With clouds of witnesses. If that is so, then could not

However, when the Lord Jesus comes again, the Bible says He is coming with clouds – plural.[58] What, or who, are these clouds that circle Him as He returns?

In Hebrews 12:1 we read that we are "surrounded by so great a cloud of witnesses." This is referring to believers who have gone on before us to be with God. These clouds are faithful redeemed witnesses.

When Enoch prophesied of the Second Coming, He said, "Behold, the Lord comes with ten thousands of His saints" (Jude 14). Daniel saw "One like the Son of Man, coming with the clouds of heaven."[59]

Revelation 19:11-15 also describes the Second Coming. The armies in heaven are following Christ. They bring judgment on the ungodly. And in Second Thessalonians 2:7,8 "the Lord Jesus is revealed from heaven with His mighty angels." As we have seen, the word "angels" refers not only to "angelic beings," but also to God's messengers – Old Testament priests,[60] and New Testament pastors.[61]

In addition, the word "cloud" in Scripture is also used to describe the presence and glory of God. At the dedication of Solomon's Temple "the house of the Lord was filled with a cloud … for the glory of the Lord filled the house of God" (2 Chr 5:13,14).

Our Lord Jesus Christ will come again with the great heavenly hosts, and with clouds of great glory.

"I was in the Spirit " (1:10)

The first and foremost reason God has sent the Holy Spirit is to reveal the Lord Jesus Christ, because He said:

> "However, when He, the Spirit of truth has come, He will guide you into all truth; for He will not speak on His own authority, but whatever He hears He will speak; and He will tell you things to come.
> He will glorify Me, for He will take of what is Mine and declare it to you."
> (John 16:13,14)

It is impossible to understand God's Word apart from the illumination that comes from the Holy Spirit. The Holy Spirit takes truth about Jesus, and declares – reveals – it to us. Like John, we must be "in the Spirit" to understand the fullness of truth about Jesus which is contained in Revelation. It is impossible to perceive spiritual truth by the effort which is

---

this cloud which received Him out of their sight at His ascension also be a "witness" – one who had been taken bodily into heaven? I suggest it could have been Enoch. There could have been a "glory cloud" also; the Bible does not specifically tell us. We will identify the "two men" of Acts 1:10 when we study Revelation chapter 11 in **HERE COMES THE BRIDE! Volume Two.**

[58] See also 1 Thess 4:17; Mark 13:26.
[59] Dan 7:13.
[60] Mal 2:7.
[61] Rev 1:20.

contained in Revelation. It is impossible to perceive spiritual truth by the effort of human reasoning alone. As Jesus taught His disciples, understanding must come through the blessing of revelation to our spiritual senses:

> "Blessed are your eyes for they see, and your ears for they hear."
> (Matt 13:16)

> "Blessed are you, Simon Bar-Jonah, for flesh and blood has not revealed this to you, but My Father who is in heaven." (Matt 16:17)

One of the great themes of the Bible is the Spirit and the Word. The Spirit and the Word were active in the re-creation. The Spirit of God moved, and God spoke the Word.[62] The Holy Spirit conceived the Word in the virgin's womb.[63] The Spirit moved to give us the written Word, the Bible.[64] The Holy Spirit and the Word are both active in the process of our regeneration.[65]

It is in the Book of Revelation that some of the greatest themes of Scripture are brought to their climactic conclusion. This is certainly true concerning "the Spirit and the Word." Because John was in the Spirit, He saw Jesus – the Living Word – in all the fullness of His glory and beauty. Though John was still a prisoner on Patmos, his spiritual eyes and ears were so anointed He experienced visions and words describing the ascended Christ, the condition of the churches in his day, and an overview of events for the next 3,000 years!

John was "in the Spirit" throughout the whole time he received this Revelation. He testifies of this four times. Each time he uses the phrase "in the Spirit," John is about to see a new series of visions:

a. 1:10 – "I was in the Spirit":
 * visions of Christ our great High Priest, the seven churches.

b. 4:2 – "I was in the Spirit":
 * visions of God's throne, the four living ones, the 24 elders, the seven spirits of God, the sealed book, the opening of the seals, the Great Tribulation, the sun-clad pregnant woman.

c. 17:3 – "he [the angel, verse 1] carried me away in the Spirit":
 * visions of a woman sitting on a scarlet beast, Babylon the Great, the fall of Babylon, the marriage of the Lamb, the Great White Throne Judgment.

d. 21:10 – "he carried me away in the Spirit":

---

[62] Gen 1:2,3.
[63] Matt 1:20.
[64] 2 Tim 3:16; 2 Pet 1:21.
[65] John 3:3,5; 1 Pet 1:23.

- visions of the Bride-city, its gates, foundations, and walls, the river of life, the final words.

The apostle John had to be "in the Spirit" to receive the Revelation. We have to be "in the Spirit" to study and comprehend the Revelation. As Jesus said to Peter, flesh and blood – man's efforts unaided by the Holy Spirit – cannot reveal spiritual truth.[66]

"On the Lord's day" (1:10)

The phrase "on the Lord's day" can mean one or all of three things:

a. The first day of the week:

In honour of the fact that the Lord Jesus rose from the dead on the first day of the week, the New Testament Church assembled together on this day – our Sunday – to break bread, fellowship, and receive offerings.[67]

b. The day of Christ's coming:

Much of what John sees and hears is about the Second Coming of Christ and the events surrounding His coming. So John is saying here that because he was in the Spirit, he was able to see 2,000 years into the future, all the way to that great day when our Lord comes again, His 1,000-year reign on the earth, and right into eternity.

c. The seventh day of God's week of redemption:

John sees in the Spirit the 1,000-year reign of Christ, which is God's ultimate purpose for this earth. God's dealings on this earth climax with the seventh day of God's week of redemption, the millennium.[68]

Before we study the detailed appearance of Jesus in Revelation chapter one, we must first consider this statement: "the seven Spirits which are before His throne."

---

[66] Matt 16:17.
[67] Matt 28:1; Acts 20:7; 1 Cor 16:1,2.
[68] See Chapter 10, "God's Week."

Chapter 15

The Sevenfold Spirit Of God

> "John, to the seven churches which are in Asia: Grace to you and peace from Him who is and who was and who is to come, and from the seven Spirits who are before His throne." (Rev 1:4)

The Fullness of the Holy Spirit

God's revealed will for His people is that they receive the fullness of the Holy Spirit:

> "That He would grant you, according to the riches of His glory, to be strengthened with might through His Spirit in the inner man …
> …that you may be filled with all the fullness of God." (Eph 2:16,19)

Later in Ephesians, the subject of being filled with the Spirit opens the longest teaching concerning the Bride of Christ in the New Testament:

> "Be filled with the Spirit …I speak concerning Christ and the church." (Eph 5:18-33)

There are three stages in the Christian's growth in the Holy Spirit – graces of the Spirit, gifts of the Spirit, and the glory of the Spirit. The work of the Holy Spirit begins with salvation, when a person is born of the Spirit.[1] The nine graces of the Spirit, called fruit of the Spirit in Galatians, commence growing in the new believer's life as soon as he receives the Lord Jesus into his heart.[2] Next the believer is baptized into the Holy Spirit. Sometimes the New Testament calls this receiving the earnest, or guarantee, of our inheritance in Christ. God's power, revealed as nine miraculous gifts of the Holy Spirit in Corinthians, is now available to the Christian.[3] The glory of the Spirit is His sevenfold fullness, soon to be poured out upon His people. Seven is the number of completeness. At the end of the age the Lord will manifest the fullness and completeness of His power and glory through His Bride. Romans 8:19 will be fulfilled: "For the earnest expectation of the creation eagerly waits for the revealing ('manifestation' – *KJV*) of the sons of God."

The Bible also speaks of Satan's counterfeit of the sevenfold Spirit of God. Jesus taught concerning "seven unclean spirits," which are the fullness of evil (Matt 12:45).

---

[1] John 3:1-8.
[2] Gal 5:22,23.
[3] 1 Cor 12:8-10.

Both Old and New Testaments provide wonderful teachings and illustrations of the three stages of Christian growth. I can summarize some of these illustrations for you in the following chart:

Figure 25: The Graces, Gifts, and Glory of the Holy Spirit

ILLUSTRATION	GRACES 9 fruit of the Spirit (Gal 5:22,23)	GIFTS 9 gifts of the Spirit (1 Cor 12:8-10)	GLORY 7-fold Spirit of God (Rev 1:4; Isa 11:1-3)
Growing in the Holy Spirit	Born of the Spirit (John 3:3,5)	Earnest of the Spirit – down payment, guarantee of inheritance (2 Cor 1:22; Eph 1:13,14)	Fullness of the Spirit (Eph 4:13, 5:18)
Moses' Tabernacle	Outer Court	Holy Place	Holy of Holies
Feasts of Israel	Passover	Pentecost	Tabernacles
Fruitfulness (Matt 13:8-23)	30-fold	60-fold	100-fold
Growing in the Lord (1 Jn 2:12-15)	Children	Young men	Fathers

Zechariah, Isaiah, and Revelation

Teaching concerning the sevenfold Spirit of God is found in three books of the Bible: Zechariah, Isaiah, and Revelation. The main theme of Zechariah's prophecy is "restoration," of Isaiah's "redemption," and, of course, the Book of Revelation is a book of "revelation."

We also find hidden in these three books allusions to the three stages of the Feast of Tabernacles, which are Trumpets, Day of Atonement, and Tabernacles:

1. "Trumpets" in Zechariah – "The Lord God will blow the trumpet" (Zech 9:14).

2. "Day of Atonement" in Isaiah – the "birthing" of the Bride of Christ: "Who has heard such a thing? Who has seen such things? Shall the earth be made to give birth in *one day*? Or shall a nation be born at once? For as soon as Zion was in labor, She gave birth to her children" (Isa 66:8). And: "It shall come to pass in *that day* ... the yoke shall be destroyed because of the anointing" (Isa 10:27 – *KJV*).

3. "Tabernacles" in Revelation – the great harvest: "And another angel came out of the temple, crying with a loud voice to Him who sat on the cloud, 'Thrust in Your sickle and reap, for the time has come for You to reap, for the harvest of the earth is ripe.'

So He who sat on the cloud thrust in His sickle on the earth, and the earth was reaped" (Rev 14:15,16).

We can view this in snapshot form in *Figure 26*.

Figure 26: **The Feast of Tabernacles as Pictured in the Books that Contain References to the Sevenfold Spirit of God**

Book of the Bible	Zechariah	Isaiah	Revelation
Main theme of book	Restoration	Redemption	Revelation
Part of Feast of Tabernacles pictured	Trumpets	Day of Atonement	Tabernacles
Scripture references	Zech 9:14	Isa 66:5-11; 10:27	Rev 14:14-16

The Sevenfold Spirit of God in Zechariah

The first reference to the sevenfold Spirit in Zechariah reads:

> "Hear now, O Joshua the high priest, you and your colleagues who [usually] sit before you – for they are men who are a sign or omen [types of what is to come] – for behold, I will bring forth My servant the Branch.
> For behold, upon the stone which I have set before Joshua, upon that one stone are seven eyes or facets [the all-embracing providence of God and the *sevenfold radiations of the Spirit of God*]. Behold, I will carve upon it its inscription, says the Lord of hosts, and I will remove the iniquity and guilt of this land in a single day." (Zech 3:8,9 – *Amp*)

"I will bring forth My servant the Branch" is, of course, a prophecy concerning the coming Messiah. (This prophecy is repeated in Isaiah 11:1 and Jeremiah 23:5.) The "stone" in verse nine is also prophetic of Messiah. The Lord Jesus said of Himself: "The stone which the builders rejected has become the chief cornerstone."[4] On this one stone are seven eyes, "the sevenfold radiations of the Spirit of God." This, as we will see, is the anointing that was upon Messiah during His earthly ministry. The removal of iniquity in one day is a prophecy concerning the fulfillment of the Day of Atonement to the Church, the day when the Lord's "glorious church,"[5] His "holy nation, His own special people"[6] will be cleansed, and receive His fullness.

This stone with seven eyes is also spoken of in Zechariah 4:10:

---

[4] Matt 21:42, quoting Psa 118:22.
[5] Eph 5:27.
[6] 1 Pet 2:9.

> "Who [with reason] despises *the day* of small things? For these seven shall rejoice when they see the plummet in the hand of Zerubbabel. [These seven] are the eyes of the Lord which run to and fro throughout the whole earth." (*Amp*)

This verse contains another reference to "the day," which again, I believe, is the day of fulfillment in the Church of the Day of Atonement. The Lord who fulfilled the day of Passover and the day of Pentecost to His Church will also make the Day of Atonement a glorious experience for His people. In this verse He speaks of the rejoicing associated with the Feast of Tabernacles, especially when the plummet is seen.

A plummet is a line used in building to test, measure and adjust the perpendicular part of a structure. (The context of the book of Zechariah is the rebuilding of the temple of God after "the 70- years' captivity" in Babylon.)

In Revelation chapter 11 we read the true temple of God, the Church, is examined by being measured. The plummet? The measuring line? It is "the measure of the stature of the fullness of Christ" (Eph 4:13). (The last sentence of Zechariah 4:10 is quoted in Revelation 5:6.)

The Sevenfold Spirit of God in Revelation

There are four references in the Book of Revelation to the seven Spirits of God, or, what I prefer to call "the sevenfold Spirit of God."[7]

1. **Revelation 1:4 – "John, to the seven churches which are in Asia: Grace to you and peace from Him who is and who was and who is to come, and from the seven Spirits who are before His throne."**

Very early in his vision of the Lord, John speaks of the seven Spirits who are before Christ's throne. This emphasizes the importance of this great subject. Revelation 1:4 also has a practical application. We must spend time at the throne of God to receive this unique and powerful anointing.

2. **Revelation 3:1 – "And to the angel of the church in Sardis write, 'These things says He who has the seven Spirits of God and the seven stars ...'"**

Jesus has the seven Spirits of God. And the stars – God's ministers – need this sevenfold anointing to bring the Church to the fullness of Christ (Eph 4:11-13). The Psalmist wrote that God "makes ... His ministers flames of fire" (Psa 104:4–*NAS*). On the day of Pentecost there were 120 fires burning, but one Holy Spirit. May the fire that fell that day never go out![8]

---

[7] *NIV – margin.*
[8] Acts 2:3.

THE SEVENFOLD SPIRIT OF GOD

3. **Revelation 4:5 – "And from the throne proceeded lightings, thunderings, and voices. Seven lamps of fire were burning before the throne, which are the seven Spirits of God."**

The phrase "seven lamps of fire" is a clear reference to the lampstand in the tabernacle of Moses. The lampstand was the only source of light in the Holy Place. One lampstand, made from one piece of solid gold, but with seven fiery lamps. Always remember the Lord Jesus is emphasizing in the first three chapters of Revelation that the primary ministry of a local church is to be a lampstand – a fire shining brightly in the darkness.

4. **Revelation 5:6 – "And I looked, and behold, in the midst of the throne and of the four living creatures, and in the midst of the elders, stood a Lamb as though it had been slain, having seven horns and seven eyes; which are the seven Spirits of God sent out into all the earth."**

The Lamb which had been slain, and lives again, is pictured as having "seven horns" (fullness of authority) and "seven eyes" (fullness of knowledge, wisdom and power) "which are the seven Spirits of God sent out into all the earth." One Lamb; seven eyes. The Sevenfold Spirit of God, now before the throne, will very soon be manifested in Christ's Bride throughout the earth.

The Sevenfold Spirit of God in Isaiah

To further identify the sevenfold Spirit of God we must now go to Isaiah, the book of redemption. Isaiah 11:1 opens with the wonderful prophecy:

> "There shall come forth a Rod (*margin*, 'Shoot') from the stem (*margin*, 'stock or trunk') of Jesse,
> And a Branch shall grow (*margin*, 'be fruitful') out of his roots."

This is, of course, the same Branch spoken of by the prophet Zechariah. It is a prophecy concerning the coming Messiah. Isaiah 11:2 continues:

> "The Spirit of the Lord shall rest upon Him."

When our Saviour came from Heaven to earth, He was conceived by the Holy Spirit. Thus He was born of the Holy Spirit from His mother's womb. When Jesus was baptized in water, the Bible records, "while He prayed, the heaven was opened, and the Holy Spirit descended in bodily form like a dove upon Him" (Luke 3:21,22). Jesus was "filled with the Holy Spirit" at the Jordan. He was "led by the Spirit." He returned to Galilee "in the power of the Spirit."[9] When He came to Nazareth, He went "into the synagogue on the Sabbath day, and stood up to read. And He was handed the book of the prophet Isaiah. And when He had opened the book, He found the place where it was written:

---

[9] Luke 4:1,14.

> 'The Spirit of the Lord is upon Me
> Because He has anointed Me
> To preach the gospel to the poor;
> He has sent Me to heal the brokenhearted,
> To proclaim liberty to the captives
> And recovery of sight to the blind,
> To set at liberty those who are oppressed;
> To proclaim the acceptable year of the Lord.'" (Luke 4:16-18)

[Here Jesus is quoting from Isaiah chapter 61, verses 1 and 2. Notice at that time He did not quote all of Isaiah 61:2. He will fulfill the next phrase, "to proclaim ... the day of vengeance of our God" at His Second Coming. In Luke chapter four He quotes only the phrases that apply to the ministry of His first coming.]

Doctor Luke continues the narrative:

> "Then He closed the book, and gave it back to the attendant and sat down. And the eyes of all who were in the synagogue were fixed on Him. And He began to say to them, 'Today this Scripture is fulfilled in your hearing.'" (Luke 4:20,21)

Jesus boldly proclaimed, right there in the synagogue located in the town in which He was brought up, that He was the fulfillment of Isaiah's redemptive prophecy!

In chapter 11 verse two, Isaiah had prophesied that the Spirit of the Lord would be upon Messiah. Then, in verses two through four he teaches the sevenfold qualities of the Spirit of the Lord. During His earthly ministry, Jesus radiated every one of these seven:

1. **"The Spirit of wisdom"**: Paul teaches that Christ Jesus "became for us wisdom from God."[10] To the Colossians he wrote that all the treasures of wisdom are hidden in Christ.[11] In His life and teachings while here on earth, the Lord Jesus was the epitome of wisdom.

2. **"The Spirit of understanding"**: John records that "[Jesus] knew all men, and had no need that anyone should testify of man, for He knew what was in man" (John 2:24,25).

3. **"The Spirit of counsel"**: One of the great prophetic titles of Messiah is "Counsellor."[12] He demonstrated this as He counselled His disciples, Nicodemus, the Samaritan woman at the well, the woman taken in adultery, and countless others.

---

[10] 1 Cor 1:30.
[11] Col 2:3.
[12] Isa 9:6.

4. **"The Spirit of might"**: Another prophetic title of Messiah is "Mighty God."[13] Concerning the Spirit of might upon the Lord's Christ, Peter preached at the house of Cornelius:

> "How God anointed Jesus of Nazareth with the Holy Spirit and with power, who went about doing good and healing all who were oppressed by the devil, for God was with Him." (Acts 10:38)

5. **"The Spirit of knowledge"**: "Christ, in whom are hidden all the treasures of …knowledge." (Col 2:3)

6. **"The Spirit of the fear of the Lord"**: Luke the physician records that on a number of occasions when the Lord Jesus healed someone, those who witnessed the miracle were filled with fear and awe. For example, when Jesus forgave the sins of the lame man and healed him, "they were all amazed, and they glorified God and were filled with fear, saying, 'We have seen strange things today!'" (Luke 5:26). When Jesus raised the widow's son to life, "fear seized them all (*margin*), and they glorified God, saying, 'A great prophet has risen up among us' and, 'God has visited His people'" (Luke 7:16). Again, when Jesus cast devils out of the Gadarene demoniac, the whole multitude "were seized with great fear" (Luke 8:37).

7. **"[The Spirit of] righteousness"**: Anointed with the fullness of the Spirit of righteousness, Jesus also became our righteousness (1 Cor 1:30).

When Jesus was filled with the Holy Spirit, the Spirit of the Lord came upon Him, and He was anointed with the Sevenfold Spirit of God. His was a unique and special anointing. The intensity of this anointing was greater than any person had ever received. Jesus Christ was the first man on earth to be anointed with the Sevenfold Spirit of God. David had prophesied of Messiah:

> "You love righteousness and hate wickedness;
> Therefore God, Your God, has anointed You
> With the oil of gladness *more* than Your companions." (Psa 45:7)

When He was on earth, by the power of the Sevenfold Spirit of the Lord, Jesus ministered, died, and rose again.[14] He has become "the Head over all things to the church, which is His body, the fullness of Him who fills all in all" (Eph 1:21, 22).

When, as high priest, Aaron's head was anointed, the oil ran down onto his priestly garments.[15] In the same way, the anointing poured upon our Great High Priest, Jesus Christ, will run down to His body, the Church. The Sevenfold Spirit of the Lord that anointed Christ will flow down upon His Bride.

---

[13] Isa 9:6.
[14] Acts 10:38; Heb 9:14; Rom 8:11.
[15] Psa 133:2.

The Graces, Gifts, and Glory of the Spirit

At present, the Church enjoys the *graces* of the Holy Spirit – love, joy, peace, longsuffering, kindness, goodness, faithfulness, gentleness, self-control – all the fruit of the Spirit.[16]

The Church also enjoys the *gifts* of the Holy Spirit listed in 1 Corinthians 12:8-10. Wonderful though these are, when the Lord fulfills the Day of Atonement to His Bride, she will be anointed with the Spirit of the Lord – the Sevenfold Spirit of God! The miraculous gifts of the Spirit are special, but they are fragmentary. When the Spirit of the Lord – the fullness of the Spirit – the Sevenfold Spirit of God anoints Christ's Church, God's power will be continuously seen. After the Day of Atonement, during the Feast of Tabernacles, God's *glory* will be manifested as never before. The contrast between the gifts and the glory of the Spirit is like the difference between a faucet and a river. A faucet is turned on and off. A mighty river flows constantly. I am not, in any way, belittling the gifts of the Spirit. But the Sevenfold Spirit will be so much more glorious.

Contrasts between the Gifts and the Sevenfold Spirit

We thank God for the gift of "the word of wisdom." Because wisdom is knowledge applied, a word of wisdom is a miraculous word from God concerning the future. Not so much words of prediction, but powerful insight into God's future plans and purposes. But when God's people are anointed with the Sevenfold Spirit of God, the Spirit of wisdom will be manifested.

The gift of "discerning of spirits" is the miraculous ability to perceive whether the Holy Spirit, the human spirit, or an evil spirit is at work when a miracle, or what is claimed to be a miracle, occurs. But when God's people are anointed with the Sevenfold Spirit of God, the **Spirit of understanding** will be experienced, causing Christ's Bride to have the same level of perception and discernment that the Master had during His earthly ministry.

The gift of "prophecy" is God speaking to His people through supernaturally inspired speech, in a language known to the speaker, giving "help, encouragement, and comfort."[17] But the anointing of the **Spirit of counsel** will cause a river of encouraging and comforting words to flow.

The gift of "miracles" is the supernatural ability, given by the Holy Spirit, to do miracles in the Name of the Lord Jesus Christ – miracles that glorify Him. The gift of "healings" is the power of God to heal the sick. We praise God for these gifts. But when the Church is anointed with the Sevenfold Spirit of God, she will receive the **Spirit of might**.

The "word of knowledge" is a revelation of facts from the past, or the present, that could not be known by natural means. Can you imagine what will happen when God's people are anointed with the **Spirit of knowledge**?

---

[16] Gal 5:22,23.
[17] 1 Cor 14:3 – *TEV*.

The "gift of tongues" is the miraculous ability to speak to God,[18] glorifying and magnifying Him,[19] in a language not known to the speaker. In the church assembly this gift must always be accompanied by the gift of "interpretation of tongues." This gift sometimes operates as "varieties of tongues (or languages)."[20] This occurs when a Spirit-filled Christian speaks in a language he has never learned. When this happens, the fear of God falls upon those who hear. This is what took place on the fulfillment of the day of Pentecost.[21] And when the Church is anointed with the Sevenfold Spirit of God, the **Spirit of the fear of the Lord** will be manifested in a greater, more powerful measure.

The "gift of faith" is the miraculous ability to believe for, and receive, miracles. The "gift of faith" receives miracles. (The "gift of miracles" does miracles.) Abraham's faith was accounted to him as righteousness.[22] And when operating in the Biblical way, the gift of faith always focuses attention on the righteousness of God. The anointing of the Sevenfold Spirit of God will be an anointing with the **Spirit of righteousness**. Faith levels and assurance will increase,[23] the Church will be stable and immovable,[24] and the purity and righteousness of the Lord will be seen as never before.

As the Bride of Christ enjoys the fulfillment of the Feast of Tabernacles, she will experience this prophecy of Isaiah:

> "The Lord is exalted, for He dwells on high;
> He has filled Zion with justice and righteousness.
> Wisdom and knowledge will be the stability of your times,
> And the strength of salvation;
> The fear of the Lord is His treasure." (Isa 33:5,6)

This contrast between the nine gifts of the Spirit, and the Sevenfold Spirit of God is summarized in Figure 27 on the next page.

The Seven Compound-Redemptive Names of God

As we have seen, the Sevenfold Spirit of the Lord anointed Jesus Christ for His earthly ministry. This anointing demonstrated the Father's Name and Nature in the Son. Jesus confirmed this many times:
- "I have come in My Father's Name." (John 5:43)
- "The works that I do in My Father's name, they bear witness of Me." (John 10:25)
- "I and My Father are one." (John 10:30)
- "I have revealed Your name." (John 17:6 – *margin*)

---

[18] 1 Cor 14:2.
[19] Acts 2:11, 10:46.
[20] 1 Cor 12:28.
[21] Acts 2:6-12.
[22] Gen 17:10; Rom 4:3.
[23] Luke 17:5; Isa 32:17.
[24] 1 Cor 15:58.

Figure 27: Comparison of the nine Gifts of the Spirit with the Sevenfold Spirit of God

Nine Gifts of the Spirit	Sevenfold Spirit of God
Feast of Pentecost	**Feast of Tabernacles**
Word of wisdom	1. Spirit of wisdom
Discerning of spirits	2. Spirit of understanding
Prophecy	3. Spirit of counsel
Miracles and Healings	4. Spirit of might
Word of knowledge	5. Spirit of knowledge
Tongues and Interpretation	6. Spirit of the fear of the Lord
Faith	7. Spirit of righteousness

The apostle Paul also declared: "In Him dwells all the fullness of the Godhead in bodily form" (Col 2:9 – *margin*).

Jesus prayed to His Father: "The glory which You gave Me I have given them" (John 17:22). In Paul's words: "Christ in you, the hope of glory" (Col 1:27).

The redemptive Names and Nature of God the Father are shown in His seven Hebrew compound Names. These Old Testament Names reveal God the Father meeting every need of sinful man, from his lost state to his total and complete redemption.

Thus we see a wonderful progression as we study the Godhead:

- The Sevenfold compound-redemptive Names of **the Father**;

- The Sevenfold Name and Nature of the Father manifest in **the Son**;

- The Sevenfold fullness of redemption given to His Bride by **the Spirit**.

This truth is illustrated in *Figure 28* on the next page.

Figure 28: **The Relationship of the Sevenfold Spirit of God with the Seven Compound-Redemptive Names of the Lord**

Nine Gifts of the Spirit	Seven-fold Spirit of God	Seven Compound-Redemptive Names of God
Word of wisdom	1. Wisdom	1. **Jehovah-Jireh**: "The Lord will see," or "provide." (Gen 22:13,14)
Discerning of spirits	2. Understanding	2. **Jehovah-Shalom**: "The Lord send peace," or "The Lord our peace." (Judg 6:24)
Prophecy	3. Counsel	3. **Jehovah-Raah**: "The Lord my Shepherd." (Psa 23:1)
Miracles and Healings	4. Might	4. **Jehovah-Rapha**: "The Lord Who heals." (Exo 15:26)
Word of knowledge	5. Knowledge	5. **Jehovah-Nissi**: "The Lord our Banner." (Exo 17:15)
Tongues and Interpretation	6. Fear of the Lord	6. **Jehovah-Shammah**: "The Lord is present," or "The Lord is there." (Eze 48:35)
Faith	7. Righteousness	7. **Jehovah-Tsidkenu**: "The Lord our righteous-ness." (Jer 23:6)

The Seven "I AMs" of Jesus

Nearly 20 years ago, I was teaching the Book of Revelation to the church we pioneered in San Diego, when I received the following letter from Meri, one of my students:

"Pastor Graham,

"I was very moved by your teaching in the Revelation class on the seven-fold Spirit of God and the relationship to the Gifts of the Spirit and the seven Names of God.

"As you spoke I feel the Lord revealed another application of the seven Spirits – the relationship to the seven "I AMs" of Jesus in the Gospel of John. Thank you for allowing me to share."

Figure 29 on the next page is Meri's chart with a few minor additions. I appreciate her diligent study of God's Word. This application sheds further light on the Sevenfold Spirit of God with regard to the Person, anointing and ministry of our Lord Jesus Christ:

Figure 29: **The Relationship between the seven-fold Spirit of God, the Compound-Redemptive Names of God, and the "I AMs" of Jesus**

Seven-fold Spirit of God	Seven Compound-Redemptive Names of God	Seven "I Ams" of Jesus in John's Gospel
1. Wisdom	Jehovah-Jireh – "Provider"	1. **Bread of life** (John 6:35)
2. Understanding	Jehovah-Shalom – "Peace"	2. **Door (salvation brings peace)** (John 10:7,9)
3. Counsel	Jehovah-Raah – "Shepherd"	3. **Good Shepherd** (John 10:11)
4. Might	Jehovah-Rapha – "Healer"	4. **Resurrection and Life** (John 11:25)
5. Knowledge	Jehovah-Nissi – "Banner"	5. **Light** (John 8:12)
6. Fear of the Lord	Jehovah-Shammah – "Present"	6. **Way, Truth, and Life** (John 14:6)
7. Righteousness	Jehovah-Tsidkenu– "Righteousness"	7. **Vine** (John 15:1-5)

Grace and Peace

> "To the seven churches …Grace to you and peace from Him who is and who was and who is to come, and from the seven Spirits who are before His throne." (Rev 1:4)

Notice that both the Lord Jesus Christ, and the Sevenfold Spirit minister grace and peace. In this chapter we have only had room to skim the surface of the depths of this vast subject, the Sevenfold Spirit of God. But I trust you have been blessed and encouraged. God is raising up a Church which will be anointed, as Jesus was, with all of God's fullness. This Church will be on fire for Jesus, and shine gloriously and brightly in the dark days to come. This Church, anointed with the Sevenfold Spirit of God, will minister grace and peace to all who will "hear what the Spirit is saying to the churches."

We now move on to the detailed appearance of the Lord Jesus in Revelation chapter one.

PART THREE   THE CHRIST

Chapter 16

Here Comes the Bridegroom! (II)

Revelation chapter 1 (continued)

The Christ, The Church, The Christian

As we continue our study of Revelation chapter one, we are going to do so under three headings:

- I.   The Christ
- II. The Church
- III. The Christian

I. THE CHRIST (1:13-16)

John, in the Spirit on the Lord's day, heard behind him a loud voice, as of a trumpet. He turned to see the voice, and saw the Lord standing in the midst of seven golden lampstands. In the words of Charles Haddon Spurgeon, John saw "The Christ of Patmos."[1]

Jesus reveals Himself in Revelation chapter one as the "Son of Man" (verse 13). This title speaks of the fact that the Word was made flesh, and dwelt among us.[2] It emphasizes His humanity. In the book of Daniel, the Old Testament companion book of Revelation, Daniel also describes seeing the Son of Man:

> "I was watching in the night visions
> And behold, One like the Son of Man,
> Coming with the clouds of heaven!
> He came to the Ancient of Days,
> And they brought Him near before Him.
> Then to Him was given dominion and glory and a kingdom…"
> (Dan 7:13,14)

---

[1] Spurgeon, *op.cit.* Sermon title – page 7.
[2] John 1:12.

On the other hand, Christ's title, the "Son of God," speaks of His deity. He always was, is, and always will be, God.[3]

The phrase "the Son of Man" occurs 85 times in the Gospels with regard to the Master, and of these, 83 times it is He Who is speaking. In the Gospels Jesus called Himself the Son of Man with regards to His mission ("the Son of Man has come to seek and to save that which was lost"[4]), His death ("the Son of Man [will] be three days and three nights in the heart of he earth"[5]), His resurrection ("the Son of Man ... will rise again"[6]), and His Second Coming ("Therefore you also be ready, for the Son of Man is coming at an hour you do not expect."[7])

The Bible says the first martyr of the Church, Stephen, as he was being stoned to death, saw Jesus as the Son of Man:

> "But he, being full of the Holy Spirit, gazed into heaven and saw the glory of God, and Jesus standing at the right hand of God,
> and said, 'Look! I see the heavens opened and the Son of Man standing at the right hand of God!'" (Acts 8:55,56)

In Revelation chapter one the Lord Jesus is about to commend, correct, and command His churches. He appears as the Son of Man, because, while He lived here on earth, He identified with frail flesh. He was tempted, tired, thirsty, hungry, sad, disappointed, mocked, rejected, and finally crucified. Therefore, "He can sympathize with our weaknesses."[8]

The Appearance of Jesus – the High Priest of the Churches

1. His Garment:

> "The Son of Man, clothed with a garment down to the feet." (1:13)

In the Old Testament, the priestly garments of Aaron, the High Priest, were called "garments for glory and for beauty."[9] Into the High Priest's garments were woven bright and beautiful colours – blue, purple, and scarlet.

But on the Day of Atonement the High Priest was commanded to wear "the holy linen tunic ... linen trousers ...a linen sash ... the linen turban" (Lev 16:1-4). When our Lord Jesus Christ, our Great High Priest after the order of Melchizedek, came to earth, He humbled Himself, and put aside the glory of heaven to become a

---

[3] Titus 2:13.
[4] Luke 19:10.
[5] Matt 12:40.
[6] Matt 20:18,19.
[7] Luke 12:40.
[8] Heb 4:15.
[9] Exo 28:2.

man. To pay the full price for our atonement, He "became obedient to the point of death, even the death of the cross" (Phil 2:5-8).

Ezekiel had a vision of a Man clothed in linen, leading five other men in the sealing of the righteous (Eze 9:1-7). Daniel had a vision of a Man clothed in linen (Dan 10:5-9, 12:7). The body of Jesus was wrapped in linen when He was taken down from the cross (Luke 23:53). The seven angels that poured out the seven plagues were "clothed in pure bright linen" (Rev 15:6). The Bride of Christ is "arrayed in fine linen, clean and bright" (Rev 19:8). "The armies in heaven, [are] clothed in fine linen (*margin*, 'pure white linen'), white and clean." (Rev 19:14) "The fine linen is the righteousness of saints." (Rev 19:8b – *KJV*) The Bible teaches Christ is our righteousness (1 Cor 1:30).

His garment, then, speaks to us of the purity we can receive through faith in Him.

The garment to the foot also suggests the right of the Lord Jesus Christ to govern and judge. This robe is not only His attire as our Great High Priest – but also His robe of judicial authority. He is about to judge and to give His verdict on the condition of the seven churches.

2. His Girdle (Chest band, or Sash):

"Girded about the chest with a golden band ('sash' – *NIV*)" (1:13).

The Greek word for "girdle" or "band" is *zone*, from which we get our English word "zone," meaning "girdle, belt, area, or encircling an area with a band or stripe." This sash speaks to us of seven major aspects of our wonderful Lord Jesus.

i. His Deity

First and foremost, it is a golden sash. In tabernacle language, the fact that it is made of gold speaks of His deity. This golden girdle reminds us that although John sees our Lord Jesus Christ as the Son of Man, He is the Eternal Son of God.

ii. His Service

This belt or sash also speaks to us of service. Even today in India, waiters and doormen at hotels still proudly wear their brightly-coloured, identifying sashes.

The classic example of the relationship between the girdle and serving is when the Son of Man washed His disciples' feet. The Bible says Jesus "laid aside His garments, took a towel ('servant's towel' – *Amp*) and girded Himself" (John 13:3).

In the same way Jesus commanded His disciples to remember Him in the breaking of bread, which we still do to this day, He also commanded His disciples to wash one another's feet:

"For I have given you an example, that you should do as I have done to you." (John 13:15)

The observance of foot-washing is an important sacrament demonstrating humility and service in the Church.[10] How sad that many Christians have never participated in this blessed sacrament!

iii. His Readiness to Help Us

Thirdly, the fact that our Lord is girt about with a golden girdle speaks of His readiness to help us, and act on our behalf today. A man in the East uses the girdle to bind up his long flowing robes. Girdles are not usually worn indoors. It is only when he is outdoors – walking, moving about, or engaged in manual labour – that he adjusts his robe with his sash. So the fact that Jesus has a golden girdle signifies He is still ready and able to serve and help those who are His servants. Blessed thought indeed!

iv. His Righteousness and Faithfulness

Fourthly, this girdle-belt indicates that whether as servant or judge, our Lord Jesus will always be righteous and faithful in His dealings with His people. As Isaiah says:

> "Righteousness will be his belt
> and faithfulness the sash around his waist." (Isa 11:5 – *NIV*)

Later, the prophet gives further understanding of the symbolism of faithfulness and authority signified by the robe and girdle (sash):

> "On that day I will send for my servant Eliakim son of Hilkiah;
> I will invest him with your robe, gird him with your sash; and hand over your authority to him. He shall be a father to the inhabitants of Jerusalem and the people of Judah.

---

[10] A "sacrament" is a religious act or ceremony that often uses natural things to demonstrate spiritual truth. The observance of a sacrament – that which is done outwardly – is a sign or symbol of the inner workings of God's redemption and grace. Sacraments are not formal, lifeless church traditions, but acts, remembrances and ceremonies that demonstrate Biblical covenant relationships with God, and others. The eight sacraments to be observed in the New Testament Church, each a celebration of covenant, are:

1. Worship
2. Baptism in water
3. Communion – the breaking of bread
4. Foot-washing (1 Tim 5:10)
5. Confirmation (Acts 14:22, 15:32)
6. Marriage
7. Dedication of children
8. Giving of tithes and offerings

I will lay the key of the house of David on his shoulder; what he opens no man shall shut, and what he shuts no man shall open." (Isa 22:20-22 – *NEB*)[11]

v. His Majesty and Authority

Have you ever seen on television pictures of the Queen of England at special State occasions? When she opens the British parliament with her speech from the throne, in addition to her crown and scepter, she wears a regal golden sash from her shoulder to her waist. This sash sets her apart as the head of the royal family of Great Britain, and sovereign over the nations she rules.

The sash Jesus wears in John's vision speaks of the fact that He is King of kings and Lord of lords, and He rules and reigns supreme over all – from the vastness of the universe to the smallest details in our lives.

vi. His Supply

The next thing to note about this band, or sash, is this – it was usually hollow, and therefore served as a purse, as well as an article of clothing.[12] It was the place where a man kept his money. It was his purse, his "wallet." This golden girdle then may represent the "purse" of the Lord Jesus. The fact that it is golden can assure us it is full of wealth unequalled, and riches unsurpassed. Jesus has everything we need in abundant supply. We can safely trust and depend on Him. On August 31, 1959, I resigned from secular employment, which had provided me with a weekly paycheck. Ever since, Pamela and I have lived by faith in Him. Yes, there have been trials and testings. But the Lord of the harvest has been faithful. He has never failed to supply our needs.[13]

vii. His Love

Lastly, notice the placement of His girdle. It is around the chest of our Lord, close to His heart, thus speaking of His abounding love for His children. In the words of Dr G. Campbell Morgan:

> "Jesus moves amid the churches with the robe reaching to His feet,
> marking the fact that He is the sole Governor of His people, having the right
> to pass His verdict upon their service, and reward or punish them as He will.
> The golden girdle about the breasts reveals the fact that every judgment He
> pronounces, and every sentence He passes, is based upon His infinite love
> and faithfulness. Christ is the one supreme Head, Ruler, Governor, among

---

[11] Hilkiah was the father of Eliakim, who was overseer of the king's household in the reign of King Hezekiah.
[12] Called "money belts" (Matt10:9; Mark 6:8).
[13] Phil 4:18,19.

His people, and all His headship, and His rule, and His government are based upon His infinite and unfailing compassion."[14]

[Revelation chapter 15 tells us the seven angels that came out of the temple having the seven plagues, are also described as "clothed in pure bright linen, and having their chests girded with golden bands" (Rev 15:7). They are sent by God.]

3. His Head

"His head and hair were white like wool, as white as snow" (1:14).

The Lord Jesus Christ is the Head of the Church:

"He [God the Father, verse 17] gave Him [Christ] to be head over all things to the church,
which is His body, the fullness of Him who fills all in all." (Eph 1:22,23)

"He (the Son, verse 13) is the head of the body, the church." (Col 1:18)

Not only is our Lord Jesus the Head of the Church. He is the Head of all principality and power:

"For in Him dwells all the fullness of the Godhead bodily (*margin*, 'in bodily form');
And you are complete in Him, who is the head of all principality and power (*margin*, 'rule and authority')." (Col 1:9,10)

The head, of course, is the source of all intelligence, bodily control and direction. It is the command center of life.

The Word of God instructs us not to stop "holding on to Christ, who is the head. Under Christ's control the whole body is nourished and held together by its joints and ligaments, and grows as God wants it to grow." (Col 2:19 – *TEV*)

In Solomon's song the Shulamite describes the head of her Beloved King: "His head is like the finest gold."[15] We will see the further significance of this when we superimpose John's description of Jesus upon the tabernacle of Moses.

When the Lord Jesus appears in Revelation 19:12, "on His head were many crowns." He is indeed Head over all!

---

[14] Morgan, *op.cit.* – page 14.
[15] Song 5:11.

4. His Hair

Just as measurements, substances, and created things have meaning in Scripture, so do colours. White always speaks of righteousness. This is established in both Old and New Testaments. Isaiah the prophet said:

> "'Come now, and let us reason together,'
> Says the Lord,
> 'Though your sins are like scarlet,
> They shall be as white as snow;
> Though they are red like crimson,
> They shall be as wool.'" (Isa 1:18)

As we have already seen, concerning the Bride of Christ, Revelation 19:8 says:

"And to her was granted that she should be arrayed in fine linen, clean and white (*margin*, 'bright'): for the fine linen is the righteousness of saints." (*KJV*)

We should never forget the only righteousness we have is our Lord Jesus Christ. We must be constantly reminded that our righteousness is in Christ alone:

"But of him are ye in Christ Jesus, who of God is made unto us wisdom and righteousness, and sanctification, and redemption:
That, according as it is written, He that glorieth, let him glory in the Lord."
(1 Cor 1:30,31 – *KJV*)

There are three other things we can learn from our Lord's appearing with "hair white like wool, as white as snow." Firstly, the Bible has this to say about gray (white) hair:

> "The splendor of old men is their gray head." (Prov 20:29)

> "The silver-haired head is a crown of glory,
> If it is found in the way of righteousness." (Prov 16:31)

We are commanded to observe and honour those with white hair:

> "You shall rise (*margin*, 'observe') before the gray headed and honor the presence of an old man." (Lev 19:32)

This is not just because of their age – but because of the wisdom they have acquired from life's experiences. Jesus is about to judge the seven churches. He will judge with wisdom.[16] He will judge with righteousness, according to the prophet's words, "with righteousness He shall judge."[17]

Secondly, white hair can sometimes be the result of deep grief. For Jesus, as the Son of Man, was "A Man of sorrows and acquainted with grief."[18]

In the Song of Solomon the Beloved King's hair is described by his bride: "His locks are wavy, and black as a raven."[19] But when John sees the Beloved King, he sees His hair "white like wool, as white as snow." Why the difference?

Jesus conducted His earthly ministry between the ages of about 30 and 33 years. Yet the Jews said he looked nearly 50 years old.[20] Did He look older than he was because of the sorrow He bore even before the cross? We know that on the cross "He [bore] our griefs and carried our sorrows."[21] Could that be one of the reasons for His appearance to John with white hair?

It is a medical fact that extreme shock or trauma can cause a person's hair to turn white rapidly and prematurely. It was observed in the Second World War that during the German blitz of England, many who saw the death and devastation in London's streets turned white-haired almost overnight.

When we went through the tragedy and trauma of our beautiful 24-year-old daughter Debbie being killed by a drunk driver, my hair turned white very quickly.

Thirdly, we must note the similarity between the visions of Daniel and John:

> "I watched till thrones were put in place,
> And the Ancient of Days was seated;
> His garment was white as snow,
> And the hair of His head was like pure wool." (Dan 7:9)

Here our blessed Lord Jesus is called "the Ancient of Days." He is without beginning or ending. As the Eternal Son of God He does not age! Again, His white hair speaks to us of His eternal experience and wisdom.

In Revelation chapter one, the Son of Man, standing in the midst of the seven churches, is about to pronounce judgment upon them – with wisdom and righteousness. He *is* wisdom and righteousness.[22]

---

[16] The British custom is for lawyers and judges to wear white woollen wigs and black gowns while officiating in court. This indicates their authority and wisdom in upholding the laws of the land. This custom is also observed in our home country of New Zealand.
[17] Isa 11:4.
[18] Isa 53:3.
[19] Song 5:11.
[20] John 8:57.
[21] Isa 53:4.
[22] 1 Cor 1:30,31.

5. His Eyes

"His eyes [were] like a flame of fire." (1:14)

The Bible has much to say about God and fire. In fact, it says, "Our God *is* a consuming fire" (Heb 12:29).

The Bible also has much to say about God's eyes: "His eyes [were] like torches of fire" (Dan 10:6). "His eyes were like a flame of fire." (Rev 19:12)

As Jesus prepares to judge His churches, His piercing eyes of fire see everything. Nothing is hidden from His eyes. The wise man said:

> "The eyes of the Lord are in every place,
> Keeping watch on the evil and the good." (Prov 15:3)

And the writer to the Hebrews warns:

> "There is no creature hidden from His sight, but all things are naked and open to the eyes of Him to whom we must give account." (Heb 4:13)

The challenge to us is this: God is looking for those who will go on to maturity and perfection in Him:

> "For the eyes of the Lord run to and fro throughout the whole earth, to shew himself strong in the behalf of them whose heart is perfect toward him."
> (2 Chr 16:9 – *KJV*)

6. His Feet

"His feet were like fine brass, as if refined in a furnace … and when I saw Him, I fell at His feet as dead." (1:15, 17)

As we learned in our study of Moses' tabernacle, brass speaks of judgment against sin and self. In Bible times fine brass – an alloy of two-thirds copper and one-third zinc – was made by heating and mixing the metals at extremely high temperatures in a fiery cauldron.

It is no wonder John saw the feet of the Lord as brass. For this is what the Bible says about the nail-scarred feet of Christ in His resurrection and ascension glory:

> "He raised Him from the dead and seated Him at His right hand in the heavenly place,
> far above all principality and power and might and dominion, and every name that is named, not only in this age but also in that which is to come. And He put all things under His feet." (Eph 1:20-22)

These are the feet about to walk through the churches, stamping out everything that displeases Him. These are the feet at which John fell down as dead.

7. His Voice

"His voice [was] as the sound of many waters." (1:15)

In our missionary travels we have been privileged to visit some of the most awesome sights and sounds of God's creation. I instantly recall Niagara Falls as I think of John hearing the voice of the Lord as the sound of many waters.

Pamela and I were provided with raincoats as we joined a group aboard a small boat that went very close to the base of the Falls. No other voice could be heard. For the thunderous sound of the powerful waters was overwhelming.

The Lord is about to speak to the churches. He will speak with resounding clarity, drowning out all other voices.

John says that he turned to *see* the voice that spoke with him. Having turned, he saw the seven lampstands, which are the voice of God on the earth – and the Son of Man, the voice of God to the Church.

8. His Hand

"He had in His right hand seven stars … He laid His right hand on me." (1:16:17)

As we have seen, the Lord tells John these stars are God's anointed messengers – pastors – of the seven churches to whom He is about to speak. It is important to note these messengers of the seven churches are in His hand.

Every church leader should walk humbly, knowing, "It is a fearful thing to fall into the hands of the living God" (Heb 10:11). And every church member should obey the command, "Do not touch My anointed ones, and do my prophets no harm" (Psa 105:15).

We will discuss the significance of the Lord laying His right hand on John when we look at John's reaction to the vision He saw.

9. His Mouth

"Out of His mouth went a sharp two-edged sword."(1:16)

This sharp, two-edged sword is, of course, the Word of God:

> "For the word of God is living and powerful, and sharper than any two-edged sword, piercing even to the division of soul and spirit, and of joints and marrow, and is a discerner of the thoughts and intents of the heart." (Heb 4:12)

This sword divides between soul and spirit – between that which originates with the carnal desires of man, and that which originates with the Holy Spirit moving in a believer's spirit that is kept clean by the blood of the Lamb. Just as, after examination, the animals offered in sacrifice upon the brazen altar were cut and divided by the blade of the priest, so the sword of the Spirit examines and separates each thought and intent of our hearts.

The Greek word used here for "discern" appears only in this verse, and nowhere else in the New Testament. *Kritikos* signifies that which relates to judging (*krino*, "to judge"). From this Greek word we get our English words "critic" and "critical." God's Word passes judgment on everything we purpose or think.

Not only does the Lord wield this sword through the seven churches. In Revelation 19:15 it says of Him, "Out of His mouth goes a sharp (*margin*, 'sharp two-edged') sword, that with it He should strike the nations."

I like to think of this two-edged sword representing the judgment of God on one side of the blade, and the mercy of God on the other.

This sword is an essential part of every Christian's armour: "Take ... the sword of the Spirit, which is the word of God" (Eph 6:17). No soldier of the cross will be an overcomer without his sword!

10. His Countenance

"His countenance was like the sun shining in its strength." (1:16)

The Greek word used here, *opsis,* is not usually translated as "face," but "appearance." His whole appearance was like the sun shining in its strength. When we considered the subject "Sun, Moon and Stars,"[23] we saw that the sun speaks to us of the glory of God the Father. Here in Revelation the Son is reflecting the glory of His Father. The prophecy of Malachi is being fulfilled:

> "But to you who fear My name
> The Sun of Righteousness shall arise
> With healing in His wings." (Mal 4:2)

This glory seen by John in Revelation chapter one is the same glory he had seen with Peter and James when Jesus was transfigured before them: "His face shone like the sun, and His clothes became as white as the light."[24]

---

[23] See Chapter 10, "God's Week."
[24] Matt 17:1,2.

This is the same glory that was seen when He rose from the dead: "His countenance was like lightning, and his clothing as white as snow."[25]

This is the same glory that was seen by the apostle Paul when he met Jesus on the road to Damascus – an encounter that radically changed his life. Paul testified to King Agrippa: "'At midday, O king, along the road I saw a light from heaven, brighter than the sun.'"[26] This is the same glory that will be seen when He destroys Babylon the great: "After these things I saw another angel [the Angel-Messenger, Jesus[27]] coming down from heaven, having great authority, and the earth was illuminated with his glory."[28]

This is the same glory which will be seen at His Second Coming: "Then will they see the Son of Man coming in a cloud with power and great glory."[29]

This is the sun-glory He shares with His Bride at the fulfillment of the Day of Atonement: "Now a great sign appeared in heaven: a woman clothed with the sun."[30]

When we superimpose the vision of the Lord Jesus seen by John upon the articles of furniture in the tabernacle of Moses, a wonderful picture emerges (see *Figure 30* on the next page). Also, when we compare John's vision of the Lord with the tabernacle furniture a clear pattern emerges, as can be seen in the following list:

The Lord Jesus Christ	**The Tabernacle of Moses**
1. Feet like brass	1. The altar of brass
2. His whole body clothed with fine linen, speaking of purity	2. The washstand of brass, for cleansing and purifying
3. Messengers to seven churches in His right hand	3. The lampstand – symbol of the churches
4. About to speak to local churches	4. The table of showbread – symbol of communion table around which a local church assembles
5. Golden sash around chest	5. The golden altar; His heart of intercession for us
6. His head; countenance shining like glory of the sun	6. The ark of the covenant; the glory

---

[25] Matt 28:3.
[26] Acts 26:13.
[27] See Chapter 14, "Here Comes the Bridegroom!"
[28] Rev 18:1.
[29] Luke 21:27.
[30] Rev 12:1.

What a vision of Jesus John experiences! And as the Lord begins to speak to each individual church in chapters two and three, He reaches back to John's vision, presenting one or more aspects of His appearance applicable to the need of that particular church.

Figure 30: The Lord Jesus Christ as Seen in the Tabernacle Pattern

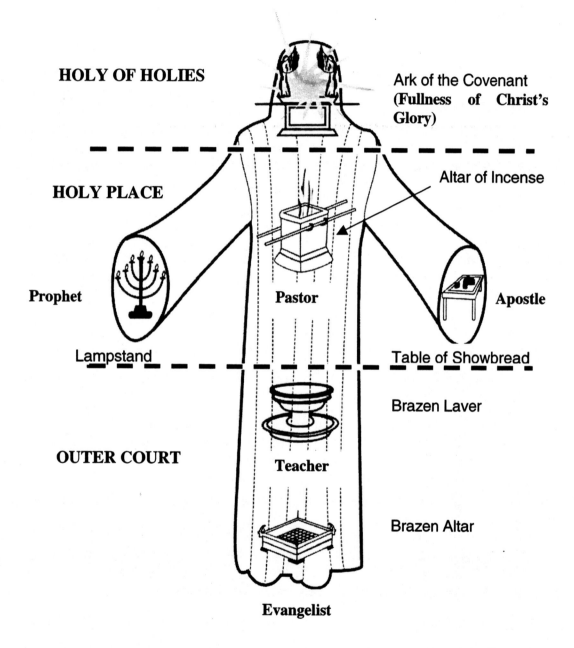

II. THE CHURCH (1:11,12,20)

"The seven churches which are in Asia ... I saw seven golden lampstands ... the mystery of the seven stars which you saw in My right hand, and the seven golden lampstands ... the seven lampstands which you saw are the seven churches." (1:11,12,20)

The lampstand is already described in Chapter 13 of this book. God wants each local church to give light. But five of the seven churches have allowed darkness to enter in, and the Lord commands them to repent.

"In Asia"

The term "Asia" has had various meanings throughout the centuries. Today, when we hear this word, we might think of South Asia (Pakistan, India, Bangladesh, Sri Lanka), or South-East Asia (Thailand, Vietnam, Laos, Cambodia), or Central and East Asia (China, Korea, and Japan). But at the time John received the Revelation, Asia was the name of the Roman province located in the westernmost part of what is still sometimes known as Asia Minor ("Little Asia"), or modern-day Turkey. In New Testament times Asia was the largest and most important of all the Roman provinces of that area. Ephesus was the capital city of the province of Asia.

The seven churches to which the Lord spoke were all located in the west-central area of this province [see *Figure 4*]. Beginning at Ephesus in the southwest and moving northward, we come to Smyrna and Pergamos; turning south-east we find Thyatira, Sardis, Philadelphia, and Laodicea. A circle enclosing these seven cities would have a radius of only 60 miles.[31]

It is understandable why the Lord chose churches in Asia to be representative and prophetic of conditions then and now. The apostle John had lived in this province for many years, mainly at Ephesus, and was probably well known to the churches of that area.

Lydia, the first convert in Philippi, was from Thyatira in Asia,[32] and Epaphras laboured for the Lord at Laodicea.[33] The Apostle Paul traveled extensively in the province of Asia. On his third missionary journey he spent a long time (probably 3½ years) in Ephesus.[34] Even before Paul completed that missionary journey, the Bible records, "all who dwelt in Asia heard the word of the Lord Jesus, both Jews and Greeks."[35] When God began to work "unusual miracles by the hands of Paul" in Ephesus, his opponents accused him with these words:

> "You see and hear that not only at Ephesus, but throughout almost all Asia, this Paul has persuaded and turned away many people [from the worship of the goddess Diana], saying they are not gods which are made with hands." (Acts 19:11-27)

---

[31] It is interesting to note in passing that the apostle Paul also wrote letters to seven local churches. Paul wrote letters to assemblies in the following cities (in the order they appear in the Bible): Rome, Corinth (2), Galatia, Ephesus, Philippi, Colossæ, Thessalonica (2). Both Paul and John wrote to the church at Ephesus.
[32] Acts 16:14.
[33] Col 2:1, 4:12-16.
[34] Acts 19:20, 20:16,17.
[35] Acts 19:10.

"The Mystery"

In verse 20 we find the word "mystery" which appears regularly throughout the New Testament. "Mystery" (margin, 'hidden truth') is used 27 times in the New Testament, and four times in the Book of Revelation.

The English word "mystery" in the New Testament is translated from the Greek word *mustērion*, and means "that which is known to the initiated, *mustes*" (from *mueō*, to initiate into the mysteries).

In common usage in the English language today, the word "mystery" means something that is hidden, inexplicable, hard to solve, or obscure. But in Greek, "mystery" means just the opposite. It means not to hide, but to show. It means not to be inexplicable, but to explain. It does not mean difficult to solve, but simple to comprehend. It does not mean to obscure, but to reveal.

For example, the derivative *mueomai*, found in Philippians 4:12, is translated:

> "I am instructed" (*KJV*), and
> "I have learned the secret" (*NAS* and *NIV*).

To be "initiated" does not mean membership in some exclusive group, but the illumination that comes upon God's Word from His Spirit, a blessing all Christians can enjoy. About this word, W.E. Vine says:

> "In the New Testament it denotes, not the mysterious (as with the English word), but that which, being outside the range of unassisted natural apprehension, can be made known only by Divine revelation, and is made known in a manner and at a time appointed by God, and to those only who are illumined by His Spirit."[36]

In English, "mystery" denotes *knowledge withheld*.

In Greek, "mystery" denotes *truth revealed*. The terms especially related to the word "mystery" are – "made known," "revealed," "preached," "manifested," "understand." This is illustrated in the following two verses:

> "The mystery which has been hidden from ages and from generations, but now has been *revealed* to His saints." (Col 1:26)

> "Behold, I *show* you a mystery." (1 Cor 15:51 – *KJV*)

In Revelation 1:20, Jesus clearly explains the mystery of the seven stars and the seven golden lampstands. The mysteries of the New Testament, including the Book of

---

[36] Vine, *op.cit.*

Revelation, are not truths God wants to hide from us. On the contrary, He wants to reveal to us the contents of this Book.

All it requires is that we be initiated – be joined to God's redeemed, Spirit-filled people – and have a burning desire to follow Him all the way He leads us.

III THE CHRISTIAN (1:12-17)

In this third section of Revelation chapter one, we want to look at John's response to the vision. We may not, as John did, see the Lord with our natural eyes. But if we see Him with the eyes of our spirit, as He is revealed in this chapter, we will, I believe, respond as John did. A vision of His glory produces a personal response.

Five major things happened to John in the latter part of this chapter:

Verse 12	1.	"I turned"
	2.	"I being turned" (*KJV*)
Verse 17	3.	"I saw"
	4.	"I fell"
	5.	"He laid His right hand on me"

1. "I turned"

The main purpose of God's Word is to turn us. To turn us from sin, or anything that displeases God, and to Him. Jesus spoke His parables so that people "should turn" ("should be converted" – *KJV*; Greek, "to turn about"). This is not just speaking of the experience of initial salvation, when we are "converted to Christ." As we journey through life, from time to time the Lord must turn us by making a "mid-course correction" to the direction in which we are headed. The Bible calls this repentance (Greek, "a change of mind"). To repent means to change our mind, so that God can change our heart. We can change our mind. Only God can change our heart.

John turned to see. He couldn't do it in his own strength. Neither can we.

Then John testifies, "And *being* turned, I saw."

2. "Being turned" (*KJV*)

The prophet Jeremiah records that Ephraim understood He needed God to turn Him:

> "I have surely heard Ephraim bemoaning himself and I was chastised, as a bullock unaccustomed to the yoke: turn thou me, and I shall be turned; for thou art the Lord my God.
> Surely after that I was turned, I repented ..." (Jer 31:18,19 – *KJV*)

Jeremiah prays a similar prayer in Lamentations:

> "Turn thou us unto thee, O Lord, and we shall be turned; renew our days as of old." (Lam 5:21 – *KJV*)

When God does the turning, we are indeed turned. Why don't we pray, "Lord, turn me"? When John was turned, He saw the Glorious Lord. So will we.

3. "I saw"

When God turns us, He begins to reveal Himself anew to us. When John was turned, He saw the Son of Man in His tenfold glory and beauty. In Revelation nearly 50 times John testifies, "I saw." (He says "I heard" 25 times). John's response to what He saw?

4. "I fell"

John testifies, "When I saw Him, I fell at His feet as dead."[37] There are too many Christians today who have "I" trouble. "I" must fall dead at His feet, so "I" can say with Paul:

> "I have been crucified with Christ; it is no longer I who live, but Christ lives in me; and the life which I now live in the flesh I live by faith in the Son of God, who loved me and gave Himself for me." (Gal 2:20)

"When I saw Him, I fell at His feet as dead." Dead people are silent. When we fall at His feet as dead, we will be too. No pleading. No complaining. No asking. No arguing. Just listening for His awesome voice. Dead people do not move either. No rushing here and there. No important activities. No schedule. No appointments. No distractions. Prostrate. Still. Attentive only to Him.

When Daniel saw the vision of the ram and the goat, what was his reaction? "And I, Daniel, fainted and was sick for days." Why? He says, "I was astonished (*margin*, 'amazed') by the vision" (Dan 8:27).

But there is more to this verse: "afterward I arose and went about the king's business." He was still astonished, but, like John, when touched he rose up, and got on with the

---

[37] It is of interest that in the Bible, when people were overwhelmed by the awesome presence of God, they fell forwards on their faces, bowing, kneeling, or falling prostrate before their Lord. Just to mention some instances of this: Abraham (Gen 18:2), Lot (Gen 19:1), Eliezer (Gen 24:26), the children of Israel (Exo 4:30,31), Moses (Exo 34:8), Joshua (Josh 5:13-15), Ruth (Ruth 2:10), David (Psa 95:6), Ezekiel (Eze 44:4, "the glory of the Lord filled the house of the Lord; and I fell on my face"), Daniel (Dan 10:9), the leper (Mark 1:40), the father of the boy with epilepsy (Matt 17:14), our Lord Jesus Christ (Matt 26:39), the two Marys at the resurrection (Matt 28:11), the apostle Paul (Eph 3:14), the apostle John (Rev 1:17), the 24 elders (Rev 4:10).

The only person I can find of whom it is specifically written that, when he was overwhelmed, he fell backwards was Eli, the grandfather of Ichabod, who "fell off the seat backward ... and his neck was broken and he died" (1 Sam 4:18).

king's business. When visions, circumstances, problems or anything else amaze us, let's follow their example – rise up, and get on with kingdom business.

When Daniel saw the vision of the man clothed in linen, wearing a golden sash around his waist, he was looking at what John saw nearly 700 years later – the Lord Jesus Christ in His ascension glory. His reaction to this vision? Very similar to John's. This is the way Daniel describes his experience:

> "And I, Daniel, alone saw the vision, for the men who were with me did not see the vision; but a great terror fell upon them, so that they fled to hide themselves.
> Therefore I was left alone when I saw this great vision, and no strength remained in me; for my vigor was turned to frailty (*margin, Literally,* 'ruin') in me, and I retained no strength.
> Yet I heard the sound of his words; and while I heard the sound of his words I was in a deep sleep on my face, with my face to the ground." (Dan 10:7-9)

When the Bride of Christ sees her Beloved Bridegroom on the Day of Atonement, I think her reaction may be very similar to Daniel's and John's. But their experience did not end with them fearful and weak.

5. "But He laid His right hand upon me"

John's words sound like Daniel's, when the angel Gabriel touched Daniel, and spoke with him:

> "Suddenly, a hand touched me, which made me tremble on my knees and on the palms of my hands.
> And he said to me, 'O Daniel, man greatly beloved, understand the words that I speak to you, and stand upright, for I have now been sent to you.'
> While he was speaking this word to me, I stood trembling.
> Then he said to me, 'Do not fear, Daniel, for from the first day that you set your heart to understand, and to humble yourself before your God, your words were heard; and I have come because of your words.'"
> (Dan 10:10-12)

Daniel was told not to fear. So was John. If we are serving the Lord with everything we are, and everything we have, we do not need to fear anything we read in the Book of Revelation.

It is specifically recorded that the Lord Jesus laid His *right* hand upon John. In the Bible, the right hand is the hand of blessing, power, and authority. This is why David sang:

> "The Lord said to my Lord,
> 'Sit at My right hand,
> Till I make Your enemies Your footstool.'" (Psa 110:1)

The prophet Isaiah records that God said:

> "Listen to Me, O Jacob,
> And Israel, My called:
> I am He, I am the First,
> I am also the Last.
>
> Indeed My hand has laid the foundation of the earth,
> And My right hand has stretched out the heavens ..." (Isa 48:12,13)

And Paul taught the Ephesian church:

> " ... the working of His mighty power
> which He worked in Christ when He raised Him from the dead and seated
> Him at His right hand in the heavenly places." (Eph 1:19,20)

The Christ. The Church. The Christian.

- Have you seen, with the eyes of your spirit, the Glorious Christ as He really is?

- Have you seen the Church as Christ wants her to be, in these days of the preparation of His Bride?

- Have you, as a Christian, prayed for Him to turn you? Have you fallen before Him, and experienced His nail-scarred hand upon you?

I pray that all of us will ask the Lord to turn us, so that we can see the glory and beauty of our wonderful Lord Jesus. As we fall before Him with our faces to the ground, let us not be afraid. He will surely lay His nail-pierced hand upon us, to bless and revive us.

Now we are ready to see how the Lord appears to the seven churches, to commend, rebuke, and encourage each assembly.

PART FOUR

Revelation chapters 2 and 3

THE CHURCHES

| PART FOUR | THE CHURCHES |

Chapter 17

Introducing the Letters to the Seven Churches

Revelation chapters 2 and 3

THE "SEVENS" OF REVELATION

The number seven appears 54 times in Revelation.

In the Book of Revelation we see the unfolding of eight major "sevens." An understanding of this truth will aid us immensely in viewing Revelation as one harmonious whole.

John describes the visions in order, just as he saw them. I believe there is no need to drastically change the order of the chapters. Rather, the eight main "groups of seven" comprise a panoramic picture that commences with the first generation of the Church, and ends with the triumphant Second Coming of Christ, after which we are given a brief look into eternity. It is as if John saw a videocassette of Church history, with special emphasis on the last days, the Great Tribulation, the Second Coming, the Millennium, then eternity.

As we will see as we progress through Revelation, each major seven comes out of the seventh (the last) of the previous group of seven. This is illustrated in the two-part chart on the next page.

THE LETTERS TO THE SEVEN CHURCHES

While each of the seven letters contained a message for a specific local church, these letters were not exclusively for the church named. Nor were they sent as individual letters to separate churches. Everything John saw in the whole Book of Revelation was to be sent to every church: "'Write down what you see, and send the book to these seven churches'" (Rev 1:11).

We must view Paul's epistles in the same way. Each of his letters contained a message for the particular church to which he was writing. But also, Paul's letters contain God's eternal Word for the whole Church of every age.

Figure 31: **The Main Groups of Seven in Revelation**

1	2	3	4
SEVEN CHURCHES	SEVEN SEALS	SEVEN TRUMPETS	SEVEN COMPANIES
[Christ in the midst of seven lampstands]	[The seven-sealed book is opened]	[The seven trumpets sound]	[Some individuals, some composite]
Rev ch's 1-3	*Rev ch's 4-7*	*Rev ch's 8-11*	*Rev ch's 12 and 13*
1. Ephesus	1. White horse	1. Hail, fire, blood	1. Sun-clad Bride
2. Smyrna	2. Red horse	2. Burning mountain cast into sea	2. Fiery red dragon
3. Pergamos	3. Black horse	3. Star falls	3. Man child
4. Thyatira	4. Pale horse	4. Sun, moon, stars	4. Michael
5. Sardis	5. Martyrdom	5. Locust plague	5. The remnant
6. Philadelphia	6. Great earthquake, sun black, moon	6. 200 million troops like locusts	6. The beast (the Antichrist)
7. Laodicea	7. Silence in heaven, Marriage of Lamb	7. Kingdom of God and His Christ	7. Another beast (the False Prophet)

5	6	7	8
SEVEN BEINGS	SEVEN BOWLS	SEVEN JUDGMENTS	SEVEN NEW THINGS
[Some individuals, some composite]	[7 bowls, or vials, of the wrath of God]	[God's 7 judgments on His enemies]	[God makes all things new]
Rev ch 14	*Rev ch's 15 and 16*	*Rev ch's 17-20*	*Rev ch's 21 and 22*
1. Lamb & 144,000	1. Loathsome sores	1. Religious Babylon	1. New Heaven
2. Angel (Enoch)	2. Blood on the sea	2. Political Babylon	2. New Earth
3. Second angel	3. Blood on rivers	3. Kings of the earth	3. New Jerusalem
4. Third angel, with loud voice	4. Scorching heat of sun	4. Beast and False Prophet	4. New nations of saved, walk in light
5. Fourth angel	5. Darkness and pain	5. The Devil	5. New river
6. Fifth angel	6. Euphrates dried up	6. Judgment Seat	6. New tree of life
7. Sixth angel	7. Hail and earthquake	7. White Throne	7. New throne

There are seven distinct ways we can examine the letters to the seven churches.[1] We can consider them:

1. Naturally:

As we have already noted, each church was, of course, located in a city existing in that day. While **HERE COMES THE BRIDE!** is not a book about secular

---
[1] These headings are adapted from a recorded message by Kevin Conner.

history, anthropology, or archaeology, by noting the conditions prevailing in each city, we can gain valuable understanding of the environment in which the church was planted, and the forces with which the early Christians had to contend.

2. Locally:

The churches in Ephesus, Smyrna, Pergamos, Thyatira, Sardis, Philadelphia, and Laodicea were actual local assemblies. Despite relentless persecution from both Romans and Jews, those who had become believers in Jesus of Nazareth gathered together in His Name, knowing that He was in their midst. Where possible we will try to discover how Christ's church was pioneered and established in each city.

3. Representatively:

The letters to the seven churches must also be considered representatively. That is, the conditions found in each local assembly represent conditions that were in other churches – churches that existed then, churches that exist now, and other churches that will exist until the end of the Church age.

4. Universally:

The word "Church" is found in only one of the four Gospels – Matthew, the Gospel of the Kingdom. In His teaching about the Church, our Lord clearly distinguishes between the worldwide Church and a gathering of believers in one geographical place. When He says. "I will build My church," [2] He is speaking of His Church *universal* – His "called-out ones" of every nation, generation, and denomination. But when He says, "Tell it to the church ... where two or three are gathered together in My name, I am there in the midst of them," [3] He is talking about His church *local*.

More than 60 years after the day of Pentecost there were probably hundreds of churches located in cities and towns all over the known world. But in Revelation, the Lord chose to speak with just seven churches, located in what is today western Turkey. Although the seven churches were local assemblies, they also represent conditions in Christ's universal Church – both in Bible days, and throughout Church history.

5. Historically:

Many Bible teachers believe the seven churches represent seven ages of Church history. This conclusion is reached by taking the churches in the order in which they appear in Revelation, and comparing the individual conditions of these churches with seven successive periods of Church history.

---

[2] Matt 16:18.
[3] Matt 18:17-20.

In his excellent compilation of Bible lessons, *The Shepherd's Staff*, Ralph Mahoney writes concerning the historical view:

> "The historical, or 'all of history' view, sees the visions of the Book of Revelation as a preview of history from John's time until the end of the Church age. Most Protestant reformers supported this view.
>
> "Of these, some believed each one of the seven churches in Revelation 2 and 3 represented a progressive forecast of seven periods that would unfold from John's time until the end of the Church age.
>
> "For example, what we read about the first of the seven churches (Ephesus) would reveal what the Church would be like the latter years of John's life at the end of the first century.
>
> "What was written about the last of the seven (Laodicea) would reveal what the Church would be like in the last part of the Church age, just before Jesus returns to earth. The others would represent the time periods between Ephesus (the first) and Laodicea (the last)."[4]

Some expositors who have strong convictions about this historical/dispensational viewpoint refer to the way the lamp in the tabernacle of Moses was lit as an illustration of their reasoning. The priest took fire from the brazen altar into the holy place. God Himself had lit the fire on the altar with fire from heaven. The priest lit the first lamp. He then lit the second lamp from the flame of the first. The third lamp received its fire from the second lamp, and so on, until all the seven lamps of the lampstand were burning. The original outpouring of the Holy Spirit and fire on the day of Pentecost, which came from Jesus Himself, has continued to empower His Church through the centuries.

The Book of Revelation does not specifically state that the seven churches are typical or prophetical of seven major historical time periods. But there does appear to be a definite pattern of similarity when we compare the churches with the chronology of conditions that have prevailed during the nearly 2,000 years of the Church.

Some authors teach that not only do the seven churches represent seven periods of church history. They believe just as each local church in Revelation chapter one had a particular angel, or messenger, so each of the Church ages has a special messenger. I think there may be an element of truth in this; it is, at least, of historical interest. I can best summarize this historical/dispensational view with the following table:

---

[4] *The Shepherd's Staff*, edited by Ralph Mahoney; World MAP, Burbank, California, 1993, *Section G1, Eschatology* – page 3.

Ralph Mahoney is the Founder of World Missionary Assistance Plan. Through teaching seminars, magazines, and his excellent teaching manual, *The Shepherd's Staff*, thousands of pastors and preachers in Third World nations have been encouraged in their ministries.

Figure 32: **Historical Viewpoint of the Letters to the Seven Churches**

Church	Ephesus	Smyrna	Pergamos	Thyatira	Sardis	Philadelphia	Laodicea
YEARS	34-100 AD	100-312	312-606	606-1517	1517-1750	1750-1900	1900-Great Tribulation
CHURCH AGE	Apostolic Age	Persecuted Age	Imperial (State) Church Age	Papal (Roman) Age	Reformation (Restoration) Age	Holiness Missionary-Evangelistic Age	Pentecostal-Charismatic and Apostate Age
MESSENGER	Paul	Irenaeus	Martin	Columba	Luther	Wesley	Paul [5]

A further addition to the historical viewpoint – a number of expositors see a comparison between the seven kingdom parables in Matthew chapter 13 and the seven churches in the Book of Revelation. These expositors teach that in addition to the personal and practical lessons Jesus taught, there was also a strong prophetic element in the seven kingdom parables. Each parable typified one of seven "Church ages."

One such expositor is Earl L. Moore. While his dates differ from those I have given above, concerning the prophetic element of the kingdom parables he couples them with the "seven church ages" as shown in *Figure 33* on the next page.[6] (I have matched the duration of each age from *Figure 32*.)

6. Personally:

These letters are not just messages to churches. They are also to individual Christians. In fact, the Book of Revelation begins with a promised blessing to individuals, and ends with a solemn warning to individuals:

> "Blessed is he who reads and those who hear the words of this prophecy, and keep those things which are written in it; for the time is near." (Rev 1:3)

> "For I testify to everyone who hears the words of the prophecy of this book: If anyone adds to these things, God will add to him the plagues that are written in this book;

---

[5] No. This is not a misprint. I mean the same apostle Paul who was a "special messenger" to the Church of the first century. While the identity of the messengers to church ages two through six may be open for discussion, I think there is little doubt about church ages one and seven. I will explain this when we look at Revelation chapter 13 in **HERE COMES THE BRIDE! Volume Two**.

[6] *Revealing the Christ of the Revelation* by Earl L. Moore; E.B.T. Church Publications, Indianapolis, Indiana, no date.

Earl L. Moore was the son of pioneers of the "Pentecostal Movement" which swept around the world shortly after its beginnings in the early 1900s. Pastor Moore was baptized at the age of six and called to the ministry when he was ten. He was ordained in 1942, and traveled extensively throughout America as well as many foreign countries, teaching the Word of God.

Figure 33: **Comparison Between the Kingdom Parables and the Seven Churches**

Church	Ephesus	Smyrna	Pergamos	Thyatira	Sardis	Philadelphia	Laodicea
Parable	Sower	Wheat and tares	Mustard seed	Leaven	Hidden treasure	Pearl of great price	Dragnet
Reference	Matt 13:1	Matt 13:24	Matt 13:31	Matt 13:33	Matt 13:44	Matt 13:45	Matt 13:47
Church age	1st Age	2nd Age	3rd Age	4th Age	5th Age	6th Age	7th Age
Years	34-100 AD	100-312	312-606	606-1517	1517-1750	1750-1900	1900-Great Tribulation
	Sower Church Age	Sowing of Tares among the Wheat Church Age	Mustard Seed and Growth Church Age	Leaven Added Church Age	Hidden Treasure Church Age	Pearl of Great Price Church Age	Dragnet Church Age
	[Apostolic Church]	[Persecuted Church, Mixture]	[State Church]	[Papal Church]	[Reformation Church]	[Holiness, Missionary and Evangelistic Church]	[Apostate Church, but Great Harvest and Revival]

and if anyone takes away from the words of the book of this prophecy, God shall take away his part from the Book of Life, from the holy city, and from the things which are written in this book." (Rev 22:18,19)

This personal emphasis is very clearly stated in each of the letters: "He [every individual] who has an ear, let him hear ... to him who overcomes" (Rev 2:7). The Lord has a personal message for you, and for me, through the words of these letters – indeed, through every word of the Book of this prophecy.

7. Practically:

The commendations, corrections, and challenges to each church are extremely practical. They speak to us right where we live. The practical steps we must take to rid ourselves of things displeasing to God are clearly stated – "remember," "repent," "be faithful," "do not fear," "hold fast," "hear," "overcome."

"OVERCOMING" – THE MAIN THEME OF THE SEVEN LETTERS

Many books have been written on the letters to the seven churches. I consider the very best of these to be *The Overcomer*, by Rob Wheeler. The subtitle of his book is *The Bible formula for being in the glorious church as seen from the seven churches of the Book of*

Revelation.[7] Unfortunately, this book is currently out of print. I am grateful to Rob for giving me permission to glean some thoughts from it for this book.

As we will see as we progress through the Book of Revelation, there are many frightening predictions and prophecies contained in its 22 short chapters. But before these things happen – mountains moving, stars falling, atomic warfare, horrible beasts and the dragon arising – God has, in the opening chapters of Revelation, an important, practical, life-saving message for *His Own people*.

For the Lord's judgments begin in the house of God.[8] In the words of the Old Testament companion book of the Revelation, Daniel, first "the sanctuary shall be cleansed."[9]

Twenty-two times – once for each chapter – the Lord encourages us to overcome every pressure that would hinder us from being a part of His glorious Church. This overcoming is not a result of knowing who the man child is (interesting though that may be). Rather, it is the result of an ever-increasing intimacy with Christ.

> "He who overcomes shall inherit all things (*margin*, 'I shall give him these things'), and I will be his God and he shall be My son." (Rev 21:7)

Every one of the seven churches was encouraged to overcome – even those for whom the Lord had no rebuke. Overcoming is the main message of the letters to the seven churches. To enable us to be overcomers, God allows situations in which we learn to be victorious. Each time we overcome in a negative situation, a difficult problem, a temptation, or a challenging relationship, we are maturing. As a result, we enter into a closer, deeper relationship with Him.

Overcomers – or Overcome?

It is not sufficient to only know the doctrines in the Book of Revelation. It's what we do when circumstances change or things go wrong – how we react to family pressures, disappointments, stress, tests in relationships, temptation, contradiction, perplexity, frustration, sadness, loss – that demonstrates whether we are overcomers, or overcome. Learning to be an overcomer is one of the most important ingredients of preparation to be in the Bride of Christ.

God knows how we will react under pressure. Our problem is we don't know. Therefore, the Lord will allow us to be tested by negative circumstances – circumstances that sometimes bring out the worst in us – so we can learn to look to Him for help in overcoming painful emotions, wrong attitudes and ungodly responses. When we experience negative circumstances, we must remember God is not punishing us; He is processing us,

---

[7] *The Overcomer* by Rob Wheeler; Orama Christian Fellowship Trust, Great Barrier Island, New Zealand, June 1980.
[8] 1 Pet 4:17.
[9] Dan 7:14.

preparing us, loving us, strengthening us, that we may be a part of the glorious Church, with no "spots" of anger, or "wrinkles" of pride.[10]

If we do not learn to overcome in the small, daily experiences of life, we will never overcome the really big things that await us in the coming years.

If we learn to overcome now, we will certainly, through the Lord's strength and grace, overcome then. I am convinced there are going to be only two kinds of Christians in the last days – the overcomers, or the overcome; the wise, or the foolish; those built on rock, or sand; the Bride of Christ, or the remnant of her seed. The awesome truth is that every day we are, by our responses, attitudes and actions, determining our own destiny.

"But I have failed," I hear someone say. "I've blown it. I was in this situation and I was overcome." Don't be discouraged. We cannot change the past. But we *can* change the future. If you have been overcome, there is grace with God to forgive, to cleanse, to heal memories of past failures and hurts, and to restore your soul.

However, when you are strengthened, God may allow the very same set of circumstances to come your way again! But then you'll be able to say, "I remember that temptation. This is what I've learned. I won't be overcome this time. I am learning, in every situation, to be an overcomer!"

Seven Main Areas to be Overcome

It is interesting to note that every major force we have to overcome today is found in one, two, or more of the seven churches of Asia:

	Church	Overcoming
1.	Ephesus	**ATTITUDES**
2.	Smyrna	**AFFLICTION**
3.	Pergamos	**ASSOCIATIONS**
4.	Thyatira	**AUTHORITY**
5.	Sardis	**APATHY**
6.	Philadelphia	**ARDUOUS CIRCUMSTANCES**
7.	Laodicea	**AFFLUENCE**

---

[10] Eph 5:27.

Seven Churches Study Plan

For brevity and clarity we will look at each church under the same 14 headings. We will start each heading with the letter "C." Here are the main points of interest we will look at in our studies of the seven churches:

1. Commission

At the commencement of each letter, John receives the commission to write to the messenger of that particular church.

2. City

It is interesting to look at the nature of the city in which each church is located. This helps us understand more clearly what Christ is saying to the church. We will also consider the meaning of each city's name under this heading.

3. Consequences

A brief look at what remains today of each city helps us see the consequences of the church's response to Christ's words.

4. Church

Under this heading we will seek to discover, where possible, the origin and circumstances of each assembly in Bible days.

5. Character

How Christ reveals Himself to each church usually gives us the key to what He is going to say. In writing to each local church, He usually emphasizes one or more of His character aspects from John's vision of the Son of Man.

6. Conduct

Christ says to each church, "I know your works." He says the same to us today. He knows our conduct. He knows every thought and every deed.

7. Commendation

It is so beautiful to see the grace of our Lord Jesus Christ in His dealings with each church. Before He lists His complaints, He recognizes and commends those things they are doing well.

8. Complaint

He identifies faults in five of the seven churches. And as we meditate in God's Word, He will identify our individual sins.

9. Correction

How wonderful is our Lord! He never rebukes without giving a remedy. He not only points out what is wrong – He tells how the fault can be corrected and overcome.

10. Call

To five of the seven churches there is a call to repentance. The first words of this call read, "Repent, or else!" To repent means to change our minds, so that God can change our hearts.

11. Caution

There are wonderful promises of blessing to those who repent and overcome. But also there are punishments promised to those who do not overcome. For example, to the Ephesian church He says, "Repent and do the first works, or else I will come to you quickly and remove your lampstand from its place – unless you repent" (Rev 2:5).

12. Counsel

In some cases, the Wonderful Counselor[11] gives counsel to the church, speaking firmly but lovingly to them.

13. Challenge

He challenges each church to overcome every problem and difficulty.

14. Compensation for Conquerors

There are very specific rewards for those who obey Him and overcome. Here is an interesting observation – usually, the worse the condition of the church, the greater the promise to the overcomer!

Now we will look at each of the seven churches. And as we do, I pray that the Lord will speak to each one of us personally, and place a burning desire within our hearts to please Him, to be overcomers, and to enter into the fullness of relationship He desires to have with us.

---

[11] Isa 9:6.

| PART FOUR | THE CHURCHES |

Chapter 18

The Falling "Mother Church"

Ephesus ... Overcoming Attitudes

Revelation 2:1-7

¹ "To the angel (*margin*, 'or messenger') of the church of Ephesus write, 'These things says He who holds the seven stars in His right hand, who walks in the midst of the seven golden lampstands:
² I know your works, your labor, your patience, and that you cannot bear those who are evil. And you have tested those who say they are apostles and are not, and have found them liars;
³ And you have persevered and have patience, and have labored for My name's sake and have not become weary.
⁴ Nevertheless I have this against you, that you have left your first love.
⁵ Remember therefore from where you have fallen; repent and do the first works, or else I will come to you quickly and remove your lampstand from its place – unless you repent.
⁶ But this you have, that you hate the deeds of the Nicolaitans, which I also hate.
⁷ He who has an ear, let him hear what the Spirit says to the churches. To him who overcomes I will give to eat from the tree of life, which is in the midst of the Paradise of God.'"

1. Commission

John was commissioned by the Lord Jesus Christ, "To the angel (*margin*, 'messenger') of the church of Ephesus write ..."

2. City

Ephesus was an ancient Greek city located about 35 miles south of the modern city of Izmir in present-day Turkey. Colonists from Athens founded Ephesus in the early 1000s B.C. The city became famous for its Temple of Artemis, or Diana as she was called. This temple, located at the head of the harbour of Ephesus, is considered one of the Seven Wonders of the Ancient World. However, this temple was a place of blasphemous idolatry and sexual promiscuity and perversion – so much so that in Roman times, the city was given over to idol worship and immorality. As a consequence of the widespread worship of Diana at Ephesus, a large factory in the city made portable shrines of the goddess. Devotees purchased these shrines, set them up in their houses, and carried them when they traveled.

The Persians conquered Ephesus in the 500s B.C. Two hundred years later, in the 300s B.C., the city became a major trading and banking center under the Greeks. Ephesus grew in importance when it became the capital of the Roman province of Asia. It was during this time that a large and flourishing Christian church was established in Ephesus, which became the leading Christian community in Roman Asia. But the city was later looted by the Goths, Arabs, Turks, and finally the Mongols in 1403. It was abandoned, and lay deserted until archaeologists uncovered it in the late 1800s.

Ephesus was first excavated by an Englishman named Wood, 1869-74; then by the British Museum, 1904-5; and by Austrian expeditions in 1894 and 1930. The ruins of the Temple of Diana, the theatre (into which the mob who seized Paul rushed[1],) the stadium, or circus (probably the place where Paul fought with wild beasts[2]), and some of the streets were uncovered.

Also found were the remains of a Roman bathhouse, said to cover over 100,000 square feet, constructed entirely of marble, with many rooms – steam rooms, cold rooms, lounge rooms – evidence of the luxury and magnificence of the city in Roman times. The ancient ruins of a once-great system of aqueducts, with huge arches that supported clay water pipes, have also been uncovered.

A second large temple was unearthed, which contained a statue of Domitian. This statue is five times life-size. Domitian was the Roman Emperor who called himself "god," and who banished John to Patmos.

In July 2001, our local newspaper, *The San Diego Union*, printed an article about Ephesus in its Travel section. It reported that during summer Ephesus is jammed with tourists, who marvel at the ruins of this ancient, white-marble city. The correspondent described his visit to the centerpiece of Ephesus, the magnificent Celsus Library. A coloured photo of this amazing building accompanied his article. To illustrate the magnificence of Ephesus, this temple of learning, built in A.D.135, was once the second largest library in the world (after the one built at Alexandria in 300 B.C.). Beyond the steps and the two-story columned facade of the ancient structure, the Celsus Library had niches for 12,000 hand-written scrolls.

As with many of the names of places and people in the Bible, the interpretation of the word "Ephesus" has both positive and negative meanings. On the positive side, this city's name means "Beloved, desirable." But on the negative side it means "To let go, permission, to relax."

---

[1] Acts 19:29. This theatre was capable of holding more than 21,000 people, and is claimed to be the largest ever built by the Greeks.
[2] This stadium, where the Ephesians held their shows, was found to be 850 feet long by 200 feet wide.

3. Consequences

Of the seven cities containing the churches the Lord Jesus speaks to in Revelation chapters two and three, four now lie in ruins. The cities of Ephesus, Pergamos, Sardis, and Laodicea are all desolate. Only Smyrna, Thyatira, and Philadelphia still exist as modern cities.

Ephesus was once such a center of commerce it was called "The Market of Asia." But the entire city, together with the magnificent temple of Artemis, was destroyed by the Goths in A.D. 262. The city never regained its glory, or its "first love." As late as A.D. 431 a group of Christian bishops held a council in Ephesus. But the remains of Ephesus were regularly under siege.

Despite its ancient prominence, and a renewed interest today in its ruins, Ephesus as a living city exists no more. The city's once-great seaport is today only a marsh covered with reeds. With the exception of the small Turkish village nearby at Ayasaluk, only a vast expanse of desolate ruins remain. The consequences of disobedience are very serious. The Lord warned the church at Ephesus what would happen, and its candlestick has been removed.

4. Church

It is important to see how a strong Biblical foundation was laid at the commencement of the Ephesian church. The first mention of Ephesus is in Acts 18:19. After spending one and a half years teaching the Word at Corinth, Paul the apostle "came to Ephesus," and "entered the synagogue and reasoned with the Jews."

Next Apollos, "an eloquent man and mighty in the Scriptures, came to Ephesus."[3] Of Apollos, it is written, "This man had been instructed in the way of the Lord; and being fervent in spirit, he spoke and taught accurately the things of the Lord, though he knew only the baptism of John."[4] Aquila and Priscilla were also in Ephesus, and when they "heard him, they took him aside and explained to him the way of God more accurately."[5]

Apollos went on to Corinth, and Paul returned to Ephesus, where he found about twelve disciples. In the New Testament, when the word "disciple" is used for any except those who are true followers of Jesus Christ, it is specifically stated. (For example, "the disciples of John.") Therefore we can conclude these disciples at Ephesus were followers of the Lord Jesus, and, as such, had repented of their sins, and been cleansed by His blood. However, when Paul asked them, "Into what then were you baptized?" they replied they had only been baptized into John's (the Baptist's) baptism. When they heard that John's baptism was a signpost pointing towards Jesus Christ, "They were baptized in the name of the Lord Jesus."

---

[3] Acts 18:24.
[4] Acts 18:25.
[5] Acts 18:26.

Paul also asked: "Did you receive the Holy Spirit when you believed?" To this question they replied, "We have not so much as heard whether there is a Holy Spirit." If all Christians automatically receive the gift of the Holy Spirit when they believe in Jesus Christ, why should the apostle Paul have asked believers this question? Here we see that one may be a disciple of Jesus without having received the Holy Spirit as God's gift. Then Paul "laid hands on them, [and] the Holy Spirit came upon them, and they spoke with tongues and prophesied."[6]

The first pastor of the Ephesian church was Paul. He served the Ephesian church for over three years, and under his leadership the church grew rapidly.[7] From Ephesus the Gospel spread throughout the whole province of Asia – "all the people who lived in the province of Asia, both Jews and Gentiles, heard the word of the Lord."[8] It is probable that it was during this time Paul had a miraculous escape from Roman persecution, as John would many years later. Writing to the Corinthians, Paul says, "I have fought with beasts at Ephesus."[9] He seems to allude to this again in his Second Letter to Corinth, "For we do not want you to be ignorant, brethren, of our trouble (*margin*, 'tribulation') which came to us in Asia: that we were burdened beyond measure, above strength, so that we despaired even of life. Yes, we had the sentence of death in ourselves ... God ... delivered us from so great a death."[10]

Paul had great love for the Ephesian church. This is demonstrated in the Biblical accounts of his departure from the church, and his final meeting with, and his exhortation to, the elders of the church.[11] The Ephesian church is the only one of the seven churches in Asia to receive letters written by both John and Paul. Paul's letter was written during his first captivity at Rome.[12] Most scholars agree he wrote it about A.D. 62, approximately 34 years before John received the Revelation.

Paul's letter to the Ephesians contains the longest passage in Scripture on the Bride of Christ – chapter 5, verses 22-33. The six chapter divisions in Ephesians contain six teachings about the Church. In the light of what Jesus said to the Ephesian church through John, it is interesting to note what He said to this church through Paul. This can be summarized in the table on the following page.

The second pastor at Ephesus was Timothy.[13] It is believed the third pastor of the Ephesian church was Onesimus. Onesimus was originally from Colossæ. He was a slave of Philemon, but had escaped to Rome, where Paul led him to Christ.[14] The fourth pastor at Ephesus was the apostle John. And so, in a sense, John is writing to his own "home church."

---

[6] Acts 19:1-7.
[7] Acts 20:31.
[8] Acts 19:10 – *TEV*.
[9] 1 Cor 15:32.
[10] 2 Cor 1:8-10.
[11] Acts 20:1, 17-38.
[12] Acts 28:16.
[13] 1 Tim 1:3; 2 Tim 1:18.
[14] Onesimus means "profitable." See the book of Philemon.

Figure 34: **Summary of the Book of Ephesians**

Chapter	Reference	Church Pictured as	Made Up of Many
One	Verses 22 and 23	BODY	Parts (hands, feet, tongue, etc.)
Two	Verses 21 and 22	TEMPLE	Stones
Three	Verse 15	FAMILY	Members (father, mother, children, grandparents)
Four	Verses 13 - 16	PERFECT MAN	Joints
Five	Verses 22 – 33	BRIDE	Members
Six	Verses 10 - 18	ARMY	Soldiers

Despite persecution and opposition, the church at Ephesus continued to grow – so much so that the very influential Roman philosopher and writer, Pliny the Younger, wrote letters to the Emperor Trajan describing the Christians and asking what to do about them. These letters are the earliest accounts about Christians written by a pagan.[15] Because these letters between the Emperor Trajan and Pliny the Younger (who later became governor of Bithynai) have survived, we are assured that profession of faith in Christ was a capital offence. If a person was discovered to be a Christian, he or she was given an opportunity to renounce Christ, and worship the Emperor. Refusal to do so resulted in execution.[16]

5. Character

The Lord Jesus Christ, in speaking to the Ephesian church, emphasizes two aspects of His character and appearance from Revelation chapter one:

   a. "He who holds the seven stars in His right hand"
   This is language the Ephesian church understood. Jesus has already interpreted what He means by these stars, and the Ephesians had been well taught by Paul concerning the five ascension gift ministries.[17]

   b. "Who walks in the midst of the seven golden lampstands"

   Paul had also written to them about the pattern of the local church. But even though they knew the pattern, and are highly commended by the Lord, He is going to put His finger on an attitude which cannot exist in a church or in an individual desiring to be a part of the glorious Church – the Church of which Paul had written to them over 30 years earlier.

---

[15] *The World Book Encyclopedia*, Field Enterprises Educational Corporation, 1972; Volume 15, "P" – pages 509–510.
[16] *Eerdmans' Handbook to the History of Christianity*; Lion Publishing, Berkhamsted, England, 1977 – page 72.
[17] Eph 4:8-16.

6. Conduct

As He says to each local church (and individual,) He says to the church at Ephesus – "I know your works."

We all know that our sins were washed away, not by our own works, but because of our faith in the finished work of Jesus upon Calvary.[18] And we know the first principle of the doctrine of Christ is "repentance – turning from – dead works."[19] Dead works can be described as anything we do that does not draw upon God's life and power as its source of origin, continuation, and completion.

But the Bible emphasizes once we are saved we must do good works – works that do draw upon God's life and power as their source of origin, continuation, and completion. Compare this verse:

> "Not by works of righteousness which we have done, but according to His mercy He saved us, through the washing of regeneration and renewing of the Holy Spirit." (Titus 3:5)

with this verse:

> "This is a faithful saying, and these things I want you to affirm constantly, that those who have believed in God should be careful to maintain good works. These things are good and profitable to men." (Titus 3:8)

The Lord gives this solemn warning about works and rewards:

> "But if any one builds upon the Foundation [Jesus Christ], whether it be with gold, silver, precious stones, wood, hay, straw,
> The work of each [one] will become (plainly, openly) known – shown for what it is; for the day (of Christ) will disclose and declare it, because it will be revealed with fire, and the fire will test and critically appraise *the character and worth of the work each person has done.*
> If the work which any person has built on this Foundation – any product of his efforts whatever – survives (this test), *he will get his reward.*
> But if any person's work is burned up [under the test], he will suffer the loss (of it all, *losing his reward*), though he himself will be saved, but only as [one who has passed] through fire." (1 Cor 3:12:15 – *Amp*, emphasis mine)

Today we find in the Church two extremes concerning works. The first is those who are always busy doing works for the sake of "being busy doing works." I work very long hours, and I assure you I am not advocating laziness. But remember, it is not how active we are – it is how productive we are that counts.

---

[18] Eph 2:8,9.
[19] Heb 6:1.

The second extreme is those who do next to nothing, and have a kind of "super-spiritual" attitude that says, "I'll just let the Lord do it." Of course, without Him we can do nothing.[20] But there is a pertinent allegory found in Solomon's song: The Shulamite says that she is ready to sleep; she has taken off her robe, and washed her feet. So she does not answer her Bridegroom's voice, or his knock at the door, immediately. When she finally does get up she says, "I opened for my beloved, but my beloved had turned away and was gone."[21]

How tragic it would be to hear teaching about the Bride of Christ and the Book of Revelation and then get lazy, or isolate ourselves from the Lord's work. "Faith by itself, if it does not have works, is dead."[22] As we have already seen, the brides in the Old Testament who are prophetic pictures of the Bride of Christ, often found their bridegrooms while working in the field, or at the well. The words of Jesus are so relevant here: "I must work the works of Him who sent Me while it is day; the night is coming when no one can work."[23]

7. Commendation

The Lord gives eight commendations to the church at Ephesus. This is the greatest number to any of the seven churches:

- **a. "I know your works":** Good works are both spiritual and practical, and often personally inconvenient. But the Lord knows each time we give someone a ride to church, or help in the maintenance of the church property. He knows when we work extra hours on the job so we can go on a summer missions trip. He knows when we take a cooked meal to that elderly Christian man. He sees when we vacuum the church sanctuary.

- **b. "I know your labour":** This is not talking about work in the normal course of Christian life and service. The Greek word gives the sense of "toil resulting in extreme weariness" – "work resulting in extreme trouble, exhaustion, inconvenience, and even embarrassment." In Paul's words, "I have worked much harder;"[24] and, "in weariness and toil, in sleeplessness often."[25]

    There were times when, in His humanity, Jesus was exhausted. He sat down at the well.[26] He fell asleep at the back of a boat in the midst of a storm.[27] In His letter to the Ephesian church, the Lord commends them twice for their labours.

---

[20] John 3:27, 6:63, 15:5.
[21] Song 5:2-6.
[22] Jas 2:17.
[23] John 9:5.
[24] 2 Cor 11:23 – *TEV*.
[25] 2 Cor 11:27.
[26] John 4:6.
[27] Mark 4:38.

c. "I know your patience (*margin, 'perseverance'*)": Patience is not the ability to sit quietly and wait. Rather, it is the ability to endure, to persevere, in the midst of trials and pressure. The Greek word *hupomonō* literally means "to abide under." Bible patience can be defined as "a continuing endurance which only grows stronger through trials and under pressures." We are exhorted to "Glory in tribulations, knowing that tribulation produces perseverance" (Rom 5:3). And in Hebrews we are told:

> "You need to persevere, so that when you have done the will of God, you will receive what He has promised." (Heb 10:36)

The first three commendations to the Ephesian church are, "I know your (a) works, (b) labour, and (c) patience. But soon Jesus will identify the heart of their problem – "You have left your first love."

The church at Thessalonica received the same three commendations as the church at Ephesus – but each with something added. The Thessalonians had not left their first love, and in 1 Thessalonians 1:3 they are commended for their:

i. work of *faith*;
ii. labour of *love*;
iii. patience of *hope*.

The difference between these two churches was this: The Ephesian church was an older, established church, with a longer tradition and successful growth, and while commended by the Lord, was carrying on in the present because of a passionate love for Jesus they had experienced in the past.

By contrast, in the Thessalonian church:

i. Their work was the work of *faith*. It is one thing to give and work out of an abundance of resources. It is totally different to give and work out of a faith which is alive because of first love;
ii. Their labour was a labour of *love*. In the Ephesian church it was just "labour." They had fallen from their first love. But not the Thessalonians.
iii. Their patience – endurance – was a patience of *hope*. They had the thrill of triumphant expectation in their hearts. This resulted in an eagerness to serve their Lord fervently.

In the first letter to the Corinthians, these three qualities – faith, hope and love – are spoken of this way: "And now abide faith, hope, love, these three; but the greatest of these is love." May the light of our love for our precious Lord Jesus never grow dim.

The fourth commendation to the Ephesian church was:

d. **"You cannot bear (*margin*, 'endure') those who are evil":** Here was a clean and holy church, located in a city filled with evil and iniquity. Not only do they not do evil. They cannot endure evil people. Paul had warned the Ephesian elders more than 35 years earlier: "From among yourselves men will rise up, speaking perverse things, to draw away the disciples after themselves."[28] The Lord Jesus commended the Ephesians for not tolerating such men in the Christian churches throughout the city of Ephesus.[29]

e. **"You have tested those who say they are apostles and are not, and have found them liars":** The Ephesian church recognized the ministry of true apostles sent to them by the Lord – such as Paul, Timothy, and John – and discerned those who claimed to be apostles but were not.

Today there are two extremes of teaching about apostles. The Greek word *apostolos* literally means "one sent forth." So one extreme believes that everyone who "goes out" to serve the Lord is a "sent one" and so everyone who goes out is an apostle. The other extreme believes that apostles finished with the death of John, the last of the original 12, and there have been no apostles since. Both of these extremes are incorrect.

When the Bible says, "God has appointed these in the church: first apostles," it is not speaking of order of rank, but of chronological order.[30] In addition to the first 12 apostles of the Lamb, there are a number of other apostles named in the New Testament. But after some time, apostolic ministry – indeed, the fullness of all the five ascension gift ministries – was lost to the church. With the commencement of the Reformation these ministries began to be restored. In my lifetime, during the five decades since the Second World War, I have observed an amazing restoration – a restoration that still continues to grow in power, intensity, and worldwide impact. This is illustrated in the diagram on the following page.

Just as there were many true apostles and false apostles in the era of the Early Church, so there will be many true and false apostles in these Last Days. Therefore it is essential to know how to identify true apostles.

There are 10 main characteristics of true, Scriptural apostles:

- *Apostles have a foundational ministry in God's Word:* True apostles have the ability to teach God's Word in an organized and understandable way. The Early Church "continued in the apostles' doctrine (*margin*, 'teaching')."[31] Christians are informed, strengthened, built up, encouraged, and challenged when they sit under the preaching and teaching of a true apostle.

---

[28] Acts 20:30.
[29] Bible historians believe the Ephesian church had grown to where there were many meeting places throughout the city.
[30] 1 Cor 12:28.
[31] Acts 2:42.

Figure 35: **The Loss and Restoration of the Ascension Gift Ministries**

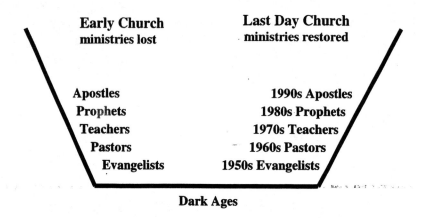

- *Apostles pioneer, and establish, new local churches:* True apostles are fathers – spiritual fathers of people, ministers, and churches. The apostle Paul could write to the Corinthian church: "Am I not an apostle? Am I not free? Have I not seen Jesus Christ our Lord? Are you not my work in the Lord? If I am not an apostle to others, yet doubtless I am to you. For you are the seal (*margin*, 'certification') of my apostleship in the Lord."[32]

  To this same church Paul also wrote: "For though you might have ten thousand instructors in Christ, yet you do not have many fathers; for in Christ Jesus I have begotten you through the gospel. Therefore I urge you, imitate me."[33]

  Apostles often work together with prophets in the pioneering and establishing of new churches. These ministries become part of the foundation of that local assembly. As Paul wrote to the Ephesians, "Having been built on the foundation of the apostles and prophets, Jesus Christ Himself being the chief cornerstone" (Eph 2:20).

- *Apostles have God-given authority concerning the pattern of the local church, and its government and order:* True apostles are not, nor should they behave like, dictators. They are servants of the churches. But, though he was a servant of the churches, Paul wrote to the Corinthians, "The rest I will set in order when I come."[34]

- *Apostles display genuine humility and sacrifice:* Paul was an apostle with great ability and authority, but when he was shipwrecked he "gathered a bundle of sticks and laid them on the fire."[35] He was willing to humbly serve in any way.

---

[32] 1 Cor 9:1,2.
[33] 1 Cor 4:15,16.
[34] 1 Cor 11:34.
[35] Acts 28:3.

Writing again to the Corinthian church (2 Corinthians 11:22-33) Paul lists some of the hardships, suffering, and sacrifices he had experienced in the course of his apostolic ministry – beatings, shipwreck, hunger, robbers, and much more. He also told the Corinthians, "For I think that God has displayed us, the apostles, last, as men condemned to death; for we have been made a spectacle (*margin*, 'theatre') to the world, both to angels and to men."[36]

- *Signs, wonders, and miracles follow an apostle's ministry:* Paul could also write, "Though I am nothing, truly the signs of an apostle were accomplished among you with all perseverance, in signs and wonders and mighty deeds."[37]

- *An apostle is recognized as such by other apostles:* In Galatians 2:9, we read that Peter, James and John, all pillars in the church, recognized Paul's ministry. Any self-proclaimed ministry unrecognized by pillars in the church is dangerous, and out of order.

- *An apostle has the ability to function in each of the other four ascension gift ministries when necessary:* For example, Paul was a prophet to Timothy[38], a teacher at Corinth[39], an evangelist at Athens[40], and a pastor at Ephesus.[41]

- *An apostle has the ability to recognize potential ministry, develop, encourage, and place that ministry:* Paul sent Tychicus to Ephesus[42], Epaphroditus to Philippi[43], Artimas or Tychicus to Titus[44]. The apostles at Jerusalem sent Peter and John to Samaria.[45]

- *An apostle has the authority and ability to correct, when necessary, other ministers:* When the controversy about circumcision arose, Paul and Barnabas went to the apostles and elders at Jerusalem about this question. During the discussion, all four spokesmen were apostles.[46] On another occasion Paul withstood Peter to his face because Peter would not eat with Gentile Christians.[47]

- *An apostle will suffer intense opposition, criticism, persecution and rejection:* Paul was not only persecuted by the Jews and jailed by the Romans. He was criticized and rejected by some of his own spiritual children![48]

---

[36] 1 Cor 4:9.
[37] 2 Cor 12:11,12.
[38] 2 Tim 1:6.
[39] 1 Cor 4:17.
[40] Acts 17:22.
[41] Acts 20:31.
[42] Eph 6:21.
[43] Phil 2:25.
[44] Titus 3:12.
[45] Acts 8:14.
[46] Acts 15:1-21.
[47] Gal 2:11-20.
[48] For example, 2 Cor 10:10.

One of the reasons for the opposition and rejection suffered by true apostles and prophets is that these two are going to have a special ministry in the Last Days:

> "Rejoice over her, O heaven, and you holy apostles and prophets, for God has avenged you on her [Babylon]!" (Rev 18:20)

It does not say pastors, teachers, evangelists, elders, deacons, or congregations were to rejoice – important though all these people be. It says "apostles and prophets." God is going to equip mighty apostles and prophets for a very powerful ministry in these last days, and give them a special part in the fight against evil, and the tearing down of Babylon.

The Lord commended the Ephesian church for their discernment. They were not deceived by those who called themselves apostles but were, in reality, liars.

The sixth commendation the Lord gave the Ephesian church was for their perseverance and patience –

f. **"You have persevered and have patience"**: Here the Lord is, in effect, saying to the Ephesians: "In the midst of this city polluted by every kind of sin and iniquity you have borne the reproach of living a Christlike life, and you are enduring patiently. Even though they persecute, torture, and kill you for not burning incense to the Emperor, you have stood firm."

g. **"You have laboured for My name's sake and have not become weary"**: They remembered what they had been taught by Paul. At their water baptism they had received their coming Bridegroom's Name. Colossæ was not far away, and they had, I'm sure, read in Paul's epistle to the Colossian church, "Whatever you do in word or deed, do all in the name of the Lord Jesus, giving thanks to God the Father through Him."[49] So, knowing the power of the Name of the Lord Jesus Christ, they gladly laboured for His Name's sake.

h. **"You hate the deeds of the Nicolaitans, which I also hate"**: Note it says the Ephesian church hated their deeds, not the people. The word "Nicolaitan" comes from two Greek words, *nikao*, which means "to conquer, or overthrow," and *laos*, meaning "the people, or the laity." Neither the Bible nor history give us much information about what the deeds of the Nicolaitans were, but the Lord Jesus said He hated their deeds.

The Nicolaitan heresy was possibly named after Nicolas, a native of Antioch who converted to Christianity from the Jewish religion. Some early Church writers hold that this sect was started by Nicolas, and promoted by his followers. Irenaeus, who wrote late in the second century (nearly 100 years after the Book of Revelation was written by John), stated that the Nicolaitans *were* founded by Nicolas, the proselyte

---

[49] Col 3:17.

of Antioch mentioned in Acts 6:5. Irenaeus went on to say that Nicolas indulged in adultery, and that the Nicolaitans "lived lives of unrestrained indulgence."[50]

Students of Bible history are united in the belief that the doctrine and the deeds of the Nicolaitans were an extreme form of Gnosticism.[51] Supporters of this deadly doctrine claimed that since their bodies were physical, and therefore evil, only what their spirits did was important. Therefore, they felt free to indulge in sexual immorality, eat food offered to idols, and do anything with their bodies that would satisfy their carnal, ungodly lusts.

To summarize, the Nicolaitans seemed to have held three heretical doctrines:

i. They believed that it was lawful for Christians to eat food which had been sacrificed to idols.

ii. They committed the immoral excesses of the heathen, using as their excuse the false teaching that a person's spiritual and physical natures were completely separate, thereby giving them license to sin. These first two abominations were in direct opposition to the decree of the church rendered in Acts 15:20 and 29.

iii. Many Bible historians believe they tried to establish a "Holy Order of Men." This was a form of ecclesiasticism whereby men were proclaimed to be so "holy" they were able to dominate and rule the spiritual life of the people, and overthrow the right of the laity to approach God directly through Jesus Christ.

> The word "minister" means, in any language, "to serve." As the apostle Paul wrote, "Not that we have dominion (*margin*, 'rule') over your faith, but are fellow workers for your joy; for by faith you stand."[52] A true minister has no desire for prominence or domination, but does all he can to serve God's people, and help strengthen their personal relationship with the Lord.

These three things were done, it must be remembered, not simply as an indulgence of fleshly appetites and pride, but as part of a religious sect that professed itself to be Christian! No wonder the Bible warns, "But there were also false prophets among the people, just as there will be false teachers among you.

---

[50] *Against Heresies* by Irenaeus, I, xxxvi, 3; III, xi, 1.
[51] The Gnostics took their name from the Greek word *gnosis*, which means "knowledge." They professed to have special and unique insights into secret truths about God, man, and life. The Gnostics taught that Jesus was not really the Son of God. They taught matter was evil and spirit was good. Since God was spirit (and therefore good), He could not have created a material world that was evil. They further argued that since spirit and matter could not intermingle, Christ and God could not have united in the person of Jesus. One of the main reasons John wrote his first letter was to expose Gnostic heresy with such statements as "Every spirit that does not confess that Jesus Christ has come in the flesh is not of God" (1 Jn 4:3).
[52] 2 Cor 1:24.

They will secretly introduce destructive heresies, even denying the sovereign Lord who bought them – bringing swift destruction on themselves" (2 Pet 2:1 – *NIV*).

The church at Ephesus was successful in withstanding the work of the Nicolaitans, but, unfortunately, as we shall see, the church at Pergamos was not.

8. Complaint

There was only one complaint against the Ephesian church, but in the light of all they knew and had experienced, it was a very serious one. They had fallen, and left – not lost – their first love. Despite all Christ's commendations of this church, they had left the most important ingredient of any relationship – first love:

> "But I have this [one charge to make] against you: that you have left (abandoned) the love that you had at first [you have deserted Me, your first love]."[53] (Rev 2:4 – *Amp*)

The apostle Paul had, in his letter to the Ephesian church, emphasized the importance of love in marriage, and in the relationship between Christ and His Church.[54] But now, over 30 years later, they had left their first love.

What is first love? First love is not only the intensity and passion of the love we felt for Jesus at the beginning of our relationship with Him. Rather, it is the *sum total of all the love* we have experienced in that relationship from the first day we met Him, until now. Over the years our coming Bridegroom has demonstrated His love to us countless times, through good experiences and bad. As a result, our love for Him, and our relationship with Him, keeps growing and maturing.

I remember vividly the thrill I felt when I first met Pamela in September 1953. I remember the love I felt for her on our wedding day. Through the years our love for each other has grown and matured. It is the sum total of all the love we have experienced and given to each other, during very happy times, and also through difficult times.

If the Ephesian church has left their first love, they are now in their second love. What is second love? Second love is anything that takes the place of our first love relationship with the Lord. Possibly the Ephesians loved the work they did for the Lord more than the Lord Himself.

"I have this against you, that you have left your first love." These are the attitudes the Ephesian church had to overcome. When a Christian falls out of fervent love for his Lord, it affects every area of his life. Unless a serious attitude adjustment is made, he will be

---

[53] The phrase used in the *King James Version* is "I have *somewhat* against thee." The word "somewhat" is in italics, and does not appear in the original. It softens the Lord's complaint and rebuke, whereas this rendering from the *Amplified Bible* brings out the point clearly.
[54] Eph 5:22-33.

overcome by the cares of this life. And when our first love for the Lord has been restored, we need to check our attitude of first love in every area of our life. Have we left our first love for the people of God? Have we left our first love for our husband? Our wife? Our children?

9. Correction

These are the three serious adjustments the Lord commands the Ephesian church to make – Remember, Repent, Repeat ("do the first works").

"Remember therefore from where you have fallen." Remember every occasion the Lord showered His special love upon you. Remember His constant love through the years. Read the Gospels and experience again His great love demonstrated on the Cross. Remember the love of Christ you have experienced while in prayer, while reading the Bible, while in church services. Remember the love of Jesus that flowed through you when you told someone about Him. Remember the release of His love when you were able to forgive that person who had hurt you. Remember!

10. Call

"Repent." Change your mind, so that God can change your heart. Correct your attitudes. Turn from the drudgery of routine Christianity. Turn away from anything that will hinder the rekindling of the fire of God's love in your heart.

11. Caution

In these seven letters there is a "Repent – or else" judgment caution for five churches. The Lord cautions the Ephesian church, "Repent … or else I will come to you quickly and remove your lampstand from its place – unless you repent."

Ephesus was a prosperous commercial metropolis, the capital city of Asia. Today it lies in ruins. The Ephesian church was the largest in the world. It is probable that some individual Christians responded to this message from Christ, but tragically, as a church they did not respond. Today there is no Christian church in Ephesus. There is no Ephesus. Their lampstand was removed.

12. Counsel

"Repeat – Do the first works." Not dead, religious works. But when you've made your attitude adjustment, pray again, inspired by your first love. Read the Bible again with your heart filled with first love for the Lord. Give willingly of your time and finances to the Lord's Kingdom. Do the first works in the same way you did before you left your first love.

Love for Christ is more than an emotion. It is devotion – obedience that springs from love for Him. He said, "If you love me, keep (*margin,* 'you will keep') My commandments."[55]

---

[55] John 14:15.

13. Challenge

It was a challenge for the Ephesian church to return to their first love. But they had been taught how to do it. Before his teaching on marriage and the Bride of Christ, Paul gave the Ephesian church the keys to loving with first love[56]:

a. "Be filled with the Spirit": It is the Holy Spirit Who sheds abroad the love of God in our hearts (Rom 5:5);

b. Praise and worship God: "speaking to one another in psalms and hymns and spiritual songs, singing and making melody in your heart to the Lord;"

c. Be thankful: "Giving thanks always for all things to God the Father;"

d. Remember the power there is in the Lord's Name: "in the name of our Lord Jesus Christ;"

e. Fear God: "Submitting to one another in the fear of God (*margin*, 'Christ')."

These are personal, practical steps we can take to see our first love for Jesus rekindled and restored.

14. Compensation for Conquerors

Every one of the seven churches was given this commandment – "He who has an ear, let him hear what the Spirit says to the churches." This statement was also used by Jesus in the Gospels – "He who has ears to hear, let him hear!"[57]

How the Lord will compensate – reward – those who hear Him and overcome these attitudes is truly wonderful. Eating of the tree of eternal life. The tree of life was lost in the garden as a result of the fall.[58] Thus the promise to those who overcome in the Ephesian church reminds us of the very first bride and bridegroom, Eve and Adam. The tree of life is restored in the last chapter of Revelation.[59] This reminds us of the last Bride and Bridegroom, the glorious church and Christ.

What will the tree of life give? Enthusiasm. Victory. Joy. Vigour. Strength. And ultimately, eternal life. Surely these are the signs of someone enjoying first love!

"To him who overcomes." Overcomes what? Overcomes the lukewarm attitude in the heart of a Christian who has fallen from his first love. Overcomes the attitude of complacency that can spoil our love for the Lord. Overcomes the attitude that forgets the immense price the Lord paid at Calvary.

---

[56] Eph 5:18-21.
[57] For example, Matt 11:15; Luke 8:8.
[58] Gen 3:22.
[59] Rev 22:2.

Thank God for knowledge, growth, and maturity. Rejoice in every opportunity the Lord gives to serve Him. But, wherever He takes you, never leave your first love behind. Always take your first love with you. Don't leave home without it!

Jesus taught that the first and great commandment is centered on first love: "You shall love the Lord your God with all your heart, with all your soul, and with all your mind."[60] If this is the first and great commandment, could it be that the first and great sin is to break this commandment? Think on this.

Let us guard our hearts, and allow nothing to cause our fall from first love. If you sense you have fallen from your first love, don't feel condemned. David prayed, "Restore to me the joy of Your salvation."[61] You can make these words your prayer. As your joy is restored, so will your love. By the Holy Spirit we can overcome every attitude that would tempt us to put Christ second.

The next of the seven churches had to overcome not attitudes, but affliction.

---

[60] Matt 22:37-39.
[61] Psa 51:12.

PART FOUR   THE CHURCHES

Chapter 19.

The Persecuted, Suffering Church

Smyrna ... Overcoming Affliction

Revelation 2:8-11

¹ "And to the angel (*margin*, 'or messenger') of the church in Smyrna write,
² 'These things says the First and the Last, who was dead, and came to life:
³ I know your works, tribulation, and poverty (but you are rich); and I know the blasphemy of those who say they are Jews and are not, but are a synagogue (*margin*, 'congregation') of Satan.
⁴ Do not fear any of those things which you are about to suffer. Indeed, the devil is about to throw some of you into prison, that you may be tested, and you will have tribulation ten days. Be faithful until death, and I will give you the crown of life.
⁵ He who has an ear, let him hear what the Spirit says to the churches. He who overcomes shall not be hurt by the second death.'"

1. Commission

At the commencement of this Second Letter, John was commissioned by the Lord Jesus Christ: "And to the angel (*margin*, 'or messenger') of the church in Smyrna write ..."

2. City

At the time of the writing of the Book of Revelation, Smyrna was, naturally speaking, a splendid, beautiful city. Located 40 miles north of Ephesus, and situated on the Ægean Sea at the mouth of a small river, Meles, Smyrna was one of the finest cities of Asia. It was called "the lovely – the crown of Ionia – the ornament of Asia."

The Ionian Greeks had sailed across the Ægean Sea from Greece to the western coast of Asia Minor (present-day Turkey) to escape invasion. The Ionians in Asia Minor became the cultural leaders of the Greeks in the 600s and 500s B.C., and established a number of prominent cities, the greatest of which were Ephesus, Miletus,[1] and Smyrna. From an

---

[1] See Acts 20:15,17; 2 Tim 4:20.

historical point of view, it is important to note that during the time the Ionians lived in this area, what is known today as Western literature and philosophy originated.

After it had been conquered and inhabited by various invaders, Ionia was freed by Alexander the Great in the late 300s B.C. Nevertheless, Ionia was dominated politically by others – first Alexander's successors, and later, of course, by the Romans. Smyrna, a city of over 100,000 people in Roman times, became one of the most glorious cities in all Asia. It was very well planned, the streets being laid out at right angles. It contained many magnificent buildings, including a large public library. There was also a huge, handsome building surrounded with elaborate porticos which served as a museum. This building was consecrated to the Greek poet Homer, who, according to the proud tradition of the people of Smyrna, lived in their city, some saying he was born there.[2] His two epic poems, the *Iliad* and the *Odyssey*, were very influential, because Homer's portrayals of their gods formed the religious views of the Greeks. The church in Smyrna had to continually contend with Greek religion and culture.

Because of the strong Greco-Roman influence, at the time the letter to Smyrna was written there were three major, and many smaller, Greek and Roman temples in the city. There was a large temple to Jupiter, called Zeus by the Greeks, who was the chief Greek and Roman deity. (When the cripple at Lystra was healed through the ministry of Paul and Barnabas, the people cried out, "'The gods have come down to us in the likeness of men!' And Barnabas they called Jupiter, and Paul, Mercury."[3]) There was also a temple built for the worship of Cybele, more commonly known as Rhea, who, in Greek mythology, was the goddess of the growth of natural things. The Romans called Rhea *Magna Mater* ("Great Mother"). The religious ceremonies in both of these temples involved drunkenness, debauchery, and immorality. These two temples were, together with other lesser temples, situated on a magnificent road that displayed so much gold, both in temples and statues, it was called "The Golden Way."

In the third major temple, every citizen of Smyrna was required to burn incense at a statue of the Roman Emperor. Refusal to worship the Emperor as god resulted in imprisonment, torture, then death. These First Century churches were surrounded by so much idolatry, it is little wonder that John concludes his longest letter with the commandment, "Little children, keep yourselves from idols" (1 Jn 5:21).

This city's name means "myrrh, or, crushed myrrh," "anointing," "bitter." How prophetic and descriptive of the church located there! For the Christians of Smyrna lived in the midst of intense pressure, opposition, affliction, and persecution.

3. Consequences

Smyrna was destroyed by an earthquake in A.D.178, but was quickly rebuilt. Smyrna was among the few Asian cities to withstand Turkish attacks, and was one of the last to fall to the Muslims.

---

[2] Halley, *op.cit.* – page 536.
[3] Acts 14:11,12 – *margin*.

Since the 600s B.C. many different peoples have ruled Smyrna, including the Greeks, the Romans, the Seljuk Turks, the Moguls, and the Ottoman Turks. Since 1424, except for a brief period following the First World War, when the city was given to Greece for administration (from 1919 to 1922), the Turks have controlled Smyrna.

Smyrna continues to this day to be a prosperous Turkish port, an important railroad centre, and a bustling rich hub of trade. The city, now called Izmir by the Turks, is the capital of Izmir *vilayet* (province), and lies about 200 miles southwest of Istanbul. The metropolitan area of the city has a population of well over 600,000. The church at Smyrna remains faithful to Christ to this day.

4. Church

We do not know how this church began. Because both Paul, and his enemies, reported that the Gospel had been preached through the whole of Asia, it is believed that during his time as pastor of the Ephesian church, Paul sent out teams to witness in every city.[4] This seems most likely.

5. Character

Christ reaches back to chapter 1, verse 17 for the two main aspects of His character He wants to emphasize to the Smyrnæan church:

a. "These things says the First and the Last"

Here the Lord is saying to these believers, "I know the beginning and the end of your situation. You are going through hurtful circumstances which you think, because of My apparent silence, I know nothing about. But I know the end result. That is why I have not intervened, and why it appears to you that I am silent."

He is also reminding the church of Smyrna of His words in chapter 1, verse 8:

"I am the Alpha and the Omega, the Beginning and the End, says the Lord, who is and who was and who is to come, the Almighty."

God does not always reveal to us what lies ahead. But here He is assuring a church that is going through acute persecution and suffering that, though they may not understand what is happening right now, He *is* the Almighty, and He *does* have everything under control. He is the Author and Finisher of their faith. He is the One Who Himself endured contradiction – circumstances which on the surface appear to be the opposite of that which God says in His Word.[5]

The believers in Smyrna were suffering, afflicted, persecuted, and facing all kinds of contradiction, and our Lord wrote the shortest letter of the seven to

---

[4] Acts 19:10,26.
[5] Heb 12:1-3

them! This apparent lack of communication could be easily misinterpreted: "We don't have much. We are just a poor suffering church. Jesus doesn't have a lot to say to us."

But the truth is just the opposite! This is a church in which the Lord has nothing to complain about, nothing to correct. His silence is not a mark of disapproval. Rather, it is a sign of His approval.[6]

b. "These things says ...[He] who was dead, and came to life"

Rather than deny their Lord by burning incense to an idol of Caesar, Christians were dying for their faith in Smyrna. So our Lord reminded them there is life after death! Just as He rose triumphant from the dead, so will all who trust in Him. There is a startling similarity between what Jesus went through – persecution, suffering and death – and what this church is going through. To a church in which many are being killed just for believing in Christ the Messiah, this reminder of His resurrection must have been a great encouragement.

6. Conduct

The Lord says to this suffering church, "I know your works." Although they may not think so, He does know the persecution they are enduring, and how they conduct themselves as a result of it.

7. Commendation

Examining the church at Smyrna, the Lord Jesus commends them for five things:

a. "I know your works":
In the midst of unspeakable persecution, every day they were working out this verse in their lives:

"This is a faithful saying, and these things I want you to affirm constantly, that those who have believed in God should be careful to maintain good works. These things are good and profitable to men." (Titus 3:8)

b. "I know your tribulation":
The Greek word *thlipsis*, translated "tribulation," actually means "to suffer affliction." It refers to sufferings due to the pressure of circumstances, or the antagonism of people who oppose us. When this word is used of the present experience of believers in Christ, it denotes almost invariably the pressure and affliction, beyond which they can normally endure – affliction that comes upon them from without.

Tribulation. Affliction. Pressure. Yet the Lord has no complaint about this church. Could we call the church at Symrna a "perfect church"? If so, one of the tests of

---

[6] See chapter 14, "The Silences of God" in Pamela Truscott's book, *Prayer – from a Discipline to a Delight*.

perfection is to be an overcomer while under pressure! Could we say the church at Smyrna was a "glorious church"? Then one of the tests to be in the glorious church is overcoming in the midst of affliction.

The Lord Jesus says to the church at Smyrna, "*I* know your tribulation. *I* know your affliction. *I* know your pressure." The Greek word used for "to know," *oida*, is from the same root as *eidon*, "to see." It is a perfect tense verb with a present meaning. Here "to know" signifies, primarily, to have seen or perceived; hence, to have absolute, full and complete knowledge of that which has been seen. Once again, He is reassuring them – "I really have seen your situation, and know it completely."

Jesus knew and understood personally the intense stress and emotional tension of pressure. He had experienced it. He agonized in prayer in Gethsemane. It was there He was captured. He stood as a prisoner before Pilate, Herod, and later, Pilate again. He was forsaken and denied by His Own disciples. He was brutally whipped. He felt forsaken on Calvary's Cross, as His Father could not look upon the enormity of the sin Jesus bore there. Yes, He understands pressure. He knows what you are going through.

c. **"I know your poverty":** In the New Testament there are a number of Greek words translated "poverty" and "poor." The word used here, *ptōcheia*, does not mean a person is down to their last dollar. It has a much stronger meaning than that. It is used to describe the degree of the poverty Jesus voluntarily experienced on our behalf.[7] It means "totally destitute, and completely stripped of everything, resulting in an utterly beggarly state." Only those who have seen beggars in poor countries such as India can visualize this.

Surely the Lord will now severely chastise the church at Smyrna for their lack of faith? Certainly He will scold them for not rebuking this condition of abject poverty. Now He will complain that they have not turned back two pages in their Bibles and claimed the promise of Third John verse two.

But no. He's commending them. The Lord has no complaint about this church.

It is important we note that the church at Smyrna is not complaining to God, either. They have the same attitude as Job. Job was a man who "was blameless and upright, and one who feared God and turned away from evil."[8] He went from being "the greatest of all the people of the East" to the poorest.[9] Yet in his sickness and poverty the Bible says of Job "he fell to the ground and worshipped." It also records he did not react or complain: "In all this Job did not sin nor charge God with wrong" (Job 1:22).

---

[7] 2 Cor 8:9.
[8] Job 1:1, *margin*.
[9] Job 1:3-21.

The church in Smyrna could be described in the words of James: "Listen, my beloved brethren: Has God not chosen the poor of this world to be rich in faith and heirs of the kingdom which He promised to those who love Him?" (Jas 2:5). They were poor in goods, but rich in faith!

Jesus warned against the "deceitfulness of riches."[10] Is the Lord against riches and prosperity? No. Speaking of the latter days[11], Jeremiah prophesies God's people shall so prosper that the nations shall fear and tremble:

> "Then it shall be to Me a name of joy, a praise, and an honor before all nations of the earth, who shall hear all the good that I do to them; they shall fear and tremble for all the goodness and all the prosperity that I provide for it." (Jer 33:9)

Our Lord Jesus said we will prosper if we give:

> "Give, and [gifts] will be given you, good measure, pressed down, shaken together and running over will they pour into [the pouch formed by] the bosom [of your robe and used as a bag]. For with the measure you deal out – that is, with the measure you use when you confer benefits on others – it will be measured back to you." (Luke 6:38 – *Amp*)

And John the revelator warns us that true prosperity is dependent on spiritual prosperity:

> "Beloved, I pray that you may prosper in all things and be in health, just as your soul prospers." (3 Jn 2)

God was able to display a great truth through the example of the Christians in Smyrna: real contentment and blessing are not determined by what we have, but who we are. Over 2,000 years earlier, He had demonstrated this in Job. His ultimate intention was to make Job a "double-portion man."[12] But first He allowed him to become destitute. Why? Because *God is seeking people who will love and serve Him for Who He is, and not just for what He does, or what He gives.*

I have been released from personal guilt by this truth. During the first few years we lived in India we were almost destitute. I have never described publicly how bad our situation was. People simply would not believe it. I felt embarrassed and responsible for the conditions in which we lived. My wife never complained once. On the contrary, we both felt so honoured to be serving Jesus we often didn't realize how miserable we were! From the example of the church in Smyrna, and the Lord's commendation to them, I have been set free. I have learned it is not a shameful thing to be destitute. In fact, I read in Scripture that

---

[10] Matt 13:22; Mark 4:19; Luke 8:14.
[11] Jer 30:24.
[12] Job 42:8.

those who were destitute because they served God are commended for their faith.[13]

We must all learn the lesson Paul describes in Philippians:

> "I have learned to be satisfied with what I have.
> I know what it is to be in need, and what it is to have more than enough. I have learned this secret, so that anywhere, at any time, I am content, whether I am full or hungry, whether I have too much or too little.
> I have the strength to face all conditions by the power that Christ gives me."
> (Phil 4:11-13 – *TEB*)

The next commendation to this church is:

d. **"But you are rich"**: God does not measure the extent of our riches by the abundance of our money or possessions. Having plenty of external, material things does not mean a person is blessed, spiritual, or happy. Indeed, if money and possessions become our primary goal, then we, like the rich young ruler, disqualify ourselves from the blessing of God.[14] But if money and possessions are just instruments we use to bless others and further the kingdom of God, then the Lord will supply our every need, plus an abundance for His church and His work.

Because the believers in the church at Smyrna would not worship the idol of the Emperor, most of them were unable to qualify for employment. But, although they were unemployable and therefore poor in this world's goods, God assures them that they are rich. They are like Moses, who "Esteem[ed] the reproach of Christ greater riches than the treasures in Egypt" (Heb 11:26 – *KJV*). They were partakers of "the unsearchable riches of Christ,"[15] and "the exceeding riches of His grace."[16] They were experiencing true riches and power: "That He would grant you, according to the riches of His glory, to be strengthened with might through His Spirit in the inner man" (Eph 3:16). These Christians were laying up for themselves "treasures in heaven."[17]

The fifth commendation our Lord gave the Smyrnæan church was for their ability to overcome in the midst of the opposition, reviling, and persecution they received not only from the Greeks and Romans – but also from the Jews:

e. **"I know the blasphemy of those who say they are Jews and are not, but are a synagogue (*margin*, 'congregation') of Satan"**: As we have noted, the early Christian church was made up of Jews and Gentiles who had received Jesus

---

[13] Heb 11:37.
[14] Mark 10:21.
[15] Eph 3:8.
[16] Eph 2:7.
[17] Matt 6:20.

Christ as their Saviour and Lord. In contrasting the unsaved Jew and the saved Jew, Paul makes this clear statement:

> "For he is not a Jew who is one outwardly, nor is circumcision that which is outward in the flesh;
> but he is a Jew who is one inwardly; and circumcision is that of the heart, in the Spirit, not in the letter; whose praise is not from men but from God."
> (Rom 2:28,29)

Jewish synagogues have their origin in the Babylonian captivity. Without a temple in which to worship, the Jews built synagogues (literally, "a bringing together") where they prayed, read, sang their Scriptures, and preached. After the captivity, there were "the temple" and "the synagogues."[18]

Describing his persecution of the church before he met the Lord Jesus, the apostle Paul said, "In every synagogue I imprisoned and beat those who believed on [Christ]."[19] After his conversion, Paul preached in synagogues, and as a result, some Jews turned to Christ and became a part of local churches.[20] But those Jews who rejected the Messiah persecuted and blasphemed the church. They spoke contemptuously about the Lord Jesus, and slandered His followers. They refused to employ Christians, thus increasing the economic stranglehold on the church.

The Jews had brought back from Babylon idolatrous and immoral practices. The synagogues allowed themselves to be further corrupted by the idol worship and sexual promiscuousness of the Greeks and Romans. The Jews became tools of the devil in ridiculing, opposing, and attacking the church. They blasphemed Jesus in such a satanic manner, He called them "the synagogue of Satan."[21] The members of the church at Smyrna had to overcome, with Christlike meekness and forgiveness, affliction and rejection from fellow-citizens, neighbours, and even their own family members who were still members of the synagogue.

There are two basic heresies that emanated from the synagogue of Satan, both of which are extremely harmful to the cause of the Church. The first is false doctrine concerning the Second Person of the Godhead, our Lord Jesus Christ. The second is the mixture of law and grace. Almost every false religious system can be traced to one of these two heresies:

i. **False doctrine concerning the Person of Christ:** Confusion and error concerning Him is the greatest hindrance of all to people coming into a personal relationship with God. Some deny He ever lived. Others say He was a good prophet who was killed by the Romans. Yet others say He is

---

[18] See Acts 24:12.
[19] Acts 22:19; 26:11.
[20] For example, the church at Ephesus. See Acts 18:4.
[21] Note that the only two references to "the synagogue of Satan" are in letters to the churches concerning which the Lord had no complaint – Smyrna and Philadelphia.

a god, and put his statue or picture up with a host of other gods. If any of the basic facts about the Lord Jesus are denied – that He is the eternally-existent Son of God, born of a virgin, Who lived a sinless life as recorded in the Gospels, and shed His perfect blood on the Cross for our sins, rose bodily from the grave, ascended to heaven, sent the Holy Spirit, and is coming again, and that repentance from sin and faith in Him is the only way to God the Father – then there is no hope of salvation. Lack of belief in His uniqueness, holiness, and deity result in idolatry and immorality. This is, I am sure, what happened at the synagogue in Smyrna.

ii. **A mixture of law and grace:** The Bible makes it abundantly clear that salvation is by grace alone, through personal faith in the Lord Jesus Christ.[22] However, the journey from salvation by race to salvation by grace was a long one for the early Church. Peter's vision on the housetop was a turning point.[23] The council at Jerusalem issued decrees.[24] But Judaizers arose, both in the church, and outside the church. Those within the church taught that, in addition to believing on Jesus, Christians should also keep the law of Moses. Those outside the church denied Jesus was the Messiah, blaspheming His Name and persecuting His people.

8. Complaint, 9. Correction, 10. Call, 11. Caution

When we consider all that the church in Smyrna was suffering, it is absolutely amazing the Lord Jesus has not a word of complaint against them. There are no faults to correct. There is no call to repentance. Nor is there a judgment threatened. But there is some gracious counsel, and a strong exhortation for them to be overcomers.

12. Counsel

a. "Do not fear any of those things which you are about to suffer"

When we read the counsel of Christ to the Smyrnæan church, it seems as if their situation is going from bad to worse. The words of the Lord concerning their future seem so contrary to His promises about healing, prosperity, life, freedom, and blessing.

Only two of the seven churches are without complaint from the Lord. These two churches give us a prophetic picture of the overcoming, mature, glorious church. The church in Smyrna must overcome the stress, opposition, and pressure of affliction they suffer because they have put their trust in Christ.

---

[22] Eph 2:8,9.
[23] See Acts chapter 10.
[24] See Acts chapter 15.

The church in Philadelphia must overcome the stress and pressure of opposition they suffer because of their trust in His Word and His Name. Both churches were under terrible pressure. Therefore, we learn from these two churches that one of the major secrets of going on to perfection is learning how to overcome the pressures and stress of opposition.

God promises in His Word He is going to have an overcoming and perfect church. But churches and individuals will have various areas in which they must overcome – love for the Lord, stress, affliction, opposition, temptation, finances, standing for the truth, not denying His Name, and many more. The Lord will allow situations to arise in our lives that must be overcome. Take a simple example: a new believer is baptized in water in the Name of our Lord Jesus Christ. Joy and victory immediately follow. But soon he experiences opposition and contradictions. Why? God is desiring to bring him to maturity. The truth of death, burial and resurrection with Christ, and the power of His Name, is being worked out in a practical way in his life.

Some want to eliminate the word "suffering" from the Christian vocabulary. "Only believe," they say. God says the opposite, "Not only believe." This whole verse reads, "For to you it has been granted on behalf of Christ, not only to believe in Him, but also to suffer for His sake" (Phil 1:29). Learning to be an overcomer in suffering is an integral part of our growth in maturity.

b. "Indeed, the devil is about to throw some of you into prison, that you may be tested ('tried' – *KJV*)"

I cannot say I fully comprehend this. But just as God gave the devil permission to test Job, so He gives the devil permission to test the Smyrnæan church. In this verse, the Greek word translated "tested" is *peirazō*, and means literally "to try, tempt, pierce through." The Lord is not pronouncing a sentence of punishment on this church. He has no complaint. Rather, He is allowing them to experience fiery trials to purify and mature them further:

> "In this [salvation] you greatly rejoice, though now for a little while, if need be, you have been grieved (*margin*, 'distressed') by various trials,
> that the genuineness of your faith, being much more precious than gold that perishes, though it is tested by fire, may be found to praise, honor, and glory at the revelation of Jesus Christ." (1 Pet 1:6,7)

c. "You will have tribulation ten days"

Here the word for "tribulation" means primarily "a pressing, pressure" – also "affliction, anguish, distress, anything which burdens the spirit." Tribulation denotes something or someone from the outside bearing down on the believer.

This is not referring to the stress you feel when your automobile gets a flat tyre. This does not mean the pressure you experience when you need to finish your laundry and your washing machine breaks down. Nor the frustration of knowing your parking meter is running out. How can we call our small every-day challenges "pressure" in the light of the suffering, persecution, and punishment of the Christians in Smyrna?

Tribulation is real, and it will happen to us. Jesus promised it:

> "These things I have spoken to you, that in Me you may have peace. In the world you will have tribulation; but be of good cheer, I have overcome the world." (John 16:33)

I am not convinced the "ten days" is a period of ten literal days, 240 hours. As we learned in our chapter on Bible Numerics, ten is the number that represents trials and testings.[25] I am inclined to believe the Lord is informing the church at Smyrna that there will be a time limit on their afflictions and persecution.[26]

Two examples in Scripture of a period of ten days are found in Daniel and Leviticus. Both references describe a time of testing. Daniel said to the Babylonian steward, "Please test your servants for ten days, and let them give us vegetables to eat and water to drink." The result? "At the end of ten days their features appeared better and fatter in flesh than all the young men who ate the portion of the king's delicacies."[27]

The other example is the ten-day period that was the time of preparation during the feast of Trumpets.[28] There was no ten day period in the feast of Passover. Nor in the feast of Pentecost. But in the feast of Trumpets, on the first day of the seventh month, there was a holy convocation where trumpets were blown. This was followed by ten days of preparation.

On the tenth day of this seventh month was the Day of Atonement – the day of affliction of soul, and the offering made by fire – the Day of the Lord's appearing.[29] As we have seen, we are living in the time of the fulfillment of the festival of Trumpets. It is during this season that God is testing our soul – our mind, emotions, will, purpose, intellect, affections, and motivations. God is examining our discipline, reactions, and emotional responses, in preparation for bringing us into the fullness of the blessing of the Day of Atonement.

---

[25] See Chapter 11, "Numbers In The Bible."
[26] Some scholars teach the ten days is symbolic of the ten Roman Emperors who most vigorously persecuted the early Church.
[27] Dan 1:6-15.
[28] See Chapter 12, "The Festivals of Israel."
[29] Lev 23:23-32.

13. Challenge

Two huge challenges faced the church in Smyrna:

a. "Do not fear any of those things which you are about to suffer"

Do not fear! We are living in an age when we see all around us the fulfillment of the Lord's prophecy, "Men's hearts failing them from fear."[30] Despite all that the believers at Smyrna are suffering, and will suffer, they are encouraged not to fear.

b. "Be faithful until death"

Shouldn't that read, "Be faithful until I get you out of prison"? No. For it takes more faith to die for the Lord in prison – or to die by being crucified, or mauled by wild beasts – than it does to be set free from prison. Hebrews chapter 11 is often called the "Heroes of faith" chapter. The first 35 verses record the great faith exploits of many well-known Bible characters. Verse 36 begins with the words, "Still others," and then describes in graphic detail *their* faith exploits: These "others had trials of mockings and scourgings, yes, and of chains and imprisonment. They were stoned, they were sawn in two, were tempted, were slain with the sword. They wandered about in sheepskins and goatskins, being destitute, afflicted, tormented." And God commends them for their faith.

Not long ago Pamela and I were fellowshipping with the president of a prominent American Christian organization. During the course of our conversation he said, "Graham and Pamela, I am persuaded that the American church has been lulled into such a false sense of security and materialism, that it is totally unprepared for suffering or persecution. I think the unsaved are more prepared for it than the Church!" I agree. I am not prophesying gloom and doom. I am saying we desperately need to learn how to overcome stress, pressure, and affliction. Paul could say this about his sufferings:

> "[Even] now I rejoice in the midst of my sufferings on your behalf. And in my own person I am making up whatever is still lacking and remains to be completed [on our part] of Christ's afflictions, for the sake of His body, which is the Church." (Col 1:24 – *Amp*)

This does not mean that Christ did not suffer sufficiently, but rather, there will be Christians who will walk the pathway that Jesus walked in order that they may be like Him. Peter puts it this way:

> "For what credit is it if, when you are beaten for your faults, you take it patiently? But when you do good and suffer, if you take it patiently, this is commendable before God.

---

[30] Luke 21:26.

For to this you were called, because Christ also suffered for us, leaving us an example, that you should follow His steps." (1 Pet 2:20,21)

The time has come for us to begin to pray this prayer:

"But what things were gain for me, these I have counted loss for Christ.
Yet indeed I also count all things loss for the excellence of the knowledge of Christ Jesus my Lord, for whom I have suffered the loss of all things, and count them as rubbish, that I may gain Christ
and be found in Him, not having my own righteousness, which is from the law, but that which is through faith in Christ, the righteousness which is from God by faith;
That I may know Him and the power of His resurrection, and the fellowship of His sufferings, being conformed to His death." (Phil 3:7-10)

This is not negative. To be ravished with a desire to know Jesus, and be like Him, is the highest longing any Christian can have.

It is difficult to conceive how many of our brothers and sisters in Christ were martyred in the cities of Asia. Multiplied thousands more, from the apostle Paul to Ignatius, bishop of Antioch, were sent to Rome, the capital of the Empire, to be executed there. just for being a Christian. Seven letters of Ignatius, written when on his way to his death in Rome (about A.D.110-115), survive from the beginning of the second century. In these letters he speaks of others who "preceded me from Syria to Rome for the glory of God." One of his letters is addressed to Polycarp, bishop of Smyrna, who in turn became a martyr at approximately 86 years of age (about A.D.156-160).

The execution of Polycarp was carefully recorded by one of his disciples. The proconsul urged Polycarp to deny Christ: "Swear, and I will set you free: execrate [utter curses against] Christ," to which Polycarp bravely replied: "For eighty-six years I have been His servant, and He has never done me wrong: how can I blaspheme my King Who saved me?" ... The proconsul sent the crier to stand in the middle of the arena and announce three times: "Polycarp has confessed that he is a Christian." Then a shout went up from every throat that Polycarp must be burnt alive.

When the pyre was ready, Polycarp prayed: "O Father of Thy Beloved and Blessed Son, Jesus Christ, through whom we have come to know Thee, the God of angels and powers and all creation, and of the whole family of the righteous who live in Thy presence; I bless Thee for counting me worthy of this day and hour, that in the number of the martyrs I may partake of Christ's cup, to the resurrection of eternal life of both soul and body in the imperishability that is the gift of the Holy Spirit ..." When he completed his prayer, his executioners lit the fire, and a great flame shot up. He was burned alive.[31] Polycarp was indeed "faithful until death."

The Bible contains many exhortations to faithfulness. Paul wrote to the church at Corinth, "Moreover, it is [essentially] required of stewards that a man should be found faithful – proving himself worthy of trust" (1 Cor 4:2 – *Amp*). In *The Living Bible* this verse reads: "Now the most important thing about a servant is that he does just what his master tells him to."

During the battle that brings about the fall of Babylon, the ten kings and the beast "will make war with the Lamb, and the Lamb will overcome them, for He is Lord of lords and King of kings; and those who are with Him are called, chosen, and faithful" (Rev 17:14). "Called, chosen, and faithful." This faithfulness is further rewarded when the Lord returns: "Well done, good servant; because you were faithful in a very little, have authority over ten cities" (Luke 19:17).

c. "and I will give you the crown of life"

"Faithful unto death." Job was able to say in the midst of his many afflictions, "Though He slay me, yet will I trust Him."[32] In the midst of incredible pressure he overcame, and received a double portion from the Lord.[33]

The worst thing that could happen to us in our afflictions is that we could die, right? Wrong! Paul said, "For to me, to live is Christ, and to die is gain ... I [have] a desire to depart and be with Christ, which is far better" (Phil 1:22,23). We should not desire death nor should we fear death. The crown of life is the victor's crown of *eternal* life – the "imperishable crown"[34] – given to all who endure:

> "Blessed is the man who endures temptation; for when he has been approved, he will receive the crown of life which the Lord has promised to those who love Him." (Jas 1:12)

Or, in the words of our Lord Jesus:

> "And you will be hated by all for My name's sake. But he who endures to the end will be saved." (Matt 10:22)

So what is the challenge to the believers in Smyrna? What have they to overcome? Affliction – and the misunderstanding that because they were experiencing pressure and contradictions, God was not with them. Some Christians have been

---

[31] Adapted from *Eerdmans' Handbook to the History of Christianity, op.cit.* – page 81; citing Eusebius, *History of the Church* IV 15.
[32] Job 13:15.
[33] Job 42:8.
[34] 1 Cor 9:25.

taught that if circumstances are against you, you must be out of the will of God. But the truth is this – there are times when it can seem that everything is against you, yet you are still in the will of God. Conversely, there are times when everything appears to be going well for you, and yet you are out of the will of God. Both good times and bad times have their own challenges and temptations, and we must learn to be overcomers in all circumstances.

14. Compensation for Conquerors

Although the Lord has no complaint against the church in Smyrna, He exhorts them to listen to His Spirit: "He who has an ear, let him hear what the Spirit says to the churches." This is followed by a wonderful promise to each Christian who overcomes affliction – those who overcome both the attack, and the temptation to feel sorry for themselves. **"He who overcomes shall not be hurt by the second death."**

Jesus taught there will be two resurrections. As we will see in our future studies, these two resurrections are separated by 1,000 years.[35]

> "Do not marvel at this; for the hour is coming in which all who are in the graves will hear His voice
> and come forth – those who have done good, to the resurrection of life, and those who have done evil, to the resurrection of condemnation." (John 5: 28,29)

The first death is natural death, the death of the body. The church at Smyrna was very familiar with this. However, the second death is when all who have not received Christ will be cast into the lake of fire for everlasting punishment:

> "Blessed and holy is he who has part in the first resurrection. Over such the second death has no power, but they shall be priests of God and of Christ, and shall reign with Him a thousand years ...
> Then Death and Hades were cast into the lake of fire. This is the second death."
> (Rev 20:6,14)

The message of our Lord Jesus to the church in Smyrna is not a "negative" Gospel. It is a "reality" Gospel – it describes the real conditions of millions of our brethren throughout the world today who are being hated for His Name's sake. In many nations of Africa and Asia Christians live under intense pressure. They are being persecuted, beaten, and killed because they believe in Jesus. Fortunately, most of them had never heard that if they came to Jesus they would live comfortably and prosperously ever after. Thus believers in these nations are far better prepared for affliction than members of the Western Church.

When we were resident missionaries in India, those who wanted to be baptized into Christ had to go before a magistrate and receive a certificate of permission. I would always ask them two questions in the waters of baptism: "Will you live for the Lord Jesus Christ for the remainder of your life? Are you willing to die for Him?" I was not being

---

[35] Rev 20:5.

melodramatic in asking this question. For some were killed – even by members of their own families – for their faith. In the past few years there has been an alarming increase in persecution of the Church in India. Church buildings have been firebombed. Christians beaten, drowned, crucified, and burned alive. They have been willing to die for Him.

The Word of God declares:

> "Many are the afflictions of the righteous,
> But the Lord delivers him out of them all." (Psa 34:19)

"Many are the afflictions of the righteous." But when the Lord has completed His intended work of grace, in His Own time, and in His Own way, He will deliver His people from every affliction – sometimes, by taking them to Himself in Heaven.

The church in Smyrna had to overcome affliction. The church in Pergamos had to overcome wrong associations.

PART FOUR   THE CHURCHES

Chapter 20

The Church with Doctrinal Error

Pergamos ... Overcoming Associations

Revelation 2:12-17

¹² "And to the angel (*margin*, 'or messenger') of the church in Pergamos write,
'These things says He who has the sharp two-edged sword:
¹³ I know your works, and where you dwell, where Satan's throne is. And you hold fast to My name, and did not deny My faith even in the days in which Antipas was My faithful martyr, who was killed among you, where Satan dwells.
¹⁴ But I have a few things against you, because you have there those who hold the doctrine of Balaam, who taught Balak to put a stumbling block before the children of Israel, to eat things sacrificed to idols, and to commit sexual immorality.
¹⁵ Thus you also have those who hold the doctrine of the Nicolaitans, which thing I hate.
¹⁶ Repent, or else I will come to you quickly and will fight against them with the sword of My mouth.
¹⁷ He who has an ear, let him hear what the Spirit says to the churches. To him who overcomes I will give some of the hidden manna to eat. And I will give him a white stone, and on the stone a new name written which no one knows except him who receives it.'"

1. **Commission**

Once again, John receives the commission from the Lord to write to this local church: "And to the angel (*margin*, 'or messenger') of the church in Pergamos write ..."

2. **City**

The ancient Greek city of Pergamos, also known as Pergamum and Pergamon, was situated about 12 miles from the west coast of Asia Minor, in the province of Mysia[1] (located in modern-day Turkey). Later, from about 283 to 133 B.C., it became the capital

---
[1] Acts 16:7,8.

of the kingdom of Pergamum. This city first acquired prominence when the Macedonian general Lysimachus chose its acropolis, a citadel 1,000 feet above sea level, as a stronghold for his treasures, which he entrusted to the governor of Pergamos.

Pergamos grew into a glorious and important city, compared to Alexandria and Antiochia. It is believed that in this city the art of making parchment was discovered, which was called, in Latin, *pergamena* ("paper of Pergamos").[2] The city boasted a vast library of 200,000 volumes, which, however, was removed by Mark Antony (82-30 B.C.), the friend of Caesar, and given as a present to Cleopatra, whom Antony later married. In addition, during this period many of the city's art and sculpture masterpieces were transferred to Rome.

After the death of Alexander the Great in 323 B.C., the kingdom of Pergamos was taken over by Attalos, and the Attalian dynasty ruled the kingdom for approximately 150 years (283-133 B.C.). During this era, under the sumptuous excesses of the Attalian princes, who also wielded religious power and authority, Pergamos was raised, as regards splendor, to the first city of Asia. It became an important trade, industrial, scientific and art center. In 133 B.C. the king of Pergamos bequeathed his kingdom to the Romans, under whose control Pergamum remained one of the chief cities of Asia Minor.

The city was addicted to idolatry and debauchery, and its grove, which was one of the wonders of Pergamos, was filled with statues and altars.[3] Eventually, Pergamos became a city in which there was a union of the following: a pagan cathedral city, a university town, a center of great political power, a royal residence (embellished by a succession of kings who all had a passion for expenditure and ample means to gratify it), and a city of many temples, all devoted to idols and sensuousness.

At the time the Lord's letter was written to the church in Pergamos, in their city were the headquarters of three major powers, all vehemently opposed to Christianity:

   a. *Pergamos was a centre of Roman political power:* Because Pergamos was such a political power in a Roman province, emperor worship was strictly enforced on all its citizens. Refusal to burn incense at the altar in the temple erected to the Roman Caesar resulted in imprisonment, torture, and ultimately, death.

   b. *Pergamos was the seat of power for the Babylonian priesthood:* The Babylonian religion and priesthood originated with Nimrod, who was so opposed to the true God, Jehovah, he used hungry leopards to hunt down those who believed in Him. The beginning of his kingdom was Babel[4] (Greek, "Babylon"). Nimrod's city was the commencement of political Babylon. Nimrod's tower was the commencement of spiritual Babylon, a religion of astrological predictions, occult

---

[2] The skin of a very young calf, sheep, or goat was dressed and prepared in a special way rendering it fit for writing on.
[3] An elaborate replica of the altar of Pergamos, based on archaeological findings, is in the Berlin State Museum, Germany.
[4] Gen 10:8ff.

mysteries and witchcraft, priests with great ecclesiastical power and authority over their people, and the worship of human beings. This subject continues right through the Bible until the destruction of both Babylons, which is described in the Book of Revelation.[5]

When the Babylonian empire fell to Cyrus king of the Medes and Persians on October 13, 539 B.C. it is believed that the high priest of Babylon, and many other Babylonian priests, together with all their regal and ecclesiastical trappings, were absorbed into the Medo-Persian captivity. From that time the decline and ultimate decay of the once-great city of Babylon began, and by the year 280 B.C. the city had become a desert wasteland. It was about this time the Babylonian high priest, together with a number of other Babylonian priests, fled to Pergamos, taking their mystical religion with them. Some scholars believe that this Babylonian high priest was none other than Attalos, the founder of the Attalian dynasty.

The power of the Babylonian priesthood would, by the end of the first century A.D. move to the city of Rome. However, this transfer of power really commenced when the fourth prince of the Attalian dynasty, Attalus III Philometor, gave his kingdom to the Romans in 133 B.C. When the letters to the seven churches were written, Pergamos was still the seat of power and authority for the religion of Babylon. This is the main reason why the Lord Jesus said to the church in Pergamos: "You dwell where Satan's throne is."

c. *Pergamos was the headquarters for the worship of Æsculapius:* In the city there were many large and ornate temples – the temple of Zeus (also called Jupiter) which housed the most magnificent altar ever seen until that time, of Athene, and of Dionysos (also called Apollo). One of the most powerful – mainly for its mystical and demonic power – was the temple of Æsculapius, the god of healing in Greek and Roman mythology.

---

[5] In **HERE COMES THE BRIDE! Volume Two** I will trace Babylon's line from Genesis to Revelation. In these Last Days all the rebellion, witchcraft, and controlling wickedness of the spirit of Babylon are joining together to form a political, financial, and religious system to take over and control the world. This system is diametrically opposed to the Lord Jesus Christ and His Church. Some important references:
• Isaiah chapters 13 and 14 – Prophecy against Babylon, and its coming fall;
• Isaiah chapters 47 and 48 – Prophecy against Babylon's witchcraft, astrologers, pleasures, and its coming fall;
• Daniel chapters 1 to 5 – The glory of Babylon, and prophecy of its fall;
• Zechariah chapter 5 – Prophecy of the rebuilding of the land of Shinar (Babylon, see Gen 10:10);
• Revelation chapter 17 – A woman called Babylon;
• Revelation chapter 18 – A city called Babylon.

Those who wish to make a detailed study of Babylon are referred to *The Two Babylons* by Alexander Hislop. The copy in my study is the Second American Edition, and was published by Loizeaux Brothers, Inc., Neptune, New Jersey, in 1959.

It is important that I state here I hold those who work in modern medicine in high esteem. I am privileged to count as friends a number of medical doctors. We encouraged our daughter Debbie in her nursing studies and career.

In the days when the letter to Pergamos was written, nothing was understood of the practice of medicine as we know it, with its hygiene, anaesthetics, surgical procedures, and medicines. Rather, the methods of healing were mystical, involving the worship of idols and secret things, prayers to evil spirits, trances – and what was done to the human body was in total opposition to modern medical science.

In art and sculpture, Æsculapius was pictured bearing a staff with a serpent entwined around it. The serpent was the ancient symbol of health, because it could shed its skin and appear young again.[6]

Pergamos was the world headquarters for the mystical worship of Æsculapius. The city's inhabitants were daily reminded of this, for the symbol of this god was stamped on one side of their coins.

The name Pergamos has two major meanings: "citadel, berg, castle, highly elevated," and "married to power," "thoroughly married." The significance of this will become apparent as we continue our study of the church at Pergamos.

3. Consequences

The Arabs conquered and looted Pergamos in 716, when Pergamos lost the last vestiges of its political power. Tamerlane the Tartar, a Mongol Turk descended from Genghis Khan and a very devout Muslim, attacked the city in 1401. The subsequent Turkish rule resulted in a shrinking of the Greek population.

By 1675 there were no more than 20 Christian families left in the city. The number of Greeks continued to dwindle, and after the Asia Minor Catastrophe in August 1922 the Hellenic population of Pergamos escaped as refugees to Greece. The city gradually fell into ruin, and is now a scene of desolation.

The ruins of ancient Pergamos surround the modern Turkish town of Bergama, and among the most impressive remains are a Roman theatre, amphitheatre, and race track.

4. Church

Once again, there is no direct record in Scripture concerning the commencement of this church. As with the church in Smyrna, it was probably begun from Ephesus,[7] because Pergamos was only 50 miles north of Smyrna.

---

[6] The serpent-entwined staff of Æsculapius is used in modified form as a symbol by the United States Department of Health, Education, and Welfare.
[7] Acts 19:10,26.

5. Character

The Lord Jesus Christ reaches back to the first chapter of Revelation, verse 16, and emphasizes just one aspect of His character from that vision to the church in Pergamos: **"These things says He who has the sharp two-edged sword."**

Notice the sword of the Lord is in His mouth, not in His hand. This, of course, is speaking of the power of His Word:

> "For the word of God is living and powerful, and sharper than any two-edged sword, piercing even to the division of soul and spirit, and of joints and marrow, and is a discerner of the thoughts and intents of the heart." (Heb 4:12)

God's sharp sword can cut, sever, separate, divide – and discern! This is exactly what the believers in Pergamos need. They must separate themselves from wrong and harmful associations with those who try to justify their sin by teaching false doctrine. Only God's Word, as a two-edged sword, can bring separation, cleansing, and holiness. They must overcome sin, not make excuses for it.

The Lord wants to do "spiritual surgery" in Pergamos. Sometimes it is necessary for a surgeon to use his scalpel to save a patient's life. Covering the problem with a strip of sticking plaster won't do. Counseling won't cure it. The doctor must cut out the offending flesh. In doing so, he causes a wound that will heal, thus bringing health to the body. In *The Message*, Hebrews 4:12 reads:

> "God means what he says. What he says goes. His powerful Word is sharp as a surgeon's scalpel, cutting through everything, whether doubt or defense, laying us open to listen and obey. Nothing and no one is impervious to God's Word. We can't get way from it – no matter what."

The Lord tells this local church that they are associating with people of whom He does not approve. These teachers of false doctrine must be separated and removed from their midst. If they are not cut away, their teachings will destroy the church. "The sword of the Spirit, which is the word of God" must be allowed to cut away every hindrance to growth and holiness in order for them to become overcomers.

6. Conduct

To the statement "I know your works" the Lord adds these words to the church at Pergamos – "[I know] where you dwell, where Satan's throne is."

The Greek word for "throne" is *thronos*, which literally means "a throne, a seat of authority." The Devil had set up a throne for himself in Pergamos, and right there in that very same city a Christ-honouring church had been established. What a wonderful victory for the New Testament Church!

As we draw our attention to "Satan's throne," we need to remember it appears from Scripture that angels have ranks, or orders of authority.[8] We have already considered the rebellion and fall of Satan and his angels.[9] Fallen angels now fight against God in corrupting mankind. The fallen angels have maintained their rank and order of authority under Satan's leadership. Therefore, Satan appoints prince evil spirits to rule over nations.[10] This is because Satan is not omnipresent. He has a place for his throne upon the earth. When John wrote the letter to this church Satan's throne was there in Pergamos – because, as we have seen, at that time Pergamos was the seat of power of the Babylonian priesthood.

Victory over Satan

There is a great need for balance as regards the subject of Satan and spiritual warfare. We need to know that the Devil and his demons are real. We are in a spiritual battle:

> "Put on all the armour that God gives you, so that you will stand up against the Devil's evil tricks.
> For we are not fighting against human beings, but against the wicked spiritual forces in the heavenly world, the rulers, authorities, and cosmic powers of this dark age." (Eph 6:11,12 – *TEV*)

But not every problem we face is a direct result of Satan's activities, or demonic influence. We need to remember two very important things: Firstly, we should use discernment, maturity, love, grace, and compassion when praying for people.

Secondly, we cannot blame the Devil for our own carnality or spiritual laziness. Rather, we must be vigilant to realize our need to die daily, to discipline ourselves, and to grow in our knowledge of Christ Jesus. The Christian life is not a series of simplistic, quick fixes obtained by binding and casting out the Devil.

Just as he had in Bible days, so today the Devil has thrones on earth for himself, and his chief assistants. There is an important satanic throne in the capital city of every nation on earth. There are other thrones in various places. And because Satan is "the prince of the power of the air" there is a sense in which all of us, to some extent, dwell where Satan's seat is.[11]

But just as in Revelation the promises of God were to overcomers, so today the Lord promises His blessing to overcomers. And is not this one of the most encouraging truths in the Bible – that by His death and resurrection Jesus Christ overcame Satan, and, with the Lord reigning supreme in our hearts, we too can overcome Satan?

---

[8] For example, Eph 6:12.
[9] See Chapter 10, "God's Week."
[10] For example, Dan 10:13.
[11] Eph 2:2.

Jesus overcame the Devil in the wilderness.[12] Jesus gave the seventy power to overcome the Devil.[13] At the Cross Jesus "disarmed principalities and powers."[14] "He stripped all the spiritual tyrants in the universe of their sham authority at the Cross."[15]

After His triumphant resurrection from the dead He told His disciples, "These signs will follow those who believe: In My name they will cast out demons."[16] John declares, "For this purpose the Son of God was manifested, that He might destroy the works of the devil."[17] This promised victory is ours through our Lord Jesus Christ: "You have overcome the wicked one."[18]

In these days we see an increase in the onslaught of the powers of darkness. But we need not fear. Our Lord Jesus Christ has overcome the power of the Devil. And He can make us overcomers.

7. Commendation

The fact that the believers in the Pergamos church lived where Satan's seat was, is both an observation of their conduct and a commendation. Thus there are three ways in which the Lord commends this church:

a. "I know your works, and where you dwell, where Satan's throne is ... where Satan dwells":

It is difficult for us to contemplate, but this church was living in a city where temples to false gods stood on every street corner and in every public square.

In these temples, sexual vice was not only condoned, but was, in most temples, promoted as an act of "worship." Everyone living in Pergamos was confronted with this daily.

Also, because Pergamos was such an important political city in the Roman province of Asia, emperor worship was compulsory. In addition, Pergamos was the seat of power of the Babylonian priesthood, with all its accompanying mysticism, idolatry, control, and sexual perversion. "I see where you live, right under the shadow of Satan's throne."[19] That a church was established and functioning in Satan's territory was indeed commendable.

The Lord had further commendations for the church at Pergamos:

---

[12] Matt 4:1-11.
[13] Luke 10:19.
[14] Col 2:14,15.
[15] Col 2:15 – *TM*.
[16] Mark 16:17.
[17] 1 Jn 3:8.
[18] 1 Jn 2:14.
[19] Rev 2:13 – *TM*.

b. "You hold fast to my Name":

Earlier we saw the significance of the fact that on the fulfillment of the Day of Pentecost to the New Testament Church, Peter received the revelation of the Name of God – the Lord Jesus Christ.[20] We also saw that betrothal, or engagement, in Bible days, was a binding covenant. The members of the church at Pergamos had received the Name of their heavenly Bridegroom the day they were baptized in water – "Is it not they who slander and blaspheme that precious name by which you are distinguished and called [the name of Christ invoked in baptism]?" (Jas 2:7 – *Amp*)

The New Testament Church was commanded – as are we – to, "Let every detail in your lives – words, actions, whatever – be done in the name of the Master, Jesus" (Col 3:17 – *TM*). How they loved and revered His Name:

> "Therefore God also has highly exalted Him and given Him the name which is above every name,
> that at the name of Jesus every knee should bow, of those in heaven, and of those on earth, and of those under the earth,
> and that every tongue should confess that Jesus Christ is Lord, to the glory of God the Father." (Phil 2:9-11)

But everyone around them hated that Name with a passion! The Greeks, the Romans, the Jews – the whole city – reviled that Name. When the disciples of Jesus of Nazareth were first called Christians at Antioch, it was a term of derision.[21] Nowhere was this derision more noticeable than in Pergamos. Here Christians were arrested, jailed, tortured, and killed. And yet, despite the risks, the threats, the persecution, Jesus commended them because, as He said to them, "you hold fast to my Name." In the Greek language, there are many words for "hold." The word used here, *tēreō,* is very significant. It means "to watch, to keep, to observe, to preserve, to give heed to." What a commendation!

"But you continue boldly in my Name; you never once denied my Name, even when the pressure was worst, when they martyred Antipas, my witness who stayed faithful to me on Satan's turf." (Rev 2:13 – *TM*)

c. "and [you] did not deny My faith even in the days in which Antipas was My faithful martyr, who was killed among you, where Satan dwells":

Thirdly, the Lord commends the Pergamos church for their faith.

They had heard the Gospel, and at great personal cost they had left the idolatry and sexual perversions of their temples, or the unbelief and sins of their Jewish synagogues, and placed their faith in the Lord Jesus Christ. The world system

---

[20] Chapter 10, "God's Week."
[21] Acts 11:26.

around them was rotten to the core. But it could not cause these faithful followers of Jesus to deny their faith. They were about to learn of a situation they needed to overcome. But as far as faith was concerned, they were overcomers:

> "For whatever is born of God overcomes the world. And this is the victory that has overcome the world – our (*margin*, 'your') faith.
> Who is he who overcomes the world, but he who believes that Jesus is the Son of God?" (1 Jn 5:4,5)

Antipas was assuredly one of many martyrs from the church at Pergamos. He could have been one of the early pastors of this church. The church members could have lost their faith because their leader was killed by the enemies of Christ. Maybe he was killed by the Roman prelate for not worshipping Caesar. Maybe he was killed by the Babylonian priesthood for refusing to participate in their mysterious worship. Maybe the priests of the temple of Æsculapius killed him because they heard that people were being healed when prayed for in the Name of Jesus Christ by Pastor Antipas.

Perhaps members of the synagogue of Satan decided to get rid of him. However Antipas was martyred, despite his murder – together with constant death threats to themselves – this church did not deny their faith.

The truth is, that it requires more faith to go through a trial than to be delivered from it. We saw this when we looked at the "heroes of faith" in Hebrews chapter 11. Like Jesus, when we face contradictions, we must endure.[22] For true faith is not found in simplistic formulas and quick-easy religious methods. Faith is not demonstrated by shouting Bible verses at difficult situations hoping they will go away.

In the Book of Acts, James was put in jail, and beheaded. Peter was put in the very same jail, and an angel came and set him free.[23] Who had faith? Both of them!

Faith is the fundamental quality of our relationship with God. The writer of Hebrews states:

> "Without faith it is impossible to please Him, for he who comes to God must believe that He is, and that He is a rewarder of those who diligently seek Him." (Heb 11:6)

The Greek word for faith is *pistis*, and means "firm persuasion, a conviction based on hearing, trust, faithfulness, fidelity, firm conviction." The Bible definition of faith is found in Hebrews 11:1:

---

[22] Heb 12:1,2.
[23] Acts 12:2; 3-18.

"Now faith is the realization of things hoped for, the confidence of things not seen." (*Margin*)

"The fundamental fact of existence is that this trust in God, this faith, is the firm foundation under everything that makes life worth living. It's our handle on what we can't see." (*TM*)

For holding on to their faith under extreme pressure, the Lord commends the church at Pergamos: "You are true to me, and you did not abandon your faith in me."[24]

"Faith toward God" is listed as one of the seven "elementary principles of Christ" (Heb 6:1,2). Each of these elementary principles has five distinct aspects – there are five types of repentance, five different baptisms, five separate ministrations of the laying on of hands, and so on. The five aspects of faith are:

a.	Saving Faith:	Eph 2:8,9 –	Trusting the Word
b.	Faith, the Fruit of the Spirit:	Gal 5:22,23 –	Obeying the Word
c.	Faith, the Gift of the Spirit:	1 Cor 12:9 –	Speaking the Word
d.	Doctrinal Faith:	Jude 3 –	Teaching the Word
e.	The Spirit of Faith:	2 Cor 4:13 –	The Word of Faith Perfected

As the church in Pergamos experienced, when the fruit of faith grows in the garden of our hearts, this fruit is sometimes watered with tears, strengthened in storms, refined in testing – but never wavers in contradictions.

"You did not deny My faith."[25] When we face contrary circumstances, may the same be written of us.

8. Complaint

The Lord has two very serious complaints concerning the church at Pergamos. The first concerns the doctrine of Balaam:

"But I have a few things against you, because you have there those who hold the doctrine of Balaam, who taught Balak to put a stumbling block before the children of Israel, to eat things sacrificed to idols, and to commit sexual immorality."

---

[24] Rev 2:13 – *TEV*.
[25] Rev 2:13 – *Amp*.

The second is the doctrine of the Nicolaitans:

"Thus you also have those who hold the doctrine of the Nicolaitans, which thing I hate."

If ever there was a situation which answers those who say, "It doesn't matter what you believe. Doctrine is not important," this is it. The importance of sound doctrine is foremost[26] – what we believe totally governs the way we behave. This is why Paul exhorted Timothy, "Take heed to yourself and to the doctrine."[27]

Here is a church in the New Testament which, having been commended for its steadfastness and faith, is now being rebuked by the Lord Jesus for allowing into their fellowship those who hold wrong doctrines – doctrines which the Lord says, "I hate." The Lord is careful to point out it is not the whole church which believes these false doctrines, but that there are some who have association and fellowship with those who do believe them.

This is what the Lord is saying here: "You are allowing into your assembly those who believe and practice these hateful doctrines. You have people in your midst who claim to be Christians, and yet, so they may eat food sacrificed to idols and commit sexual immorality, hold doctrines by which they excuse their sin. By their wrong beliefs they justify their wrong behaviour. By their incorrect creeds they defend their incorrect conduct. Though you as a whole congregation do not hold to these doctrines, you are allowing some to do so. You are not confronting the situation. You are not dealing with it. You are not making it clear to those with these deceitful doctrines that they need to repent, or you will excommunicate them from your church. If you don't act, these heresies could spread to others in your assembly. So if you love those of your brothers and sisters who are in this error, confront them soon. Otherwise I will come to you quickly, and I Myself will fight against them with the sword of My mouth."

a. The Doctrine of Balaam

It is hard to imagine how such an abominable teaching as the doctrine of Balaam could creep into a New Testament church. This teaching later became known as the "Antinomian heresy" which, simply put, says, "If you name the Name of Christ, and you are in the faith, your conduct does not matter. There is no connection between your spirit and your body (Gnosticism again). Once you are saved, you can live your life as you please. God's covenants can never be broken; sin cannot violate a covenant." Thus the doctrine of Balaam can be defined, "Taking the things of God, the world, and the devil, and mixing them together using false interpretations of Scripture to justify sinful behaviour."

I have summarized the doctrine of Balaam in chart form (see *Figure 36*, pages 256-257). The story of Balaam is found in Numbers chapters 22 through 25.

---

[26] 2 Tim 4:3; Titus 1:9,2:1.

[27] 1 Tim 4:16.

Balaam was a man hired by Balak, king of Moab, to prophesy against the children of Israel. He wanted Balaam to curse this nation that had come up out of Egypt. He believed that if such a curse was pronounced upon them, Israel would be weakened, thus enabling Balak to defeat them, and drive them out of the land.

God appeared to Balaam and warned him not to go. Balak sent his princes back to Balaam, offering him silver, gold, and great honour if he would curse Israel.

Balaam, lured by the offer of Balak to hire him, started on his way, only to be spoken to by his ass, and also by the Angel of the Lord. Balaam offered to go back, but the Angel said he must now go forward. He met King Balak, who took him to three different mountains, and three times offered sacrifices, asking Balaam to curse Israel. But although Balaam was a soothsayer who practiced divination,[28] God caused him to prophesy blessings on Israel, not curses. Balak became angry and sent Balaam away without rewarding him. Ultimately, Balaam was killed with the sword.[29]

But that is not the whole story. Numbers chapter 25 opens with these alarming words: "Now Israel remained in Acacia Grove, and the people began to commit harlotry with the women of Moab. They [the Moabites] invited the people [of Israel] to the sacrifices of their gods, and the people ate and bowed down to their gods. So Israel was joined to Baal of Peor, and the anger of the Lord was aroused against Israel."[30]

Balaam had just blessed the children of Israel. Yet the next thing we read is that the very same people Balak, King of Moab, wanted to destroy are bowing down to his idols. The Moabite girls have persuaded the Israelite boys to join them in their lewd and immoral idol-worshipping feasts. They are associating together. They are mixing the sins of Moab with the people of God. The Lord so hated this association between Israel and Moab he slew 42,000 Israelites.[31]

How could this possibly happen? It happened because of the counsel of Balaam!

> "Look, these women caused the children of Israel, through the *counsel of Balaam*, to trespass against the Lord in the incident of Peor." (Num 31:16)

When Balaam was unable to curse Israel, he went home, his passions still driven by greed for the wages of unrighteousness. If Balaam was unsuccessful in pronouncing weakness over Israel, he would weaken them another way. So he corrupted God's people by counseling them to associate with the Moabites – to fall down before Moab's idols, and have sex with their women. He counseled Israel with this false teaching – they could break the Ten Commandments,

---

[28] Josh 13:22.
[29] Num 31:8.
[30] Num 25:1-3.
[31] Num 25:9

because, Balaam said, according to the words of blessing he had prophesied over them, mixing with the Moabites could not possibly harm them. Little wonder that the Lord, speaking through the prophet Micah concerning what He requires, says:

> "O My people, remember now
> What Balak king of Moab counseled,
> And what Balaam the son of Beor answered him,
> From Acacia Grove (*margin*, 'Shittim') to Gilgal,
> That you may know the righteousness of the Lord
> He has shown you, O man, what is good;
> And what does the Lord require of you

Figure 36A: The Doctrine of Balaam
(Revelation 2:14)

OLD TESTAMENT			NEW TESTAMENT		
Balaam (Num 22-26, 31:16)	**Nimrod** (Gen 10 & 11)	**Lucifer** (Isa 14; Eze 28)	**Pergamos** Doctrine of Balaam (Rev 2:14)	**Thyatira** Jezebel (Rev 2:20-24)	**Acts 15** (N.T. Commandments)
Sexual (Fleshly Lust) 1. Commit whoredom with the daughters of Moab. (Num 25:1)	No restraint (Gen 11:6) including sexual impurity and perversion.	"Iniquity of thy traffic" (Eze 28:18) "Tabrets and pipes" (v13) "Perfect in beauty" (v12)	1. Committed fornication.	Taught and seduced the Lord's servants to commit fornication.	Abstain from fornication.
Material (Pride and Covetousness) 2. Asked to speak for rewards. (Num 22:7)	"Mighty upon the earth" (1 Chron 1:10) including wealth.	"I will exalt my throne," (Isa 14:13)	2. Stumbling blocks. Mixture from Babylonian religion.	She called herself a prophetess.	Abstain from things strangled and from blood.
Devotional (Worship) 3. BALAAM "I will promote thee unto very great honor" (Num 22:17) ISRAEL – Bowed down to Moab's gods. (Num 25:2)	"Let us make us a city, tower, and name." Pride, idolatry, pagan occult worship. First worship of human beings.	"I will be like the most high" (Isa 14:14)	3. Ate things sacrificed to idols.	Taught and seduced the Lord's servants to eat things sacrificed to idols.	Abstain from pollution of idols.

But to do justly, And to love mercy
And to walk humbly with your God?" (Mic 6:5,8)

As Dr Judson Cornwall writes in his last book, *Forbidden Glory*, in the chapter entitled "Pride and Ministry":

"Balaam's problem was not that he was false, but that he was mixed. He could contact God, and apparently, also contact the demonic realm, for God is not in the business of cursing or carrying out curses. Balaam had a reputation for successfully bringing spiritual curses on others, and that's a form of witchcraft.

Figure 36B: **The Doctrine of Balaam (continued)**
(Revelation 2:14)

NEW TESTAMENT					
N.T. Babylon (Rev 17 & 18)	**Temptation In** (1 Thess 5:23)	**Temptation By**	**Temptation How** (1 John 2:16)	**Temptation Practical**	**Temptation Overcoming** (Rev 21:7; 1 John 5:4)
1. Full of abominations and filthiness of her fornication. (Rev 17:4)	BODY	FLESH	Lust of the flesh (Realm of natural bodily needs)	Females (Girls)	"Greater is He that is in you, than he that is in the world". (1 John 5:4)
2. Merchants and merchandise – gold, silver, precious stones (Rev 18:11-13)	SOUL	WORLD	Lust of the eye (Realm of emotional needs)	Finances (Gold)	"This is the victory that overcometh the world, even our faith". (1 John 4:1-4)
3. Beast (Rev 17:8) is worshipped and his image (Rev 13:4,12)	SPIRIT	DEVIL	Pride of Life (Realm of motivation of our lives – our self-righteousness as opposed to God's righteousness)	Fame (Glory)	"You have overcome the wicked one". (1 John 2:13,14)

> "The most dangerous prophet in the world is one who is a mixture. He or she may accurately hear from God and share divine words with us – thereby producing in us a strong confidence. About that time, he or she shifts into another spirit realm and declares lies, condemnation, and false doctrine. Because we have heard truth from them, we often fail to judge the message by God's Word and discern the spirit force that is at work in the individual speaking. I believe Balaam falls into this category. Sometimes he spoke for God, but at other times he spoke for demonic forces. Probably there were times when he spoke just for Balaam." [32]

The church at Pergamos was tolerating persons who falsely taught, as Balaam had done centuries before, that idolatry and immorality could be wilfully committed by God's people because God would excuse such sins. The human body and spirit were totally different, they taught. The body was evil, the spirit good. Therefore, it does not matter what the body does, because God excuses any sins of the flesh. But when the church leaders had met at Jerusalem, these subjects had been dealt with once and for all, Judas and Silas had personally taken the ruling to the Gentile churches in Asia:

> "It seemed good to the Holy Spirit and to us not to burden you with anything beyond the following requirements:
> You are to abstain from food sacrificed to idols, from blood, from the meat of strangled animals and from sexual immorality. You will do well to avoid these things." (Acts 15:28,29 – *NIV*)

Balaam is also mentioned in the New Testament. We read of those who "have run greedily in the error of Balaam for profit," and also those who "have forsaken the right way and gone astray, following the way of Balaam the son of Beor who loved the wages of unrighteousness." [33] The doctrine of Balaam. Serving God out of greed. Putting a stumbling block before the people of God. Witchcraft. Counseling God's people to mix their faith with idolatry and immorality. Justifying sin by using false doctrine. Denying that Jesus Christ is the Eternal Son of God. These are very serious matters.

We must be careful in this day and age that nothing of the doctrine of Balaam be allowed to enter our churches. I know we live in a sin-sick world, and we are commanded to be witnesses in it. But let us be victorious overcomers. Do not be

---

[32] *Forbidden Glory – Portraits of Pride*, by Judson Cornwall. McDougal Publishing, Hagerstown, Maryland; 2001 – page 101.

For over 50 years Dr Judson Cornwall has faithfully served the Lord as pastor, teacher, author, and traveling ambassador for Christ. He is the author of nearly 60 books. At the time of this writing (December 2001), he is at his home in Phoenix, Arizona, dying of bone cancer.

When we moved from India to the United States in 1977, we felt we needed a trusted senior American minister to be our pastor. Judson graciously consented to be that man. For almost 25 years he has encouraged, corrected, advised, and pastored us. Dr Cornwall officiated at the Memorial Service for our daughter, Debbie. Thanks for everything, Jud. We will miss you, but we'll see you again soon.

[33] Jude 11; 2 Pet 2:15.

polluted by mixture. Never allow the spirit of the world to dilute the Gospel's authority and power.

b. The Doctrine of the Nicolaitans

The second complaint of the Lord to the church at Pergamos was, that in addition to those who held the doctrine of Balaam, they also had in their midst those who held the doctrine of the Nicolaitans. We saw that the Lord Jesus commended the church at Ephesus because they hated (as He did) the *deeds* of the Nicolaitans. In the church at Pergamos He says He hates the *doctrine* of the Nicolaitans.

The word "Thus," or, in some translations, "Likewise," at the beginning of verse 15 would indicate there are similarities between the doctrine of Balaam and the doctrine of the Nicolaitans. Once again, the Lord says to the church at Pergamos that as a church they are not teaching, nor practicing, the extreme Gnosticism of the doctrine of the Nicolaitans. But they do allow people who hold this doctrine to be in their midst and associate with them.

9. Correction

For the church at Pergamos, there is only one answer to their problems – they must separate themselves from these evil forces. They must discipline those who hold to these heresies, correct them, or exclude them from the church. Otherwise judgment will be swift and heavy.

10. Call

As with five of the other churches in Asia, the call to the church in Pergamos is to repent. With godly sorrow they must confess they have harboured heretics, and turn from all wrong associations, wrong doctrine, idolatry and sexual sins. It is interesting to note that we also are commanded to flee from these things: "My beloved, flee from idolatry."[34] "Flee sexual immorality."[35] "Flee also youthful lusts."[36]

11. Caution

The judgment caution for this church is "Repent, or else I will come to you quickly and will fight against them with the sword of My mouth." Notice the Lord's grace to the church, even in judgment: "I will come to *you* ... I will fight against *them*." Later in Revelation when John beholds the Lord Jesus coming again in power and great glory, he sees a sharp, two-edged sword projecting from His mouth ... the sword of His Word to smite the nations who reject Him.[37]

---

[34] 1 Cor 10:14.
[35] 1 Cor 6:18.
[36] 2 Tim 2:22.
[37] Rev 19:15.

12. Counsel

His counsel to the church in Pergamos is, as it is to the other churches, "He who has an ear, let him hear what the Spirit says to the churches." Open the ears of your spirit. This is not just a letter to the church in Pergamos, but to all Christians in all churches.

13. Challenge

The believers in all seven churches are challenged to become overcomers. Living in the midst of such abject debauchery and idolatry, how easy it would have been for the church at Pergamos to give in to the temptation, pressure, and persecution they experienced daily. But the Lord has special promises for those who will overcome.

14. Compensation for Conquerors

The two promises to those who will overcome in contradictions and temptations are:

a. "To him who overcomes I will give some of the hidden manna to eat."

The hidden manna refers to the pot in the ark of the covenant which contained a sample of the bread, "manna," God gave the children of Israel in the wilderness.[38] Today we can eat of the "hidden manna" in three ways:

i. Reading and studying the Bible, which is "solid food;"[39]
ii. Fellowshipping with Jesus, Who said He was the Living Bread come down from heaven;[40]
iii. Breaking bread together in remembrance of Him.[41]

This promise concerning the hidden manna also has a prophetic significance. When the Lord fulfills the Day of Atonement to His Bride, only those Christians who are overcomers will participate in the glorious Day of His appearing. This, as we have seen, will occur at the communion table when His people are breaking bread in remembrance of Him. That the eating of the hidden manna is a collective experience is indicated in the Lord's words, "To him who overcomes I will give some of the hidden manna to eat."

When Jesus referred to Himself as the Bread of Life, there is a twofold interpretation – spiritual, and physical. Those who eat and drink of Him will certainly pass from spiritual death to spiritual life – "everlasting life."[42] But there is a very strong suggestion that there are some who will not taste physical death either:

---

[38] Exo 16:33.
[39] Heb 5:14.
[40] John 6:51.
[41] Matt 26:26; 1 Cor 10:16,17.
[42] John 6:27.

"I am the bread of life ...
This is the bread which comes down from heaven, that one *may eat of it and not die.*
I am the living bread which came down from heaven. If anyone eats of this bread, *he will live forever.*" (John 6:48,50,51 – emphasis mine)

What a wonderful promise to those who will rise up and be overcomers in these Last Days!

b. "And I will give him [the overcomer] a white stone, and on the stone a new name written which no one knows except him who receives it."

There are a number of historical customs involving a white stone. By applying Biblical principles, we find in each there is an element of truth pertaining to this wonderful promise to the overcomer:

•• *In courts of law* – In ancient times a white stone meant innocence and acquittal. Jurors displayed a black stone for "guilty" and a white stone for "innocent." Of course, we are guilty – but Jesus has washed away our sin and guilt and we are justified by faith in Him.[43]

•• *The reward of victory* – Those who commanded armies in victory were given a white stone by their rulers on their return from battle. This white stone carried with it certain privileges in the city. (It was something akin to the custom in today's culture where the mayor gives a prominent person "the key of the city.") God has promised victory for those who will trust in Him: "In the Messiah, in Christ, God leads us from place to place in one perpetual victory parade."[44]

•• *Freedom and citizenship* – In Bible days, freedom and citizenship were important issues to each individual.[45] When a man became a free citizen he was, in some places, given a white stone. This stone enabled him to move about freely, and was similar to "identification papers" or a "passport." Paul says we "are no longer strangers and foreigners, but fellow citizens with the saints and members of the household of God" (Eph 2:19).

•• *The "tessara hospitalis"* – When two close friends were about to part, they would inscribe both their names on a white stone, and divide the stone in two. The two friends may never meet again, but the halves of the stone would be bequeathed to their sons. Sometimes whole generations would pass without any meeting. The relationship was continued only through letters and "word-of-mouth" messages. But when two descendants of the original friends did

---

[43] Rom 5:1.
[44] 2 Cor 2:14 – *TM*.
[45] See, for example, Paul the apostle's conversation with the chief captain in Acts 22:27,28.

meet, if they possessed the complementary halves of the white stone, the friendship was immediately renewed. Jesus has called us His friends.[46]

•• *Engagement* – There is a custom that is still prevalent in the countries of the Indian subcontinent. Two young people fall in love, but are forbidden to marry by their families. They make a secret pledge of betrothal, and take a piece of jewelry made of white stone, and write something on it in code. It may be a term of endearment, or a secret message, but the inscription will not be understandable to anyone except themselves. When they finally meet again, maybe years later, their appearance will have changed. But when the two pieces of white stone are fitted together, the secret word – the "new name" – is again complete, and they are reunited.[47] Paul says we are engaged to be married: "I promised your hand in marriage to Christ, presented you as a pure virgin to her husband."[48]

Concerning the "new name written" in the promise to the overcomer, we have established that God's Name – the Lord Jesus Christ – is received at water baptism. However, I would not be surprised if, in eternity, our Lord Jesus Christ is further honoured, exalted, and rewarded by the Father. Our heavenly Bridegroom will, in eternity, share a portion of that with those who are overcomers. "And I will write on him My new name."[49] Who knows the fullness of what eternity will reveal!

The letter of the Lord Jesus to the church in Pergamos teaches the necessity to overcome wrong associations. The next church – Thyatira – must learn how to overcome false authority.

---

[46] John 15:13-15.
[47] This features prominently in M. M. Kaye's excellent book about princely families in Nineteenth Century British India, *The Far Pavilions*.
[48] 2 Cor 11:2 – *TM*.
[49] Rev 3:12.

PART FOUR   THE CHURCHES

Chapter 21

The Compromising Church

Thyatira ... Overcoming Authority

Revelation 2:18-29

¹⁸ "And to the angel (*margin*, 'messenger') of the church in Thyatira write, 'These things says the Son of God, who has eyes like a flame of fire, and His feet like fine brass:
¹⁹ I know your works, love, service, faith, and your patience (*margin*, "perseverance"); and as for your works, the last are more than the first.
²⁰ Nevertheless I have a few things against you, because you allow that woman Jezebel, who calls herself a prophetess, to teach and seduce My servants to commit sexual immorality and eat things sacrificed to idols.
²¹ And I gave her time to repent of her sexual immorality, and she did not repent (*margin*, "does not want to repent").
²² Indeed I will cast her into a sickbed, and those who commit adultery with her into great tribulation, unless they repent of their deeds.
²³ I will kill her children with death, and all the churches shall know that I am He who searches (*margin*, "examines") the minds and hearts. And I will give to each one of you according to your works.
²⁴ Now to you I say, and to the rest in Thyatira, as many as do not have this doctrine, who have not known the depths of Satan, as they say, I will put on you no other burden.
²⁵ But hold fast what you have till I come.
²⁶ And he who overcomes, and keeps My works until the end, to him I will give power over the nations –
²⁷ He shall rule them with a rod of iron; They shall be dashed to pieces like the potter's vessels – as I also have received from My Father;
²⁸ and I will give him the morning star.
²⁹ He who has an ear, let him hear what the Spirit says to the churches.'"

1. Commission

Each letter contained a message to every church, and to each individual believer. But once again, John is commissioned to write to one specific person, the senior minister of the local church in one city: "And to the angel (*margin*, 'messenger') of the church in Thyatira write …"

2. City

Thyatira was the least impressive of the seven cities listed in Revelation chapters 2 and 3. Thyatira was located on the road from Pergamos to Sardis (37 miles to the southeast), approximately 50 miles (80 kms) northeast of Smyrna. It was situated in the confines of Mysia[1] and Ionia, a little south of the river Hyllus, and at the northern extremity of the valley between Mount Tmolus and the southern ridge of Temhus. It lay on very flat land, thus making it extremely hard to defend.

The ancient city was founded by Lydians and named Pelopia, and later, Euhippia. Selucus Nicator, one of the generals of Alexander the Great, took control of the city in the Third Century B.C. and changed its name to Thyatira. During the following centuries Thyatira was ruled from Pergamum; thus, although Greek culture and religion were still powerful, by 100 B.C. the Roman influence was very apparent. The strange thing is that while Greece, when conquered by the Romans, ceased to be a political power, Greek culture still formed the foundations of the imperial Roman way of life. As the Roman writer Horace observed, "Captive Greece captivated her conqueror." Thus Hellenistic art, literature, government and religion thrived through most of the Roman period, especially in the larger cities.

Some of the earliest settlers of the city were Jews. In fact, history records there was a large colony of Jewish settlers known to be living in the city throughout the centuries. Thyatira was one of many Macedonian colonies established in Asia Minor as a result of the destruction of the Persian empire by Alexander the Great.

Dyeing formed an important part of the industrial activity of Thyatira, as it did in Colossæ and Laodicea. To this day, the waters of what was the city of Thyatira are said to be so well adapted for dyeing that in no other place can the scarlet cloth, from which fezes[2] are made, be so brilliantly or so permanently dyed, as here. A businesswoman by the name of Lydia, Paul's very first European convert was, the Bible says, "a seller of purple from the city of Thyatira," (Acts 16:14), "a dealer in expensive textiles,"[3] whom Paul led to Christ in Philippi.

While not a magnificent city like Ephesus or Pergamos, Thyatira was, nonetheless, an extremely prosperous one. This was due to the many corporate guilds of tradespeople – trade unions of potters, tanners, cloth manufacturers, dyers, and garment makers. These trade guilds promoted idolatry, excessive drinking, and sexual impurity.

---

[1] Acts 16:7,8.
[2] A fez (named after a town in Morocco) is a cap made of fine red cloth, which fits close to the head, with a tassel of blue silk or wool at the crown, worn by men in Turkey and other countries of the Middle East and Northern Africa.
[3] *TM*

Indeed, like the other cities of Asia, Thyatira was filled with pagan idolatry and sensuousness. In the city there was a famous temple to Artemis (Diana), the goddess of the Ephesians. The name of a priestess of Artemis has been found in the inscriptions among the limited ruins of the city that remain.

The main temple in Thyatira was dedicated to the worship of Apollo, the sun-god, who was second in power only to his father Zeus. Zeus was the supreme divinity among the Greeks, and was, at the time, generally recognized by the Romans as the equivalent of the supreme Roman god, Jupiter. Apollo was worshipped as the sun-god under the surname Tyrimnas. This "incarnation" of Apollo was no doubt introduced by the Macedonian colonists, for the name is Macedonian. In fact, Tyrimnas, the god who ruled by force, became the patron deity of the city in the form of the sun-god, and was a constant reminder to the populace of their victorious past in winning battles against invaders. Images of Apollo – both idols and pictures – were shown with bright flames shining out from his head and body, and his feet were depicted as shining brass. The manner in which the Lord Jesus Christ was about to reveal Himself to the Thyatiran church would be very significant, as it was impossible for the inhabitants of Thyatira to walk out the door without seeing images of the sun-god.

The temple of Apollo was the place where Emperor worship, mandatory in Thyatira, was carried out. The religion of Babylon, with all its mysticism and demonic influence, was mixed with idol worship at this temple. Apollo was also known as the "averter of evil" – worship him, the temple priests said, and no misfortune would befall you, and you would be delivered from everything bad. The priests at this temple also presided over religious law and atonement, issuing judgments and fines for making amends, and giving orders demanding restitution. While in demon-induced trances, using communion with evil spirits and horoscope-like methods, these priests would convey the sun-god's knowledge of the future. They would, in this way, claim to make known the will of Zeus, Apollo's father (both Zeus and Jupiter were known as "the Father"), to the worshippers.

The temple of Apollo the sun-god had a powerful grip on the total life of the city of Thyatira – not only spiritually, but also economically. For no-one could belong to the trade guilds, which controlled the commerce of the city, unless they worshipped at the temple of Apollo. Anyone who refused to join the idolatrous, immoral feasts and sexual orgies at the temple was completely barred from being a union member. Non-union-members could not work nor trade. Thus, in order to be a part of the commercial life of the city, it was essential to be a practicing, paid-up, pagan idolator and fornicator. Even before Lydia came to Christ, the Bible says she "worshipped God."[4] So it is possible she was carrying on her business in Philippi in order to escape the evil strictures of involvement in the commerce of her hometown.

While the principal deity of Thyatira was Apollo, followed closely by Diana, the city boasted a third religious superstition that was very powerful, and extremely strange. Outside the city walls was a temple dedicated to Sambatha, a woman who was a sorceress and fortuneteller, and considered by the people to be a prophetess. In the ancient writings

---

[4] Acts 16:14.

she is sometimes identified as Chaldaean (from Babylon), sometimes Jewish, sometimes Persian. This temple was located in the midst of an enclosure designated "the Chaldaeans' court," which, according to historical and archaeological records, was a place of unspeakable idolatry and immorality.

There is ample evidence to show that Thyatira was a very cosmopolitan city in which there was a great amalgamation of races. It is believed by some scholars that Sambatha, while probably Jewish, embraced every religion practiced in Thyatira. By her false prophecies she was trying to combine all the various religions into one. She may be the woman whom the Lord Jesus called "Jezebel," who called herself a prophetess, who was possessed by a seducing spirit, and was tolerated in the Christian church. She deceived and encouraged some in the church to participate in practices that the Lord described as "the depths of Satan."

The name Thyatira comes from two words that mean "sacrifice" and "continual." Some scholars add that Thyatira also means "ruled by a woman."

This historical background of Thyatira is of immense assistance in helping us, nearly 2,000 years later, understand the pressures and challenges Christians who lived in that city had to overcome.

3. Consequences

History records that in A.D. 366 Valeus the Eastern emperor gained a victory over Procopius in Thyatira. Despite the fact Arabs and Turks attacked Thyatira repeatedly through the centuries, each time it was destroyed the city was rebuilt. Because these new structures were erected over the ruins of Thyatira, much of its history lays buried underground. Only the temple of Apollo, an ancient church, a colonnaded road, and some small items from the ancient city remain. Today, over the site of Thyatira is the town of ak-Hissar ("white castle"), which still has a reputation for the manufacture of scarlet cloth. The city, which is located in the territory that is now Anatolian Turkey, presently has a population of about 50,000. Little or no evidence remains to indicate there was a large church here in the apostolic era. Its candlestick has been well and truly removed.

4. Church

Once again neither the Bible nor history tell us how this church was started. Lydia, who came to Christ under Paul's ministry in Philippi, was wealthy enough to own a home in Philippi,[5] and another in her hometown, Thyatira. Being a woman of influence, she could have had a part in the founding of this church. Luke wrote to Theophilus that while Paul was ministering at Ephesus, "all who dwelt in Asia heard the word of the Lord Jesus, both Jews and Greeks."[6]

---

[5] Acts 16:15.
[6] Acts 19:10.

5. Character

While speaking to the church in Thyatira, the Lord Jesus emphasizes three major aspects of His character:

a. "These things says the Son of God"

This is the first time in the Book of Revelation the Lord Jesus has called Himself "the Son of God." When John turned to see the vision of Christ in chapter one, he saw "One like the Son of Man." Yet the glory of that vision spoke clearly that He was the Son of God.[7] It is only now, in this central letter of the seven, He makes use of this title of supreme power and authority. The situation has become so serious in the church at Thyatira that He wants them to know without any doubt that He, the Son of God, is speaking to them. He Who is the Head of the Church. He, the only One to Whom all might and authority has been given. He Who declared "All authority has been given to Me in heaven and on earth" (Matt 28:18). For this is the church that must overcome false authority.

Now the Lord Jesus reaches back into chapter one for two more aspects of His character:

b. "Who has eyes like a flame of fire"

It is essential the church at Thyatira realize that the Lord sees and knows everything:

> "For nothing is secret that will not be revealed, nor anything hidden that will not be known and come to light." (Luke 8:17)

This is not an image of the sun-god pictured with fire coming out of his head and body. This is the fire of the One True and Living God. Fire gives light, and He Who is the Light of the world has eyes like fire which pierce all hidden darkness.[8] The flames of God's fire cleanse and purge: "Our God is a consuming fire."[9]

c. "And His feet like fine brass"

We have already seen, when studying the altar and washstand made of brass in the tabernacle of Moses, that in the Bible brass speaks of judgment against sin, self, and mixture.[10] By revealing Himself in this way, the Lord Jesus is announcing to the church in Thyatira that He is coming in judgment. He gave time for repentance. Now it is time for judgment.

---

[7] Rev 1:13.
[8] John 9:5.
[9] Heb 12:29.
[10] See Chapter 13, "The Tabernacle Of Moses."

When we superimpose the Lord Jesus Christ upon the tabernacle of Moses, His head is on the ark of the covenant, and His feet on the brazen altar. (See *Figure 30*). The "fire" of the Shekinah glory from His eyes; the brass of judgment at His feet.

The five articles of furniture in the Outer Court and the Holy Place remind us of the five ascension gift ministries the Lord has set in His church. These five ministries are God's chosen "governments,"[11] His "authorities" in His Church – yet the people's servants. Indeed, all six articles of furniture in the tabernacle of Moses make a beautiful prophetic picture of Christ, the Head of the Church, and His ministries.

In the Book of Exodus, chapters 25 through 30, Moses is given commandments for the construction of each individual piece of tabernacle furniture. The order of making the articles of furniture seems, on casual reading, to be out of sequence. God commences in the Most Holy Place with the ark of the covenant. Then He moves on to the Holy Place and the table of showbread. Next, the lampstand. Then He moves Moses' attention to the front gate of the tabernacle, and gives instructions for the building of the brazen altar. After this, He returns to the Holy Place and the incense altar made of gold, then back to the Outer Court again and the brazen washstand. It seems haphazard, but when we turn to the New Testament, we see the order for making the tabernacle furniture, and the order in which God lists the five ministries in Ephesians 4:11, is identical!

When we studied Moses' tabernacle, we saw the ark of the covenant is a picture of the Lord Jesus Christ in all His power and glory. He is the Perfect Apostle, Prophet, Evangelist, Pastor and Teacher.

Leaving the Holy of Holies, the first article of furniture Moses was commanded to make was the table of showbread. The first ministry listed in Ephesians 4:11 is the apostle. The first and foremost ministry of the apostle is to lay a firm foundation of sound doctrine in churches and individuals. This he does by feeding them with the bread of God's Word. There were 12 loaves on the table of showbread. Jesus chose 12 apostles of the Lamb at the commencement of His earthly ministry, and in the Last Days He will raise up 12 apostles of the Bride. These two groups of 12 will make up the 24 elders of Revelation chapter four.

The second piece of furniture seen in the Holy Place is the lampstand. The burning oil in the lampstand gave light in the Holy Place, illuminating the table of showbread and the altar of incense. True prophets give prophetic illumination – in accordance with God's Word – and challenge us in our ministry of prayer and praise.

After the lampstand God instructs Moses to build the brazen altar, and to place it in the Outer Court. Here blood was shed to cover the sins of the people. This pictures the evangelist who preaches the good news that the blood of Jesus washes our sins away.

---

[11] 1 Cor 12:28 – *KJV*.

Moses was told how to construct the golden altar of incense for the Holy Place. This speaks to us of the ministry of the pastor. True pastors shepherd their people, and lift them up in prayer. Note the position of the incense altar – close to the very heart of God.

Last, but certainly not least, we return to the Outer Court and the brazen washstand. Just as the priests washed their hands and feet there, so the ministry of God's Word through the teacher washes us. This washing – to cleanse and sanctify God's people – is an essential part of preparing to be in the glorious church, the Bride of Christ.[12]

We can summarize these thoughts in the following chart.

Figure 37: **Summary of Christ and His Five Ministries as Typified in Moses' Tabernacle**

Ministry (Eph 4:8-11)	Furniture in Moses' Tabernacle (Exo 25-30)	Main function of each ministry in the Church
The Lord Jesus Christ (v 10)	Ark of the Covenant	Head over all; Supreme Authority over Church
1. Apostle	Table of Showbread	Governs
2. Prophet	Lampstand	Guides
3. Evangelist	Brazen Altar	Gathers
4. Pastor	Altar of Incense	Guards
5. Teacher	Brazen Washstand	Grounds

6. Conduct

As the Lord Jesus says to each local church, He says to the Christians in Thyatira, "I know your works."

We are about to be shocked over the apparent lack of morals in this church. We are about to be appalled at the sexual indulgences considered acceptable conduct in their lifestyle. How could one depraved woman deceive with such persuasive authority? Who could entice some members of this church to go to "the depths of Satan"? What was the reason this church received the longest letter of the seven?

But how gracious is the Lord Jesus! He is about to pronounce striking judgment – but first comes His commendation. He has come to correct, yet He does not overlook the qualities He can commend.

---

[12] Eph 5:26,27.

7. Commendation

In verse 19 we find there are six positive qualities the Lord Jesus recognizes in the church of Thyatira. It is interesting to note the qualities He commends repeatedly.

- a. **"I know your works"**: He does not name these works, or give a list of them. He declares He knows them, and He knows the motivating forces behind these good works.

- b. **"[I know your] love"**: Their good works were motivated by love. They had read Paul's letter to the church at Corinth: "Trust steadily in God, hope unswervingly, love extravagantly. And the best of the three is love."[13] They had read John the Revelator's letter too:

    > "Whoever believes that Jesus is the Christ is born of God, and everyone who loves Him who begot also loves him who is begotten of Him.
    > By this we know that we love the children of God, when we love God and keep His commandments." (1 Jn 5:1,2)

- c. **"[I know your] service"**: Here was a church in which Jesus recognized their service – their ministry to the Lord, and to one another in the church.

- d. **"[I know your] faith"**: Like the church at Pergamos, they had not denied their personal faith in the Lord Jesus Christ, despite all the pressures and temptations to do so.

- e. **"[I know your] patience (*margin*, 'perseverance')"**: Here was a church which endured and persevered through difficult circumstances. The Lord sets great value on this quality in His people. He spoke of it to the church at Ephesus, and now commends the church at Thyatira for possessing it.

- f. **"as for your works, the last are more than the first"**: Their good works are increasing: "You are now doing more than you did at first" (*NIV*).

Yes, the Lord knows exactly what is happening in Thyatira. But good works, manifestations of the fruit of the Holy Spirit, and patient endurance cannot compensate for something in their midst that is so structurally, governmentally, spiritually and morally wrong. In order to indulge in the pleasures of the flesh, some in the church had submitted to, and compromised with, false authority. This must be overcome.

8. Complaint

> **"Nevertheless, I have this against you: You tolerate that woman Jezebel, who calls herself a prophetess. By her teaching she misleads my servants into sexual immorality and the eating of food sacrificed to idols.**

---

[13] 1 Cor 13:13 – *TM*.

> **I have given her time to repent of her immorality, but she is unwilling."**
> **(verses 20, 21 – *NIV*)**

Although in some translations the beginning of verse 20 reads "I have a few things against you,"[14] in reality, there is only one complaint against the church in Thyatira – "You tolerate that woman Jezebel." From verse 20 to verse 24 the Lord elaborates the facts of this complaint, emphasizing their error in tolerating this misleading, false authority.

The Tale of Two Women

The story of the church in the city of Thyatira is the tale of two women – Lydia and Jezebel. As we have already seen, Lydia was led to Christ in the city of Philippi by the apostle Paul. She and her household were baptized, after which she invited Paul and Silas to stay in her home. When Paul and Silas were beaten and imprisoned, upon their release they again "entered the house of Lydia; and when they had seen the brethren, they encouraged them."[15] As I said earlier, it is very probable Lydia was involved in the establishing of the church in Thyatira.

The second woman in Thyatira, Jezebel, could not have been more different. The Lord Jesus likens her to an Old Testament woman named Jezebel who lived in the late 800s, B.C. She was the daughter of Ethbaal, king of the Zidonians, and the wife of Ahab, king of Israel. The account of Ahab and Jezebel is found in 1 Kings chapters 16 through 22. Jezebel's bloody death is recorded in 2 Kings chapter 9.

Jezebel was a dominating, ambitious, sinful woman who was married to a feeble man. The Lord Jesus reaches into the Old Testament and uses the name "Jezebel" to describe the woman who is being tolerated by the church at Thyatira. Because she, like the devilish Jezebel of old, who had introduced the abominations of Baal worship into Israel, was introducing the same vile practices of idolatry and immorality into the Christian church.[16] The Master uses Old Testament Jezebel to graphically illustrate this New Testament woman's character, and the evil influence she was exerting in this church.

Ahab's wife Jezebel was without doubt a teacher and worshipper of Baal. The worship of Baal was Nature-worship, and by Jezebel's time had become utterly degraded. Jezebel, a Zidonian, set herself up as the authority in Israel and said, in effect, "I do not ask that you stop worshipping your Jehovah. But let us all worship Baal as well. We can worship God and His creation together. We can unite the two forms of worship." Jezebel was the first ecumenical leader. She did not seek to do away with the worship of Jehovah God. Rather, she added something vile to true worship in order to pollute it. But the ultimate evil purpose of this unscrupulous woman was to set aside the worship of Jehovah altogether, and replace it with the worship of Baal.

---

[14] For example, *KJV, NKJV*.
[15] Acts 16:14,15,40.
[16] 1 Ki 16:31-33.

Likewise, the notorious woman in the church in Thyatira, whom the Lord called "Jezebel," was teaching and seducing God's servants to commit sexual immorality and eat things sacrificed to idols. She was compromising the pure Word of God by adding something vile to the pure worship of the Lord Jesus Christ.

Ahab's wife, Jezebel, so despised her husband that she wrongfully took to herself his authority – power which was not hers. She usurped the king's authority. She controlled him. She told him, "You now exercise authority over all Israel. But you, my husband, are too weak and spineless to even take Naboth's vineyard. I'll get it for you."[17] As queen, she could have all the vineyards she needed. But she was so greedy for material gain she lied about Naboth, had him killed, and stole his vineyard. Her reputation for ruthlessness was such, that when the prophet Elijah heard Jezebel planned to murder him, the Bible says "he arose and ran for his life."[18]

By contrast, Lydia of Thyatira was used by the Lord as a foundation upon which the work of the Lord grew. Jezebel of Thyatira caused the work of the Lord to fall. One woman was a blessing. The other was a curse.

This letter from the Lord Jesus is focused on overcoming false authority. Jezebel of Thyatira probably had a following of influential people in the city. She was attracted to the growing cause of Christianity and had attached herself to the church, but at the same time she militantly insisted on advocating idolatry and immorality be mixed with the Gospel, claiming prophetic inspiration from God for her teachings. It does not say that the church had made Jezebel a member. Nor does it say they had given her an official position of authority. But it does say they tolerated her, they put up with her, they acquiesced to this compromising situation, and wouldn't do anything to change it. They had accepted a personality rather than a principle. Their church had been weakened. So now, as we shall see, this evil teacher and seducer is about to be judged. But first, we must take a quick look at what the Bible says concerning the ministry of women.

The Ministry of Women[19]

Under the Old Covenant, we find many women are recorded as having ministries of great and godly influence. There is the ministry of Moses' sister, Miriam the prophetess.[20] Deborah was both prophetess and judge of the whole of her country.[21] Huldah was another very powerful prophetess.[22] Queen Esther saved her nation.[23] No wonder David the Psalmist sang, "The Lord gives the command; the women who proclaim the good tidings are a great host" (Psa 68:11 – *NAS*).

---

[17] 1 Ki 21:7.
[18] 1 Ki 19:3.
[19] For further studies on this subject, see my book *What Does the Bible Teach About Women's Ministry?*
[20] Exo 15:20.
[21] Judg 4:4.
[22] 2 Ki 22:14; 2 Chr 34:22.
[23] Esther chapter 8.

In the New Testament, we find that God chose a woman, Anna the prophetess, to be the first person to preach publicly about Jesus after His birth.[24] The woman at the well was the first to testify of Christ in Samaria.[25] The first messengers of the resurrection of Christ were women.[26] Aquila's wife, Priscilla, helped her husband in his teaching ministry.[27] Philip had four daughters who prophesied.[28] Phoebe was a minister of the church at Cenchrea.[29] Junia was of note among the apostles.[30] Clearly, men and women are one in Christ by the power of the Cross, which is manifest in our baptism into Christ:

"For as many of you as were baptized into Christ have put on Christ.
There is neither Jew nor Greek, there is neither slave nor free, there is neither male nor female; for you are all one in Christ Jesus." (Gal 3:27,28)

The problem in the church in Thyatira was not one of gender, but of message and method. This woman, whom the Risen Lord calls Jezebel, is teaching a message and lifestyle diametrically opposed to the teaching of the Bible. And in deceiving and seducing people in the church with these damnable heresies, she is taking on an authority that is not rightfully hers, thus usurping the authority of the senior pastor of the church.

Every minister, whether man or woman, should be firmly planted in a good local church. All should be covered by and accountable to senior ministry. I do not say this in any sectarian or dictatorial sense, but rather, it is the Bible pattern for the safety, strengthening, and blessing of every ministry.

The Ministry of Prophets

One of the Lord's many complaints about this woman Jezebel is that she called herself a prophetess. When we studied the letter to the church at Ephesus, we looked briefly at the ministry of apostles. Now we would do well to pause and consider the ministry of prophets. For there is considerable confusion, especially in Charismatic circles, as to what a prophet is and does.

On the negative side, there have been, are, and will be false prophets. The Lord Jesus foretold that in the end times "many false prophets will rise up and deceive many."[31] There were false prophets in the apostolic era.[32] John wrote that many false prophets had gone out into the world.[33] And as we shall study in **Volume Two** of this book, there will arise a person called "the false prophet," who is spoken of in Revelation chapters 16,19, and 20.

---

[24] Luke 2:36-38.
[25] John 4:4-42.
[26] Matt 28:8,10.
[27] Acts 18:24-26.
[28] Acts 21:9.
[29] Rom 16:1,2.
[30] Rom 16:7.
[31] Matt 24:11.
[32] Acts 13:6.
[33] 1 Jn 4:1.

However, on the positive side, in these Last Days, as the outpouring of the Holy Spirit continues and increases, we can gladly anticipate an increase in the pure prophetic flow, and in the ministry of God's true and holy prophets.[34]

As we have seen, the prophet is the second ascension gift ministry listed in Ephesians 4:11. The prophet has received a gift from the ascended Christ, with which he or she is to serve the Lord, the church, and, in some isolated cases, an entire nation. Like the apostle, the prophet has a deep understanding of the Bible, particularly the mystery of Christ (Eph 3:4,5).

A prophet has a foundational ministry in the establishing of new churches, and in the sending forth of missionaries, often working together with apostles (Eph 2:20) and teachers (Acts 13:1). The prophet has the gift of prophecy matured to a remarkable degree. And most importantly, a prophet is not a prophet because he calls himself a prophet, but because mature ministers and churches recognize and receive him as such.

My definition of the gift of prophecy is simply this: "Prophecy is a supernatural utterance, inspired by the Holy Spirit, in a language known to the speaker." Each of the nine manifestation gifts of the Spirit listed in 1 Corinthians 12:8-10 operates at three distinct levels. We can summarize these three aspects of prophecy in the following chart:

Figure 38: The Three Levels of the Operation of Prophecy

"Now concerning spiritual gifts, brethren, I do not want you to be ignorant." (1 Cor 12:1)

Different Aspects	Definition	Who will Operate
1. **Spirit** of prophecy (Rev 19:8)	Simple but inspired utterance testifying of, and glorifying, the Lord Jesus	ALL believers (1 Cor 14:31)
2. **Gift** of prophecy (1 Cor 10:9)	Deeper and more mature inspired utterance from the Lord for exhortation ("stirring up"), edification ("building up"), and comfort ("cheering up"). (1 Cor 14:3)	SOME believers (1Cor 12:10)
3. **Ministry** of a prophet (Eph 4:11)	Inspired teaching of the Word. Prophetic utterances which confirm and sometimes even create. Involved in starting and establishing churches, usually together with an apostle.	FEW believers (1 Cor 12:28, 29)

9. Correction

The opportunity for this false prophetess Jezebel to repent has been rejected. The time for correction and judgment has arrived.

---

[34] Acts 2:17.

a. "Indeed I will cast her into a sickbed"

The Greek word for "bed" is *klinē* from which we get our English word "recline." In addition to a bed, it also denotes a couch for reclining at meals. Jezebel had seduced church members to attend trade guild banquets, where they would recline on couches and eat a lavish feast, get drunk, watch the entertainment, worship the Roman Caesar (by falling down before the statue of Apollo burning incense to it), and commit fornication. This is Gnostic teaching sunken to its very lowest and most corrupt level – "If your spirit is in fellowship with God, it does not matter what you do with your body." Extreme Gnosticism taught that one could only have profound insight into the deep mysteries of Satan by experience and experiment. By this false teaching idolatry and immorality were justified. In fact, this heresy denied the sinfulness of sin, affirming that within the things that seem to be evil are things that are good. They were seduced into believing the only way to deal with the flesh was by indulging it. By this they could prove that nothing they did harmed them. This denial of evil blinded the servants of God to the truth. Christ now counteracts. He will cast Jezebel and those with her into a different kind of *klinē* – a bier – a bed not of opulent couches and cushions, but of wood, used to carry corpses to their graves.

b. "And those who commit adultery with her into great tribulation"

Jezebel is about to experience her destruction. Her bed of sin is to be exchanged for a bed of severe sickness and death. We are here reminded of Paul's warning to the church at Corinth. Because they did not discern the Lord's body, both in the communion emblems and in their Christian brothers and sisters, Paul declared: "For this reason many are weak and sick among you, and many sleep (*margin*, 'are dead')."[35]

The Lord's words about "great tribulation" are also prophetic. As we have noted briefly, during the three and a half years of the Great Tribulation, the glorious Church, the overcomers, will be protected, and enjoy intimate fellowship with Christ. But those Christians who are overcome will go into the Great Tribulation where they will either deny their faith by taking the mark of the beast, or die for their faith. In dying for their faith they do not lose their salvation, but they do lose their lives. We will study this in more detail in **Volume Two** of this book.

c. "I will kill her children with death"

Some of those whom Jezebel had seduced into temporary association with her wicked ways would be struck down with extreme sickness, and go through a time of unspeakable affliction and distress. But her children – those who united with her wholeheartedly in a permanent, submissive, immoral relationship – the Lord Jesus will deal with more severely. These took total license to live as they pleased under the cloak of Christianity. They have "known the depths of Satan"

---

[35] 1 Cor 11:30.

(verse 24). They are Jezebel's children. The Lord will kill them. Now please use your imagination just for a moment. Can you begin to picture the reaction of the people as this letter is read to the congregation? Some in the church now realize the Lord Jesus has just pronounced their death sentence. What a dramatic effect the reading of this letter must have had in Thyatira! What reverence. What solemnity. What godly fear. What a church service!

10. Call

a. "Unless they repent of their (*margin*, 'her') deeds"

They must repent – turn from this wickedness immediately. Otherwise, the sickbed and great tribulation!

b. "All the churches shall know that I am He who searches (*margin*, 'examines') the minds and hearts. And I will give to each one of you according to your works."

Not only was this letter to be read in Thyatira. All the churches would hear its message. The Lord reminds all the churches He is the One Who examines them – their minds, the center of their thoughts and will – and their hearts, the seat of their emotions, purpose, and motivations. His methodical investigation reveals true character, and brings all to light, whether good or evil. Can you imagine the heart-searching as the Lord says "I will give to each of you according to your works"? Each believer's mind would be racing to remember any works done that were even remotely associated with Jezebel and her teaching. For Jezebel had assured her followers that they could not truly appreciate grace until they really experienced sin. She had so perverted the Gospel message she had seduced them into believing her message – a Christian must plunge into the cesspool of iniquity to serve Christ better. Of course, the Bible teaches just the opposite: "Shall we continue in sin that grace may abound? Certainly not! How shall we who died to sin live any longer in it?" (Rom 6:1,2)

11. Caution

"Now to you I say, and to the rest in Thyatira, as many as do not have this doctrine, who have not known the depths of Satan, as they say, I will put on you no other burden."

Now Christ is not addressing Jezebel and her deluded followers, but rather the pastor, together with those who have remained faithful in the Thyatiran assembly. These are they who have not believed her doctrine, nor experienced the sin her doctrine engendered. Nor had they consented to its toleration. The phrase "I will put on you no other burden" reminds us of the words to the churches in Asia from the counsel at Jerusalem:

"For it seemed good to the Holy Spirit and to us, to lay upon you no greater burden than these necessary things:
that you abstain from things offered to idols, from blood, from things strangled, and from sexual immorality. If you keep yourselves from these, you will do well." (Acts 15:28,29)

This church should have taken better notice of "these necessary things" when that letter first arrived from Jerusalem!

12. Counsel

"But hold fast what you have till I come"

Those who had remained faithful, and not compromised their beliefs or their conduct, are exhorted to hold fast to that which they have. Christ exhorts the godly remnant to hold fast the Word of God that had kept them from deception and evil. Jezebel taught that the sacrifice of Christ on Calvary was not enough. Continual sacrifices at idolatrous altars were necessary. But nothing can be added to or taken away from God's Word, and Christ's sacrifice. They are complete. And we are "complete in Him."[36] So they were to hold on tenaciously to the truth of God's Word, opposing all wrong doctrine and evil practice. Hold on, Christ says, until My manifestation. This is the way you will overcome Satan.

This same counsel – to "hold fast" – comes to you and me today. "Test all things; hold fast what is good. Abstain from every form of evil." (1 Thess 5:21,22) And as the writer to the Hebrew Christians commands:

"Let us hold fast the confession of our hope without wavering, for He who promised is faithful." (Heb 10:23)

13. Challenge

After all this church has experienced, they are still challenged to be overcomers. And so are we! We are challenged to be overcomers, and to minister to others that they may be overcomers too. We must not allow any compromise with the standards of the world. We rob people of blessing if we lower our standards about marriage or morality. It is imperative we declare to His people the whole counsel of God.[37] We must preach what the Bible says about excessive debt, greed, selfishness, deception, and all sin. Any doctrine, philosophy or seducing spirit that makes it easier to sin, whether by excusing it, minimizing it, or denying its existence is from the pit of hell. Not only those who teach and seduce the servants of God to sin in these matters are guilty, but also any church or ministry that tolerates such teaching is guilty also. It may be old-fashioned. It may sound harsh. But let us say it loud and clear – Christians who tolerate "Jezebel" and do not

---

[36] Col 2:10.
[37] Acts 20:27.

repent will be swiftly judged by God. Let us then obey the Lord's challenge to "hear what the Spirit says to the churches."

14. Compensation for Conquerors

a. "And he who overcomes, and keeps My works until the end, to him I will give power over the nations–He shall rule them with a rod of iron; they shall be dashed to pieces like the potter's vessels–as I also have received from My Father."

Notice this contrast: "Those who commit adultery with her into great tribulation, unless they repent of *her* deeds," with "He who overcomes and keeps *My* deeds."[38] This clearly is the criterion for the overcomer – repent of Jezebel's deeds and keep doing God's deeds.

As we shall see, the promise "To him [the overcomer] I will give power over the nations" has several shades of meaning. One is certainly the promise of the Holy Spirit's power to take the Gospel to the nations of the earth. Before the Lord Jesus comes again, we will see the greatest missionary explosion in history, with multitudes coming to Christ.

This promise to the overcomer is, of course, a promise of godly authority. Today overcomers are being trained by the Holy Spirit to rule and reign with the Lord. There are a number of Greek words in the New Testament translated "rule." In each of the following verses the word is *poimainō* which means "to act as a shepherd, tend flocks, to guide, to govern." A rod of wood – the shepherd's staff – indicates the loving care of the shepherd. A rod of iron speaks of firm and uncompromising judgment. In the Book of Revelation there are three people, or groups of people, who are shown to be ruling with a rod of iron:

i. The Christians who are overcomers (2:27, quoting Psa 2:8,9) – *the Bride of Christ*;

ii. The man child (12:5) – *the offspring of the Bride and Bridegroom;*

iii. The Lord Jesus Christ (19:16) – *the Heavenly Bridegroom.*

We will study this subject in more detail in **Volume Two** of this book.

b. "And I will give him the morning star"

Some in the church of Thyatira had been seduced and had fallen into unspeakable darkness. The Lord Jesus has had to be very specific in revealing this darkness, and very severe in judging it. But now he promises light to the overcomer. "I will give him the morning star." What a tremendous promise to those in this church

---

[38] *NAS.*

who had remained loyal to their Lord, maintaining a Christian lifestyle in a city where they were constantly bombarded with satanic temptations.

The morning star appears on the horizon while it is still dark, and is the herald of a bright new day. The phrase "the morning star" appears only three times in Scripture, once in Job, and twice in Revelation.

When God answers Job, He asks him a number of questions about the creation of the earth. One of these questions is:

> "To what were its foundations fastened?
> Or who laid its cornerstone,
> When the morning stars sang together,
> And all the sons of God shouted for joy?" (Job 38:6,7)

As we have seen in a previous chapter of this book, God's original creation was perfect.[39] This could be a reference to the Lord Jesus Christ and the angels singing praise to God, and shouting for joy, when they saw the beauty of creation before it was marred by sin.

The second time the "morning star" is mentioned is this promise to the overcomer. Lastly, at the end of Revelation, we are told Who the Morning Star is: "I Jesus ... am ... the Bright and Morning Star" (Rev 22:16). Brightness. Glory. Light. No more darkness. The rewards to the overcomers will be eternal. What a contrast to the darkness uncovered in Thyatira.

The letter of the Lord Jesus to the church in Thyatira teaches the necessity to overcome false authority. Now we travel 37 miles south to Sardis. The church in Sardis must learn how to overcome apathy.

---

[39] See Chapter 10, "God's Week."

PART FOUR   THE CHURCHES

Chapter 22

The Dead Church

Sardis ... Overcoming Apathy

Revelation 3:1-6

¹ "And to the angel (*margin*, 'messenger') of the church in Sardis write, 'These things says He who has the seven Spirits of God and the seven stars: 'I know your works, that you have a name that you are alive, but you are dead.
² Be watchful, and strengthen the things which remain, that are ready to die, for I have not found your works perfect before God.
³ Remember therefore how you have received and heard; hold fast and repent. Therefore if you will not watch, I will come upon you as a thief, and you will not know what hour I will come upon you.
⁴ You have a few names even in Sardis who have not defiled their garments; and they shall walk with Me in white, for they are worthy.
⁵ He who overcomes shall be clothed in white garments, and I will not blot out his name from the Book of Life; but I will confess his name before My Father and before His angels.
⁶ He who has an ear, let him hear what the Spirit says to the churches.'"

1. Commission

In the year 94 or 95 A.D. the apostle John had been arrested in the port city of Ephesus, mainly because of the amazing growth and influence of the Christian church in that city. John, of course, refused to burn incense to the Roman Emperor, Caesar Domitian, and so was shipped in chains to the island of Patmos, where, despite his advanced years, he was put to work in the quarries. It was here that the Lord Jesus, Whom John had not seen with his eyes for 60 years, appeared and gave him important messages for seven of the churches in Asia. The fourth church, Thyatira, was to overcome a mixture of idolatry, immorality and the Christian faith – a mixture introduced into the church by false authority. The fifth church, at Sardis, is called to overcome apathy, indifference, and the deadness of their backslidden condition. "And to the angel (*margin*, 'messenger') of the church in Sardis write ..."

2. City

The strategic city of Sardis was founded probably as early as the beginning of the Iron Age. In apostolic days it was the main metropolis and capital of Lydia, a region in the Roman province of Asia, with the city of Smyrna to the west, Thyatira to the north, and Philadelphia to the southeast.

Sardis was situated on a narrow plateau 1,500 feet above sea level, about two miles south of the river Hermus, just below the range of Mount Tmolus. The city was virtually inaccessible. It was the ancient residence of the kings of Lydia, the last of whom was Crœsus, who was known for his immense wealth. Crœsus was so rich, that when Cyrus of Persia captured Sardis in 546 B.C., it is said he took $600,000,000 worth of treasures from the city.[1] Historians believe Crœsus minted the very first coins during his opulent reign.

Sardis was conquered in 504 B.C. by the Ionians, assisted by the Athenians. In 395 the Greeks defeated the Persians in the vicinity of the city. In 334 Sardis surrendered to Alexander the Great. In 283 it was taken by Seleucus, and in 214 sacked by Antiochus the Great, after which it came under the dominion of Pergamos. Finally, in 189 it was given up to the Romans. The city was leveled by a devastating earthquake in the year 11 A.D. and later rebuilt by the Roman Emperor Tiberius Caesar. But much of the greatness of Sardis under the Roman Empire was due to its past reputation.

From very early times the area around Sardis was known for its extremely rich and fertile soil. Because of its convenient location, it became a commercial city of strategic import. Prosperous businesses flourished in the city. The art of dyeing wool – wool that was used in the manufacture of carpets – is said to have been invented here. The city obtained much wealth from textile manufacturing and the dyeing industry. Sardis also became famous for its jewelry trade. There are two special varieties of the sardine, or sardius stone. One is a brownish red (like a chalcedony), the other a transparent red (like a cornelian). Because of its transparent brilliance, this stone was a favourite for personal ornamentation among the ancients. Not only this – because of the gem's hardness, it was used in making expensive engraving seals. This red sardine or sardius stone is mentioned a number of times in the Bible, including Revelation 21:20, where it forms the sixth foundation of the wall of the heavenly Jerusalem.[2]

The distances between the seven cities of Asia were not great, and so, at the time these letters were written to the seven churches, similar religious, cultural and political influences were at work in each city. At the time of the Lord's letter Sardis was a morally degenerate, pagan city. The cult of Caesar worship was prominent. There were apostate Jewish synagogues, and Greek and Roman temples with the accompanying idolatry and immorality. The patron deity of Sardis was Cybele, who, it was believed by the adherents to this mysterious cult, had power to restore life to the dead. The massive temple of

---

[1] This calculation was made in 1947, so the amount is in 1947 U.S. dollars. The money taken would be many times this in today's dollars.
[2] See also Exo 28:17, 39:10; Eze 28:13.

Cybele still bears witness today, in its fragmentary remains, to the wealth and architectural skill of the people who built it. Also among the ruins of the city, the magnificent temple to Artemis, Diana of the Ephesians, survives in part from the fourth century B.C. On the north side of the acropolis, overlooking the valley of the Hermus river, are the ruins of an outdoor theatre nearly 400 feet in diameter, attached to a stadium which is almost 1,000 feet across.

Over 600 years before John wrote this letter, Sardis was one of the richest and most powerful cities in the world. It was a military stronghold, and a major stop on the main commercial route through Asia Minor. But the history of the city of Sardis is one of unwarranted overconfidence and complacency. For although the inhabitants thought themselves to be invincible, on at least two occasions the cliffs of clay that made the city seem impregnable were scaled by invading armies and the city was conquered – by Cyrus of Persia in 546 B.C. and Alexander the Great in 334 B.C. The people of Sardis were too complacent to keep watch, so on both occasions their city was taken by surprise and humiliated by military defeat. The opposing armies attacked at night by quietly scaling the city's steep fortress walls.

Sardis may have been named for the red gemstones mined in the area, the name "sard" (Greek, *sardios*) being derived from the name of this precious stone. Some Bible scholars believe the name "Sardis" means "the remnant" or "that which remains," from the Hebrew *sarad*, translated in our English Bible as "remain,"[3] or from the Hebrew *sarid*, also translated as "remain."[4] The name of this city could also mean "measured," from the Hebrew *sered*, a carpenter's measuring rule or line.[5]

3. Consequences

After the fall of the Roman Empire, Sardis slowly lost both its affluence and influence. It was attacked and conquered by the Arabs in A.D. 716. It was destroyed in 1403 by Tamerlane, the leader of the Berlas Turks. There are considerable remains of the ancient city around the tiny village of Sert-Kalessi, a station on the railway from Smyrna to Philadelphia. The only remaining indication that followers of Jesus once lived here is that, adjacent to the fourth century B.C. ruins of the temple of Artemis, lie the ruins of a fourth century A.D. Christian church.

4. Church

Some Bible historians believe that the apostle John was the founding minister of this assembly. If this be so, how it must have grieved him to have to tell the church in Sardis it was in the same condition as its city! They had ceased to be watchful. They had been conquered by apathy. They were living on their past reputation.

---

[3] Josh 10:20.
[4] For example, Num 24:19; Deut 2:34.
[5] Isa 44:13.

5. Character

The aspects of the Lord's character revealed to each church gives us not only the key to the condition of the church, but also the answer to its problems. The emphasis to the church in Sardis is twofold:

a. "These things says He who has the seven Spirits of God"

We have already studied the seven Spirits of God, or the Sevenfold Spirit of God, in this book.[6] There we saw the phrase "the seven Spirits of God" represents the fullness of the power and ministry of the Holy Spirit. This is what the church at Sardis needs to reverse a dead situation, and restore resurrection life to them. This dead church must be revived! Only God's Holy Spirit can do this.

b. "[He who has] the seven stars"

Jesus identified the seven stars He held in His hand as the local senior ministers of these Asian churches. Imagine for a moment the Head of the Church holding the Sevenfold Spirit of God in one hand, and the seven ministers in the other, and bringing His two hands together to make them one. Anointed ministers are a key to the life of any local church. When the Holy Spirit indwells the church, there is the life of Jesus, for He said of the Holy Spirit, "He will glorify Me, for He will take of what is Mine and declare it to you."[7]

6. Conduct

As always, the Lord says, "I know your works." But He has more to say about their works. "I have not found your works perfect (complete) before God." They were just going through the actions of playing church. They gathered, they fellowshipped, they sang, they heard the preaching, they prayed – but they were spiritually dead. Like Samson of old, they "did not know that the Lord had departed from [them]."[8] If the Holy Spirit was withdrawn from our church services next Sunday, how many would know? Would He be missed? This is a very serious question. For all works – even Christian works – not inspired and empowered by the Holy Spirit are dead works.

7. Commendation

There is no commendation for the church as a whole at Sardis. Only the faithful few are commended for not defiling their garments. This church is not applauded by the Lord for exposing false teachers, nor for its love, patience, faith, good works, hatred of evil, discernment, or perseverance. This lack of commendation speaks as loudly as the coming complaints.

---

[6] Chapter 15, "The Sevenfold Spirit of God."
[7] John 16:14.
[8] Judg 16:20.

8. Complaint

"You have a name that you are alive, but you are dead"

Here the Judge of all is saying to His church, "You have a name that you are alive. You go through the motions of having church services. You go through the motions of reading the Bible and praying. You do things the way you used to do them when I was with you by the power of the Holy Spirit. But now it's just dead works." In *The Message* the Lord's complaint reads: "I see right through your work. You have a reputation for vigor and zest, but you're dead, stone dead."

The Lord does not complain about sins of the flesh, erroneous doctrine, deceivers in their midst, or the acceptance of unlawful authority. Outwardly everything looks great. But when the Lord looked into their hearts, there was no spiritual life.

Is it possible for Christians to become spiritually dead? Obviously, yes. Jesus said so. But how? By slacking off and sliding back.

Some Christians die spiritually because they stop reading the Bible and praying, thus starving their souls to death. Others die because they experience an offence in the church, so they become bitter and just stop attending. To be securely planted in a local church is essential for a growing, flourishing spiritual life.[9] Yet others die because they see a minister fall, and this becomes a stumbling-block for them. Yet others give up Christianity when they observe a hypocrite's lifestyle. Some find the discipline of living a Christian life too demanding, and the responsibility of church involvement too time-consuming. Hurts cause others to lose their faith in God. Pride has led many away from simple trust in Christ. Others have had the spiritual life squeezed out of them by the cares of this world. Some lose their faith because of tragedy, grief, contradictions, or discouragement. And then there are those who remain in church, go through the motions of serving God, but are totally void of spiritual life.

Whatever causes Christians to spiritually die, the good news is this – God heals backsliding and restores life. His invitation to all is: "Return, you backsliding children, and I will heal your backslidings." If we have sensed the loss of spiritual vigour, may our response be that of the people in Jeremiah's day: "Indeed we do come to You, for You are the Lord our God."[10] To those who feel spiritually dead His Word promises, "He will revive us."[11]

9. Correction

"Remember therefore how you have received and heard; hold fast and repent"

"Remember." "Received." "Repent."

---

[9] Psa 92:13.
[10] Jer 3:22.
[11] Hos 6:2.

"Remember." The previous generation of believers in Sardis had been greatly influenced, directly or indirectly, by men like John, Paul, Timothy, Silas, Peter, and Apollos. Through the preaching and writings of these early church leaders, the Christians at Sardis had been strong, faithfully living for Christ in a very immoral and idolatrous society. The church in its early decades was alive because the power of God's Word and God's Spirit worked mightily in them. They applied what they learned to their personal lives, and lived victoriously for the Lord.

But somehow this current generation had forgotten. Reality became ritual. Underneath this shallow religious reputation was a generation of men and women in Sardis, most of whom were spiritually dead. Despite the fact they were in the church, they had, like their brethren in other cities in Asia, become defiled by the sin of sexual immorality – immorality which at that time had captured the hearts and minds of the citizens of this city sold out to idolatry. As a result of this tragic choice, our Lord found them spiritually dead – and what's more, apathetic about it.

Sin destroys the lifeline we have to the heart of God:

> "Your iniquities have separated you from your God;
> And your sins have hidden His face from you." (Isa 59:2)

Separated from God we die. So the Lord commands the church in Sardis – "Remember"!

And what were they to remember? "How (not only what) they received and heard." The joy they experienced when they first heard the good news of the Gospel. The thrill of knowing that, through Christ, they were children of God. The enthusiasm with which they had once served Him. The fire that burned in their hearts when they were filled with the Holy Spirit. They were to remember they had received the good news that Christ was raised from the dead. His dead body was made alive again by the power of God. That same power could bring them to life again.[12] "Hold fast to these truths," the Lord commanded.

10. Call

"Repent." The call to repentance is clear and urgent. The Lord Jesus demands, "Turn from whatever it is that is separating you from God's life-flow so that you may live anew!" David, as he repented from his sin, cried out to God:

> "Create in me a clean heart, O God,
> And renew a steadfast spirit within me.
> Do not cast me away from Your presence,
> And do not take Your Holy Spirit from me.
> Restore to me the joy of Your salvation,
> And uphold me by Your generous Spirit." (Psa 51:10-12)

---

[12] 2 Tim 2:8; Rom 8:11.

As you read these words, if you have a desire for the Lord to renew your spirit and restore the joy of your salvation, let me assure you, if you sincerely turn from your sin, and pray this prayer of David, the Lord will most definitely answer you.

As a carpenter measures his work with a ruler, so the Builder of the Church will measure His people:

> "Rise and measure the temple of God, the altar, and those who worship there. But leave out the court which is outside the temple, and do not measure it, for it has been given to the Gentiles. And they will tread the holy city underfoot for forty-two months." (Rev 11:1,2)

Here is Moses' tabernacle language again. Those who do not press in to the Holy Place and the Holy of Holies, but remain in the Outer Court, will not measure up for the promised blessing and protection of the overcoming church. They will be trodden under foot for the 3½ years of the Great Tribulation. They will lose their lives, but, if they remain faithful to the Saviour, they will not lose their eternal salvation.

This is the reason it is so very important for the church in Sardis – and for us – to repent. The measuring ruler is "a perfect man, to the measure of the stature of the fullness of Christ" (Eph 4:13). The Lord is about to use Bridal language to the church in Sardis, but what a long way they have to go to measure up – to be overcomers!

11. Caution

    a. "Be watchful," "Wake up" *(NAS):* Centuries before, their city had been conquered because of the failure of their watchmen to stay awake. Now the church had drifted into this same self-confidence and lack of alertness. As a result they had been conquered by apathy and spiritual death. Their spiritual eyes were closed. This is serious. No wonder the Lord Jesus speaks so sharply to them. This is literally a matter of life and death:

"Up on your feet! Take a deep breath! Maybe there's life in you yet. But I wouldn't know it by looking at your busy-work; nothing of *God's* work has been completed. Your condition is desperate."[13]

The present-day Church, especially in more affluent nations, must also guard against drifting into apathy. Enjoying relative comfort and safety, her inner life force can quickly ebb away. Rituals – even Charismatic rituals – can replace the reality of God's powerful presence. In the parable of the ten virgins they all, wise and foolish, slumbered and slept while the Bridegroom tarried.

The subject of being awake and watchful is an important one in the Bible.

---

[13] *TM* – emphasis Peterson's.

Concerning the "salvation ready to be revealed in the last time,"[14] it is written:

> "And do this, knowing the time, that now it is high time to awake out of sleep; for now our salvation is nearer than when we first believed." (Rom 13:11)

Missionary outreach must increase in these days, for the Lord says:

> "Awake to righteousness, and do not sin; for some do not have the knowledge of God. I speak this to your shame." (1 Cor 15:34)

b. "Strengthen the things which remain, that are ready to die": Some in the church were not yet dead, but so far gone they were "ready to die." The only way they could be strengthened was by the power of the Holy Spirit:

> "That He would grant you, according to the riches of His glory, to be strengthened with might through His Spirit in the inner man." (Eph 3:16)

"The things that remain" refers to sound doctrine. There is no complaint here about heresy or false teaching. No attacks from those outside the church are mentioned. Satan has no need to trouble a dead church. It is interesting to note that in Sardis and in Laodicea there is no conflict with people or doctrines, inside or outside the church. Nevertheless, spiritual death is a dreadful enemy, and the church in Sardis had to overcome it.

12. Counsel

"Therefore if you will not watch, I will come upon you as a thief, and you will not know what hour I will come upon you."

This phrase is particularly poignant for a city that in the past had been captured during night attacks. The watchmen of Sardis were not on the alert. This city was defeated by their overconfidence and by their enemies catching them by surprise. To the church the Lord reiterates this element of surprise: "You will not know what hour I will come upon you."

There are several references in Scripture to Jesus coming as "a thief in the night." When asked by His disciples concerning the sign of His coming and of the end of the age, Jesus warned:

> "Watch therefore, for you do not know what hour your Lord is coming. But know this, that if the master of the house had known what hour (*margin, Lit. 'watch of the night'*) *the thief would come*, he would have watched and not allowed his house to be broken into.

---

[14] 1 Pet 1:5. This I believe to be an allusion to an event in the fulfillment of the Feast of Tabernacles to the church.

> Therefore you also be ready, for the Son of Man is coming at an hour you do not expect." (Matt 24:42-44)

Paul wrote to the church at Thessalonica:

> "But concerning the times and the seasons, brethren, you have no need that I should write to you.
> For you yourselves know perfectly that the day of the Lord so comes *as a thief in the night*." (1 Thess 5:1,2)

Peter wrote these graphic words about the Second Coming of our Lord Jesus Christ:

> "But the day of the Lord will come *as a thief in the night*, in which the heavens will pass away with a great noise, and the elements will melt with fervent heat; both the earth and the works that are in it will be burned up." (2 Pet 3:10)

It was the slumbering watchmen of Sardis who were caught unawares. In the same way, the Bible teaches it is the person who is *not* prepared to whom the Lord will come as a "thief in the night." Read the verse again: "Therefore if you will *not watch, I will come upon you as a thief*, and you will not know what hour I will come upon you." But the overcomer will be spiritually alive and alert, ready and waiting, watching for the coming of his Lord.

13. Challenge

"You have a few names even in Sardis who have not defiled their garments; and they shall walk with Me in white, for they are worthy."

Finally, some good news. There are a few – a faithful remnant – who have not defiled their garments as they walked the filthy streets of Sardis. They have walked in the *light* at all times.[15] They have walked worthy of their calling in Christ.[16] Their robes have no spots or wrinkles. They are not spotted by sin, nor wrinkled by pressure.[17] They are washed by the water of the Word. I have already listed the Christian's garments in Chapter 2 of this book. Collectively they make up the wedding garment.

Our Lord Jesus made it clear no-one can participate in the wedding of the King's Son without a wedding garment.[18] Walking with Him in white is a clear reference to the marriage of the Lamb and His wife, the Bride of Christ.[19] No wonder the Lord challenges the church at Sardis – and us – to "hear what the Spirit says to the churches."

---

[15] 1 Jn 1:7.
[16] Eph 4:1.
[17] "Not having spot or wrinkle" (Eph 5:27).
[18] Matt 22:11.
[19] Rev 19:7,8.

14. Compensation for Conquerors

There are three wonderful promises to the overcomer:

a. "He who overcomes shall be clothed in white garments"

The Lord promises, "The one who overcomes in the midst of this apathy and spiritual death will be given a white wedding garment, and be in My Bride." Remember, concerning the marriage of the Lamb the Scripture says: "His bride has prepared herself. She has been permitted to dress in fine (radiant) linen, dazzling and white – for the fine linen is (signifies, represents) the righteousness (the upright, just, and godly living, deeds, and conduct, and right standing with God) of the saints (God's holy people)" (Rev 19:7,8 – *Amp*).

b. "[He who overcomes] ... I will not blot out his name from the Book of Life"

This is a very controversial passage, but we cannot ignore it. God has a special Book. It is the Lamb's Book of Life, and is spoken of many times in the Book of Revelation.[20] In this Book are recorded all the names of those who, by faith, believe the Lord Jesus Christ is the Son of God and that He, as God's Eternal Lamb, shed His blood for their sins. They have received Him into their hearts as Saviour and Lord. As a result of their repentance, their sins have been blotted out.[21] When they gave their lives to Him, the Holy Spirit miraculously quickened their spirits, giving them spiritual life. They were "born again," or "born from above,"[22] and their names were written in the Lamb's Book of Life. Jesus described this experience with these words: "He who hears My word and believes in Him who sent Me has everlasting life, and shall not come into judgment, but has passed from death into life" (John 5:24). When the Lamb's Book of Life is opened on the final judgment day, all whose names are recorded in it will go on to live eternally with their Lord. Those who have not served Jesus will be thrown into the lake of fire.

It is the Lamb's Book of *Life*. It is absolutely essential to have the life of Christ within to have one's name written in this Book. All Bible-believing Christians would agree with this. The question arises, "Is it possible to have one's name blotted out from the Lamb's Book of Life after it has been recorded in it?" Tragically, the answer is "Yes." Jesus said so. Those in Sardis who had once served the Lord Jesus, living close to Him and keeping their spirits alive and their garments clean, but who were now dead and defiled – their names would be removed from the Lamb's Book of Life. The Bible makes it abundantly clear that no sin can enter heaven.[23] On the other hand, those who had overcome sin and spiritual death would be clothed in white garments, and their names would remain

---

[20] Rev 3:5, 13:8, 17:8, 20:12-15, 21:27.
[21] Acts 3:19.
[22] John 3:3 – *margin*.
[23] 1 Cor 6:9,10; Rev 22:15

in the Book of Life. There are many references to this in the Bible, but the example of Moses, I think, is the most vivid.

In Exodus chapter 32 Moses is praying for Israel because of their great sin. Moses pleads with God, "Lord, if You will not forgive their sin, please blot my name out of Your Book which You have written." The Lord replies that He will blot out of His Book only those who have sinned. Their names were in God's Book. Now, because of sin, He is about to blot their names out of His Book.[24]

"But," I hear someone say, "I am eternally secure in Christ." Most definitely you are! As long as you stay *in Christ*. "But," I hear another say, "Jesus said, 'I give them [My sheep] eternal life, and they shall never perish; neither shall anyone snatch them out of My hand.'"[25] Absolutely! I agree. You need never fear. No-one can ever, against your will, snatch you out of the Lord's hand. But He didn't say you can't walk out.

c. "I will confess his name before My Father and before His angels"

The Lord Jesus gives another great promise to the overcomer. He promises to confess the overcomer's name before His Father and before His angels. The words of Jesus in the Gospels shed more light on this promise: "Whoever confesses Me before men, him I will also confess before My Father who is in heaven" (Matt 10:32). By being watchful, and not defiling their garments, the faithful remnant in the church at Sardis confessed their love for Jesus before all. The word translated "confess" here is the Greek word *homologeō*, and means literally "to speak the same thing." Making clear, public confession of allegiance to Christ as one's Master and Lord, and speaking the words that God speaks, are the prerequisites for receiving the Lord's acknowledgment of our loyalty to Him.

Dead or Alive?

There is an awful possibility threatening the life of every church, and each individual Christian. The church at Sardis is our warning. This possibility is so subtle and insidious, that almost before knowing it, a church or Christian can drift into this frightful peril – apathy and dead orthodoxy.

There may be large numbers attending the church services. The finances may be flowing in. There may be much activity. The church may run many programs. The musicians may be skillful, and the preaching correct. It may have a name that it is a live church. Pastors from far and wide may esteem it; even envy it. But no-one knows except Jesus, the Head of the Church, that the life of God is no longer there. Few are getting saved, there is no real growth, no loving unity, no deep emotion, no intense zeal, no compassionate outreach. The fire of His presence no longer burns. On the outside, everything looks fine.

---

[24] Exo 32:31-33.
[25] John 10:28.

But the piercing eyes of Jesus can see the true picture – much of the church is already dead, and the rest is about to perish.

Do you hear the Lord saying to you today, "Remember the passion you had for Me years ago? It's gone. You're dead." To those barely alive, He says, "Wake up! Live again in the power and joy of the Holy Spirit!" Or, can you hear Him saying, "In the midst of temptations and pressures you've kept your clothes clean. Continue to be watchful. Be an overcomer, and you will walk with Me dressed in white. I will never blot your name out of the Book of Life, but I'll acknowledge you before Father."

The key to staying alive in Christ is to be filled with the Holy Spirit daily.[26] Walking in His fullness results in a life of love, joy, peace, laughter, tears, trials, wholesomeness, satisfaction, and success. The Lord Jesus Christ is the resurrection and the life.[27] Filled with His power we can live daily according to the promise of Jesus: "I am come that you may have life, and that you may have it more abundantly."[28]

---

[26] 2 Cor 2:14.
[27] John 11:25.
[28] John 10:10.

Chapter 23

The Weak but Faithful Church

Philadelphia ...Overcoming Arduous Circumstances

Revelation 3:7-13

⁷ "And to the angel (*margin*, 'messenger') of the church in Philadelphia write,

'These things says He who is holy, He who is true, He who has the key of David, He who opens and no one shuts, and shuts and no one opens:

⁸ I know your works. See, I have set before you an open door, and no one can shut it; for you have a little strength, have kept My word, and have not denied My name.

⁹ Indeed I will make those of the synagogue of Satan, who say they are Jews and are not, but lie – indeed I will make them come and worship before your feet, and to know that I have loved you.

¹⁰ Because you have kept My command to persevere, I also will keep you from the hour of trial which shall come upon the whole world, to test those who dwell on the earth.

¹¹ Behold, I am coming quickly! Hold fast what you have, that no one may take your crown.

¹² He who overcomes, I will make him a pillar in the temple of My God, and he shall go out no more. I will write on him the name of My God, and the name of the city of My God, the new Jerusalem, which comes down out of heaven from My God. And I will write on him My new name.

¹³ He who has an ear, let him hear what the Spirit says to the churches.'"

1. Commission

The study of the previous three churches has been somewhat depressing. How refreshing it is to consider the church of Philadelphia. John must have been much happier writing this letter, which he had been commissioned by the Lord to write: "And to the angel (*margin*, 'messenger') of the church in Philadelphia write ..."

2. City

The city of Philadelphia was founded in the year 138 B.C. by Attalus II, king of Pergamos. The king's nickname was *"Philadelphus"* which is Greek for "brother lover," because of the great love he had for his brother, Eumenes II, whom Attalus II succeeded as king of Pergamos. Thus Philadelphia is commonly known as the city of "brotherly love."

Philadelphia was located 26 miles southeast of Sardis, and 70 miles northeast of Smyrna, and, under Roman rule, it became the second city of the region of Lydia in the province of Asia. It was situated 952 feet above sea level on the lower slopes of Tmolus, on the southern side of the valley of the river Ain-é-ghiul Sou, which is probably the Cogamus river spoken of in antiquity. The original population of Philadelphia seems to have been Macedonian, but by apostolic times the religions and cultures of Greece, Rome and apostate Judaism were prominent. As we have already noted, the Lord commanded John to write the Book of Revelation when the Emperor Domitian was forcing all the inhabitants of the Roman provinces to worship him as god. In the 1900s archaeologists discovered coins made by the mint in Philadelphia during Domitian's reign (81-96 A.D.). These coins picture an image of Domitian on one side, and the idol Artemis (Diana), along with the city name, on the other. As with all the cities of Asia at that time, Philadelphia contained many pagan temples.

Although prosperous, Philadelphia was not a very large or impressive town. One reason for this could be that it was located on a main geological fault line, and several times earthquakes had nearly destroyed it. It was, however, both a fortress city and an agricultural center. The soil was good, growing excellent grapes, giving rise to a thriving wine industry. It was also well known for its manufacture of textiles and production of leather.

But what was most important about Philadelphia was its strategic location. The city of Philadelphia was about 100 miles inland from the sea, the farthest east of all the seven cities under consideration. It was thus a gateway city – the doorway to the high tableland of Anatolia and beyond. Philadelphia was on the main access road of the most important trade route in the world – the passage to the eastern nations known today as Afghanistan, Pakistan, India, Bangladesh, Myanmar (formerly Burma), and China.

3. Consequences

Even though in later centuries the Turks and Muslims flooded across Asia Minor, Philadelphia continued to have, by comparison with other cities, a number of resident Christians. It remained a Roman city and persistently resisted conquest until it was finally taken by the Turk Bazazet I in A.D. 1390. It was in the part of Asia Minor left under Turkish control by the armistice at the close of World War I.

Unlike Ephesus, which left its first love and has disappeared in a pile of ruins, Philadelphia stands today as a modern, vibrant Turkish town of 25,000 inhabitants, named Ala-Shehir, which, in the Turkish language means "the reddish city." (By a mistake due to ignorance of the language, earlier travellers reported its name as Allah-Shehir, "city of God.") Among the ruins of historic Philadelphia are the remains of a wall and about 25 ancient churches. In one area there are four strong marble pillars that once supported the dome of a church.

4. Church

Like the churches in other cities of Asia, the church at Philadelphia was probably established as the result of missionary outreach from Ephesus. The church at Philadelphia was experiencing arduous, tiring circumstances. Continuous hardships were causing this wonderful church to become weary.

The Lord Jesus comes, not to rebuke, but to encourage every believer in the church. He says to them, "Don't stop now. Carry on. You're doing a great job. You can overcome weariness, even in such difficult circumstances."

Only two of the seven churches have no words of complaint and rebuke from the Master – Smyrna and Philadelphia. The church at Smyrna faced attack from hostile, pagan people. The church at Philadelphia faced mental, emotional, and spiritual pressure from fellow countrymen.

Smyrna suffered physical persecution from the outside. Philadelphia suffered opposition from the inside – spiritual pressures and persecution from those close to them. God allowed both these churches to experience these pressures to bring them to a place of maturity, excellence, and perfection – to make them victorious overcomers.

It is the same today. Some Christians, like the believers in Smyrna, will touch maturity and go on to perfection by experiencing persecution from without. Yet others, like the Christians in Philadelphia, will, because of their dedication and obedience to the Lord, become a part of the glorious church by experiencing pressure and persecution from within.

5. Character

Four aspects of Christ's character, two of which are not found in John's vision in chapter one, are emphasized in the letter to this church:

a. "These things says He who is holy"

The Lord emphasizes first His holiness. Possibly He is reminding the Philadelphians of this aspect of His character to commend them because they had not been corrupted with the paganism that surrounded them. He also reminds us: "Be holy, for I am holy."[1]

---
[1] 1 Pet 1:16.

b. "He who is true"

Not only are the words of Jesus true. He is the truth: "I am the way, the truth, and the life."[2]

c. "He who has the key of David"

Quoted from Isaiah 22:22, this promise was first given by Isaiah the prophet to Eliakim, son of Hilkiah, the master of King Hezekiah's household:

> "The key of the house of David I will lay on his shoulder;
> So he shall open, and no one shall shut;
> And he shall shut, and no one shall open."

This quotation in Revelation is a clear reference to the authority of Christ, and is closely related to what He says next. Because the main purpose of keys is to open and shut doors:

d. "He who opens and no one shuts, and shuts and no one opens"

This continues the same thought as was prophesied by Isaiah, which we will look at in more detail under:

6. Conduct

"I know your works": Jesus knows they have worked so hard they have almost expended all their energy. Therefore, He goes on to assure them:

"See, I have set before you an open door, and no one can shut it"

Firstly, they are to "look and see" so they can behold the open door. This "open door" speaks to us of three important truths:

a. Jesus, the Open Door of Salvation

Just as there was only one door into the tabernacle,[3] so there is only One Door to salvation. Jesus clearly said: "I am the door. If anyone enters by Me, he will be saved" (John 10:9).

Notice also there was only one door to the marriage of the Bridegroom. "And those who were ready [the wise virgins] went in with him to the wedding; and the door was shut." (Matt 25:10)

---

[2] John 14:6.
[3] Exo 26:36.

b. The Open Door in Heaven

> "After this I looked [exactly what the church in Philadelphia was commanded to do], and there before me was a door standing open in heaven." (Rev 4:1 – *NIV*)

This door is opened for John – and us – so we can see "what must take place after this," and see the "throne in heaven with someone sitting on it."[4]

This door was opened for Paul and he entered into it.[5] This door was opened for Stephen.[6] This door was opened for Elijah.[7] This door was opened for Moses.[8] This door was opened for Enoch, the man who walked with God for 300 years. He was the man who so pleased God with his walk of faith that he overcame the world. God took him through this open door into His very presence.[9] Enoch was an overcomer, and is a type of the last-day overcoming Church of Jesus Christ. May the Church take her rightful place, "blessed ... with every spiritual blessing in the heavenly places in Christ."[10]

c. The Open Door of Missionary Opportunity

Paul, informing the church in Corinth about his ministry in and around Ephesus, wrote:

> "For a great and effective door has opened to me, and there are many adversaries." (1 Cor 16:9)

From prison he requested the Colossians to pray "that God would open to us a door for the word, to speak the mystery (*margin*, 'hidden truth') of Christ" (Col 2:4).

And in his second letter to the Corinthians: "When I came to Troas to preach Christ's gospel ... a door (*margin*, 'opportunity') was opened to me by the Lord." (2 Cor 2:12)

The Greek word for "door," *thura*, also means "opening" or "opportunity." Just as Philadelphia was strategically located for trade, so it could become an open door for the Gospel to travel yet further to the east.

In these momentous days, we too must constantly look for the open doors God places before us. Walking through these open doors of opportunity will not spare

---

[4] Rev 4:1,2 – *NIV*.
[5] 2 Cor 12:2-4.
[6] Acts 7:56.
[7] 2 Ki 2:11.
[8] Jude 9; Matt 17:3.
[9] Gen 5:24.
[10] Eph 1:3.

us from struggles, adversaries, and trials. But the Lord will reward our obedience and faithfulness. When we begin looking for them, we will be amazed how many doors the Lord will open for us to share the Gospel with others. We stand strategically at the beginning of the greatest spiritual awakening and harvest of souls in history.

Through open doors of prayer, giving and going we must take the Gospel to the people of our generation. They too, must have an opportunity to have their names written in the Book of Life. Jesus also holds "the keys of Hades and of Death" (Rev 1:18). And the ultimate fate of those who do not receive Christ is recorded in Revelation chapter 20:

> "And I saw the dead, small and great, standing before God, and the books were opened …
> and Death and Hades delivered up the dead who were in them. And they were judged, each one according to his works.
> Then Death and Hades were cast into the lake of fire. This is the second death.
> And anyone not found written in the Book of Life was cast into the lake of fire." (Rev 20:12-15)

Surely these solemn words should motivate us to seek open doors to witness for our Lord!

7. Commendation

Christ's commendation of the church in Philadelphia is fourfold:

a. "You have a little strength"

They were a minority group in a pagan city. It was a huge challenge to each Christian to remain loyal to Christ in the midst of such idolatry, immorality and opposition. It was draining and wearying to put up with false accusations from the synagogue of Satan. They were becoming weak. But the Lord commended them for the little strength they still had.

One of the greatest qualities a Christian can possess is the ability to keep going – even when we feel we have only a little strength left. In 50 years of serving the Lord, how often I have had these thoughts, "I dedicated my life to you, Lord, to be a missionary. That's all. I didn't sign up for all these heartaches, disappointments, sicknesses, misunderstandings, trials, sorrows, contradictions, betrayals. I'm not sure I can carry on." But His grace and strength have helped me to keep on going.

Paul the apostle pleaded three times with the Lord that the thorn in his flesh would depart from him. The Lord's reply to him contains a message we can apply personally: "My grace is sufficient for you, for My strength is made perfect in weakness" (2 Cor 12:9).

b. "You have kept My word"

The church at Philadelphia had been taught the Word of the Lord, and they lived by it. This is one of the highest commendations a Christian can receive.

c. "[You] have not denied My name"

They knew the power and protection of the Name of the Lord Jesus Christ. They experienced the truth of this promise: "The name of the Lord is a strong tower; the righteous run to it and are safe (*margin*, 'secure')" (Prov 18:10). The Lord Jesus commends them for this. As then, the powerful authority of the Name of the Lord has tremendous influence on every area of our lives today.

d. "You have kept My command to persevere –'endure patiently'" (*NIV*); "You have kept the word of my patience" (*KJV*)

The church in Philadelphia endured temptation and opposition patiently. Had this church worshipped Caesar, and taken shelter in the heathenism of Rome, they could have made life so much easier for themselves. But they did not take the easy way out. Therefore the Lord Jesus commends them for their patience.

We live in a very impatient age. In the rush and bustle of twenty-first century living, we must be reminded of our need to persevere through difficult circumstances, and to be patient in trials and testing.

In the parable of the sower, Jesus taught the need of patience, saying that those who receive the Word into their hearts must "keep it and bear fruit with patience (*margin*, 'endurance')."[11] The writer of Hebrews commands us, "Do not become sluggish (*margin*, 'lazy'), but imitate those who through faith and patience inherit the promises."[12] The fact is that patience and perseverance are produced by tribulation:

> "We also glory in tribulations, knowing that tribulation produces perseverance (*margin*, 'endurance');
> and perseverance, character (*margin*, 'approved character'); and character, hope." (Rom 5:3,4)

It is difficult, but seek to embrace your tribulations and trials as blessings in disguise, and this will produce those evasive but essential qualities – patience and endurance.

---

[11] Luke 8:15.
[12] Heb 6:12.

8. Complaint

There is no complaint against this weak but faithful church.

9. Correction, 10. Call, and 11. Caution

Consequently, there is no correction, no call to repentance, or caution for this church. But the Lord does give the church at Philadelphia counsel concerning three subjects – the synagogue of Satan, the coming hour of trial, and the importance of retaining their crown.

12. Counsel

a. "Indeed I will make those of the synagogue of Satan, who say they are Jews and are not, but lie – indeed I will make them come and worship before your feet, and to know that I have loved you."

In Philadelphia there was a Jewish community, most probably Hellenistic Jews, which vehemently opposed Christians. These apostate Jews refused to recognize Jesus as their Messiah. They actively persecuted all who had trusted in Jesus as Saviour.

In the very early years of the Church, there had been a civil, and sometimes even warm, friendship between Jews and Christians living in the Roman province of Asia. After all, they had so much in common. In the beginning they had the same Bible, because, during its infancy, the only testament the Christian Church had was the Old Testament. But this friendship did not last. The Jews, especially the Grecian Jews, turned against the Church, and became, in the graphic words of the Lord Jesus, "the synagogue of Satan."

Soon the leaders and members of the Christian assembly in Philadelphia experienced the deep agony and anguish of betrayal by those who claimed to be close to them. No wonder they had just a little strength. For nothing drains our mental, physical, emotional and spiritual strength like betrayal. It is hard, but to come to maturity and perfection we also may experience – and, hopefully, overcome – the deep hurt of being betrayed by someone close to us. We will have more to say about this in a later Chapter of this book.[13]

But the Lord Jesus does promise the Philadelphian church that the day will come when the enemies of Christ and His Church will have to acknowledge that Jesus is the Son of God, and that God loves His Church

b. "Because you have kept My command to persevere, I also will keep you from the hour of trial which shall come upon the whole world, to test those who dwell on the earth."

---

[13] See Chapter 26, "Overcoming and Healing Your Hurts."

Intense persecution, trials, and testings remained the lot of Christ's Church for over 200 years after the letters to the seven churches were written, and so I am sure these words had some form of local fulfillment. From apostolic days to the present, the enemies of the Church have persecuted it. Some of God's people have been kept. Others have died for their faith.

But in addition to these trials, verse 10 seems to refer to a specific time – "the hour of trial which shall come upon the whole world, to test those who dwell on the earth." This I believe refers to the 3½-year period of time in the Book of Revelation called the Great Tribulation, a coming period of unprecedented worldwide suffering, destruction, judgment and disaster.

There are scriptures that indicate Christians will go into tribulation.[14] Other verses teach Christians will escape it.[15] This is not a contradiction. It simply demonstrates that a believer who becomes an overcomer now will not be overcome then. But those who are overcome now will also be overcome then. Those who learn to overcome in the midst of tribulation now will not go into the Great Tribulation then. But those who do not learn to overcome today's tribulations will go into the Great Tribulation then. They will go through trials and learn some lessons then, which, until that time, they have avoided.

To put it another way: As we have seen, Christ's glorious Church – the overcomers – will be protected from the trials and tribulation of that unspeakable time of Great Tribulation. But the remnant of the Bride's seed – those who are overcome – will not be kept, but go into the Great Tribulation, where they will either take the mark of the beast, or die for their faith. I believe this is one aspect of what Jesus taught in Matthew 16:25 – "For whoever desires to save his life will lose it, but whoever loses his life for My sake will find it."

This is a very serious matter. Now is the hour in which God calls us to dedicate ourselves wholly to Him and His purposes. If we do not consecrate ourselves to Him now, we will face situations that under force will demand our dedication. I am sure we would rather give ourselves totally to the Lord through love and desire now, than under the pressure of the coming tribulation.

c. **"Behold, I am coming quickly! Hold fast what you have, that no one may take your crown."**

"Behold." "Be awake." "Remain watchful." "Don't go to sleep." "Then you will not be surprised at My coming." The Lord Jesus had told the church at Sardis of His coming. To them it was a warning. To the church that was dead it was a stern proclamation to startle them into obedience. But to the church at Philadelphia the phrase "I am coming quickly" is a promise. To the church depending on the little strength they had left, these words were a declaration to encourage and comfort

---

[14] Dan 7:21; Matt 24:21,22; Rev 13:7.
[15] Dan 12:1; Rev 12:6.

them. At the announcement of His coming, one church is threatened, the other comforted. The same is true today – Bible truths, especially about the Second Coming of Christ, affect people differently according to the condition of their lives.

The church at Philadelphia was exhorted to "Hold fast what you have, that no one may take your crown." The inference is clear – this crown can be taken. This does not indicate the losing of salvation. No one can take salvation from a believer. But one who has a crown – a winner's wreath – can disqualify himself, thus losing his reward.

The Two Judgments

The Lord Jesus taught that there will be two resurrections: the "resurrection of life," and "the resurrection of condemnation":

> "The hour is coming in which all who are in the graves will hear [the Son of man's] voice
> and come forth – those who have done good, to the resurrection of life, and those who have done evil, to the resurrection of condemnation." (John 5:28,29)

These two resurrections, together with their accompanying judgments, will be taught in **Volume Two** of this book. But here is a brief summary.

The two resurrections are separated by a 1,000-year period of time commonly known as the millennium. That which is referred to in Revelation as the "first resurrection" Jesus called the "resurrection of life." This is the resurrection of the godly dead, the saved of all ages, which takes place at the Second Coming of Christ. This first resurrection will occur at the end of the Great Tribulation and the commencement of the millennium. Concerning the first resurrection John states:

> "Blessed and holy is he who has part in the first resurrection. Over such the second death has no power, but they shall be priests of God and of Christ, and shall reign with Him a thousand years." (Rev 20:6)

The second resurrection, which Jesus called the "resurrection of condemnation," is the resurrection of the ungodly dead, the unsaved of all ages. This will take place at the end of the 1,000-year reign of Christ and his people on the earth: "But the rest of the dead did not live again until the thousand years were finished" (Rev 20:5). They will be judged at the Great White Throne (Rev 20:11). This is not a judgment to determine the guilt of the unsaved. They are already guilty and condemned. This is not a judicial trial, but a sentencing: "Anyone not found written in the Book of Life was cast into the lake of fire" (Rev 20:15).

At the first resurrection, the saved will be judged at the Judgment Seat of Christ: "We [committed Christians] shall all stand before the judgment seat of Christ ... So then each of us shall give account of himself to God" (Rom 14:10). Here the Greek word translated "judgment seat" is *bēma*, which literally means "a step for the foot." It was a raised platform, reached by steps, where judges of athletic contests could watch the performance of each contestant, and make their decision as to who would be rewarded with a crown (a wreath made of leaves) of victory.

This judgment of Christians is for rewards: "Each one will receive his own reward according to his own labour" (1 Cor 3:8). Jesus said, "For the Son of Man will come in the glory of His Father with His angels, and then He will reward each according to his works" (Matt 16:27). Works that endure the test of the fire of His Second Coming – spoken of as "gold, silver, and precious stones" by Paul – will be rewarded. The believers whose works are consumed by the fire of His Coming – "wood, hay, stubble" Paul calls them – will suffer loss of rewards, but will not lose their salvation. The Lord will not be looking at the quantity of our works, but their quality: "The fire will test each one's work, of what sort it is" (1 Cor 3:8-15).

The most important point about rewards is this – it is not what *we* get that is important, but what *He* gets. If we are faithful in our labours for Him, His kingdom will increase, and His Name will receive glory.

The Seven Crowns of Reward

Here, listed in no particular order, are the seven crowns of reward a Christian can receive – or lose!

i. **The Crown of Life**

> "Blessed (happy, to be envied) is the man who is patient under trial and stands up under temptation, for when he has stood the test and been approved, he will receive [the victor's] *crown of life* which God has promised to those who love Him." (Jas 1:12 – *Amp*)

The crown of life is the reward earned by Christians who win the battle over temptation, and who patiently and faithfully endure trials and tribulation.

ii. **The Crown of Righteousness**

> "But you must keep control of yourself in all circumstances; endure suffering, do the work of a preacher of the Good News, and perform your whole duty as a servant of God.
> As for me, the hour has come for me to be sacrificed; the time is here for me to leave this life.

I have done my best in the race, I have run the full distance, I have kept the faith.
And now the prize of victory is waiting for me, the *crown of righteousness* which the Lord, the righteous Judge, will give me on that Day – and not only to me, but to all those who wait with love for him to appear." (2 Tim 4:5-8 – *TEV*)

All who receive Christ receive His righteousness. "But of Him you are in Christ Jesus, who became for us ... righteousness."[16] This is "imputed righteousness" – righteousness given as a gift to all who turn to Him for His salvation. The crown of righteousness is the reward earned by Christians who, like Paul, run the full distance in the race of life, keep the faith, and fulfill all God's purpose for their lives.

iii. The Crown of Joy

"For what is our hope, *our joy*, or *the crown* in which we will glory in the presence of our Lord Jesus when he comes? Is it not you?
Indeed, you are our glory and joy." (1 Thess 2:19,20 – *NIV*)

The believers in Thessalonica came to Christ under Paul's ministry. They were his "crown of joy." He writes to the church at Philippi in a similar vein, calling them his "beloved and longed-for brethren, my joy and crown" (Phil 4:1).

A Christian's greatest joy is to lead people to Christ, and to see them continue and grow in the faith.[17] Jesus said there is joy in Heaven when sinners repent and receive Him.[18] The crown of joy and glory is the reward earned by the Christian who wins souls to the Lord.

iv. The Crown That Will Last Forever

"Surely you know that in a race all the runners take part in it, but only one of them wins the prize. Run, then, in such a way as to win the prize.
Every athlete in training submits to strict discipline; he does so in order to be *crowned with a wreath* that will not last; but we do it for one *that will last for ever*.
That is why I run straight for the finish line; that is why I am like a boxer, who does not waste his punches.
I harden my body with blows and bring it under complete control, to keep from being rejected myself after having called others to the contest." 1 Cor 9:24-27 – *TEV*)

---

[16] 1 Cor 1:30.
[17] 3 Jn 4.
[18] Luke 15:10.

The crown that will last forever is the reward a Christian earns when he is so spiritually fit he is a winner in all of life's circumstances. He disciplines himself, keeping his physical desires under complete control.

As *The Message* renders the first three verses of Hebrews chapter 12:

"Do you see what this means – all these pioneers who blazed the way, all these veterans cheering us on? It means we'd better get on with it. Strip down, start running – and never quit! No extra spiritual fat, no parasitic sins.

"Keep your eyes on *Jesus*, who both began and finished this race we're in. Study how he did it. Because he never lost sight of where he was headed – that exhilarating finish in and with God – he could put up with anything along the way: cross, shame, whatever. And now he's *there*, in the place of honor, right alongside God.

"When you find yourselves flagging in your faith, go over that story again, item by item, that long litany of hostility he plowed through. That will shoot adrenaline into your souls!" (Emphasis Peterson's)

v. The Crown of the Overcomer

The Lord's promise to the church at Philadelphia:

"Hold fast what you have, that no one may take *your crown.*
He who overcomes, I will make him a pillar in the temple of My God."

"Keep safe what you have, so that no one will rob you of your victory prize.
I will make him who is victorious a pillar in the temple of my God." (*TEV*)

This promise shows us the overcomer's crown is the reward earned by the Christian who lives victoriously, even in the midst of pressure and difficulties, and becomes a pillar in the church – someone others can lean on in their times of need.

vi. The Crown of Glory

"Shepherd the flock of God which is among you, serving as overseers, not by compulsion but willingly, not for dishonest gain but eagerly;
nor as being lords over those entrusted to you, but being examples to the flock; and when the Chief Shepherd appears, you will receive the *crown of glory* that does not fade away." (1 Pet 5:2-4)

The crown of glory is the Lord's reward for humble, faithful, obedient pastors of churches, and for all who work with them and support them.

vii. The Martyr's Crown

"You will have tribulation ... Be faithful *until death*, and I will give you *the crown of life*." (Rev 2:10)

The martyr's crown is the reward earned by Christians who die for their faith. There have been countless martyrs since the birth of the church.

Even to this day, in many places of the earth, believers die for Christ. And there will be many more called to make the supreme sacrifice for the cause of Christ.

Let us then obey our Lord's exhortation to the church at Philadelphia, and work to gain, and not lose, our victor's crown given to us by our Captain and Judge. When we fully accomplish the will of God in our lives, our rewards will glorify Him:

"Do not, therefore, fling away your fearless confidence, for it carries a great and glorious compensation of reward.

For you have need of steadfast patience and endurance, so that you may perform and fully accomplish the will of God, and thus receive and carry away [and enjoy to the full] what is promised." (Heb 10:35, 36 – *Amp*)

13. Challenge

Although the Lord finds no complaint about this church, he still challenges them to overcome.

14. Compensation for Conquerors

The Lord Jesus gives five wonderful promises to those in Philadelphia who will overcome weariness in arduous, difficult circumstances:

a. "He who overcomes, I will make him a pillar in the temple of My God"

"The temple of My God" means the local church. Christians are called temples of God.[19] By pillar He does not mean a decorative, ornamental pillar, but rather a strong believer who supports the local church with all his strength – someone on whom the weak can lean, and draw strength from, in their times of need. Paul told the Galatians that Peter, James, and John were pillars in the church at Jerusalem.[20] However, not just apostles, but all believers who overcome will be made pillars.

---

[19] 1 Cor 3:17, 6:16,19; Eph 2:21; Rev 11:1.
[20] Gal 2:9.

b. "he shall go out no more"

This is probably an allusion to the necessity to leave the city when it was in the grip of a powerful earthquake. It also speaks of the stability of the overcomer, who will patiently endure all things. The overcomer will not be moved.

c. "I will write on him the name of My God"

In India, pillars and gates often have the name of the owner, or the name of the benefactor who underwrote the structure, written on them. Every time one goes in or out, he is reminded of that name.

The Name of the Lord Jesus Christ was written on the believers at Philadelphia on the occasion of their water baptism. The power of that Name helped them to be overcomers.

d. "[I will write on him] the name of the city of My God, the New Jerusalem which comes down out of heaven from My God"

"Jerusalem;" "Possession of peace" in the midst of opposition, persecution and turmoil. Only overcomers dwell in the New Jerusalem, the Bride-city of our Lord Jesus Christ:

> "Then I, John, saw the holy city, New Jerusalem, coming down out of heaven from God, prepared as a bride adorned for her husband." (Rev 21:2)

e. "[I will write on him] My new name"

This may refer to some further revelation, possibly in eternity, concerning the power of the Name of the Lord Jesus Christ. This new name is a mystery. It could describe His ongoing work in our lives after Jesus comes again. We don't know what it is – yet. But we will know, because we'll be there with Him.

And finally, these words with which He commands each church:

"He who has an ear, let him hear what the Spirit says to the churches."

As we have now seen, being an overcomer has much more to it than just passing one day at a time trying to live like a Christian. It means drawing on God's power daily to overcome weariness in onerous circumstances. This is what the church in Philadelphia had to do. So do we.

| PART FOUR | THE CHURCHES |

Chapter 24

The Poor Rich Church

Laodicea ... Overcoming Affluence

Revelation 3:14-22

¹⁴ "And to the angel (*margin*, 'messenger') of the church of the Laodiceans write,
'These things says the Amen, the Faithful and True Witness, the Beginning of the creation of God:
¹⁵ I know your works, that you are neither cold nor hot. I could wish you were cold or hot.
¹⁶ So then, because you are lukewarm, and neither cold nor hot, I will vomit you out of My mouth.
¹⁷ Because you say, "I am rich, have become wealthy, and have need of nothing" – and do not know that you are wretched, miserable, poor, blind, and naked –
¹⁸ I counsel you to buy from Me gold refined in the fire, that you may be rich; and white garments, that you may be clothed, that the shame of your nakedness may not be revealed; and anoint your eyes with eye salve, that you may see.
¹⁹ As many as I love, I rebuke and chasten. Therefore be zealous and repent.
²⁰ Behold, I stand at the door and knock. If anyone hears My voice and opens the door, I will come in to him and dine ('sup' – *KJV*) with him, and he with Me.
²¹ To him who overcomes I will grant to sit with Me on My throne, as I also overcame and sat down with My Father on His throne.
²² He who has an ear, let him hear what the Spirit says to the churches.'"

1. Commission

The church at Philadelphia was delightful. The church at Laodicea is disgusting. The city of Colossæ was only six miles from Laodicea, and the epistle Paul wrote to the Colossians was also intended for the Laodiceans: "Now when this epistle is read among you, see that it is read also in the church of the Laodiceans" (Col 4:16). If the church in Laodicea had heeded the truths contained in the Colossian letter, the depths to which their church had fallen could have been prevented. The apostle John is commissioned by the Lord Jesus to write a very corrective letter: "to the angel (*margin*, 'messenger') of the church of the Laodiceans write …"

2. City

"Laodicea" was a name given to many ancient cities in the Near East. These cities were named after Seleucid queens whose name was "Laodice." John wrote to the church in the Laodicea which was founded by the Ionians about 2,000 years B.C., when it was named Diospolis. In the 19th century B.C. this relatively small village was added by the Hittites to their expanding empire. One thousand years later the Phrygians took possession, but soon after that, the Lydians took control and renamed the village Rhoas. About 250 B.C. the Syrians captured Rhoas and Antiochus II rebuilt it, renaming the town Laodicea after his wife Laodice. This name comes from two Greek words, *laos* which means "laity" or "the people," and *dikea* which means "to have the rule over." The meaning of the city's name illustrates the attitude of its inhabitants – independent, selfish, and complacent.

About 190 B.C. Laodicea was incorporated into the kingdom of Pergamum, which kingdom, as we have seen, passed into the hands of the Roman empire. As Laodicea had no real value as a garrison town or fortress, it was looked upon by the empire as a potential liability rather than an asset, especially in the light of the recurring damage caused by frequent earthquakes in the area. However, much to the empire's surprise, Laodicea developed into a wealthy city of acknowledged importance, and eventually became the capital of the Roman region of Phrygia Pacatiana.

Located approximately 40 miles east of Ephesus, Laodicea, situated on a small river called the Lycus, was part of the tri-city area of Laodicea, Colossæ, and Hierapolis. The city lay at the junction of two fertile valleys, and at the intersection of three busy trade routes.

There are four important features of the city of Laodicea that will assist us in our study of the Lord's letter to the church there. The natural situation of the city mirrors the spiritual condition of the church. Thus when correcting this church, the Lord is using language the believers would clearly understand.

a. Laodicea was a very wealthy commercial and banking city:

In apostolic times, Laodicea was considered to be one of the wealthiest cities in the world. It contained many banks, all boasting the supreme quality of their gold, which had been brought down from the interior of the region, and refined by a special process in the city. Their vaults were filled with this refined gold, as well as silver, precious stones, and Roman coins.

When Laodicea was nearly demolished by a great earthquake 30 years before John's letter, it was rebuilt by Marcus Aurelius with local money. The city refused financial assistance from the imperial government and rebuilt Laodicea by their own efforts.

b. Laodicea boasted a prosperous and unique textile trade:

Outside the city, in the fertile Lycus valley, flocks of strange-looking sheep grazed. Through a unique and secret method of cross-breeding, the local sheep farmers had developed sheep that produced a violet-black, glossy, soft wool. There was none like it in the entire world. This beautiful wool was made into coats and other outer garments which were exported far and wide. The textile manufacturers were also world-famous for devising a method of weaving without first having to make yarn or thread. The manufacture of clothing provided a considerable source of revenue for the city.

c. Laodicea was famous for its school of medicine:

The medical school in Laodicea produced world-renowned doctors. The names of Doctors Alexander Philadelphus and Zeusus were stamped on the city's coins. The medical school was famous for producing ointments, especially for the eyes and ears, the best-known of which was an eye salve composed of a mixture of a special oil with collyrium powder made from Phrygian stone. This ointment was applied to eyes as a cure for ophthalmic diseases. Large numbers of patients came to Laodicea for medical treatment, further boosting the city's economy.

d. Laodicea did not have an adequate local water supply:

The major problem in this city was, despite being situated close to the river Lycus, it lacked an adequate and convenient supply of drinking water. Archaeologists have discovered two major aqueducts, together with a sophisticated system of stone pipes, which brought drinking water to Laodicea – one from Colossæ (six miles to the south), and the other from Hierapolis (just a few miles to the north). The water in Colossæ was cold, refreshing, and pure for drinking. Nearby were snow-capped mountains, and clear, cold streams of water ran down as the snow melted. In contrast, above the nearby city of Hierapolis, a cloud of vapour, caused by steam rising from her hot bubbling springs, was always visible. These underground springs produced hot water believed to have had medicinal properties. There were large spas in Hierapolis where people would relax in hot baths, seeking relief from their aches and pains.

The purpose of having a source of hot water and another of cold was to enable Laodiceans to mix water from the two sources to the required temperature, just as we do today with a hot tap and a cold. But this elaborate system in Laodicea didn't work – by the time the cold water from Colossæ arrived in Laodicea, it was no longer cool and refreshing to drink. It had become lukewarm. And by the time the hot water from Hierapolis arrived, it had cooled off. The temperature of the water had gone down to the temperature of the air. The hot water had also become only lukewarm. As a result of this drop in temperature the smell and taste of the minerals and chemicals contained in the water increased. The taste of the water was nauseating.¹ Drinking this lukewarm water made people vomit.

Since an enemy attack on the system of aqueducts and pipes that brought hot and cold water to their city would have rendered them helpless, the Laodiceans, unlike the inhabitants of fortress cities, never really felt secure. Consequently, it was imperative for them to maintain good relationships with all their neighbouring cities and towns. This created a very tolerant, complacent, and self-sufficient spirit, which became a chief characteristic of Laodicea – a characteristic which also permeated the Christian church located there.

3. Consequences

In the early centuries of the Church, Laodicea became a Christian city of some eminence. It was the See of the bishop of Asia Minor, and a meeting-place of church councils, the most famous of which was held in A.D. 361. During the Muslim wars in the Middle Ages, the city was destroyed by invaders, and abandoned. By the seventeenth century, travellers reported only wolves and foxes inhabited the city. The ruins are now a scene of ghostlike desolation. The place is called by the Turks Eski-hissar, which means "old castle." Most prominent at the site are the ruins of a large theatre. The ruins of some beautiful and expensive houses are also still visible.

4. Church

It is very possible that the church in Laodicea could have been started as an outreach from the church at Colossæ. The Laodicean church is mentioned four times in the epistle to the Colossians.² So it is evident, that through Paul's writing to the church at Colossæ, the Lord has the church at Laodicea in mind also. It is possible that Epaphras was the founder of the church at Laodicea.³ It is further possible that Archippus was the pastor at the time of the writing of Revelation:

> "Remember me to the brothers in Laodicea and to Nympha and the church that meets at her house.
> When this letter has been read to you, have it read to the church at Laodicea too, and see to it that you too read the one that is coming from Laodicea.
> And tell Archippus, 'See to it that you continue until you fill full your ministry which you received in the Lord's work.'" (Col 4:15-17 – *Williams*)

Is this a rebuke? I am aware the letter to the Colossians was written some 30 years before this letter to the Laodiceans. Had Archippus, during his long pastorate, allowed the spirit of the city to creep into the church? Had the meaning of the city's name become the nature of the church, so that the people now ruled the church? Did they think the church

---

¹ Those who have visited the thermal region of Rotorua in New Zealand will know exactly what I am describing here.
² Col 2:1, 4:13, 4:15, 4:16.
³ Col 1:7, 4:12.

was theirs, existing for their benefit, and that now they made the rules? Had they forgotten this was Christ's Church?[4] Did they no longer believe that God-ordained ministers and elders were "overseers, to shepherd the church of God"[5]? One thing we know for sure – this church could not have fallen into such a disgraceful condition without the pastor at least being aware of what was happening.

5. Character

Four major aspects of our Lord's character are emphasized as He speaks to the Laodicean church:

a. "These things says the Amen"

The word "Amen" has come to us from the Hebrew without being translated. The root meaning of "Amen" in Hebrew is that of nursing, or building up by feeding. The word "Amen" takes us back to God as the nursing Mother, a concept alluded to by Peter: "Be like newborn babies, always thirsty for the pure spiritual milk ('of the Word' – *KJV*) so that by drinking it you may grow up" (1 Pet 2:2 – *TEV*).

In Isaiah 65:16 God is spoken of as the Amen: "He that invokes a blessing on himself in the land shall do so by saying, May the God of truth and fidelity [the Amen] bless me ... the God of truth and faithfulness to His promises [the Amen]" (*Amp*). The Lord and His Word are unquestionable truth.

We say "Amen" at the close of a prayer, or to express agreement with a meaningful statement. We are, in effect, saying, "I accept that as unquestionable truth." But frequently the Lord Jesus began his teaching with this word. It is rendered "Verily I say unto you," (*KJV*). "Truly I say to you" (*NAS*), "Assuredly, I say to you" (*NKJV*).[6] But in Greek, the word is ἀμήν – "Amen."

When Jesus introduces His teaching with this word, He is announcing, "Listen carefully. I am about to tell you something that is unquestionable truth – truth, which if you receive it, will nourish, satisfy, strengthen, and cause you to grow, just as a mother's milk does for her baby." Thus, "Amen" said by God means "it is and shall be so." "Amen" said by man means "so let it be."

To the Laodiceans the Lord Jesus is not only saying, "I teach the truth." He is saying, as He did during His earthly ministry, "I am the Truth."[7] You have not been true to Me. But you had better start changing, for I am the Truth, the ultimate Authority, the Amen.

---

[4] Matt 16:18.
[5] Acts 20:28.
[6] For example, Matt 5:18.
[7] John 14:6.

b. "[These things says] the Faithful and True Witness"

Because He is the Amen, He is, therefore, the Faithful and True Witness. He is, in effect, telling them, "The witness I am about to give concerning you will be both faithful and true."

c. "[These things says] the Beginning of the creation of God"

Having noticed the reference to Laodicea in Colossians, it is interesting to read Colossians in the light of what the Lord says to Laodicea, and to discover how this very expression, "the beginning of the creation of God," is so important in the Colossian epistle:

> "He is the image of the invisible God, the firstborn over all creation.
> For by Him all things were created that are in heaven and that are on earth, visible and invisible, whether thrones or dominions or principalities or powers. All things were created through Him and for Him.
> And He is before all things, and in Him all things consist." (Col 1:15-17)

"The beginning of the creation of God" does not mean that Jesus was the first object of creation made by God. Jesus is Eternal God, without beginning, without ending. In another place John says of the Lord Jesus, "All things were made through Him, and without Him nothing was made that was made" (John 1:3). The Lord declares Himself to be the author of all creation. Because He is about to expose their self-sufficiency and complacency, the Laodicean church needed to hear this – the Lord Jesus is the creator and possessor of everything. He comes to a church that is conceited because of its wealth and independence, and announces His wealth and independence. They should be ashamed, as the wretchedness of their wealth became apparent in the blinding splendour of His, and the sin of their independence is manifest in the glory of Him Who declared Himself to be the origin of all things, the Author of creation.

Not only is Jesus the Creator and Lord of the universe. He is the Creator and Life-Source of His New Creation, His Church, made up of everyone who has become a new creation in Christ.[8]

The Lord Jesus also appears to this church as He Who is standing at the door and knocking (verse 20):

d. "Behold, I stand at the door and knock. If anyone hears My voice and opens the door, I will come in to him and dine with him, and he with Me."

This has to be one of the most tragic pictures in the Bible. Jesus is knocking at the door of His Own church, and He isn't invited in. Yes, He is powerful enough to break the door down. But that is not how the Lord works. He wants

---

[8] 2 Cor 5:17; Gal 6:15.

His people to let Him enter because they want to, not because they have to. I am sure we have all admired Holman Hunt's painting of Jesus knocking at the door. If you look closely you will see there is no handle on the outside. The door can only be opened from the inside. Jesus is waiting for the door to be opened. This reminds us of our responsibility.

Most of us will have, at some time, used Revelation 3:20 to encourage an unsaved person to ask Jesus into his heart. I have done so countless times. That is a good application, but it certainly is not the interpretation of this verse. The context is unmistakable: Jesus is waiting to be invited into His Own house, His Own dwelling place.[9]

6. Conduct

As He says to four of the other Asian churches, so He says to the Laodiceans, "I know your works." The church's opinion of itself is so completely false. What a tremendous difference there is between their "I am" and His "you are"!

7. Commendation

I have noticed many commentators believe the Lord speaks no word of commendation to the Laodicean church. But I do not agree. Not only does the Lord commend this church, but also in doing so, He gives us a lesson which reveals the depths of His love, grace, mercy, and forgiveness. He does not condone their condition. Neither should we. But He does not condemn it. Neither should we. Through many years of Christian service, I have observed the Lord bless and restore countless people, and sometimes even churches, that many would have felt He should have abandoned. The Lord's words of commendation are:

"As many as I love, I rebuke and chasten (*margin*, 'discipline')"

"As many as I love." The Lord loves the unlovable. He commends this church and loves it – even though they make Him sick! The Lord is reminding these Christians, despite their compromises, weaknesses, and failures, He still loves them. Not only this, if they will heed His rebuke and respond to His discipline, He will forgive, restore, and make them overcomers. Did your father use the old "This-hurts-me-more-than-it-hurts-you-I'm-only-doing-this-because-I-love-you" routine when he disciplined you? Mine did. And so does our Heavenly Father! He chastens us, not out of anger, but love; not to punish us, but to discipline, correct, instruct, and bless us. This theme runs right through the Bible. For example:

> "You should know in your heart that as a man chastens his son, so the Lord your God chastens you." (Deut 8:5)

---

[9] Heb 3:6.

"Blessed is the man whom Thou dost chasten ('discipline' – *NIV*, 'instruct' (*NKJV*), O Lord,
And dost teach out of Thy law." (Psa 94:12 – *NAS*)
"My son, do not despise the chastening of the Lord,
Nor detest His correction;
For whom the Lord loves He corrects,
Just as a father the son in whom he delights." (Prov 3:11,12, quoted also in Heb 12:5,6)

"For they indeed for a few days chastened us as seemed best to them, but He for our profit, that we may be partakers of His holiness.
Now no chastening (*margin*, 'discipline') seems to be joyful for the present, but painful; nevertheless, afterward it yields the peaceable fruit of righteousness to those who have been trained by it." (Heb 12:10,11)

8. Complaint

"I know your works, that you are neither cold nor hot. I could wish you were cold or hot"

Lukewarm. Half-hearted. Tepid. Half dead. Compromising. Nauseating. This church has become like the drinking water in their city. They make Jesus sick!

I once read of a preacher who said that if you were going to compile a hymnal appropriate for use in the Laodicean church, it would include such well-known songs as, "I surrender some," "Take my life and let me be," "My hope is built on nothing much," "Sit up, sit up for Jesus," and "Be Thou my hobby."

When asked by His disciples for the signs of His coming, early in His reply Jesus said, "Because of the increase of wickedness ('the increasing crime wave' – *Williams*) the love of most will grow cold" (Matt 24:12 – *NIV*). If you and I are living in the Last Days, which I believe we are, and if the seventh church is prophetic of the Church of this age, which I believe it is, then we need to give very serious consideration to what the Lord Jesus is saying here.

Paul had warned Timothy, his son in the faith, about this condition:

"But know this, that in the last days perilous times (*margin*, 'times of stress') will come:
For men will be lovers of themselves, lovers of money ...
Having a form of godliness but denying its power ..." (2 Tim 3:1,2,5)

Because they coveted wealth, the members of this church had lowered their standards. They had changed the culture of their church to mirror the culture of their city. The citizens of Laodicea were making so much money for the Roman empire, that, as long as they paid their taxes, they were not persecuted to the extent of fellow-Christians in other

Asian cities. People felt they had the right to run their own lives, which is the attitude in most prosperous nations today. The Laodicean church had compromised truth, changed their doctrines to suit their circumstances, and made the church pleasant, comfortable, and acceptable to the community around them.

I fear some of today's churches have done the same. The secularist ethos of modern materialism has crept into the Church in Western nations with devastating consequences. Church has become too "user friendly." Instead of the Church being what Christ intended it to be, standards have been changed to embrace the culture of the day. It is not His will that a local church be a Country Club run for the sole benefit of its members. Nor should it be a Performing Arts Centre for entertainment. It is not a Political Action Group taking sides on the issues of the day. Nor is it a Protest Movement to sponsor militant demonstrations for and against emotionally charged causes. I grant you that elements of all these may, at times, be legitimately expressed in and by a church. But none of these is to be its *raison d'etre,* the purpose for which it exists. The Bible teaches the reason the church exists is:

> "to the intent that now the manifold (*margin*, 'many-sided') wisdom of God might be made known by the church to the principalities (*margin*, 'rulers') and powers in the heavenly places,
> according to the eternal purpose which He accomplished in Christ Jesus our Lord." (Eph 3:10,11)

God's purpose for His Church will be fulfilled only by a rekindling of the fire of the Holy Spirit that fell upon the waiting 120 on the day of Pentecost. God wants His people "hot."

"Neither cold nor hot." The Greek word for "cold," *psuchros*, means "very chilly," and the verb form of the same word, *psuchō*, means "to cool by blowing." A person who is spiritually cold is frozen in unbelief.

On the other hand, the Greek word for "hot," *zestos* (from which we get our English word, "zest,") means "boiling hot," from the Greek root *zeo*, "to boil, be hot, fervent." A Christian who is spiritually hot is on fire for the Lord. Filled and inflamed with fervency for Christ. Consumed with a red-hot passion and burning zeal for His Lord. After His resurrection, the Lord Jesus appeared to two disciples on the road to Emmaus. When they had shared intimate fellowship with Him, they said, "Didn't we feel on fire as he conversed with us on the road, as he opened up the Scriptures for us?"[10] They were definitely hot.

What then does it mean to be "lukewarm"? It means to be "half and half." Half-hearted towards the commands of Christ. Half-hearted towards the culture of this world. A lukewarm Christian has enough religion to get himself to church, yet not enough relationship with God to light the fire of total commitment to Him. No emotion. No passion. No enthusiasm. No urgency. No vision. No compassion. Not frozen. Not boiling. Lukewarm – a condition utterly repugnant to the Master.

---

[10] Luke 24:32 – *TM*.

An illustration of what it means to be lukewarm is found in the parable of the good Samaritan.[11] The man who went down from Jerusalem to Jericho was attacked by robbers, who wounded him, stripped him of his clothing, and left him half dead. Not dead. But not alive.

The man attacked by thieves went down from Jerusalem. "Jerusalem" means "possession of peace," and speaks of peace through living close to Jesus, Who is our Peace. When we turn from Him, we will certainly be on the road down to lukewarmness. The thieves speak of Satan and his demons.[12] They stripped him of his clothing. Like the Laodicean church, he was left naked. He was left half dead. The Laodicean church was half cold, half hot. The religious leaders of the day walked right past, ignoring the wounded man. But a certain Samaritan, a type of Jesus, came to him, showed compassion, and bandaged his wounds, pouring in oil (typical of the Spirit) and wine (typical of the Blood), brought him to an inn (a picture of the church), and took care of him. Before he left, the good Samaritan gave two days' wages (typical of two 1,000-year days) to the innkeeper (the five ministries) and said, "Take care of him; and whatever more you spend, when I come again, I will repay you." Just as the Samaritan cared for the wounded, half-dead man and restored him to health, so in these days the Lord is visiting His church anew. He desires to restore those who are lukewarm to their first love and zeal, and re-ignite the fire of God in His people.

But here is a puzzle – why did the Lord Jesus say, "I wish you were cold or hot'?[13] Because there is more hope for a person who is cold than for one who is lukewarm. It is easier to lead totally cold people to Christ, encourage them to be filled with the Holy Spirit and keep the fire of God burning in their hearts, than it is to lead a lukewarm Christian from tepid to hot. Lukewarmness is more difficult to overcome than coldness of heart. Why? Because just like the believers in the Laodicean church, a lukewarm Christian often *does not realize he is only lukewarm.*

9. Correction

"Because you say, 'I am rich, have become wealthy, and have need of nothing' – and do not know that you are wretched, miserable, poor, blind, and naked"

The problems in the Laodicean church were compounded by the fact they did not *know* how wretched, miserable, poor, blind and naked they were. Here was a group of Christians who were absorbed with the surrounding culture. Perhaps slowly, and possibly even imperceptibly, the culture of the city became the culture of the church. They were climbing the social ladder. They were advancing their careers. They were getting ahead in the world. They sported the latest expensive fashions. The Roman legions brought spoils and goods from all over the world home to Rome and her provinces and sold them on the open market. The Laodicean Christians believed that "a woman's place is in the mall,"

---

[11] Luke 10:30-37.
[12] John 10:10.
[13] Rev 3:15 – *Williams*.

and that she could afford to go on sprees of "shop-till-you-drop." In effect they said, "There is nothing we need. God has really blessed us." But the Lord's assessment of them was the complete opposite of theirs. They were totally mistaken in eight major areas:

a. You say, "I am rich"

Doesn't God promise prosperity? As with all Biblical subjects, we need to strive for balance here. John the revelator, in another place, certainly does teach it is the will of God for Christians to prosper: "Beloved, I pray that you may prosper in all things and be in health, just as your soul prospers" (3 Jn 2). The Lord's revealed will is not only our material prosperity, but also our spiritual prosperity. The Lord Jesus taught in the parable of the sower that "the cares of this world and the deceitfulness of riches choke the word."[14] He did not say the plant dies. He said it doesn't bring forth fruit.

Both Old and New Testaments state that those who are selfish, greedy and have a material mindset run a great risk of hurting themselves:

> "There is a severe evil which I have seen under the sun:
> Riches kept for their owner to his hurt." (Eccl 5:13).

> "But those who desire to be rich fall into temptation and a snare, and into many foolish and harmful lusts which drown men in destruction and perdition.
> For the love of money is a root of all kinds of evil, for which some have strayed from the faith in their greediness, and pierced themselves through with many sorrows."(1 Tim 6:9,10)

God prospers His people so that they may be free from debt,[15] and support His work with tithes and offerings.[16] Although the Laodicean believers considered themselves rich, God said they were poor. The apostle Paul, 30 years earlier, had taught them in his letter to the Colossians concerning true riches. They should have remembered:

> "To them God willed to make known what are the riches of the glory of this mystery among the Gentiles: which is Christ in you, the hope of glory." (Col 1:27)

> "For I want you to know what a great conflict (*margin*, 'struggle') I have for you and those in Laodicea, and for as many as have not seen my face in the flesh,
> That their hearts may be encouraged, being knit together in love, and attaining to all riches of the full assurance of understanding, to the

---

[14] Matt 13:22.
[15] Rom 13:8.
[16] Mal 3:8-10; Matt 23:23; Heb 7:6.

knowledge of the mystery of God, both of the Father and of Christ." (Col 2:1,2)

b. "You say I ... have become wealthy"

The church members of Laodicea, like other citizens of their city, found their security in riches and possessions. With their accumulation of money, clothes, houses, factories and farms they felt self-reliant. They were an affluent church in an affluent society with an affluent mindset. This mindset had to be overcome. Because then, as now, the danger exists that prosperity can foster self-confidence and complacency, not only in matters material, but more importantly, in matters spiritual.

We too must beware of the dangers of living a life of comfort and ease. It is a short journey from victory to defeat. Winning leads to fame. Fame leads to affluence. Affluence to indulgence. Indulgence to weakness. And weakness leads to defeat.

c. "You say I ... have need of nothing"

These church people are smug and self-sufficient. They didn't need money. They didn't need help from Rome. They didn't need help from God. They thought they had the best of all possible worlds.

The Laodicean church had totally missed the purpose of God's prosperity. They had kept their riches for themselves. This wealth was about to hurt them if they didn't change their attitudes. It is the same today. It is God's will for you to prosper, but when you do, you face a big decision. You can keep all your riches for yourself, settle down, enjoy life and become a lukewarm Christian. Or, you can obey God, support His work, and seek the Lord for the answer to the question, "Why has He prospered me?" The Bible graphically describes the two options:

> "There is one who scatters, yet increases more;
> And there is one who withholds more than is right,
> But it leads to poverty." (Prov 11:24)

How sad that instead of being a great blessing to the whole province of Asia and beyond by giving, this church corrupted itself with wealth. The great challenge to the Laodicean church was to overcome the negative effects and attitudes caused by their affluence.

d. "[You] do not know that you are wretched"

"You are wretched." The Greek word *talaipōros* means "distressed, miserable, oppressed with a burden." The burden they carried was the very same wealth that they imagined carried them. Instead of their abundance helping and lifting them, it hindered and defiled them.

e. "[You] do not know that you are ... miserable"

They were outwardly happy and satisfied, but spiritually miserable and lukewarm. The word translated "miserable" means "pitiable." The heart of the Lord was moved with pity toward them. They were so deluded. The difference between their perception of themselves, and the reality revealed by Christ, is enormous. Imagine for a moment how they felt as they listened to this letter being read to them in their Sunday church service.

All the words Christ uses in speaking to this church are words of pity. He is not angry at their condition. He is angry that they are satisfied with things the way they are.

f. "[You] do not know that you are ... poor"

This word means "to be poor as a beggar," "destitute." Only those who have visited poverty-stricken countries and been accosted by beggars – children whose arms have been cut off by their relatives, young women whose faces have been grotesquely disfigured, to evoke sympathy and gain more money – can fully envision the depths of meaning in this word. This church thought they had everything. Jesus says they possess absolutely nothing worth having.

Remember the church at Smyrna? She was materially poor, but she was spiritually rich. Laodicea, on the other hand, was materially rich but spiritually poor. The Smyrna church was richly filled with the Word and the Spirit of God. But in these areas the church in Laodicea was poor. To the natural eye, Laodicea was the rich church and Smyrna the poor church. But in the Lord's eyes, Smyrna was the rich poor church, and Laodicea the poor rich church.

g. "[You] do not know that you are ... blind"

It is ironic that in a city world-famous for its eye ointment, Christ calls His church blind. We studied earlier how the human spirit has five spiritual senses similar to the physical senses of the human body. This includes the ability to see. This church was blind – and didn't know it! Because they were blind there was no vision. Because they were blind they could not see the light.

h. "[You] do not know that you are ... naked"

In a city known worldwide for its garment industry, this church is spiritually naked. To other churches the Lord has spoken of white raiment. This church has none. They do not have the clothing that should adorn the Bride of Christ.

Jesus said only those wearing a wedding garment will enter the marriage supper of the Lamb.[17]

"I am rich." "You are poor." "I have become wealthy." "You have nothing." "I have need of nothing." "You are wretched, pitiable, blind, naked." The light of the Lord's judgment and love has revealed the true condition of this church.

10. Call

"Therefore be zealous (*margin*, 'eager') and repent"

Here the Lord is saying, "To rid yourselves of this nauseating lukewarm condition the flame of God must be re-ignited in your hearts. You must be on fire for Me again. Repent! Change your minds about yourselves. I have shown you your true condition. Change your attitudes. Turn from your love of money. Be truly sorry for your smug, complacent ways. These changes must commence immediately!" Likewise, today the Lord calls us to leave the ranks of the half-hearted, and become fully devoted to Him.

"Zealous," according to Vine, is the Greek word *zēloō*, and, together with its derivatives, means "to seek or desire eagerly," "to take a very warm interest in," "to be jealous," or to be "an uncompromising partisan."[18] The believers in Laodicea had compromised long enough. Indeed, compromising had caused them to become lukewarm. Their condition had made the Lord feel like vomiting. Now they must start back on the road to becoming "uncompromising partisans" for Jesus. They had to stop thinking about what they could get out of God, and consider what He wanted from them – "the riches of the glory of His inheritance in the saints."[19]

11. Caution

"So then, because you are lukewarm, and neither cold nor hot, I will vomit you out of My mouth"

Lukewarm Christians make Christ sick to His stomach. They make Him want to throw up. This is strong language. Does this statement shock you? It ought to. The Lord wants us to be repulsed by what repulses Him. Even in His ascended, glorified state, our Lord has feelings. Christ is not an unimpassioned company accountant, making entries in His ledger in Heaven, running the universe in a cool, calculated yet detached way. Rather, even though He is God, He has deep emotions, passionate zeal, and a loving heart.

Very literally, this phrase reads, "I am about to spew you out of my mouth." It is imminent. It's about to happen. This does not mean He is going to completely remove Christians from relationship with Himself. The Lord Jesus Christ, standing in the midst of

---

[17] Matt 22:12.
[18] Vine, *op.cit.*
[19] Eph 1:18.

the lampstands, is speaking to each church in its capacity as a *light-bearer* in this dark, sinful world.

To the Laodicean church He says, "To have light you need white-hot fiery fervency. But you are lukewarm. You are not a true example of what a Christian should be. So I am going to reject you from the ministry of witnessing for Me."

12. Counsel

"I counsel you to buy from Me gold refined in the fire, that you may be rich; and white garments, that you may be clothed, that the shame of your nakedness may not be revealed; and anoint your eyes with eye salve, that you may see."

Christ's counsel to the Laodicean church is clear – they must buy from Him refined gold, white garments, and eye salve to anoint their eyes. They must pay the price.

a. Refined gold

As we have already noted, naturally speaking, Laodicea was a very rich city. Gold refined in Laodicea, because of its purity and lustre, was a sought-after item worldwide, and high prices were paid to obtain it.

How ironic that the Lord is counseling Christians, all of whom probably owned at least some of this special Laodicean gold, to buy gold from Him. What does He mean?

Many times in Scripture gold speaks of *faith*. Writing to Christians who were suffering intense persecution for their faith, Peter said:

> "In this you greatly rejoice, though now for a little while, if need be, you have been grieved (*margin*, 'distressed') by various trials,
> that the genuineness of your faith, being much more precious than gold that perishes, though it is tested by fire, may be found to praise, honor, and glory at the revelation of Jesus Christ." (1 Pet 1:7,8)

The Laodicean church lacked faith because its members had put their trust in their money and possessions. "Just as gold is refined by fire, so your faith will be tested by fiery trials," the Lord says. "These trials are not punishment. Rather, I permit them so your faith can be purified and strengthened. One day gold will perish. But faith in Me yields eternal rewards. So stop focusing your teachings on subjects like prosperity and self-esteem, and get back to the basics. Study God's Word together, for that's how you receive faith – from the Word.[20] 'Repentance from dead works' and 'Faith towards God' are the first two of 'the elementary principles of Christ,'[21] so pay the price, and buy this everlasting gold – faith."

---

[20] Rom 10:17.
[21] Heb 6:1.

b. White garments

Garments made in Laodicea were exported everywhere. But Jesus is counseling them to buy, not the black woolen garments of their own making, but the white, linen garments of His *righteousness*, which is the wedding garment of the Bride of Christ:

> "Let us rejoice and shout for joy [exulting and triumphant]! Let us celebrate and ascribe to Him glory and honor, for the marriage of the Lamb [at last] has come, and His bride has prepared herself.
> She has been permitted to dress in fine (radiant) linen, dazzling and white – for the fine linen is (signifies, represents) the righteousness (the upright, just and godly living, deeds, and conduct, and right standing with God) of the saints (God's holy people)." (Rev 19:7,8 – *Amp*)

Here the Bride of the Lamb has prepared herself.

She has paid the price. She is wearing her dazzling white wedding gown. Not that this garment can be bought with money or religious works. No. But she has chosen to allow Christ, her righteousness, to live in her.[22] She has denied herself, and has died daily to fleshly and ungodly desires. She has chosen right standing with God, and right living. She has endured contradictions, criticisms, and pressures. She has not been enticed or influenced by the world's culture. The Lamb's "Wife has made herself ready. She was given a bridal gown of bright and shining linen. The linen is the righteousness of the saints."[23]

This church is commanded to buy these garments from their coming Bridegroom.

c. Eye salve to anoint their eyes

At Laodicea's renowned medical university a special eye salve had been developed. It is possible that some church members owned apothecary shops where this eye ointment was made and sold.

But this church was spiritually blind, and needed the anointing of the Holy Spirit. Only Jesus Christ can give this anointing.[24] John calls it "the anointing (Greek, *chrisma*) which you have received from Him" (1 Jn 2:27). It is the anointing of the Spirit which will open their spiritual eyes,[25] help them understand the Word of God,[26] give light,[27] vision, and power to be witnesses of the Gospel.[28]

---

[22] 1 Cor 1:30,31.
[23] Rev 19:7,8 – *TM*.
[24] Acts 2:33;
[25] Eph 1:18.
[26] John 16:13,14.
[27] Col 1:12.
[28] John 15:26; Acts 1:8.

Faith, Righteousness, Anointing

Faith, righteousness, and the anointing. Together, these three attributes are the only cure for lukewarmness.

In Matthew's Gospel, the Gospel of the Kingdom, the Lord Jesus taught about these three essential qualities – faith, righteousness, and the anointing. It is interesting to note He concludes each of these teachings with a warning about "outer darkness."

In Matthew chapter eight a centurion came to Jesus and pleaded with Him to heal his paralyzed servant.[29] Jesus replied that He would come and heal him. The centurion felt unworthy for Jesus to come to his home. Nevertheless, he said, he believed that by the power of Christ's words alone his servant could be healed. The centurion added that he also was a man of authority, and he therefore understood the authority and power of Jesus. Hearing these words, Jesus marveled, and said to His followers: "Assuredly, I say to you, I have not found such great *faith*, not even in Israel."

Having declared this, immediately Jesus appears to go off on a tangent by saying, "Many shall come from east and west, and sit down with Abraham, Isaac, and Jacob in the kingdom of heaven. But the sons of the kingdom will be cast out into outer darkness. There will be weeping and gnashing of teeth." Then Jesus turned again to the Centurion, telling him because he had believed, his servant was healed. What was Jesus saying? That faith in Him alone – not race, nor family background – was essential. Those without sufficient faith would be cast into *outer darkness*.

In Matthew chapter 22 Jesus taught the parable of the king who arranged a wedding for his son. The king commanded that the man who was not wearing a wedding garment – the robe of *righteousness* – be cast into *outer darkness*.[30]

Matthew chapter 25 begins with the parable of the ten virgins. The foolish did not pay the price for sufficient oil – the *anointing*. Therefore, when the door to the wedding was shut the foolish were left in darkness.[31] Then immediately Jesus begins to teach the parable of the talents. (A talent was probably worth about US$5,000.) One servant was given five talents, another two, and the third just one. The five talents could speak of the five ministries, the two talents could be a type of the two local church ministries, elders and deacons, and the one talent could refer to an individual. Each individual Christian has a ministry – some form of service in His kingdom – committed to us by the Lord. Because of a combination of fear and laziness, this third servant buried his talent in the ground and was unfruitful. It is the *anointing* that makes us

---

[29] Matt 8:5-13.
[30] Matt 22:1-14.
[31] Matt 25:1-13

profitable and fruitful for the Lord. The unprofitable servant was cast into *outer darkness*.[32]

There are two important things to note in these three parables. Firstly, each one cast into outer darkness is pictured as a believer. In Matthew chapter 8 they are "children of the kingdom." In Matthew 22, the king addresses the one without a wedding garment as "friend." In Matthew 25 the unfruitful one was a "servant" and had been given a talent.

Secondly, "outer darkness" is not hell. Being cast into outer darkness does not mean that a Christian loses his or her salvation. What is lost is the unspeakable blessing of attending the marriage supper of the Lamb. Outer darkness refers to that 3½-year period of intense darkness, the Great Tribulation, of which I have already written. Outer darkness is the same as the outer court of Revelation 11:2.

The Mighty Judge of all the earth told the church at Laodicea that if they did not regain sufficient faith, righteousness, and anointing that He would spew them out of His mouth. There seems to be a distinct parallel between "spewing out" and "casting out" into outer darkness.[33]

I have summarized this portion of teaching in the following chart.

Figure 39: **The Three Essentials for the Overcomer in the Laodicean Church Age**

1 To Overcome	2 Need	3 Christ's Counsel, "Buy"	4 Price	5 Outer Darkness	6 Christians Cast into Outer Darkness
Poverty of spirit	Faith	Gold tried in fire (1 Pet 5:7)	Prov 23:23	Insufficient faith Matt 8:8-12	Children of kingdom
Nakedness (no wedding garment)	Righteousness	White garments (Rev 19:8)	Rev 3:18	Insufficient clothing Matt 22:11-14	Friend
Blindness (without light or vision)	Anointing (releases talents)	Eye ointment (1 Jn 2:27)	Matt 25:9	Insufficient anointing Matt 25:1-30	Own servants

---

[32] Matt 25:14-30.

[33] I have already stated that "wise" Christians will be protected from the darkness of the Great Tribulation, and "foolish" Christians will go into it. There are a number of references in Revelation which speak of Christians in the Great Tribulation, for example: 6:9-11; 7:9,13-15,17; 11:2; 12:11,17; 13:7,10; 14:6,7,13; 15:1-4; 20:4. I call this company of believers "The Tribulation Saints." We will study this subject in much more detail in **HERE COMES THE BRIDE! Volume Two.**

13. Challenge

The challenge facing this proud, complacent church is to obey Christ's commands, act upon His counsel, be filled with His fire, and overcome spiritual poverty, nakedness, and blindness. The good news is this – Christ believes they can do it. For though the church in Laodicea has the hardest battle of all to fight, it is promised the greatest reward.

14. Compensation for Conquerors

"To him who overcomes I will grant to sit with Me on My throne, as I also overcame and sat down with My Father on His throne."

What an amazing promise to a church that has just been told by the Lord Jesus, "You make Me sick because of your pride, arrogance, lukewarmness, and indifference." Now He promises that those who overcome in this blind, wretched, miserable church can become co-regents of the universe with Him. But they must overcome as He overcame. When did Jesus overcome? What did He overcome? Jesus overcame the easy way out when Satan said to Him in the wilderness, "All these kingdoms of the world I will give You if You will fall down and worship me."[34] How easy! No Cross. No suffering. No death. One of His own disciples made the same suggestion to Him: "Don't go to the Cross. Think of all the good you can do if you don't die. It will be so much easier."[35] Yet again in Gethsemane He was tempted: "Father, if it be possible, let this cup pass from me." But Jesus conquered every temptation. He overcame the easy way out. He fulfilled His Father's perfect will. He went through death, was resurrected as He promised, and sat down with His Father on His throne.

This is, without doubt, the climax of the highest calling of all – the promise to rule and reign with Christ. Earthly affluence can blur our vision of the wealth of God's eternal blessings. He tells these tepid saints at Laodicea, "I conquered! I overcame! So can you! And if you do, you'll sit with Me on My throne." Therefore, **"He who has an ear, let him hear what the Spirit says to the churches."**

The letters to the seven churches in Asia teach us that there are seven basic areas that must be overcome in the lives of Christians. Let me summarize these for you as we close this section:

1. Attitudes: Our relationship with God must grow in intimacy. He must always be our first love;

2. Affliction: We must recognize that adverse circumstances and contradictions are not necessarily a sign of sin, or of being out of the will of God. No matter what happens, we must continue to love and serve the Lord fervently;

---

[34] Matt 4:8-10.
[35] Matt 16:22,23.

3. Associations: We should not form any association with people or doctrines that would harm our Christian life or testimony;

4. Authority: We should develop a Biblical perspective of authority and submission, one that will glorify Christ at home, at school, at work, and in the church;

5. Apathy: It is imperative we maintain a daily relationship with the Lord, and overcome any temptation to indifference. Nor can we rely upon the remembrance of our past experiences;

6. Arduous Circumstances: No matter how difficult the way may seem, we must carry on serving the Lord, overcoming weariness and the temptation to quit;

7. Affluence: While money is not intrinsically harmful, the love of money is. Therefore we must overcome all temptations to greed, complacency, self-sufficiency, and everything that would decrease our passion for Jesus.

As we have seen in this study, God does not and will not sovereignly make us overcomers. Yes, the Lord will help us. But there needs to be a corresponding willingness in our hearts and minds.

> "He who overcomes shall inherit all things, and I will be his God and he shall be My son." (Rev 21:7)

> "Conquerors inherit all this. I'll be God to them, they'll be sons and daughters to me." *(TM)*

This subject of becoming an overcomer is so important I invite you to join me in the next section of **HERE COMES THE BRIDE!** entitled **The Overcomer**.

PART FIVE

THE OVERCOMER

PART FIVE   THE OVERCOMER

Chapter 25

How to Be an Overcomer

The same disciple who wrote concerning overcomers in the Book of Revelation also wrote the following about overcomers in his first letter:

> "I write to you, little children,
>   Because your sins are forgiven you for His name's sake.
> I write to you, fathers,
>   Because you have known Him who is from the beginning.
> I write to you, young men,
>   Because you have overcome the wicked one.
> I write to you, little children,
>   Because you have known the Father.
> I have written to you, fathers,
>   Because you have known Him who is from the beginning.
> I have written to you, young men,
>   Because you are strong, and the word of God abides in you,
>   And you have overcome the wicked one.
>
> Do not love the world or the things in the world. If anyone loves the world, the love of the Father is not in him.
> For all that is in the world – the lust of the flesh, the lust of the eyes, and the pride of life – is not of the Father but is of the world.
> And the world is passing away, and the lust of it; but he who does the will of God abides forever." (1 Jn 2:12-17)

Without doubt, the greatest lesson we will ever learn in life is how to be an overcomer. In this chapter I want to bring to your attention a principle that will help you live victoriously for the Lord Jesus all the days of your life.

In the Scripture above, we learn that just as there are three main stages of natural growth, so there are three main stages of spiritual growth and development: "little children," "young men," "fathers." As we have already noted, the Bible is filled with exhortations for Christians to grow. For example:

> "*Grow* in the grace and knowledge of our Lord and Savior Jesus Christ." (2 Pet 3:18)

> "Having been built on the foundation of the apostles and prophets, Jesus Christ Himself being the chief cornerstone,

in whom the whole building, being fitted together, *grows* into a holy temple in the Lord,
in whom you also are being built together for a dwelling place of God in the Spirit." (Eph 2:20-22)

"Wherefore leaving the doctrine of the first principles of Christ (*margin*, 'the word of the beginning of Christ'), let us press on unto perfection (*margin*, *'full growth'*)." (Heb 6:1 – *ASV*)

Once again, a chart helps us see more clearly these three stages of Christian growth.

Figure 40: **Some Illustrations of the Three Major Stages of Christian Growth**

Illustration	First Stage	Second Stage	Third Stage
John's letter (1 Jn 2:12-14)	Little children "Babies"	Young men "Youth"	Fathers "Mature"
Parable of sower	30-fold	60-fold	100-fold
Parable of ten virgins	Foolish virgins	Wise virgins	Bride
Moses' tabernacle	Outer court	Holy place	Holy of holies
Festivals of Israel	Passover	Pentecost	Tabernacles
Book of Ruth	Orpah	Naomi	Ruth
Rains in Israel	Showers (Psa 65:10)	Former rain	Latter rain

God's revealed will is that we should grow in the Lord. God's revealed will is also that we learn to be victorious, overcoming every temptation, problem, pressure, and difficulty. "Overwhelming victory is ours through Christ." (Rom 8:37 – *LB*) "He who overcomes I shall give him these things." (Rev 21:7 – *margin*) What things? For one, the joy, privilege, and blessing of being in "the bride, the Lamb's wife" (Rev 21:9).

The important principle we must learn is this: It is obvious from John's letter that the key to growing in the Lord is learning to be an overcomer. And the key to learning how to be an overcomer is growing in the Lord. These two essential objectives are interdependent. What will hinder our growth in the Lord? Being overcome. What will hinder our becoming overcomers? Lack of spiritual growth. It is important we remind ourselves that in these last days there will be only two kinds of Christians: Those who are overcomers, and those who are overcome.

"These Three Men"

Some time ago I was reading the book of the prophet Ezekiel, and I found a phrase that is repeated four times in seven verses: *"These three men."* Four times, in a space of only seven Bible verses, God commends "these three men" (Ezek 14:14,16,18,20).

It is interesting to note in Scripture that on a number of occasions the Lord chooses "three men" for special mention. For example, Abraham, Isaac and Jacob. Peter, James and John. The three men translated bodily to heaven, Enoch, Moses, and Elijah. Three – the number of complete, perfect witness and testimony.

"These three men" in Ezekiel chapter 14 are Noah, Daniel, and Job. They lived in fellowship with God, and were righteous men. Each lived in a different period of time. As I looked afresh at their lives, I realized each was an overcomer, and, in the context of Ezekiel chapter 14, this is the reason the Lord is commending them. I call them "God's Overcomers Hall of Fame."

Three great forces were battling to overcome them: the world, the flesh, and the devil.

They faced temptation in three major areas: the lust of the eyes, the lust of the flesh, and the pride of life.[1]

Each had to overcome in all three areas of his being: soul, spirit, body.[2]

Today, we have to overcome exactly as they did. We face the same enemies and temptations that must be overcome in our lives. "These three men" in Ezekiel are men who did overcome. By their example they teach us the greatest lesson we will ever learn – how we too can be overcomers.

1. Noah

The Bible says "Noah was a just man, 'blameless, having integrity' (*margin*) in his generations. Noah walked with God" (Gen 6:9). Concerning the condition of the people of the world, among whom Noah and his family dwelt: "the Lord saw that the wickedness of man was great in the earth, and that every intent of the thoughts of his heart was only to evil continually (*margin*, 'all the day')" (Gen 6:5). And, "The earth was corrupt before God, and the earth was filled with violence" (Gen 6:11).

God commanded Noah to build an ark: a large boat that would enable Noah and his family to escape the soon-coming torrents of judgment. During this time, corruption and evil surrounded Noah. The influence of the world was strong. But Noah continued to "walk with God," and his faith did not waver.[3] He would not let his eyes lust after the sinful temptations around him. He would not allow his life to be polluted, nor his mind blinded by the influence of the wicked world in which he lived. Concerning the power of the world to blind, Paul wrote, "the god of this world has blinded the minds of the unbelieving" (2 Cor 4:4 – *NAS*).

How did Noah overcome the world? By his faith in God. He was *persuaded* that the pathway to blessing was to obey God:

---
[1] 1 Jn 2:16.
[2] 1 Thess 5:23,24.
[3] Gen 6:9.

> "By faith Noah, being divinely warned of things not yet seen, moved with godly fear, prepared an ark for the saving of his household, by which he condemned *the world* and became heir of the righteousness which is according to faith." (Heb 11:7)

Noah was strong in his soul. His thought life was not corrupted, his emotions were pure, his motivation was always to please God. By his faith he condemned and overcame the world.

Here is a great lesson we can learn from Noah. For today, just as in the time of Noah, the battle is for the minds of people. The forces of corruption in this world are fighting, through the eye-gate of men, women, and young people, to tempt and pollute them with sin. That is why John commands: "Do not love the world or the things in the world. If anyone loves the world, the love of the Father is not in him."[4] And Paul said concerning the world: "Do not be conformed to this world, but be transformed by the renewing of your mind."[5]

Jesus warned that in the last days conditions would be as they were in the time of Noah: "As it was in the days of Noah, so it will be also in the days of the Son of Man" (Luke 17:26). As Noah, we too are surrounded by evil, violence, and moral decay. Today, the Lord is preparing, not an ark of safety, but a Church. And, just like Noah's ark, the Church has only one door, and that door is the Lord Jesus Christ.[6] In the coming judgment the Lord will destroy the wicked from the face of the earth, not with water but with fire.[7] I am sure that in his day Noah was mocked and ridiculed. But he remained steadfast. He was persuaded, and through his personal faith, Noah overcame the world. Let us use the faith the Lord has given us to overcome the world.[8] "Above all, taking the shield of faith with which you will be able to quench all the fiery darts of the wicked one." (Eph 6:16) Your faith is your shield of protection in this battle against the attacks of the world and the devil.

We can summarize the first overcomer listed in "these three men," Noah	
Noah's temptation was:	The lust of the eyes;
Noah overcame:	The world;
Noah's personal victory was:	In his soul;
Noah overcame by:	His persuasion (faith).

---

[4] 1 Jn 2:15.
[5] Rom 12:2.
[6] John 10:9.
[7] 2 Pet 3:7.
[8] Rom 12:3.

2. Daniel

The main events of Noah's life took place over 2,000 years before Christ came to this earth. The next of "these three men," Daniel, lived 1,500 years after Noah, around 500 B.C.

Daniel was 17 years old when he was taken captive from Jerusalem to Babylon. He was brought to the palace to serve the King of Babylon, and commanded to eat the food and drink the wine provided by the king. The Scripture says, "But Daniel *purposed* in his heart that he would not defile himself with the portion of the king's delicacies, nor with the wine which he drank" (Dan 1:8). It is vital that we, like Daniel, have a God-glorifying purpose in our hearts. In this regard, I am challenged by the words of Paul:

> "So I run straight to the goal with purpose in every step. I fight to win. I'm not just shadow-boxing or playing around.
> Like an athlete I punish my body, treating it roughly, training it to do what it should, not what it wants to. Otherwise I fear that after enlisting others for the race, I myself might be declared unfit and ordered to stand aside."
> (1 Cor 9:26,27 – *LB*)

Daniel could have said, "I'm only young. I'm in captivity far from my own country. Jerusalem is burned to the ground. The temple is destroyed. It's no use trying to live a holy life in these modern and depressing days." But he didn't say that. Yes, he was in Babylon. But he wouldn't let Babylon get into him. Daniel would not allow his flesh to be defiled by Babylon.

I think there are two main reasons why Daniel would not defile his flesh with the king's food and drink. Firstly, Daniel would not disobey the dietary laws of Moses, in which God forbade the eating of certain foods. There were clean and unclean animals and fish, and the unclean were not to be eaten.[9] Secondly, the king's food and wine had been offered in sacrifice to Babylonian idols. God issued a commandment against idolatry.[10] And I am sure Daniel understood, just as the Apostle Paul taught, that behind every idol there is an evil spirit. Had he eaten and drank the Babylonian king's food and wine, Daniel would be having "fellowship with demons" (1 Cor 10:20).

Daniel made no secret of his faith. Though prayer to Jehovah was prohibited, he prayed openly, even though it resulted in his being cast into a den of hungry lions. He escaped unharmed. He refused to give in to the temptations of the flesh. No matter what the cost, he had made up his mind to be an overcomer. As a result this young man became one of the great prophets, receiving startling revelations of future events. God is looking for young men and women – and older ones too – who will keep themselves clean and overcome the temptations of the flesh, so that He can anoint them with His Spirit to serve

---

[9] See Leviticus chapter 11.
[10] Exo 20:3-5.

Him in these last days. Our bodies – made of flesh – are to be the temple of the Holy Spirit.[11]

We can summarize the second overcomer listed in "these three men," Daniel	
Daniel's temptation was:	The lust of the flesh
Daniel overcame:	The flesh;
Daniel's personal victory was:	In his body;
Daniel overcame by:	His purpose.

3. Job

The third of "these three men" was probably a contemporary of Abraham, who lived approximately 2,000 B.C. This man Job also was an overcomer. Noah overcame the world. Daniel overcame the flesh. Job overcame the devil.

The Biblical account of Job begins by telling us he "was blameless and upright, and one who feared God and turned away from evil" (Job 1:1 – *margin*). The record continues, "this man was the greatest of all the people of the East" (verse 3). Satan came before the Lord God, and the Lord asked Satan what he thought of Job. Satan replied that he thought Job only served God for what he could get from Him, and that God had set His heart on Job, prospering and protecting him. Then Satan said to the Lord, "But stretch out your hand and strike everything he has, and he will surely curse you to your face" (verse 11 – *NIV*).

Satan was wrong. When everything was taken from Job – his children, herds, flocks, servants, health – he did not curse God, but rather, he worshiped Him (verse 20). In fact, the Bible says "In all this Job did not sin nor charge God with wrong" (verse 22). Job overcame every temptation, loss, and criticism – so much so, the Lord rewarded him with a double portion.[12] How did Job overcome the devil? By his *perseverance:*

> "Indeed we count them blessed who endure. You have heard of the perseverance ('patience' – *KJV*) of Job and seen the end intended by the Lord – that the Lord is very compassionate and merciful." (Jas 5:10)

The Greek word for "persevere" is *hypomonē* which means "to abide under," "to endure (as in trials, or under undeserved affliction)," "to be patient." It is the same word used to describe the response of Jesus to contradictions – His ability to endure.[13] This endurance

---

[11] 1 Cor 6:19,20.
[12] Job 42:10.
[13] Heb 12:1,2.

is a quality of true love: "Love ... always protects, always trusts, always hopes, always perseveres."[14] *The Concise Oxford Dictionary* defines perseverance as "steadfast pursuit of an aim, constant persistence."[15] Job was able to endure such devastating loss because he had hope in the resurrection. This same hope can challenge and motivate us to persevere when we experience trying circumstances. Listen to just one example of Job's expressions of love and hope as he perseveres in the midst of extremely negative circumstances:

> "For I know that my Redeemer lives,
> And He shall stand at last on the earth;
> And after my skin is destroyed, this I know,
> That in my flesh I shall see God,
> Whom I shall see for myself,
> And my eyes shall behold, and not another.
> How my heart yearns within me!" (Job 19:25-27)

We can now summarize the third overcomer listed in "these three men," Job	
Job's temptation was:	The pride of life – Job had been very rich, but he did not take pride in his position or his possessions;
Job overcame:	The devil;
Job's personal victory was:	In his spirit – he did not let bitterness or anger enter his spirit. He continued to worship his Lord;
Job overcame by:	His perseverance – his patient endurance.

Noah overcame the world by his passionate *persuasion*.

Daniel overcame the flesh by his passionate *purpose*.

Job overcame the devil by his passionate *perseverance*.

"These three men" are examples to us of what it takes to be an overcomer. Let us then seek to follow their example!

"These Three Men" in the New Testament

It is important for us to note that each of "these three men" is spoken of in the New Testament – Noah and Daniel by the Lord Jesus, and Job by James. Concerning Noah, Jesus said:

> "But as the days of Noah were, so also will the coming of the Son of Man be. For as in the days before the flood, they were eating and drinking, marrying and giving in marriage, until the day that Noah entered the ark,

---

[14] 1 Cor 13:7 – *NIV*.
[15] *The Concise Oxford Dictionary* – *op.cit.*

and did not know until the flood came and took them all away, so also will the coming of the Son of Man be." (Matt 24:37-39)

We do not need to look very hard to see the conditions of Noah's day around us. On the negative side, sin, violence and corruption are everywhere. But on the positive side, there are those who, like Noah, will, through faith overcome the world.

Daniel is also spoken of by Jesus in Matthew chapter 24: "Therefore when you see the 'abomination of desolation,' spoken of by Daniel standing in the holy place ..."[16] In **HERE COMES THE BRIDE! Volume Two** we will discuss this subject in detail, as it is part of the notable seventy weeks' prophecy. The prophecies of Daniel are coming to pass in these last days.

As we have already seen, James uses Job as an example of patient endurance:

> "Take the old prophets as your mentors. They put up with anything, went through everything, and never once quit, all the time honoring God. What a gift life is to those who stay the course! You've heard, of course, of Job's staying power, and you know how God brought it all together for him at the end. That's because God cares, cares right down to the last detail."
> (Jas 5:10,11 – *TM*)

"Christ" – the Overcomer – "in You, the Hope of Glory"

Surely, one of the most wonderful things about being a Christian is "Christ ... dwell[s] in our hearts by faith" (Eph 3:17). And "Christ in you" *is* "the hope of glory" (Col 1:27). In Him alone is our hope of becoming an overcomer. In Him alone is our hope of seeing His glory on the Day of Atonement. In Him alone is our hope of being in His glorious Bride.

When our Lord Jesus Christ came to earth, He overcame every opposing power. For example, see His glorious victory in the temptation in the wilderness.

Figure 41: **How Christ Overcame Temptation in the Wilderness – Matthew 4:1-11**

	Temptation	Personal Victory In	Jesus Overcame	1 Jn 2:16	It is written in the Word of God
1.	Turn stones into bread	Body	The flesh	Lust of the flesh	"Man shall not live by bread alone"
2.	Cast self down	Soul	The flesh	Lust of the eyes	"You shall not tempt the Lord"
3.	Kingdoms of world if He will worship Satan	Spirit	The world The devil	Pride of life	"Worship the Lord your God ... serve only Him"

---

[16] Matt 24:15. See Dan 9:27.

Jesus overcame *the world*: "In the world you will have tribulation; but be of good cheer, I have overcome the world" (John 16:33). In His temptation in the wilderness He overcame every temptation of *the flesh*. Both in the wilderness, and by His death and His triumphant resurrection from the grave, He overcame the devil: "For this purpose the Son of God was manifested, that He might destroy the works of *the devil*" (1 Jn 3:8). Jesus totally overcame every enticement to sin: He "was in all points tempted as we are, yet without sin" (Heb 4:15).

The Eternal Overcomer lives within us. He has totally overcome every force that would oppose us. Therefore He Who lives within us is able to cause us to overcome in every situation! His challenge and His promise to us is:

> "To him who overcomes I will grant to sit with Me on My throne, as I also overcame and sat down with My Father on His throne." (Rev 3:21)

PART FIVE   THE OVERCOMER

Chapter 26

Overcoming and Healing Your Hurts

With the exception of when our daughter was killed in 1985, those eighteen months from the beginning of 1998 was the worst time in my life.[1]

1998 had been filled with hurtful experiences. The year began for me in Canada, where I was standing in a foot of snow burying one of my best friends – a man who had a vision that this book be written and published. Both my parents, who lived in Christchurch, New Zealand, had been ill for two years. So in addition to all our missionary travel, we had to make many unplanned trips to New Zealand in those 18 months to care for them. In May my mother died. We then received word that my Dad, who had been diagnosed as having Alzheimer's disease, had deteriorated, so again we had to travel to New Zealand to make new arrangements for his care. In July our daughter Ruthie, who so much wanted to be a mother, had a miscarriage.[2] The same month a pastor I really cared about had a complete mental and spiritual breakdown, and deeply hurt not only us, but also many others whom we loved. In September, on our way to India, I fell down some steps in London and broke a bone in my foot. Even the Bible emphasizes the pain this can cause.[3] Being either too foolish, or too proud to arrive in India on crutches, I did not go to a hospital and have my foot put in plaster. Consequently, I hopped painfully around India for six weeks. On our arrival back in California there was a fax telling us to return to Christchurch immediately. We did so, and a few days later, at the end of October, my father died.

We faced 1999 with optimism believing it would be a better year. It was worse! Pamela had a lump removed from her neck that was found to be cancerous. I began to suffer the effects of a small stroke, and for a time was unable to play my clarinet, something I dearly love to do. Another very close friend, who was our co-worker in India for over 13 years, was killed in an automobile crash, and I flew to New Zealand to speak at his memorial service. As I am not trying to evoke your sympathy, I won't describe the rest of 1999.

It was after 18 months of these repeated hurtful experiences that I was sitting in my study reading the Bible, when I read a statement Jesus made – in a verse I had memorized decades earlier:

---

[1] This chapter is being included in **HERE COMES THE BRIDE! Volume One** at the request of many who have been encouraged and helped by this teaching. This subject certainly brings one of the major truths of the Book of Revelation – the need to be an overcomer – into our daily lives.
[2] Two years ago, Ruthie blessed us with our second granddaughter, Sydney Truscott Wilson.
[3] Prov 25:19.

> "Behold, I give you the authority to trample on serpents and scorpions, and over all the power of the enemy, and *nothing shall by any means hurt you.*" (Luke 10:19)

"Excuse me, Lord?" I responded. "Nothing shall by any means hurt me? You have got to be kidding me!" I began to think about the many deep hurts I had experienced during the previous months, some of which had reduced me to tears. It was then I began to study afresh what the Bible teaches about hurts.

WHY ARE CHRISTIANS HURTING?

If Jesus really meant these words – and He did – why is it that so many Christians continue to suffer deep hurts? Why do they seem to have no ability to overcome these hurts, and be healed? They come to Christ, attend church, read the Bible, pray, do their best – but are unable to get rid of that deep inner ache.

The context of these words in Luke chapter 10, "nothing shall by any means hurt you," is the sending out of the seventy to heal the sick and to preach the kingdom of God. The seventy returned to the Lord Jesus with joy, saying that even the demons were subject to them in His Name. The context is God's kingdom, God's Word, God's healing, God's power to deliver. Why then are Christians unable to overcome and find healing for their hurts?

To be "hurt" means to be damaged emotionally, spiritually, mentally, or physically, resulting in a decrease in one's efficiency to do God's will. If we do not learn how to overcome our hurts and see them healed, these hurts, and the resultant pain and distress, will produce negative attitudes of doubt and distrust towards God, people, and past events.

As I began to study this subject in the Bible, I discovered there are at least nine different ways Christians can be hurt. When a medical doctor examines nine different people with nine different illnesses, he does not order the same treatment for each patient. Rather, he prescribes remedies to cure each particular illness. Similarly, the Bible teaches there are different cures for the nine different hurts that Christians can suffer. If we are hurt it is important we begin taking the medicine the Lord prescribes. Otherwise these injuries can damage, and even destroy, us.

Here then are the nine ways Christians can be hurt:

1. Christians can be Hurt by COMMITTING SIN

There are two major ways Christians can hurt themselves. The first of these is by committing sin. A Christian will be wounded if he engages in something of which God disapproves. I am *not* saying that all Christians who are hurting are living in sin. But disobeying God and His Word are primary causes of distress and hurt in the lives of believers:

> "If ye forsake the Lord, and serve strange gods, then he will turn and do you *hurt,* and consume you, after that he hath done you good."
> (Josh 24:20 – *KJV*)

A strange god, or an idol, is anything or anyone we esteem more highly than God.

The Prophet Jeremiah also says we will hurt ourselves if we follow other gods:

> "If you do not oppress the stranger, the fatherless, and the widow, and do not shed innocent blood in this place, or walk after other gods to *your hurt,* then I will cause you to dwell in this place, in the land that I gave to your fathers forever and ever." (Jer 7:6,7)

When we sin, we hurt ourselves: "He who sins against me injures (harms, hurts) himself" (Pro 8:36). And in the well-known prayer of Jabez: "Keep me from evil so it might not *hurt me!*" (1 Chr 4:10 – *Amp*). Have you given yourself to thoughts, speech, or actions that do not please the Lord? If so, you can be sure you will suffer until you deal with that sin.

The Cure for the Hurt of Sin

The cure for the hurts caused by our own sin is to repent, and surrender ourselves into God's hands. In repenting we turn from sin, and in turning from sin we turn from the root cause of the hurt. "He who covers his sins will not prosper, but whoever confesses and forsakes them will have mercy." (Pro 28:13) Allow the blood of the Lord Jesus Christ to cleanse from sin, begin learning how to overcome sin, and the Lord will heal your hurts.[4] You will then be able to sing in triumph the words of Paul, "Thanks be to God, who gives us the victory through our Lord Jesus Christ" (1 Cor 15:57).

2. Christians can be Hurt by SELFISHNESS and GREED

The second way Christians can hurt themselves is through selfishness and greed. Both Old and New Testaments state that those who are selfish, greedy, and have a materialistic mindset are wounding themselves. Notice the following warnings, all of which are self-explanatory:

> "There is a grievous evil which I have seen under the sun: riches being hoarded by their owner to *his hurt.*" (Eccl 5:13 – *NAS*)

> "There is one who scatters, yet increases more;
> And there is one who withholds more than is right,
> But it leads to *poverty.*" (Pro 11:24)

---

[4] Rom 6:6,7,11,14.

"But those who desire to be rich fall into temptation and a snare, and into many foolish and harmful lusts which drown men in destruction and perdition.
For the love of money is a root of all kinds of evil, for which some have strayed from the faith in their greediness, and pierced themselves through with many sorrows." (1 Tim 6:9,10)

The Cure for the Hurt of Selfishness and Greed

The cure for the pain Christians have inflicted upon themselves through selfishness and greed is to become very generous with God and others. The Bible teaches that when we honour God by bringing our tithes and offerings into the storehouse (the place where we are spiritually fed), God will rebuke the devourer – the one who tries to hurt us – for our sakes.[5] Jesus taught that as we give, so will it be given back to us.[6] As we see the Lord's miraculous provision, we will, through His grace, overcome this self-inflicted hurt.

However, even after these two problems are dealt with, there are still other ways a Christian can experience hurt.

3. A Christian can be Hurt by OFFENSES

In both Matthew's and Luke's gospels, the Lord Jesus taught that offenses must come. In Matthew He says to the world: "Woe to the world because of offenses! For offenses must come" (Matt 18:7). "Stumbling blocks are inevitable." (*NAS*) In Luke Jesus warns His disciples: "'It is impossible that no offenses (*margin*, 'stumbling blocks') should come'" (Luke 17:1).

Jesus did not say, "Offenses might come," nor, "Perhaps offenses will come." No. Jesus categorically stated, "Stumbling blocks are inevitable." "Offenses will come." The English word offense, or stumbling block, is from the Greek *skandalon,* from which we get the words "scandal" and "scandalous." Originally the *skandalon* was the name given to the part of an animal trap to which the bait for luring the prey was attached. Later, it came to mean the whole trap or snare itself. Understanding offenses is so important. Here is my definition of the word:

> "An offense is what happens when any event, experience, or person hurts us so deeply, that if we do not deal with our wounded feelings and annoyance quickly and properly, we will become trapped, and therefore hindered from going forward to reach our full potential in the Lord.
> "An offense can also be something that appears to contradict what we believe should have taken place, and thus can cause us to stumble in unbelief."

The effects of harboring an offense can be extremely detrimental to our well-being. The consequences of unresolved offenses can be stress-related illnesses or depression.

---

[5] Mal 3:8-12.
[6] Luke 6:38.

We need to recognize offenses, be aware how they happen, and find the strength to overcome the negative results of them. There are three ways offenses can occur:

a. Offenses Between Individuals

Neither strangers, nor those we know only casually, can offend us. It is those who are really close to us, those whom we trust, with whom offenses arise:

> "For it is not an enemy who reproaches me;
> Then I could bear it.
> Nor is it one who hates me who has exalted himself against me;
> Then I could hide from him.
> But it was you, a man my equal,
> My companion and my acquaintance.
> We took sweet counsel together,
> And walked to the house of God in the throng." (Psa 55:12-14)

There are many Biblical examples of offenses between individuals:

- Offenses between children and their parents: Absalom with David;
- Offenses between brothers in the same family: Jacob with Esau; Joseph's brothers were offended with him;
- Offenses between husbands and wives: Zipporah with Moses;
- Offenses between church members: Paul's words to the church at Corinth[7];
- Offenses between church leaders: Paul with Barnabas.

Offenses that are not dealt with usually cause bitterness, and bitterness spreads like a cancer, defiling many:

> "Pursue peace with all men, and the sanctification without which no one will see the Lord.
> See to it that no one comes short of the grace of God; that no root of bitterness springing up causes trouble, and by it many be defiled."
> (Heb 12:14,15 – *NAS*)

Bitter or Better?

Hurts will make us bitter, or better, depending on our reactions. The pain caused by offenses may cause sadness for a season, but remember God's Word:

---

[7] 2 Cor 11:29 – *KJV*; Phil 1:10; Acts 24:16.

"Sorrow[8] is better than laughter,
For by a sad countenance ('sadness' – *KJV*) the heart is made better.[9]"
(Eccl 7:3)

If we learn to deal with life's challenges, applying God's cures to them, and start walking in His victory, we will become better, stronger, more vital believers. We will experience success in life,[10] and joy in our newfound triumphant Christian walk.[11] If we do not learn to overcome offenses we will grow prematurely old – and bitter.

God, then, sometimes allows offenses to come, not to punish us, but to test us. He, of course, knows how we will react and respond under pressure. But we don't! Therefore the Lord allows situations – sometimes unpleasant ones – through which we learn to handle life's negative experiences. Then we in turn will be able to help others.

The Cure for Hurts Caused by Offenses Between Individuals

What can reach deep into our hearts, and pull out that painful root of offense and bitterness? The answer is found in the above verses from Hebrews chapter 12, together with an exhortation from John's first letter:

i. Pursue peace:
We must run after peace. This pursuit will bring its reward. Jesus promised: "Blessed are the peacemakers, for they shall be called sons of God."[12] And Paul taught, "For God is not the author of confusion but of peace."[13]

ii. Pursue sanctification[14]:
Maintaining the right attitude is vital. How often we want to shout, "He was wrong. I was right!" But it is not what happens that is important. It is how we react. It does not matter who was right and who was wrong. If we caused an offense, intentionally or unintentionally, we are wrong, and need to apologize. A sanctified Christian is one who has deliberately separated himself to the Lord. A spirit that is totally given to the Lord cannot carry grudges and offenses.

iii. Be filled with the love of Jesus:
"He who says he is in the light, and hates his brother, is in darkness until now.

---

[8] *Margin*, vexation *or* grief.
[9] *Margin*, well *or* pleasing.
[10] Josh 1:8 – this is the only time the word "success" occurs in the King James Version of the Bible.
[11] 2 Cor 2:14.
[12] Matt 5:9.
[13] 1 Cor 14:33.
[14] For a complete study on the subject of Sanctification, see chapter 6 of my book *You Shall Receive Power*.

He who loves his brother abides in the light, and there is no cause for stumbling ('offenses' – Greek, *skandalon* –) in him." (1 Jn 2:9,10)

Love – "the love of God [which] has been poured out in our hearts by the Holy Spirit"[15] – is the cure for offenses between individuals.

b. Taking Up the Offenses of Others

Secondly, offenses can arise in us when we take up the offenses of others. These are "shared offenses." Someone else, usually someone you care about deeply, is offended. As a result, you become offended too. In the home, the family, the workplace, the church – in any environment where people interact closely – you can, if you are not careful, become easily offended by what someone says about or does to a third party. If we share others' offenses, we become unnecessarily involved. If we are not directly involved in the problem, we cannot be part of the solution. The Bible calls this "meddling," and warns it will hurt us: "Why shouldest thou meddle to thine hurt?" (2 Chr 25:19 – *KJV*)

The Cure for Hurts Caused by Taking up the Offenses of Others

The cure for hurt caused by taking up the offenses of others is to cease being a meddler, or a busybody:

> "But let none of you suffer as a murderer, a thief, an evildoer, or as a busybody (*margin*, 'meddler') in other people's matters.
> Yet if anyone suffers as a Christian, let him not be ashamed, but let him glorify God in this matter." (1 Pet 4:15,16)

This is a very strong admonition from God's Word. Because being a meddler is listed in the same phrase as being a murderer, thief, or evildoer! Meddling cannot be listed under "Christian" behaviour. So if we are not in the "chain of command" to be a part of the answer to the problem, we should not become involved by taking up the offenses of others. It is wiser – and much safer – to mind our own business, and not take sides in other people's offenses.

c. By Becoming Offended with God

Thirdly, it is tragically possible for a believer to become offended with God. An Old Testament example of this is King Jotham. Jotham began reigning in Judah when he was 25 years old.[16] The Bible says he was a good king: "he did what was right in the sight of the Lord, according to all his father Uzziah had done." Not only this: "Jotham became mighty, because he prepared his ways before the Lord his God." But one small phrase suggests Jotham was offended with God:

---

[15] Rom 5:5.
[16] 2 Chr 27:1-6.

"he did not enter the temple of the Lord." Maybe he reasoned, "My father Uzziah became a leper as a result of his trying to offer sacrifice to God.[17] My father was trying to serve God in the temple when he got leprosy. So I'm not going to the temple." How many good people, like Jotham, no longer attend church because they hold an offense against God?

Sadly, the story of Jotham does not end there. When Jotham died his son Ahaz reigned in his stead. Ahaz was one of the worst kings of Judah. "He did not do what was right in the sight of the Lord."[18] I wonder if the father's offense carried through to his son? It appears that being offended with God, if not healed, can have dire consequences in subsequent generations.

A New Testament example of this kind of offense is found in the life of John the Baptist. On the day Jesus was baptized, John the Baptist adamantly proclaimed, "Behold! The Lamb of God who takes away the sin of the world!" (John 1:29). But later, when John the Baptist was imprisoned, he sent two of his disciples to ask Jesus, "Are you the Coming One, or do we look for another?" (Matt 11:2) The Saviour's response?

> "Jesus answered and said to them, 'Go and tell John the things which you hear and see:
> The blind see and the lame walk; the lepers are cleansed and the deaf hear; the dead are raised up and the poor have the gospel preached to them.
> And blessed is he who is not offended because of Me.'" (verses 4-6)

Doubts concerning His Lordship can result in weakening of faith, and deep offense.

The Cure for Hurts Caused by Being Offended with God

Offenses with God can only be overcome and healed by the restoration of faith and a renewed love for God's Word:

> "Great peace have they which love thy law: and nothing shall offend them (*margin*, 'they shall have no stumbling block')." (Psa 119:165 – *KJV*)

There may be someone reading this and you feel God has failed you. You may have been deeply hurt by those whom you trusted as brothers and sisters in Christ. You feel events should have gone differently. Now you don't feel like going to church. But I assure you, if you will read God's Word, study, and meditate in it, and yes, go to church to hear the Word and be encouraged by the fellowship of others, you will be able to overcome the hurts of those past offenses.

---

[17] Only the priests were permitted to burn incense to the Lord. See 2 Chr 26:18.
[18] 2 Chr 28:1.

4. A Christian can be Hurt by OPPOSITION

The fourth way a Christian can be wounded is from opposition by those outside the body of Christ. While we should not develop a siege mentality, we do know that the world system around us is against God, Jesus, the Gospel, the Bible, and Christians. And if you declare by word and deed you are a committed follower of Jesus of Nazareth, you will be opposed. You will be hurt. Neighbours, people with whom you work, even relatives who do not yet know the Lord will say things and do things that are painful. The Bible warns us this will happen, and reminds us it is portion of the price of becoming part of the glorious church:

> "Beloved, do not think it strange concerning the fiery trial which is to try you, as though some strange thing happened to you;
> but rejoice to the extent that you partake of Christ's sufferings, that when His glory is revealed, you may also be glad with exceeding joy.
> If you are reproached (*margin*, 'insulted *or* reviled') for the name of Christ, blessed are you, for the Spirit of glory and of God rests upon you. On their part He is blasphemed, but on your part He is glorified." (1 Pet 4:12-14)

Daniel, after being criticized and reviled, was cast into the lion's den. He disobeyed the king's law, which forbad praying to Jehovah. This was Daniel's testimony to the king: "'My God sent His angel and shut the lions' mouths, so that they have not *hurt* me.'"[19]

The Cure for Hurts Caused by Opposition

The way to overcome the hurts caused by those outside of the body of Christ is to become a soul-winner. Visualize those who oppose and ridicule as your mission field. In reality they are not against you. They are opposing God. As your mindset changes from hurt to seizing the opportunity to testify for your Lord, He will open the way for you to become a fruitful witness for Him. When Pamela and I first became Christians in the early 1950s most of our friends thought we had gone crazy. But over the years, the Lord gave us opportunities to tell them about Jesus, and we had the joy of seeing most of our friends turn to Him. Some entered full-time service, and are still faithfully serving the Lord.

5. A Christian can be Hurt by OTHER CHRISTIANS

More painful than the wounds we receive in the world are the injuries we receive in the Church. Of these hurts, David, the man after God's own heart, said:

> "All who hate me whisper together against me;
> Against me they devise (*margin*, 'plot') my hurt.
> 'An evil disease,' they say, 'clings to him.
> And now that he lies down, he will rise up no more.'
> Even my own familiar friend in whom I trusted,
> Who ate my bread,
> Has lifted up his heel (*margin*, 'acted as a traitor') against me." (Psa 41:7-9)

---

[19] Dan 6:1-28.

Jesus warned, when commissioning the 12 disciples, "A man's enemies will be those of his own household."[20] Tragically, this sometimes includes "the household of God."[21] Those in the "household of faith"[22] who claim to be our brothers and sisters can hurt us by their words, their deeds, and their attitudes.

The Cure for Hurts Caused by Other Christians

The only way to overcome the hurts we experience through other Christians is to practice true forgiveness. Do not keep living and reliving painful circumstances. Rather, exercise the power of forgiveness. Jesus had some strong words to say about the power of forgiveness, and the power of unforgiveness. When Peter asked the Lord concerning forgiveness, Jesus answered him with the story of the unforgiving servant, in which the master called the unforgiving servant a "wicked servant" and "delivered him to the torturers" ('tormentors' – *KJV*).[23] How many Christians today are tormented in their minds because they have not forgiven? Jesus concluded this teaching with these words: "So My heavenly Father also will do to you if each of you, from his heart, does not forgive his brother his trespasses" (Matt 18:35).

6. A Christian can be Hurt by TRAGEDY

It is impossible to express the pain that results from a tragic, traumatic experience. This hurt can be a result of the unexpected death of a close loved one, a crippling accident, a divorce, a rebellious child, or from many other negative circumstances. The pain becomes almost more than we can bear. The distress is very real, and may last a long time. While we still miss our beautiful 24-year-old daughter, Debbie, and there is an empty place in our family that no one else can fill, we have learned from experience it is possible to be healed, and to overcome this hurt also.

The Cure for the Hurt Caused by Tragedy

During the time we were pastoring the church we pioneered in San Diego, I remember calling a member of our congregation on the first anniversary of the death of his wife. During our conversation he asked, "Pastor, does the hurt and the pain ever go away?" I replied, "No, Jack, it doesn't. But let me encourage you with this. Over time we learn to draw upon the grace of God in a new way. You have experienced God's grace for salvation, Jack. You have experienced God's grace for the supplying of all your material needs. Now you have to learn to draw upon God's grace for comfort, healing, and strength in an area that is new to you. Remember, the Greek word for 'grace' is *charis*, which is God's miraculous power available to heal and overcome every hurt."

---

[20] Matt 10:36.
[21] Eph 2:19.
[22] Gal 6:10.
[23] Matt 18:21-35.

HERE COMES THE BRIDE!

Paul prayed, pleading three times for the Lord to remove the painful thorn that constantly troubled him. God answered, "My grace is sufficient for you, for My strength is made perfect in weakness" (2 Cor 12:9). God's grace is always sufficient for you and for me.

7. A Christian can be Hurt by an UNTRUE, EVIL REPORT

When it is brought to our attention that evil things – which we know are false – have been spoken against us, this can cause deep hurt. There is so much power, for good, and for evil, in the human tongue: "Death and life are in the power of the tongue" (Prov 18:21). "The tongue is a fire, a world of iniquity (*margin*, 'unrighteousness')" (Jas 3:6). There are several ways we can be hurt by what people say:

a. **By Lies:** Lying is speech which states something that is not true. Hearing things you are supposed to have said or done can be very painful: "An evildoer gives heed to false lips; A liar listens to a spiteful (*margin, Lit.* 'destructive') tongue" (Prov 17:4). "Telling lies about others is as harmful as hitting them with an ax, wounding them with a sword, or shooting them with a sharp arrow." (Prov 25:18 – *LB*)

b. **By Gossip:** Gossip is speech which shares private information with someone who is neither part of the problem, nor part of the solution. Once again, this is meddling.

c. **By Slander:** Slander is speech which tells the truth in such a way as to give a lying impression. The facts may be correct, but the way in which they are stated is designed to hurt someone's reputation, and to create questions about that person's honesty and integrity. God has this to say of slander:

> "You sit around and slander a brother – your own mother's son.
> While you did all this, I remained silent, and you thought I didn't care. But now I will rebuke you, listing all my charges against you.
> Repent ..." (Prov 50:20-22 – *NLT*)

The Cure for Hurts Caused by an Evil, Untrue Report

The only way to overcome the wounds we suffer from an untrue report is to pray for, and bless, our accusers. Our initial response is to react, to justify ourselves, and to angrily deny that which has been spoken against us. But remember what the Lord Jesus instructed:

> "I say to you, love your enemies, bless those who curse you, do good to those who hate you, and pray for those who spitefully use you and persecute you. That you may be sons of your Father in heaven." (Matt 5:44,45)

8. A Christian can be Hurt by REJECTION

Rejection is one of the most painful experiences of human relationships.

A husband leaves his wife, and she feels rejected. A man loses his job, and he feels rejected. People leave a church, and the pastor feels rejected. Children leave home, and the parents feel rejected. But if we do not learn how to overcome rejection, it will work very negative consequences in our lives. In fact, if not stopped, rejection can cause a person to descend on a speedy, and sometimes tragic, downward spiral: rejection leads to discouragement, discouragement to depression, depression to despair, and despair can lead to death – death by suicide, or as a result of physiological trauma.

The Cure for Hurts Caused by Rejection

One of the classic cases of rejection in the Bible is David's experience in 1 Samuel, chapters 29 and 30. David was rejected by King Saul, the very king whom David honoured and blessed. Not only was David rejected. He was rejected in the very thing in which he excelled – his music.

David was so discouraged with Saul, he went over to the side of the Philistines to fight for them. But there he was rejected by Achish, the leader of the Philistine army. Once again, he was rejected in something in which he excelled – his military skills.

David and his men returned to their hometown, Ziklag, only to find the city destroyed by the Amalekites. Their wives and children had been captured by the enemy. His men were so grieved and bitter they began talking about stoning David to death. Now David was being rejected by his own men – the same men who came to him when they were in distress, in debt, and discontented (*margin*, 'bitter of soul').[24] These were the same men whom David had transformed into valiant men of war. Now they are rejecting David, yet again in something in which he excelled – his leadership.

David was alone. There was no one to encourage him. What did David do? "David encouraged himself ('strengthened himself' – *NKJV*) in the Lord his God." (1 Sam 30:6 – *KJV*) David knew how to praise and worship God. He knew God's Word, and encouraged himself in the Lord's promises. He remembered God's past blessings. And as David encouraged himself in the Lord, his hurts were healed, he overcame his circumstances, and received joyous hope for the future.

David then pursued the enemy, recovered all he and his followers had lost, set free every captured person, and took his spoil of the Amalekites, thus receiving a double portion.

In the midst of rejection we will often find ourselves alone, and lonely. We must learn, as David learned, to encourage ourselves in the Lord. Then we will overcome the pain of rejection, and receive hope for the future.

---

[24] 1 Sam 22:1,2.

9. A Christian can be Hurt by BETRAYAL

It is sad to have to write this, but most Christian leaders I know have experienced, at some time in their ministry, the awfulness of betrayal. The Greek word for betrayal, *paradidōmi*, means "to deliver over treacherously." There are six major shades of meaning to the word "betrayal":

- to abandon in a crisis, thus leaving the betrayed one open to vicious attack;
- to deliver, traitorously and treacherously, to an enemy;
- to violate a trust;
- to be disloyal, extremely unfaithful;
- to place someone in great danger by giving information to the enemy;
- to "betray a confidence," meaning to expose someone by leaking private information which should be covered. "Betraying a confidence" can cause acute embarrassment, stress, and hurt.

Betrayal can also be defined as what happens when someone who has loved you, and been committed to follow you with great enthusiasm, turns against you with equal, or even greater, enthusiasm. The betrayer is so disloyal and treacherous he will do anything he can to see the betrayed one badly hurt. The word "betrayal" is used 40 times in relation to Judas Iscariot. While betrayal is an extreme method of inflicting hurt, it happens – on the job, in families, in churches, and in governments.

David, who, as we have seen, suffered rejection on a number of occasions, also experienced the intense hurt of betrayal. In 1 Samuel chapter 23 David was informed the Philistines were attacking and robbing the city of Keilah. David prayed to the Lord twice, and the Lord promised him victory. So the Scripture records, "David saved the inhabitants of Keilah" (verse 5). David then heard that Saul was again seeking to capture him, and the Lord warned him that it was the people of Keilah – the very ones whom he had just saved – who would deliver him and his men into the hands of the enemy. David escaped from Keilah just in time. Can we imagine David's distress when he learned those whom he had helped would betray him? Unfortunately, we too may be betrayed by those whom we have helped the most.

The Cure for Hurts Caused by Betrayal

The way to overcome the hurts inflicted on you by betrayal is to know the truth of Isaiah 54:17: "No weapon formed against you shall prosper." You are clothed with the armour of God.[25] The shield of faith deflects every arrow of the enemy. Victory through Christ is yours!

In Acts chapter 18 the apostle Paul traveled from Athens to Corinth. He experienced intense opposition from the Jews. Frustrated with his own people, Paul declared he would now take the message of the Gospel to the Gentiles. At this time, the Lord visited Paul and spoke with him:

---

[25] Eph 6:10-20.

> "Now the Lord spoke to Paul in the night by a vision, 'Do not be afraid, but speak, and do not keep silent;
> for I am with you, and no one will attack you to *hurt* you; for I have many people in this city.'" (Acts 18:9,10)

Just two verses later, Paul was again arrested, but the Lord protected him, and the Corinthian church was birthed from his ministry. The Lord comforts us with these same words, enabling us to overcome the dreadful hurts of betrayal.

THE MARRIAGE OF THE LAMB

In **Volume One** of this book, we have learned what the Old and New Testaments record concerning brides and marriage. We have learned the major keys that will unlock the Book of Revelation. We have studied together how the Lord Jesus Christ, our heavenly Bridegroom, appears in Revelation. We know what is meant by the Seven Spirits of God. We have been encouraged, in going through the letters to the seven churches, to be overcomers in all situations.

Now we can look forward to studying the seals, the trumpets, the bowls, the man child, the remnant, Babylon, and the 144,000. We will also look at last day events in greater detail, and see what is really happening today in the Church and in the world. We will receive, in greater detail, an answer to the question, "Does the Church go through the Great Tribulation?" I am excited that together we will study all these subjects, plus many more, in **HERE COMES THE BRIDE! Volume Two**.

As I bring **Volume One** to a close, I must again emphasize the *practical* importance of the lessons we have learned from the Book of Revelation. Our goal in studying these truths is not just to accumulate more knowledge. But rather, that our character should be changed, and our relationship with our Lord strengthened. That we see the Lord Jesus Christ anew, and become more like Him – that we stand as overcomers in our day-to-day experiences and personal circumstances – these are the greatest lessons we will learn from the Book of Revelation.

But to draw closer to the Lord, and to be overcomers, we cannot ignore our hurts. Nor can we just hope our pain will ease with time. Our wounds must be identified and healed. We dare not allow our hurts to fester and grow, for they may ultimately destroy us.

In the Book of Revelation there are wonderful promises for those who overcome: "He who overcomes shall inherit all things, and I will be his God and he shall be My son" (Rev 21:7). In the last days there will be only two kinds of Christians – those who are overcomers, or those who are overcome. Those who learn to overcome and be healed of their hurts, or those who are overcome and weakened by painful experiences. Better or bitter? Bride or remnant of her seed? Wise or foolish? Overcomer or overcome? The choice is really up to us.

The Lord has promised us: "Again there shall be heard ... the voice of joy and the voice of gladness, the voice of the bridegroom and the voice of the bride" (Jer 33:10). Can you hear the joyful sound? How will you respond?

The wind of the Holy Spirit is blowing afresh. With joyous anticipation we await three momentous events:

The revelation of the Bride of Christ – "Here Comes The Bride!"
The appearing of the Lord Jesus Christ – "Here Comes The Bridegroom!"
And their marriage.

Both Old and New Testaments teach this will be a joyous Wedding Day:

> "As the bridegroom rejoices over the bride,
> So shall your God rejoice over you." (Isa 62:5)
>
> "Hallelujah!
> The Master reigns,
> our God, the Sovereign-Strong!
> Let us celebrate, let us rejoice,
> let us give him the glory!
> The Marriage of the Lamb has come;
> his Wife has made herself ready." (Rev 19:7 – *TM*)

We can rejoice together as we prepare for the Marriage of the Lamb and His Bride!

THE APPENDIX

Appendix 1

The Differences Between a "Visitation" and a "Revival"

Every student of Last Day events must have a clear understanding of the differences between a "Visitation" and a "Revival."[1] These terms are not synonymous, nor should they be used interchangeably. We can see the contrast between the two in the following:

A Visitation

A "Visitation" is a totally sovereign act of God. At least five major things take place in a visitation:

- A Bible truth listed in "the elementary principles of Christ" in Hebrews 6:1-2, together with the experience of this truth, is restored to the Church for the first time since it was lost during the early centuries. [The early Church gradually lost these life-giving truths and experiences, and Bible doctrines and experiences were replaced with dead religious rituals.]

- One or more of the miraculous manifestation gifts of the Holy Spirit, which are listed in 1 Corinthians 12:8-10, is restored.

- One of the ascension gift ministries listed in Ephesians 4:11 is restored.

- A Visitation is worldwide in its impact. The influence of the restored Biblical truth, the gifts of the Holy Spirit, and the ascension gifted ministries, is global. [By contrast, a Revival is more local in its influence. A Revival can take place in one local church, one city, or one nation. For example, we speak of the "Welsh Revival."]

- Sadly, each Visitation was vehemently opposed by many Christians who were experiencing the blessings from the previous Visitation.

There have been three Visitations to the Church in the past 500 years.

Visitations of the Past 500 Years

1. 1517 – The "Lutheran" Visitation:

    a. The Bible truth and experience restored were the first two elementary principles listed in Hebrews 6:1,2 –

---

[1] I have adapted and expanded this teaching for **HERE COMES THE BRIDE! Volume One** from seed thoughts in an unpublished message, *The Price of the Double Portion*, by Rob Wheeler.

b. * Repentance from dead works,
* Faith towards God.
* In addition, during the 400 years until the next Visitation, one more truth was restored–Water Baptism for believers, by immersion. There was also a restoration of the experience of personal holiness, especially in the early years of the Methodist church.

c. The three vocal gifts of the Spirit were restored in a limited measure –
* Speaking in tongues,
* Interpretation of tongues,
* Prophecy.

"That the great leader of the Reformation, *Martin Luther*, was baptized in the Holy Spirit, and had the manifestations of the Holy Spirit operating in his life and ministry, there can be no doubt. In German Church history, Souer writes:

'Dr. Martin Luther was a prophet, evangelist, speaker in tongues and interpreter, in one person, endowed with all the gifts of the Holy Spirit.' (*History of the Christian Church,* Vol 3, page 406)." From *You Shall Receive Power*, Second Edition–pages 179,180.

d. During the Reformation and the 400 years that followed, the ministries of Pastors and Teachers were restored to the Church.

e. After the Reformation came many great evangelical awakenings and missionary movements which were global in their impact and influence.

f. Protestantism was bitterly fought by the Roman Catholic Church. The Jesuit order was formed to provide militant opposition to the Protestant Reformation.

2. 1900 – The "Pentecostal" Visitation

a. The truth and experience restored in this Visitation was that the promise of the baptism in the Holy Spirit (one part of the elementary principle of the "doctrine of baptisms") was for all believers. (Acts 2:39)

b. The vocal gifts of the Holy Spirit, and the teaching that they were for all believers, were fully restored. Also, there was a restoration of the gifts of healings, faith, and miracles.

c. The ministry of the Evangelist was restored.

d. The impact of this new Pentecostal Visitation was very quickly experienced all around the world. There were outpourings of the Holy Spirit in Pentecostal power in all five continents. To this day, the Pentecostal/Charismatic Movement is the fastest-growing Christian Movement on earth. [There is a whole section describing the history of the Pentecostal/Charismatic Movement in my book, *You Shall Receive Power*.]

    e. The truth that believers can receive the Holy Spirit just as Christians in the book of Acts did, was, and in some cases still is, vehemently opposed by conservative evangelicals. "These Biblical experiences are not for today, and anyone speaking in tongues is not of God, but the devil," the Pentecostals were (and sometimes, still are) told.

The words of Jesus are true 20 centuries after He said them:

"... you did not know the time of your visitation" (Luke 19:44).

3. 1948 – The "Latter Rain" Visitation:

    a. The truth and experience of the laying on of hands was restored.

    b. The gifts of a word of knowledge, a word of wisdom, and discerning of spirits, were restored.

    c. The ministry of the Prophet was restored.

    d. The "Latter Rain Visitation" was soon global in its influence, as praise and worship, and the gifts and ministries listed above were restored to Christians everywhere who were hungry for more of God.

    e. The fulfillment to the New Testament Church of the beginning of the Feast of Tabernacles, the Feast of Trumpets, took place.[2]

Sad to say, the Latter Rain Visitation was opposed and rejected by a large section of the Pentecostal movement.

4. 20?? – The Last Visitation:

    a. Just as the first of these Last Day Visitations involved the restoration of three Bible truths and experiences, so will the last:

        * Resurrection from the dead (both physical and spiritual),
        * Eternal judgments,
        * Perfection (full maturity), resulting in the manifestation of the "glorious church" (Rom 8:19; Eph 5:27).

    b. The Last Day Bride of Christ will experience the New Testament fulfillment of the Day of Atonement, and receive the Sevenfold Spirit of God. Not just gifts in their occasional operation, but a continuous flow of God's power. (See Chapter 15 of this book.)

---

[2] See Chapter 12, "The Festivals of Israel."

    c. The fully developed ministries of mature and humble Apostles will be restored.

    d. Because of the speed of modern methods of communication, the message of this Last Visitation will spread very rapidly throughout the whole earth.

    e. If the pattern of previous visitations continues, this Last Visitation will be rejected by many Evangelicals, Pentecostals, Charismatics, and even some enjoying the blessings restored in the 1948 Visitation.

A Revival

Revival is very different from Visitation, in that Revival takes place when something that has lost some or all of its life force is revived – brought back to life again. In the Greek language, the word for "revive"–*anazaō*–means "to live again."

In the Church, Revival takes place when there is a second, or third, or twentieth move of the Holy Spirit, which brings a refreshing restoration of truth and experience that was previously received in a past Visitation.

Revival comes when God's people seek Him, and pray, like David:

> "Will you not revive us again,
> That your people may rejoice in You?
> Show us your mercy, Lord,
> And grant us Your salvation." (Psa 85:6,7)

Let us, then, pray in faith for ongoing Revival, as we anticipate the next, great, Last Visitation of God before Jesus comes again.

Appendix 2

Some Questions Asked in the Book of Job

Here are just ten of the many questions asked in the book of Job. As you will recognize, these same questions are being asked by people today, 4000 years later!

	Reference	Subject	Question
1.	7:17,18	*Testing:*	"What is man, that You should exalt him, that You should set Your heart on him, That you should visit him every morning, and test him every moment?"
2.	9:2	*Justification:*	"How can a man be righteous before God?"
3.	9:24	*God:*	"Where, and Who is He?" (*KJV*)
4.	14:10	*Death:*	"But man dies and is laid away; indeed he breathes his last and where is he?"
5.	14:14	*Eternity:*	"If a man dies, shall he live again?"
6.	15:14	*Holiness:*	"What is man, that he could be pure? And he who is born of a woman, that he could be righteous?"
7.	21:15	*Prayer:*	"Who is the Almighty, that we should serve Him? And what profit do we have if we pray to Him?"
8.	22:2	*Usefulness:*	"Can a man be profitable to God, though he who is wise may be profitable to himself?"
9.	22:13	*God's knowledge:*	"What does God know? Can He judge through the deep darkness?"
10.	31:14	*Judgment:*	"What then shall I do when God rises up? When He punishes, how shall I answer Him?"

How blessed we are to know that these questions people still ask today have their answers in God's Word, the Bible!

Appendix 3

"Be not ignorant"

The phrase which commands us "Be not ignorant," or its equivalent, "I would not have you ignorant," occurs only seven times in the New Testament.

When the Holy Spirit, through the New Testament writers, uses this phrase, it obviously means that what follows is very important. "Be not ignorant" is used five times to emphasize Bible teaching, and is used twice to describe Paul's personal testimony:

"Be not ignorant"–Bible Teaching

1.	Rom 11:25	The grafting in of the Gentiles
2.	1 Cor 10:1,2	The baptism of Israel into Moses
3.	1 Cor 12:1	Spiritual gifts
4.	1 Thess 4:13	The state of the dead in Christ
5.	2 Pet 3:8	A day with the Lord

"Be not ignorant"–Paul's Personal Testimony

6.	Rom 1:13	Paul's desire to preach to the Gentiles
7.	2 Cor 1:8	Paul's troubles and persecution

Indeed, the Lord does not want us to be ignorant!

Appendix 4

Further Details of the Feast of Passover

	Actual Event in Israel Exo 12:1-14	**Fulfillment in Christ 1 Cor 5:7**	**Experience in Believer 1 Cor 5:8**
1	God spoke the Word (v 1)	Jesus is the Word (John 1:1; Rev 19:11-13)	We are epistles (2 Cor 3:2)
2	Time–appointed season (v 2)	Fullness of time (Gal 4:5)	Now is the accepted time of salvation (2 Cor 6:2)
3	Beginning of months (v 2)	New beginning (Luke 22:20; Rev 21:5)	New beginning (John 3:3; 2 Cor 5:17)
4	Speak to all (v 3)	Died for all (John 3:16)	Salvation for all (2 Pet 3:9)
5	Take every man a lamb (v 3)	Jesus is the Lamb (John 1:29; Rev 5:11-13)	Blood of the Lamb (Heb 9:22; 1 John 1:7)
6	Lamb without blemish (v 5)	Jesus, the Lamb without blemish (1 Pet 1:18,19)	Bride without blemish (Eph 5:25-27)
7	Lamb for a house (v 3)	Jesus the Son of God is Head over His Own house (Heb 3:6)	Church is the house (Eph 2:19; Gal 6:10; 1 Tim 3:15)
8	God's Name in place (Deut 16:6)	Fullness of God's Name in Lord Jesus Christ (Acts 2:36)	We receive His Name at baptism (Jas 2:7 – Amp)
9	Lamb kept 4 days, 10th to 14th day (v 3, 6)	Jesus "kept" 4 days of God's week (4,000 years, 2 Pet 3:8)	We live in day of grace, and look for Day of Atonement (Heb 9:28, 10:25)
10	Blood-stained door (v 7)	Jesus is the Door (John 10:9)	Jesus knocking at door of the Laodicean church (Rev 3:20)
11	Flesh roasted with fire (v 8)	Jesus suffered fire of God's judgment on our sin (Isa 53:6,10)	Our faith tried by fire (1 Pet 1:7)
12	Eaten with bitter herbs (v 8)	Jesus was given bitter vinegar with gall to drink (Matt 27:34)	Sometimes we must endure bitter suffering for Him (Phil 1:29)
13	Bone not broken (v 46)	Bone not broken (Psa 34:20; John 19:30-36)	Our bodies made whole through His stripes (1 Pet 2:24)
14	Eaten ready to go out of Egypt to new land (v 11)	Died, but did not stay in grave. Rose after 3 days (Mark 8:31)	Passover (our salvation) only the beginning of our Christian life. Must move on (Heb 6:1)

Appendix 5

Further Details of the Feast of Pentecost

	HISTORICAL **Actual Event in Israel**	**CHRISTOLOGICAL** **Fulfillment in Christ**	**EXPERIENTIAL** **Experience in Believer**
1	Exodus chapters 19 and 20. At Mount Sinai, 50 days after Passover	Passover Lamb ministered in Power of Holy Spirit (Matt 3:16; Acts 10:38)	Sent Spirit's Power to disciples 50 days after He fulfilled Passover (Acts 2)
2	Fire seen on mountain (Exo 19:18, 24:17)	Dove seen descending on Him (Matt 3:16)	Tongues of fire seen on disciples at Pentecost (Acts 2:3)
3	Wind shook mountain (Exo 19:18)	Taught on wind of Holy Spirit (John 3:8)	Rushing mighty wind on Day of Pentecost (Acts 2:4)
4	God spoke on mountain (Exo 19:19)	Father spoke when Jesus anointed by Spirit in Jordan (Matt 3:17)	God spoke through disciples in new tongues (Acts 2:4)
5	God came down on top of the mountain (Exo 19:19)	God "came down" and was in Christ (2 Cor 5:19; Col 2:9)	God "came into our hearts" and is in us through the Spirit's power (Col 3:4)
6	God gave 10 commandments (Exo 20)	Christ fulfilled 10 commandments (Matt 5:17; 1 Cor 5:21)	Writes new commandments to love God and others (John 12:34; Matt 22:36-40)
7	Written on tables of stone (2 Cor 3:7)	Fulfilled all the law through perfect life (John 1:7)	Written in our hearts (2 Cor 3:3; Rom 13:8-10)
8	God's Word written by God's finger (Exo 31:18)	His Name is the Word of God (John 1:1,14; Rev 19:3)	Not of letter, but of Spirit (2 Cor 3:6)
9	Ministration of death (2 Cor 3:7)	He died to bring us life (John 10:10)	Ministration of the Spirit more glorious (2 Cor 3:8,9)
10	The letter kills (2 Cor 3:6)	He was the Word anointed by the Spirit and gave life (John 1:14)	The Holy Spirit gives life to us (2 Cor 3:6)
11	3,000 disobedient slain (Exo 32:28)	Through His death on the Cross we receive life (Rom 5:10)	3,000 obedient received life through the Gospel (Acts 2:41)
12	Moses' face veiled so people could not see the glory of God (Exo 34:29-35; 2 Cor 3:13-15)	Veil over Old Testament taken away in Christ (2 Cor 3:14)	With unveiled face we behold the glory of the Lord and are changed (2 Cor 3:18)
13	Old Testament (2 Cor 3:14)	Between the Testaments. Fulfilled the Old and introduced the New (Matt 26:26-28)	We are made able ministers of the New Testament (2 Cor 3:6)

Appendix 5 continued

Further Details of the Feast of Pentecost

	HISTORICAL Actual Event in Israel	**CHRISTOLOGICAL** Fulfillment in Christ	**EXPERIENTIAL** Experience in Believer
14	Commanded to offer a new grain offering (Lev 23:16)	God did a new thing in sending His Son to the earth	Mockers said they were filled with new wine; they spoke in new tongues (Acts 2:4,13)
15	To remember they were bondmen in Egypt, and were set free (Deut 16:12)	Preached deliverance and liberty to the captives (Luke 4:18)	We have liberty through the Spirit of God (2 Cor 3:17; Gal 4:7, 5:1)
16	Commanded to make two wave loaves (Lev 23:17)	Jesus taught, "I am the Bread of life" (John 6:48)	In our identification with Christ, the church is one bread (1 Cor 10:17)
17	Wave loaves made from fine flour, that is, crushed wheat (Lev 23:17)	Jesus was "crushed" as "broken Bread" on the Cross (Isa 52:14,15; John 12:24)	God uses "crushed" and broken vessels (Psa 51:17; Matt 21:44)
18	The two wave loaves were to be baked with leaven (Lev 23:17)	Leaven speaks of sin (1 Cor 5: 6,7). Jesus became sin for us (2 Cor 5:21)	Pentecost, receiving the Holy Spirit, is not perfection. We must go on to the Feast of Tabernacles
19	The two wave loaves were to be baked with fire (Lev 23:17)	The fire of God's wrath on Christ our sin offering (Isa 53:10)	Tongues as fire (Acts 2:3) Fiery trials of faith (1 Pet 1:7, 4:12; Matt 3:11)
20	The two wave loaves, and all sacrifices, were to be waved before the Lord (Lev 23:20)	Jesus our sacrifice "waved" before the Lord as our substitute offering on the Cross	120 on Day of Pentecost "waved" and appeared to the mockers to be drunk with wine (Acts 2:13)
21	Sinai quaked greatly (Exo 19:18)	Earth quaked as Jesus died on the Cross (Matt 27:51)	All things will be tested by shaking (Heb 12:26,27)
22	Two wave loaves to be holy (Lev 23:20)	Christ was holy, without sin (1 Pet 1:19)	We should be holy… without blame before Him (Eph 1:4)
23	Pentecost a Feast of harvest (Exo 23:16)	Jesus died to bring forth a great harvest (John 12:24)	Church reaped great harvest as a result of Pentecost
24	A freewill offering to be brought (Deut 16:10)	Jesus gave Himself as a freewill offering (John 10:18)	We give ourselves and our finances freely (2 Cor 9:6-8)
25	Feast of Pentecost for all people (Deut 16:11)	Jesus said whosoever will may come and drink (Rev 22:17)	The promise of the Holy Spirit is for all (Acts 2:39)
26	Feast of Pentecost a day of rejoicing (Deut 16:11)	Jesus had a great joy set before Him (Heb 12:2)	Disciples filled with joy and the Holy Spirit (Acts 13:52)
27	Feast of Pentecost to be a time of rest (Lev 23:21)	We are to enter into His rest (Heb 4:10)	There remains a rest for the people of God (Heb 4:9-11)
28	Feast of Pentecost proclaimed as a day of holy convocation (Lev 23:21)	Jesus prayed for a coming together and unity for His followers (John 17:21)	"One accord…" (Acts 2:1). Unity through Spirit (Eph 4:3)

Appendix 6

10 Questions to Consider When Examining a Teaching, a Ministry, or a "New Spiritual Move"

While the Bible warns us not to be judgmental,[3] we are exhorted to carefully examine every teaching, ministry, and spirit. Note the following commands and warnings:

> "*Examine everything carefully;*[4] hold fast to that which is good." (1 Thess 5:21 – *NAS*)

> "Beloved, do not believe every spirit, but *test the spirits*, whether they are of God; because many false prophets have gone out into the world …
> By this we know the spirit of truth and the spirit of error." (1 Jn 4:1,6)

> "For everyone who partakes only of milk is unskilled in the word of righteousness, for he is a babe.
> But solid food belongs to those who are of full age (*margin,* 'mature,') that is, those who by reason of use (*margin,* 'practice') *have their senses exercised to discern both good and evil.*" (Heb 5:13,14)

> "'Tell us, when will these things be? And what will be the sign of Your coming, and of the end of the age?'
> And Jesus answered and said to them: 'Take heed that no one *deceives* you ('misleads you' – *NAS*)…
> … and will *deceive* many …
> … will rise up and *deceive* many …
> … to *deceive*, if possible, even the elect ('chosen ones' – *margin NAS*).
> See, I have told you beforehand.'" (Matt 24:3-5,11,24,25)

1. Is what is taught revealed in the written Word of God, preferably by two or three witnesses? Is it the "spirit of truth" (John 17:17), or the "spirit of error" (1 Jn 4:6)?

2. Does the teaching, minister, or movement exalt and glorify the Person of the Lord Jesus Christ, or is a man or woman exalted (1 Jn 4:2; John 16:14)?

3. Is it based on *charisma* or character? Does the minister have a good track record of holiness and humility and Christlikeness? Or is there self-promotion and self-grandiosity? Does the leader set himself up as a dictator, or behave like a servant? (Matt 20:27)

---

[3] Matt 7:1,2
[4] "Test all things" – *NKJV*.

4. Does it cause believers to grow in the Lord, enabling them to live victorious, overcoming Christian lives (1 Jn 4:4)? Does it produce permanent, lasting, Christ-exalting changes in people's lives?

5. Though there may be opposition, do the leaders manifest the love of Jesus at all times, even towards those who oppose them (1 Jn 3:10)?

6. Jesus said, "I will build my Church."[5] Is the Church, both local and universal, recognized, honoured, and edified (1 Cor 14:26)?

7. Does it cause Christians to make Jesus Lord over every area of their lives (Phil 2:9-11)?

8. Does it cause people to have a greater desire and boldness to share their faith with others, witnessing to the Gospel both here and abroad, through obedient praying, giving, and when called by the Lord, going (Acts 1:8)?

9. Is the proponent of the teaching, or the leader of the "movement," related to, open with, and accountable to:

   a. Local leadership for his daily Christian behaviour (lifestyle)?

   b. Peers (other ministers) locally, or out of town, for his teachings and ministry? To whom is the leader accountable? Is there a way for his/her followers to make an appeal to those peer ministries to whom the leader is accountable?

10. Does this teaching, or what is called a "move of God," grow and perpetuate itself by the Power of God's Word and the Holy Spirit, or by man's efforts (John 6:63,15:5)?

---

[5] Matt 16:18.

Appendix 7

Figure 6: Panoramic Overview of Revelation with Chapter Numbers

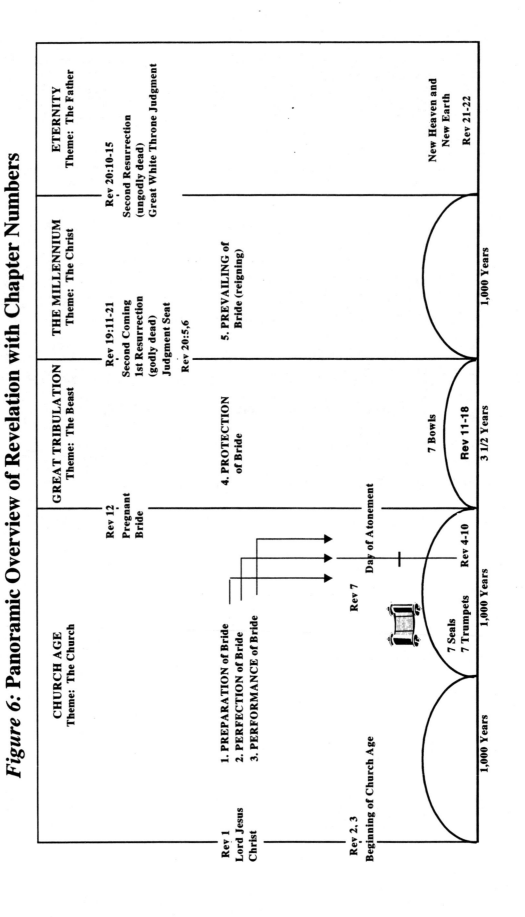

Appendix 8

Figure 13: The Seven Days of God's Week
Job 24:1; Psa 90:4; 2 Pet 3:8 – One day = a thousand years

GOD

	Father		Son — Jesus		Holy Spirit — Christ	
	Lord					
	Sun WATER Enoch →	Noah	Moses	Moon BLOOD Elijah →	Stars SPIRIT Dark Ages →	
	Day 1	**Day 2**	**Day 3**	**Day 4**	**Day 5**	**Day 6**	**Day 7**

	Day 1	Day 2	Day 3	Day 4	Day 5	Day 6	Day 7
I. Literal – God's work of Re-Creation (Gen 1)	Light – God divided the light from the darkness	Dividing the Waters Separation	Dry Land and Plants to bring forth fruit	Sun, Moon and Stars for signs, to give light	Fish and Fowls of the air Rising above the earth	Animals, man and woman A special breathing, an impartation of God. Man has dominion (Psa 8:3-6)	God rested Re-Creation complete
II. Historical – God's work of Redemption (2 Pet 3:8 & Psa 90:4 – Psalm of Moses who wrote Genesis)	Adam to Enoch 1st thousand years of history	Enoch to Abraham Noah - the flood divided the people	Abraham to Elijah Israel planted in the land	Elijah to Jesus Light (Exo 12). Lamb kept 4 days. Time of prophets All prophesied about Jesus	Jesus said "I will make fishers of men". Many fish were caught (in Acts 2:41; 4:4 etc).	Restoration of Truths as God breathes (Hos 6:2)	Reign of Christ upon the earth Millennium. (Rev 20; Luke 13:32)
III. Spiritual – God's work of Restoration Heb 6:1-3; 2 Cor 5:17; Eph 2:10.	1 – Repentance and 2 – Faith through the light of God's Word (Psa 119:130) and Jesus the Light (John 9:5) We become Lights (Matt 5:14)	3 – Water Baptism Old man is divided from new man (Col 2:11,12) (Gen 1:6) Growth (2 Pet 3:18)	Baptism in Holy Spirit Psa 1:3 Eph 3:17 Gal 5:22 John 15:16 Matt 3:10 Gal 3:29 Makes us Fruitful Witnesses (Acts 1:8)	4 – Laying on of Hands With prophecy we get special direction and confirmation – God imparts something. Healing, signs, Ministries	5 – Resurrection Life and 6 – Eternal Judgment See Acts 5 Ananias and Sapphira. Note the after-effects	7 – Perfection "One new man" (Eph 2:15) God is pouring out His Spirit and making us one. Perfection of bride at end of Day 6 (Rev 12) Dominion	Living in His sight (Hos 6:2)

The Eternal Godhead (Rom 1:20)
1 Persons: 3 Heavenly Witnesses (1 John 5:7)
2 Name: (Prov 30:4; Psa 91:14; Zech 14:9)
3 Symbol in Heavens:
4 3 Earthly Witnesses: (1 John 5:8)

Appendix 9

Figure 14: The Feasts – Festivals of Israel (Deut 16: 15,17; Lev 23)

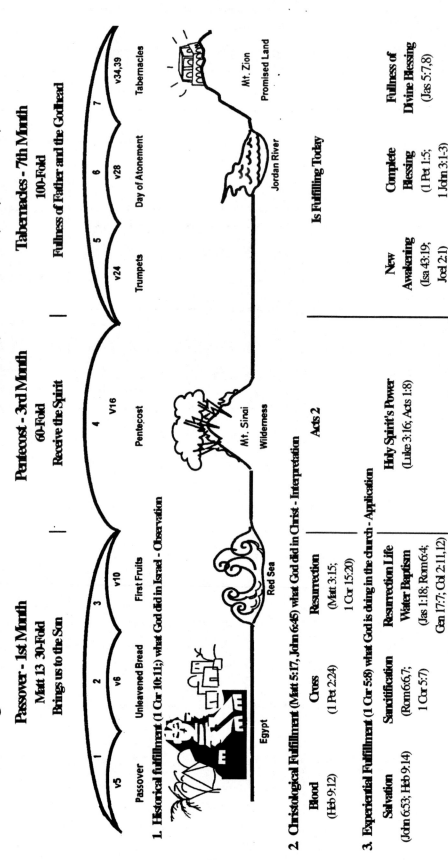

"Blessed - happy, fortunate, to be envied - are the people who know the joyful sound, who understand and appreciate the spiritual blessings symbolized by the feasts; they walk O Lord, in the light and favor of Thy countenance". (Psa 89:14 – *Amp Bible*) "Let us keep the feast" (1 Cor 5:8) "What will you do in the solemn day, and in the Day of the Feast of the Lord?" (Hos 9:5).

Appendix 10

Figure 15: **Thirty Types and Illustrations of the Three Stages of Christian Growth**

#	Lev 23, Deut 16	Passover	Pentecost	Tabernacles
1.	Time	First Month	Third Month	Seventh (last) Month
2.	Region	Egypt	Wilderness (Psa 106:12-16)	Promised Land (Zech 14:16-21; Josh 23:5; Heb 4:1-11)
3.	Location (1 Cor 10:11)	Goshen	Mount Sinai (Exo 19)	Zion (Heb 12:18,22)
4.	Noah's Ark (Gen 6:15)	Length 300 (Faithful Remnant)	Breadth 50 (= Pentecost)	Height 30 (= Full Consecration)
5.	Joseph	Dreams and Visions (Gen 37)	Overseer in Potiphar's house (Gen 39:1-6)	Ruler over King's house and all the land (Gen 41:37-45)
6.	Moses	40 Years to get Moses out of Egypt	40 years to get Egypt out of Moses	40 years leading children of Israel out of Egypt
7.	Moses' Tabernacle (Heb 9:9)	Outer Court	Holy Place	Most Holy Place (Heb 10:19)
8.	Gideon's Army (Judg 7)	32,000 Men	10,000 Men	3,000 Men
9.	Book of Ruth	Orpah	Naomi	Ruth
10.	David	Anointed by Samuel in Bethlehem (1 Sam 16:13)	Anointed King over Judah (2 Sam 2:4)	Anointed King over whole land (2 Sam 5:3-5)
11.	Rains (Psa 68:9)	Showers (Psa 65:10, 72:6)	Former Rain (Hos 6:3)	Latter Rain (Jas 5:7)
12.	Harvests	Wave sheaf (Lev 23:10-12)	Grain Harvest (Not just 1 sheaf)	Fullness of harvest- corn, wine, oil (Joel 2:23-26)
13.	Elijah (1 Ki 17,18)	Cherith (Death of famine passed over him)	Carmel (Fire fell)	Abundance of Rain
14.	Isaiah (40:9)	Cities of Judah	Jerusalem	Zion (Heb 12:18,22)
15.	Daniel (1)	Certain of the children of Israel (v3)	Daniel, Hannaniah, Mishael and Azariah (v6)	Daniel only had understanding in visions, dreams (v17)
16.	The Lord Jesus Christ (1 Pet 2:21)	Babe at Bethlehem	Child at Nazareth	Anointed Son at Jordan
17.	Sonship	Right (John 1:12)	Portion (Luke 12:42)	Double portion (Deut 21:17; 2 Ki 2:9; Heb 12:23)
18.	Growing in the Spirit	Born of Spirit (John 3:3,5)	Earnest of the Spirit (2 Cor 1:22; Eph:13,14)	Fullness of the Spirit (Eph 5:18, 3:19)
19.	Fruitfulness (Matt 13:8,23)	30-Fold	60-Fold	100-Fold
20.	Bridal Relationship (Matt 25)	Foolish Virgins	Wise Virgins	Bride
21.	Seed in Earth brings forth (Mark 4:28)	Blade	Ear	Full corn
22.	Jesus is to us (John 14:6)	Way (John 10:1,7,9)	Truth (John 16:13)	Life (John 10:10b)
23.	Branch in the vine (John 15)	Fruit (v2)	More Fruit (v8)	Much Fruit
24.	Showing forth the Spirit	Fruit of the Spirit (Gal 5:22,23)	Gifts of the Spirit (1 Cor 12:8-10)	7-Fold Spirit of God (Isa 11:2-4)
25.	Development in Christ	Servants (1 Pet 2:16)	Priests (Rev 1:6)	Kings (Rev 1:6; 1 Pet 2:9; Eph 2:6)
26.	Different Resurrected Glories (1 Cor 15:40,41)	Star Glory	Moon Glory	Sun Glory (see Rev 12 – Bride of Christ)
27.	Different stages of relationship to God	Fellowship (1 Cor 1:9)	Espoused – Engaged (2 Cor 11:2; Eph 1:13,14)	Married (Rom 7:4; Eph 4:13; Phil 3:10 "know" as Gen 4:1; Matt 1:25 Marriage relationship. Day of Atonement is Wedding Day of Christ & His Bride)
28.	Growing up in Christ (1 John 2:12-15)	Little Children (Sins Forgiven)	Young Men (have overcome by power of the Spirit)	Fathers ("you have known Him")
29.	Perfection for whole man (1 Thess 5:23)	Soul Saved (Heb 10:39)	Spirit Baptized (Acts 1:5,8; Rom 1:9)	Body Redeemed (Rom 8:23)

"Speak unto the children of Israel, that they go forward." (Exodus 14:15) "Grow in grace and in the knowledge of our Lord and Saviour Jesus Christ" (2 Pet 3:18).
"Grow up into Him in all things, which is the head, even Christ." (Eph 4:15)

Appendix 11

Figure 23: The Tabernacle of Moses in Exodus, Acts and Revelation

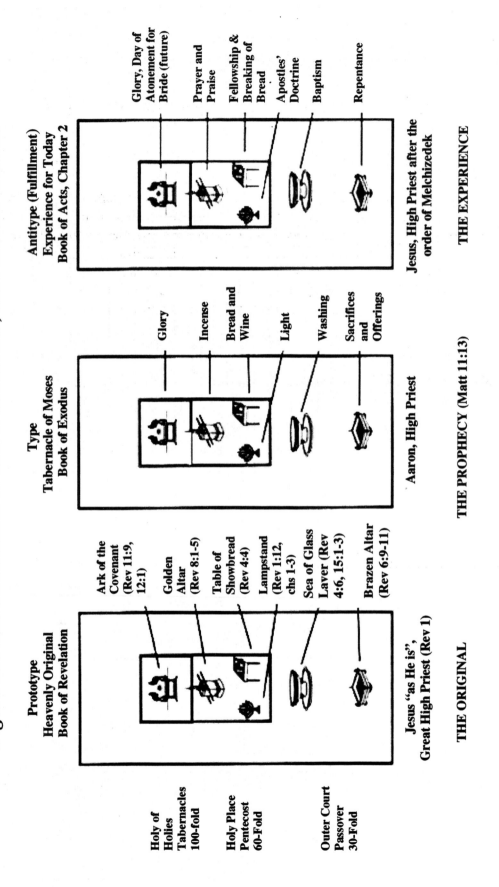

Addresses to Order Books by Other Authors

Books by Kevin Conner:

U. S. A.
City Bible Publishing
9200 N.E. Freemont
Portland, OR 97220

Australia and New Zealand
KJC Publications
PO Box 300
Vermont, Victoria 3133
AUSTRALIA

Books by Alister Lowe:

45 Leslie Parade
Slacks Creek
Brisbane, Queensland 4127
AUSTRALIA

Books by Rob Wheeler:

U. S. A.
Truscott Missions
PMB G 1
1765 Garnet Ave.
San Diego, CA 92109-3351

Australia and New Zealand
Auckland Christian Fellowship
PO Box 24-377
Royal Oak
Auckland 6
NEW ZEALAND

Books and Charts by Pastor W. H. Offiler:

Bethel Christian Ministries
2033-2nd Ave
Seattle, WA 98121
U.S.A.

About the Author

Graham Truscott and his wife, Pamela, were born in New Zealand. They met while they were in high school, came to Christ in a Wesleyan Methodist church in their late teens, and married in February 1958. They entered full-time ministry the following year, and left New Zealand for India, with their baby son, at the beginning of 1960. They spent almost 18 years as resident missionaries in India, establishing many churches in that nation. These churches continue to grow, and now number many hundreds. The Truscotts make regular ministry visits to India.

Graham and Pamela and their four children relocated to San Diego in 1977 where they pioneered another church, Restoration Temple (now known as The Life Church, Mission Bay). In April 1991 they obeyed God's call to become full-time missionaries again. The Truscotts are now Missionary Pastors to hundreds of churches and ministers around the world. Their travels for Christ have taken them to over 60 nations.

Graham is known as a missionary-statesman, Bible teacher, church planter, author, and a trainer of men and women for the ministry. In December 1999 he celebrated 45 years of preaching. His former career as a professional musician uniquely qualifies him to assist pastors and churches in the areas of church music, praise and worship. Graham is the author of numerous magazine articles, and eight published books, many of which have been translated into other languages. In 2001 the eighth English edition of his best seller, *The Power of His Presence* on the Restoration of the Tabernacle of David, was printed.

In January 1997 Graham released two CDs of his clarinet playing, titled *Bach ... to Blues ... and Back, Volumes I and II*. The 47 pieces on these albums present a wide variety of music— blues, Dixie, classical, Gospel, and hymns.

Pamela, Graham's wife of 44 years, is a mother, grandmother, and minister, and is a sought-after conference speaker. She has twice been invited to the White House, where together with other Christian Women in Leadership she met with President Reagan to discuss important issues.

In 1985 Graham and Pamela's 24-year-old daughter Debbie was killed by a drunk driver. Out of this traumatic experience Pamela wrote the book *I Cry Alone* which has been endorsed by President and Mrs George Bush, Sr, who personally distributed 800 copies.

The Truscotts continue to work out of San Diego, conducting Marriage Enrichment Seminars, Bible teaching and Prophetic conventions, and ministering in churches and Bible schools. They have dedicated the rest of their lives to encouraging ministers and churches, wherever they go, with their ministry of music, God's Word, and the anointing of the Holy Spirit.

To Order Books, Music Tapes and CDs from the Truscotts

U. S. A.:

Graham and Pamela Truscott
PMB G1
1765 Garnet Ave.
San Diego, CA 92109-3351
U. S. A.

Tel: 858-270-5118
Fax: 858-274-9461

E-mail: graham@truscottmissions.com
Website: truscottmissions.com

New Zealand and Australia:

P O Box 2336
Christchurch
NEW ZEALAND